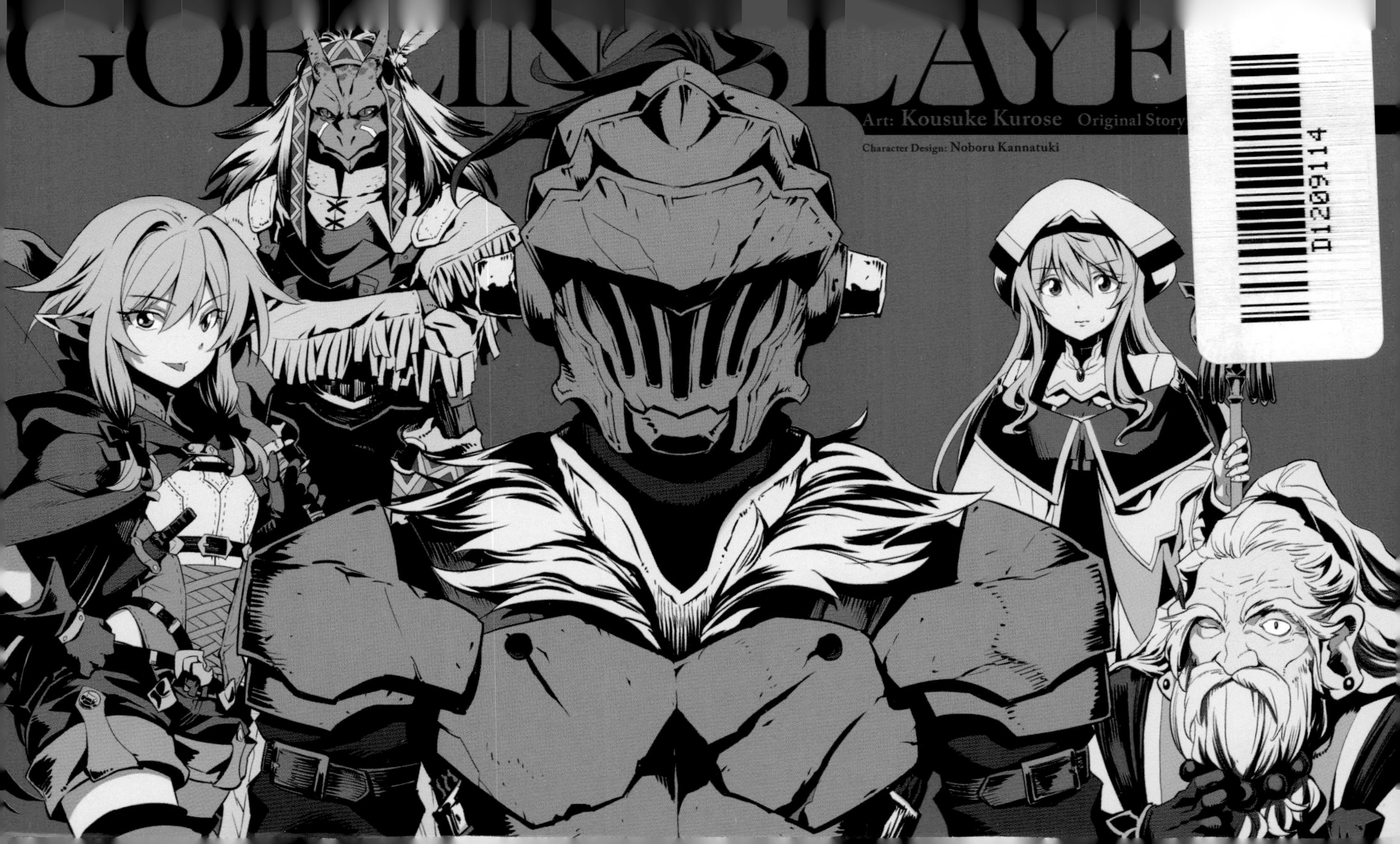
Art: Kousuke Kurose Original Story
Character Design: Noboru Kannatuki

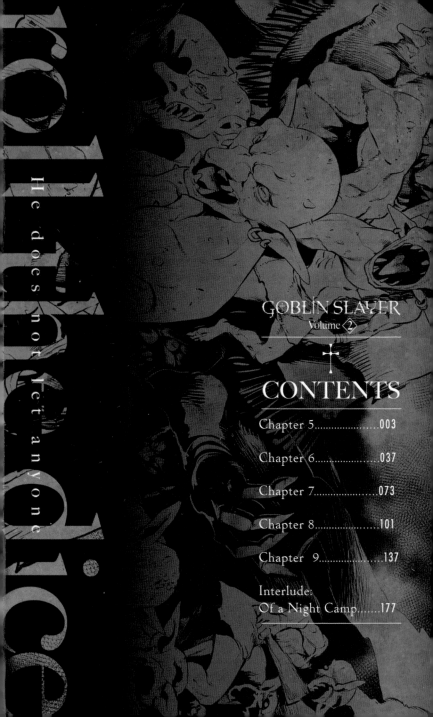

roll the dice.

He does not let anyone

GOBLIN SLAYER
Volume 2

✝

CONTENTS

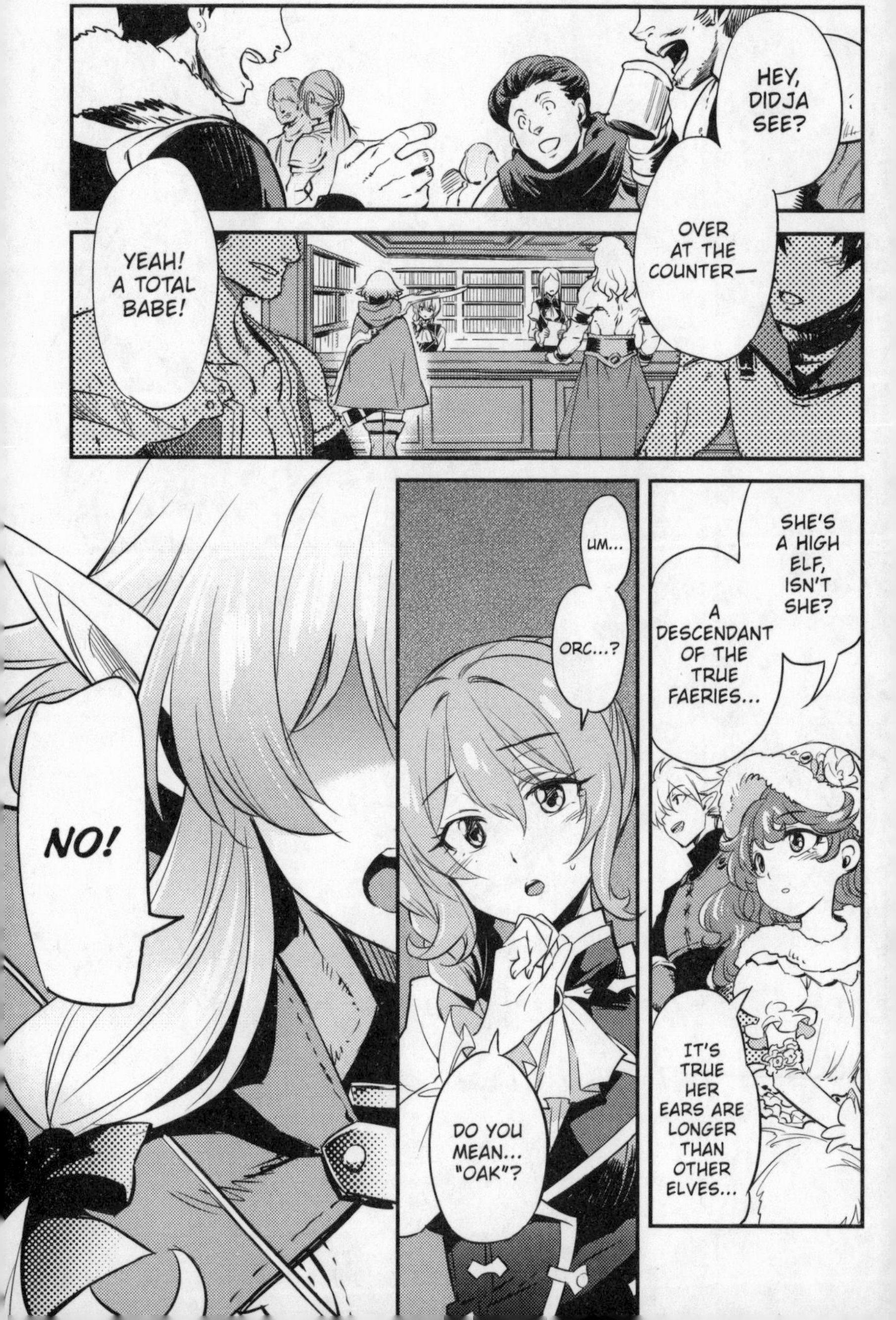
HEY, DIDJA SEE?
OVER AT THE COUNTER—
YEAH! A TOTAL BABE!
SHE'S A HIGH ELF, ISN'T SHE?
A DESCENDANT OF THE TRUE FAERIES...
IT'S TRUE HER EARS ARE LONGER THAN OTHER ELVES...
UM...
ORC...?
DO YOU MEAN... "OAK"?
NO!

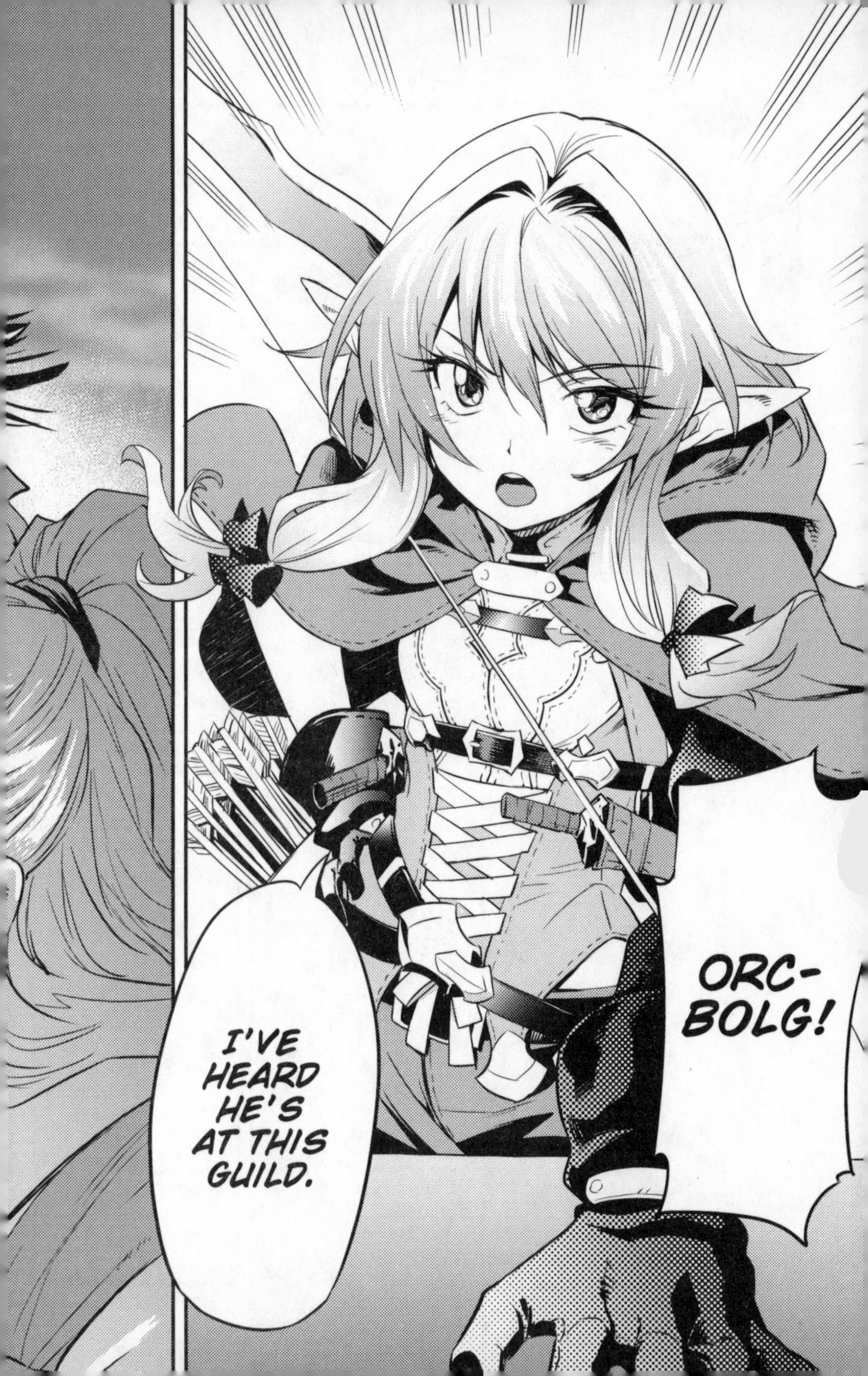
ORC-BOLG!
I'VE HEARD HE'S AT THIS GUILD.

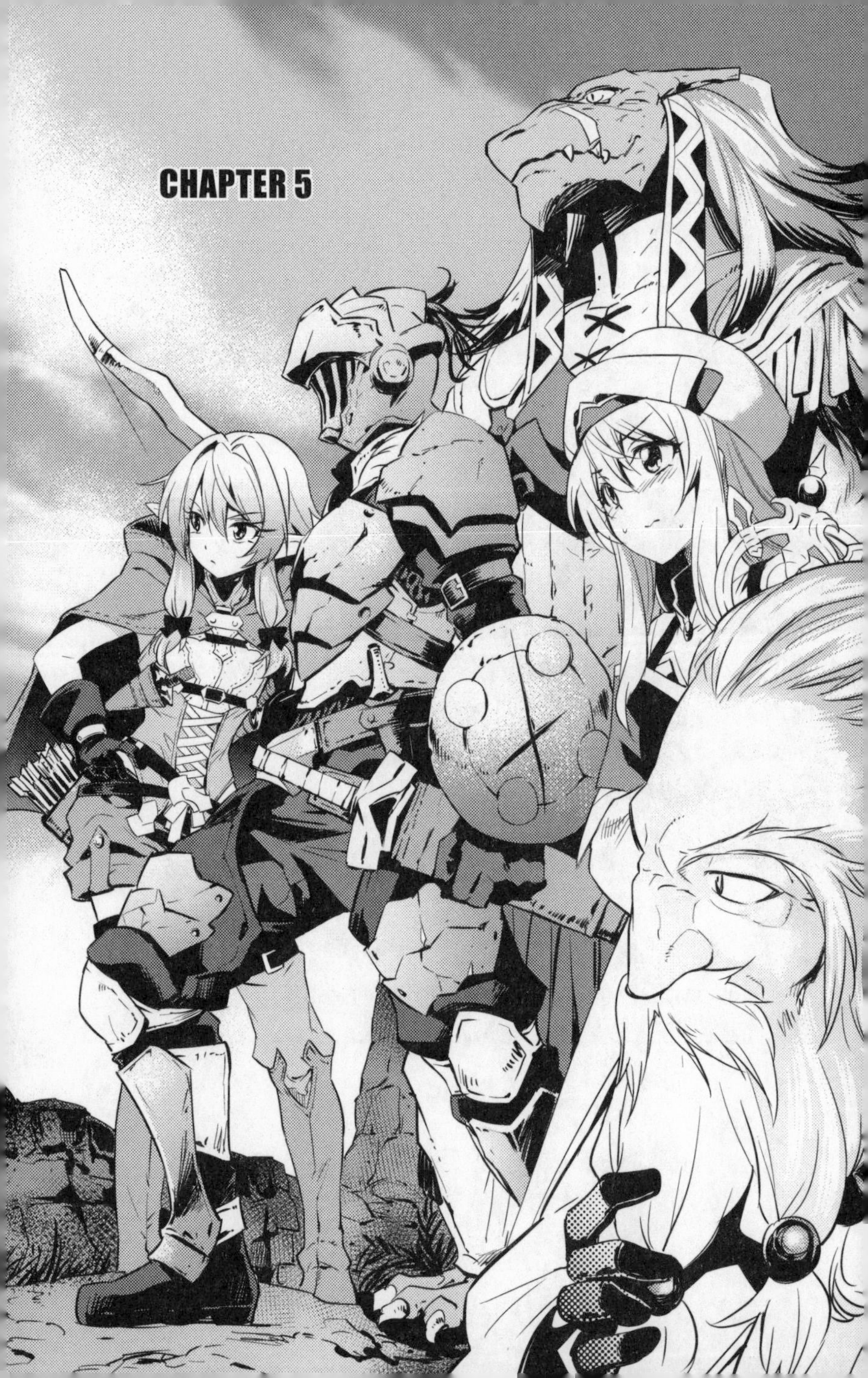
CHAPTER 5

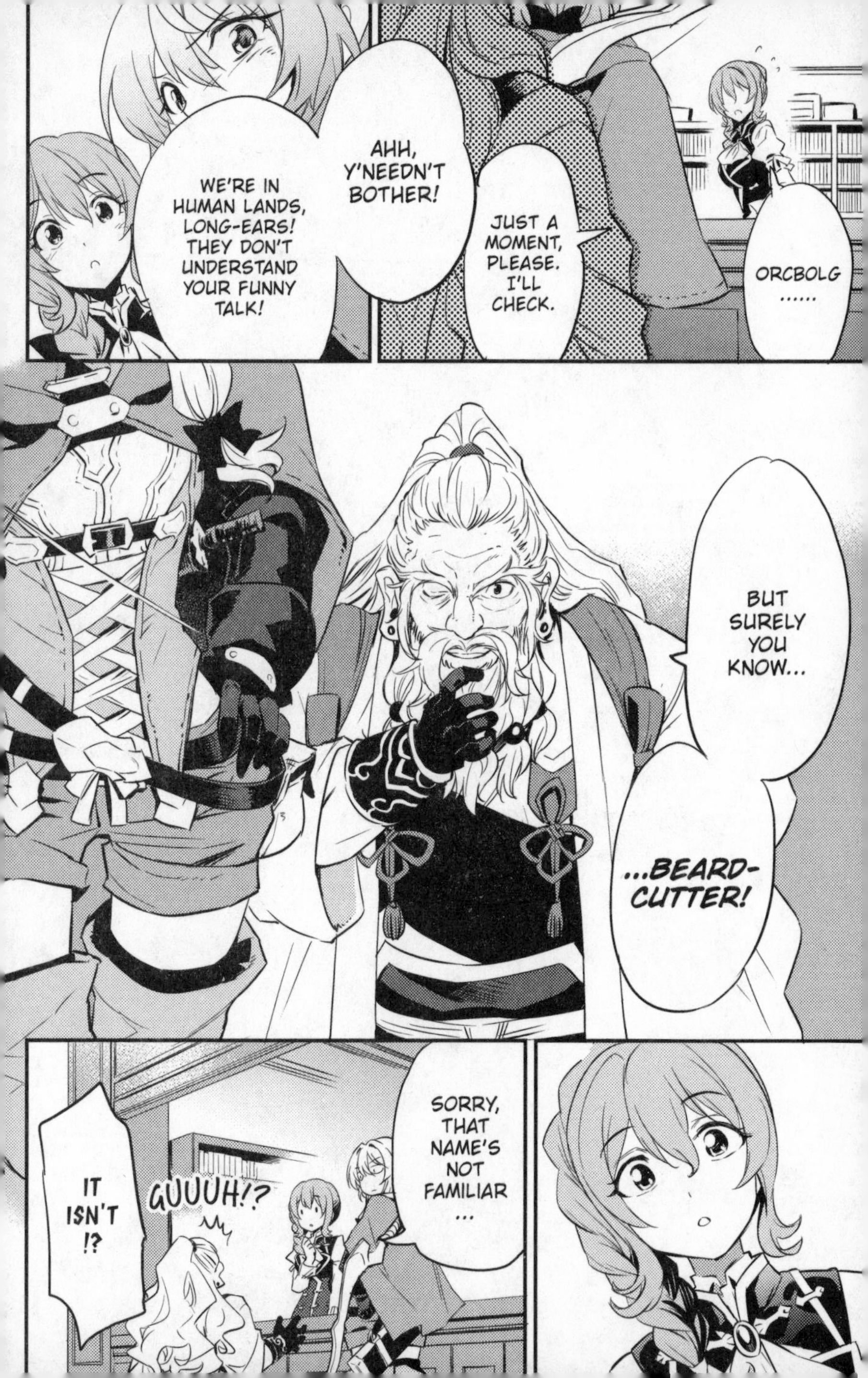
ORCBOLG ......
JUST A MOMENT, PLEASE. I'LL CHECK.
AHH, Y'NEEDN'T BOTHER!
WE'RE IN HUMAN LANDS, LONG-EARS! THEY DON'T UNDERSTAND YOUR FUNNY TALK!
BUT SURELY YOU KNOW...
...BEARD-CUTTER!
SORRY, THAT NAME'S NOT FAMILIAR ...
IT ISN'T !?
GUUUH!?

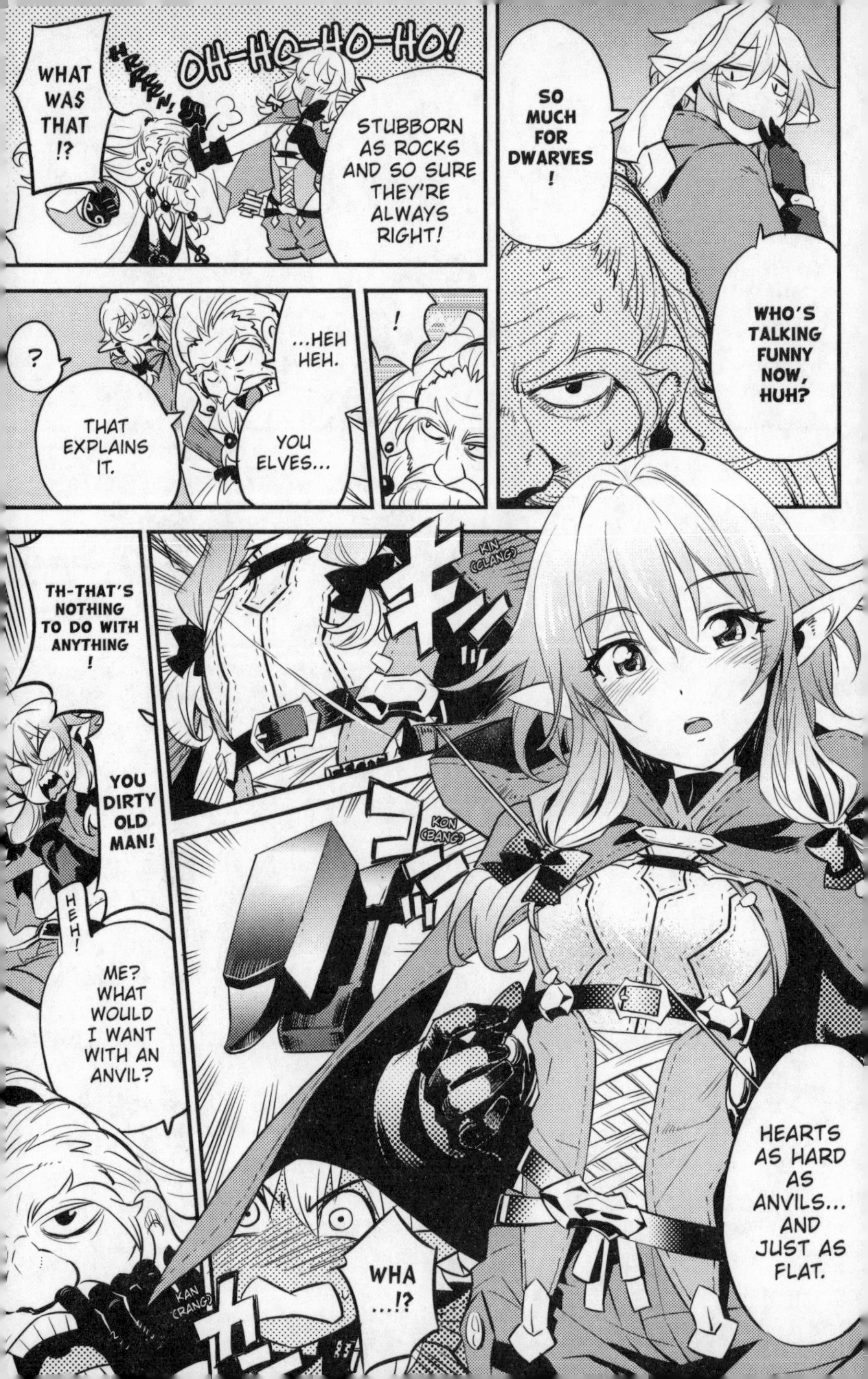
SO MUCH FOR DWARVES!
WHO'S TALKING FUNNY NOW, HUH?
STUBBORN AS ROCKS AND SO SURE THEY'RE ALWAYS RIGHT!
OH-HO-HO-HO!
HRRRN!
WHAT WAS THAT!?
!
YOU ELVES...
...HEH HEH.
?
THAT EXPLAINS IT.
KIN (CLANG)
HEARTS AS HARD AS ANVILS... AND JUST AS FLAT.
TH-THAT'S NOTHING TO DO WITH ANYTHING!
YOU DIRTY OLD MAN!
KON (BANG)
HEH!
ME? WHAT WOULD I WANT WITH AN ANVIL?
WHA...!?
KAN (RANG)

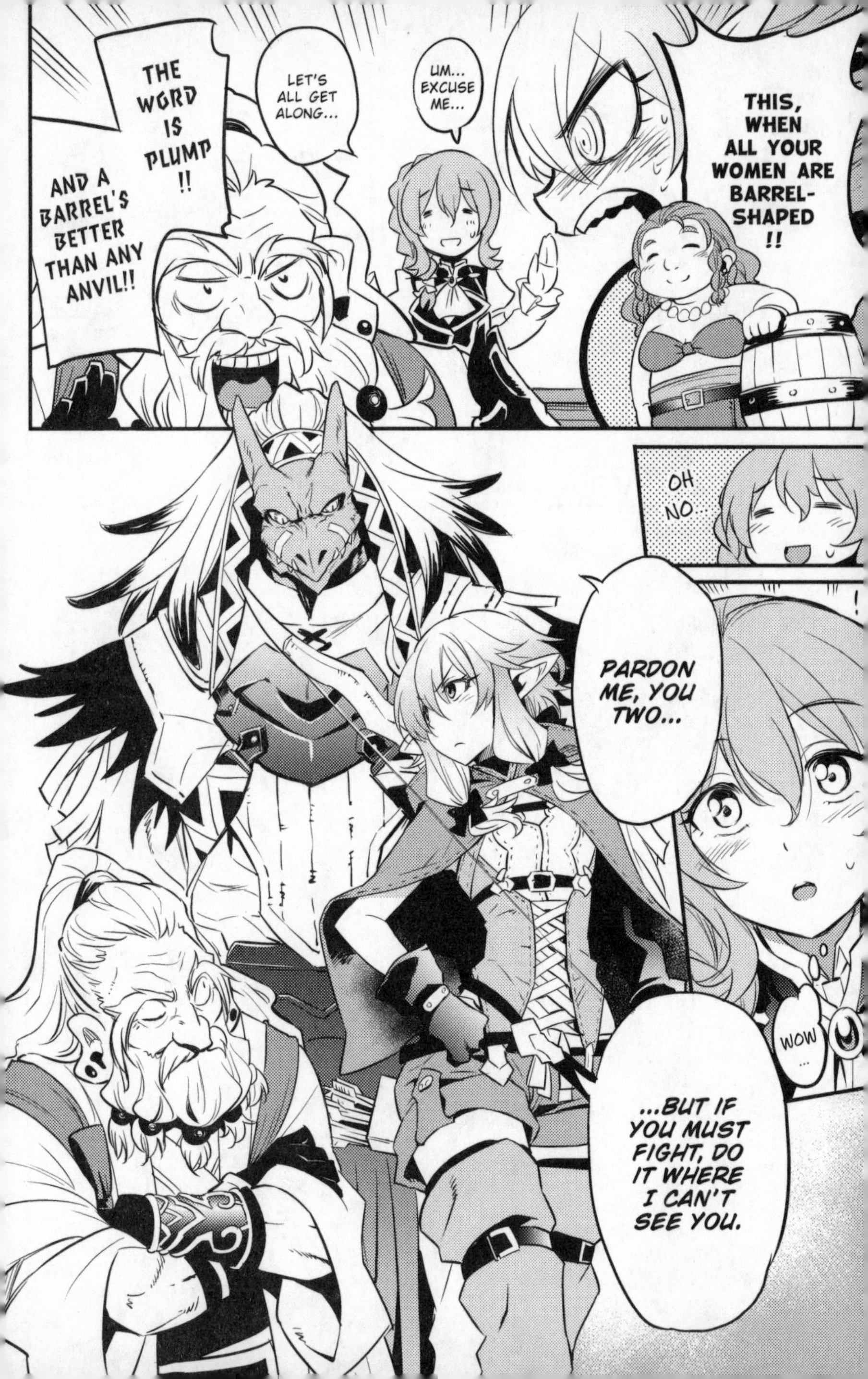
THIS, WHEN ALL YOUR WOMEN ARE BARREL-SHAPED!!
UM... EXCUSE ME...
LET'S ALL GET ALONG...
THE WORD IS PLUMP!!
AND A BARREL'S BETTER THAN ANY ANVIL!!
OH NO...
!
WOW...
PARDON ME, YOU TWO...
...BUT IF YOU MUST FIGHT, DO IT WHERE I CAN'T SEE YOU.

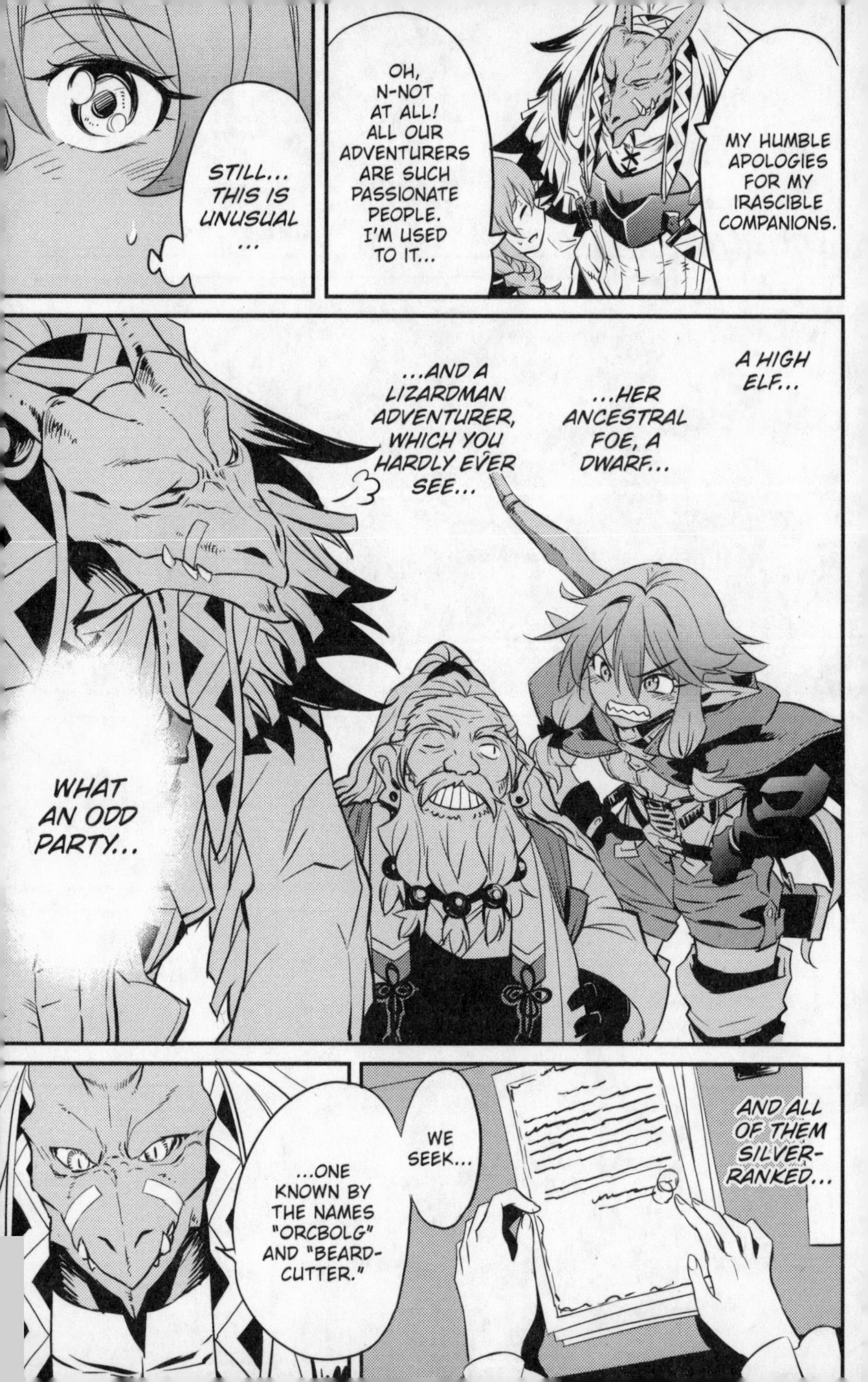
MY HUMBLE APOLOGIES FOR MY IRASCIBLE COMPANIONS.
OH, N-NOT AT ALL! ALL OUR ADVENTURERS ARE SUCH PASSIONATE PEOPLE. I'M USED TO IT...
STILL... THIS IS UNUSUAL...
A HIGH ELF...
...HER ANCESTRAL FOE, A DWARF...
...AND A LIZARDMAN ADVENTURER, WHICH YOU HARDLY EVER SEE...
WHAT AN ODD PARTY...
AND ALL OF THEM SILVER-RANKED...
WE SEEK...
...ONE KNOWN BY THE NAMES "ORCBOLG" AND "BEARD-CUTTER."

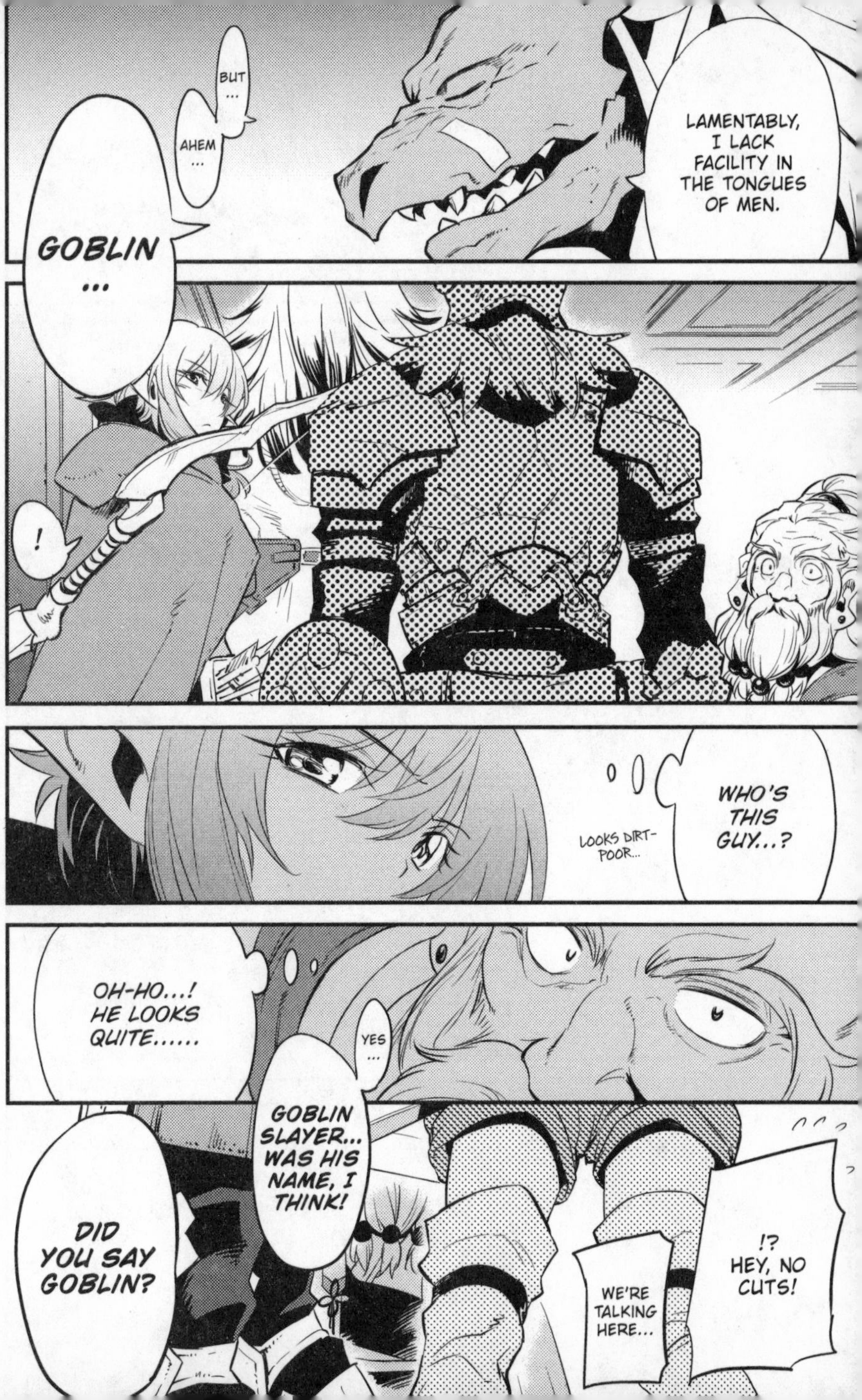
LAMENTABLY, I LACK FACILITY IN THE TONGUES OF MEN.
BUT ...
AHEM ...
GOBLIN ...
!
WHO'S THIS GUY...?
LOOKS DIRT-POOR...
OH-HO...! HE LOOKS QUITE......
YES ...
!? HEY, NO CUTS!
WE'RE TALKING HERE...
GOBLIN SLAYER... WAS HIS NAME, I THINK!
DID YOU SAY GOBLIN?

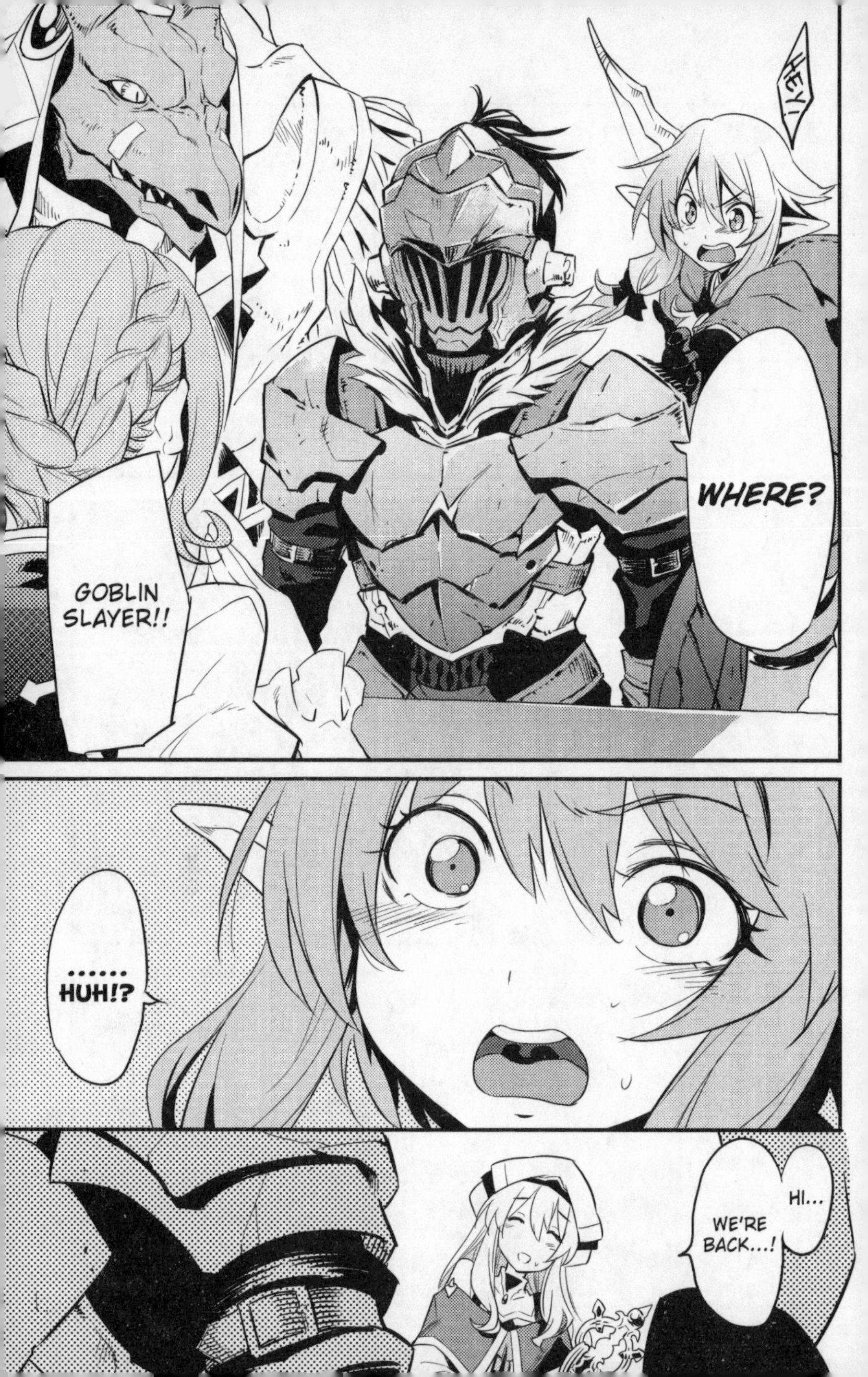
HEY!
WHERE?
GOBLIN SLAYER!!
......
HUH!?
HI...
WE'RE BACK...!

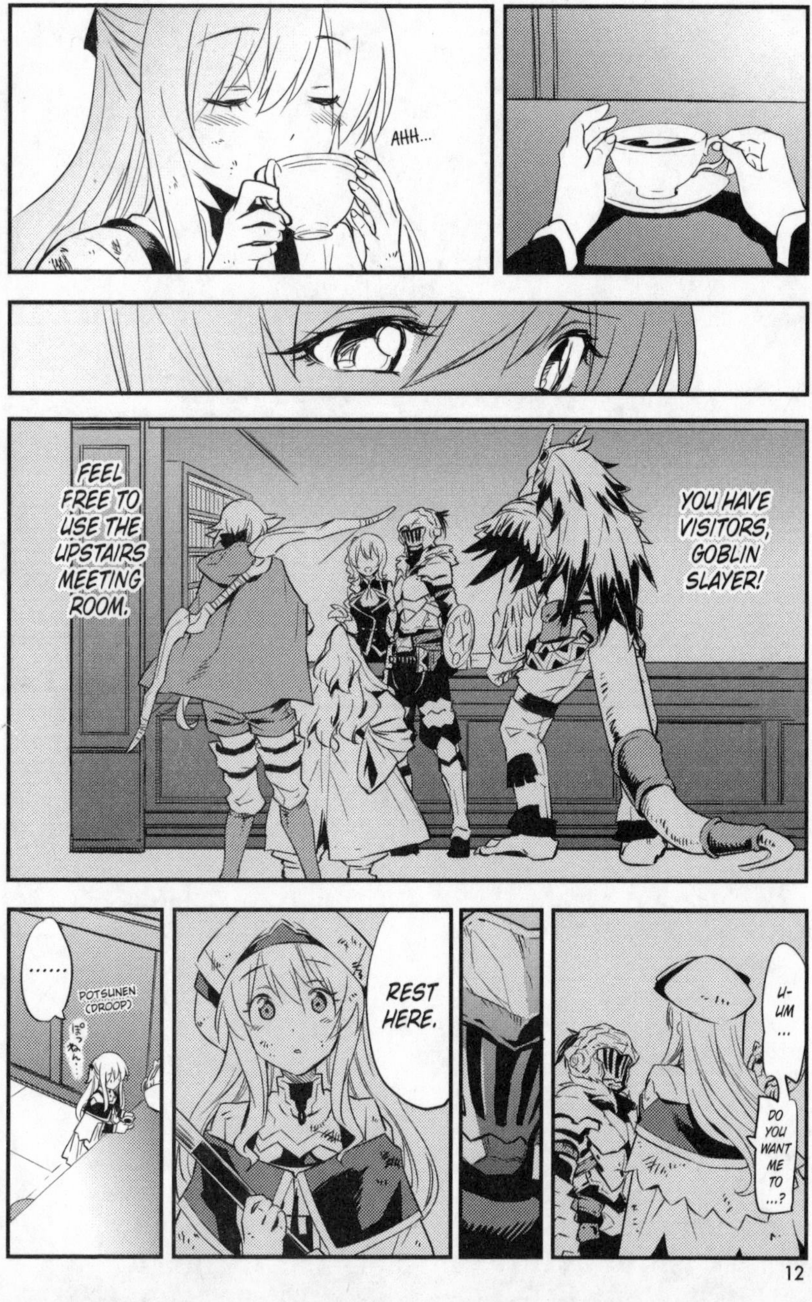
AHH...
YOU HAVE VISITORS, GOBLIN SLAYER!
FEEL FREE TO USE THE UPSTAIRS MEETING ROOM.
U-UM ...
DO YOU WANT ME TO ...?
REST HERE.
......
POTSUNEN (DROOP)

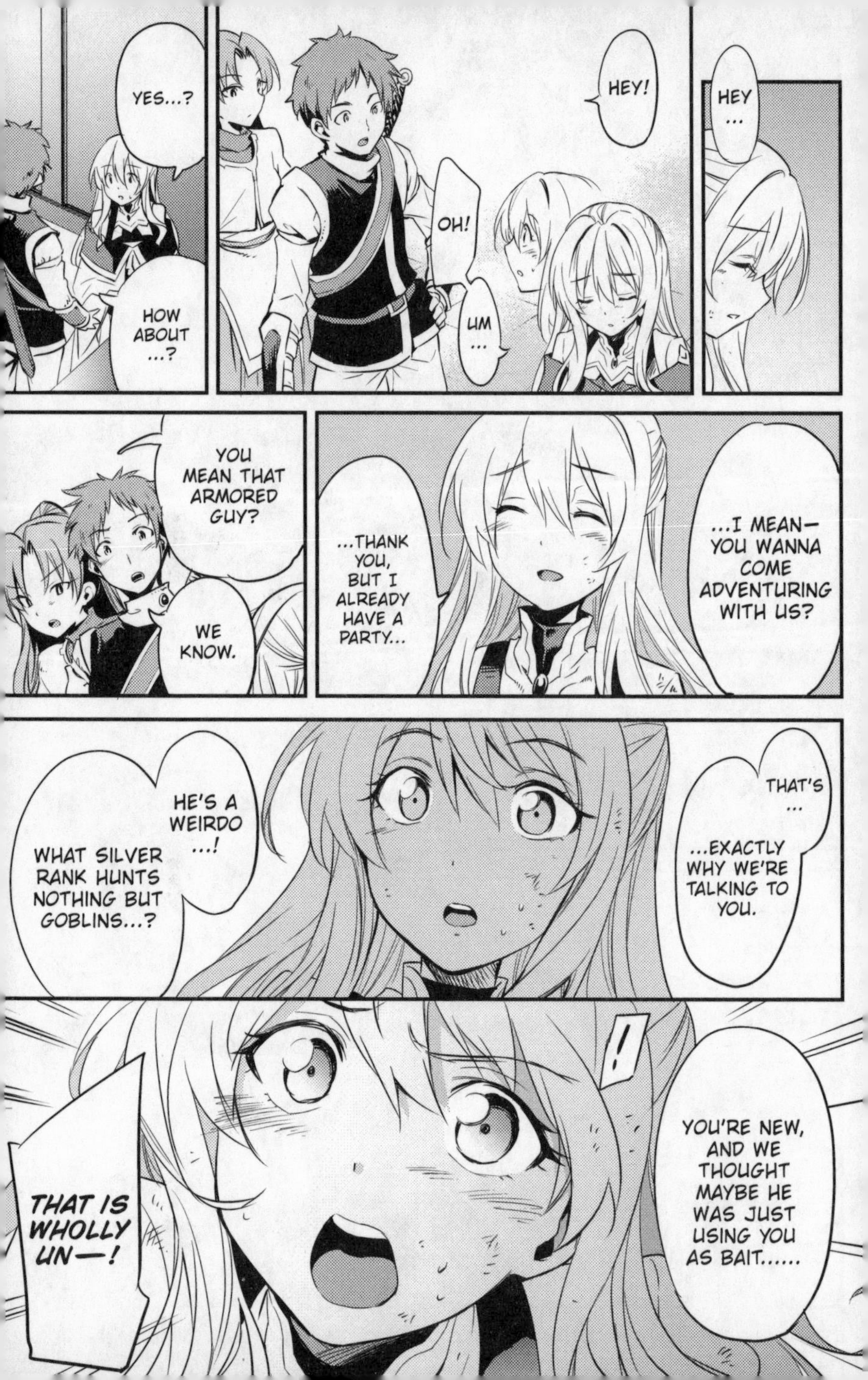
HEY ...
HEY!
OH!
UM ...
YES...?
HOW ABOUT ...?
...I MEAN—YOU WANNA COME ADVENTURING WITH US?
...THANK YOU, BUT I ALREADY HAVE A PARTY...
YOU MEAN THAT ARMORED GUY?
WE KNOW.
THAT'S ...
...EXACTLY WHY WE'RE TALKING TO YOU.
HE'S A WEIRDO ...!
WHAT SILVER RANK HUNTS NOTHING BUT GOBLINS...?
!
YOU'RE NEW, AND WE THOUGHT MAYBE HE WAS JUST USING YOU AS BAIT......
THAT IS WHOLLY UN—!

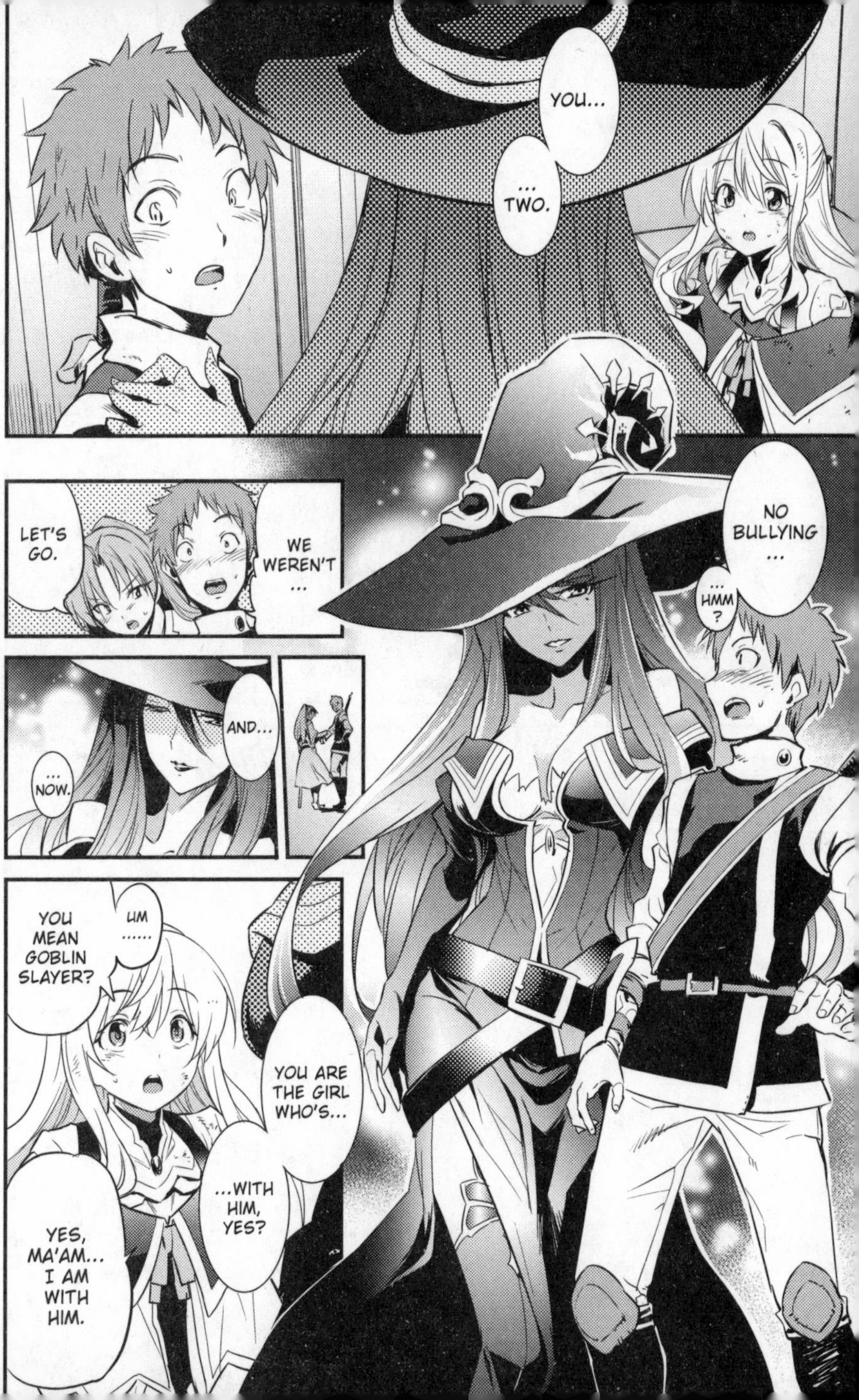
YOU...
...TWO.
NO BULLYING...
...HMM?
WE WEREN'T...
LET'S GO.
AND...
...NOW.
YOU ARE THE GIRL WHO'S...
...WITH HIM, YES?
UM......
YOU MEAN GOBLIN SLAYER?
YES, MA'AM... I AM WITH HIM.

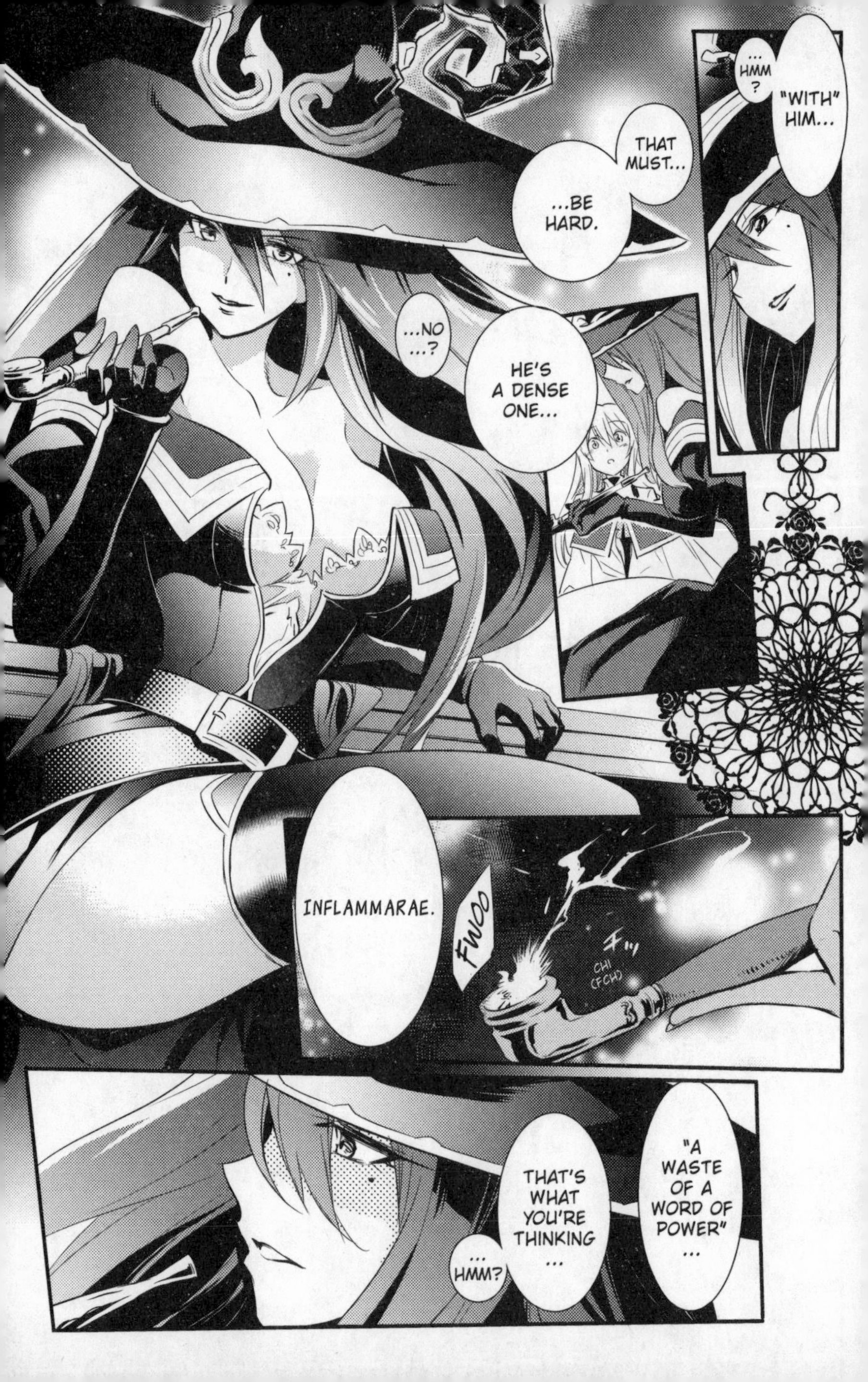
"WITH" HIM...
... HMM ?
THAT MUST...
...BE HARD.
HE'S A DENSE ONE...
...NO ...?
INFLAMMARAE.
FWOO
CHI (FCH)
"A WASTE OF A WORD OF POWER" ...
THAT'S WHAT YOU'RE THINKING ...
... HMM?

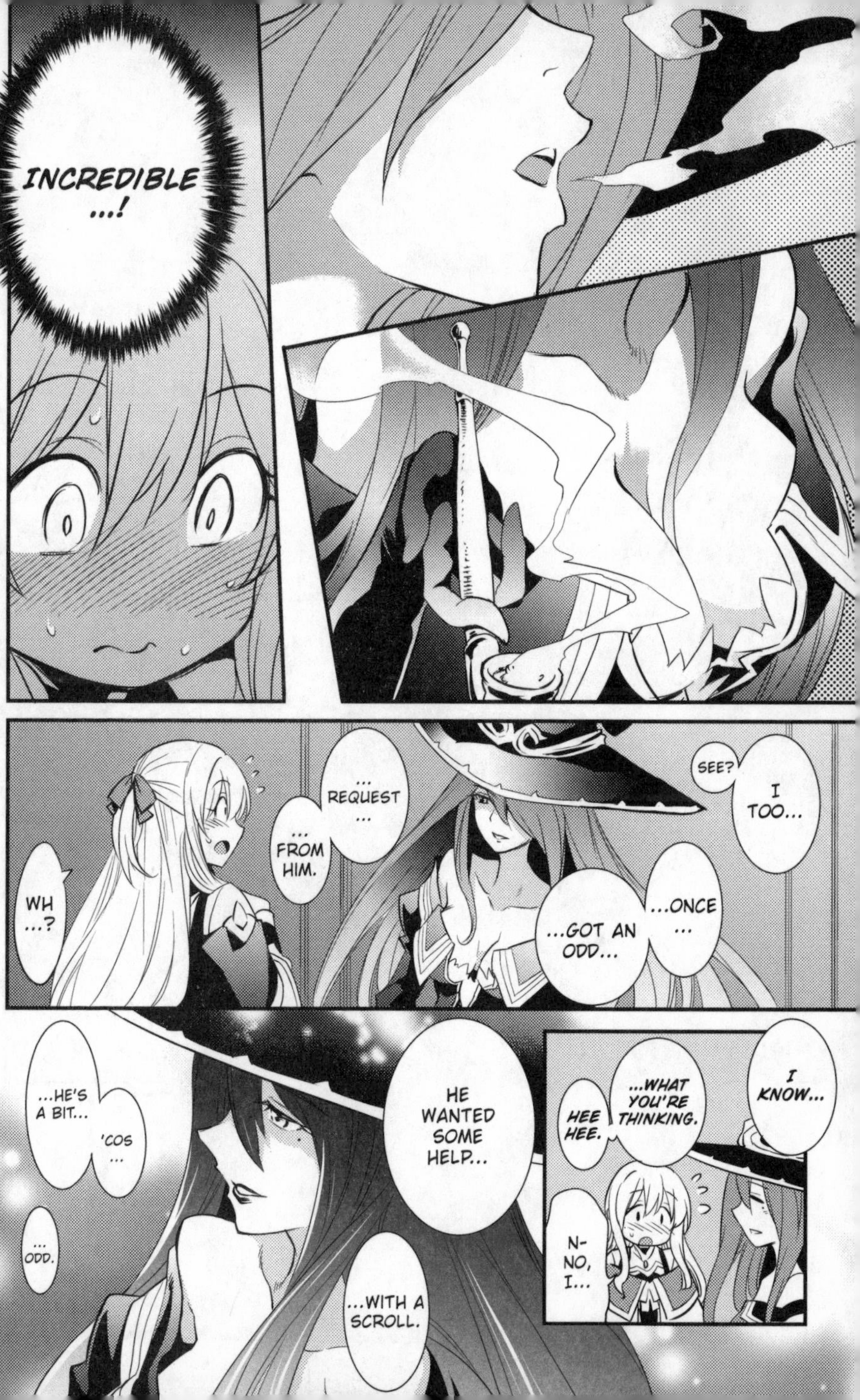
INCREDIBLE ...!
SEE?
I TOO...
...ONCE ...
...GOT AN ODD...
... REQUEST ...
... FROM HIM.
WH ...?
I KNOW...
...WHAT YOU'RE THINKING.
HEE HEE.
N-NO, I...
HE WANTED SOME HELP...
...WITH A SCROLL.
...HE'S A BIT...
'COS ...
... ODD.

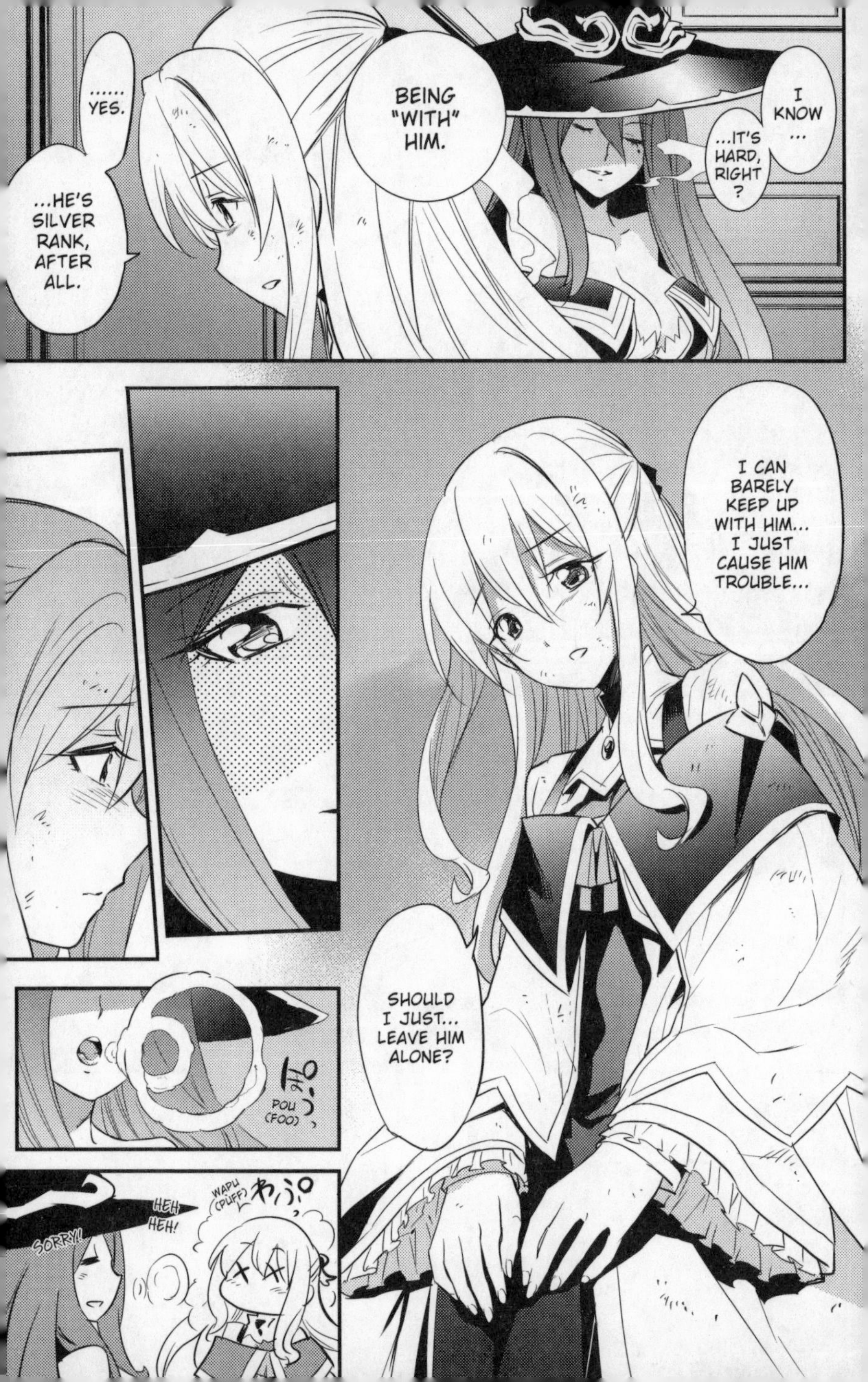
I KNOW ...
...IT'S HARD, RIGHT ?
BEING "WITH" HIM.
...... YES.
...HE'S SILVER RANK, AFTER ALL.
I CAN BARELY KEEP UP WITH HIM... I JUST CAUSE HIM TROUBLE...
SHOULD I JUST... LEAVE HIM ALONE?
ぽっ
POU (FOO)
わぷっ
WAPU (PUFF)
HEH HEH!
SORRY!

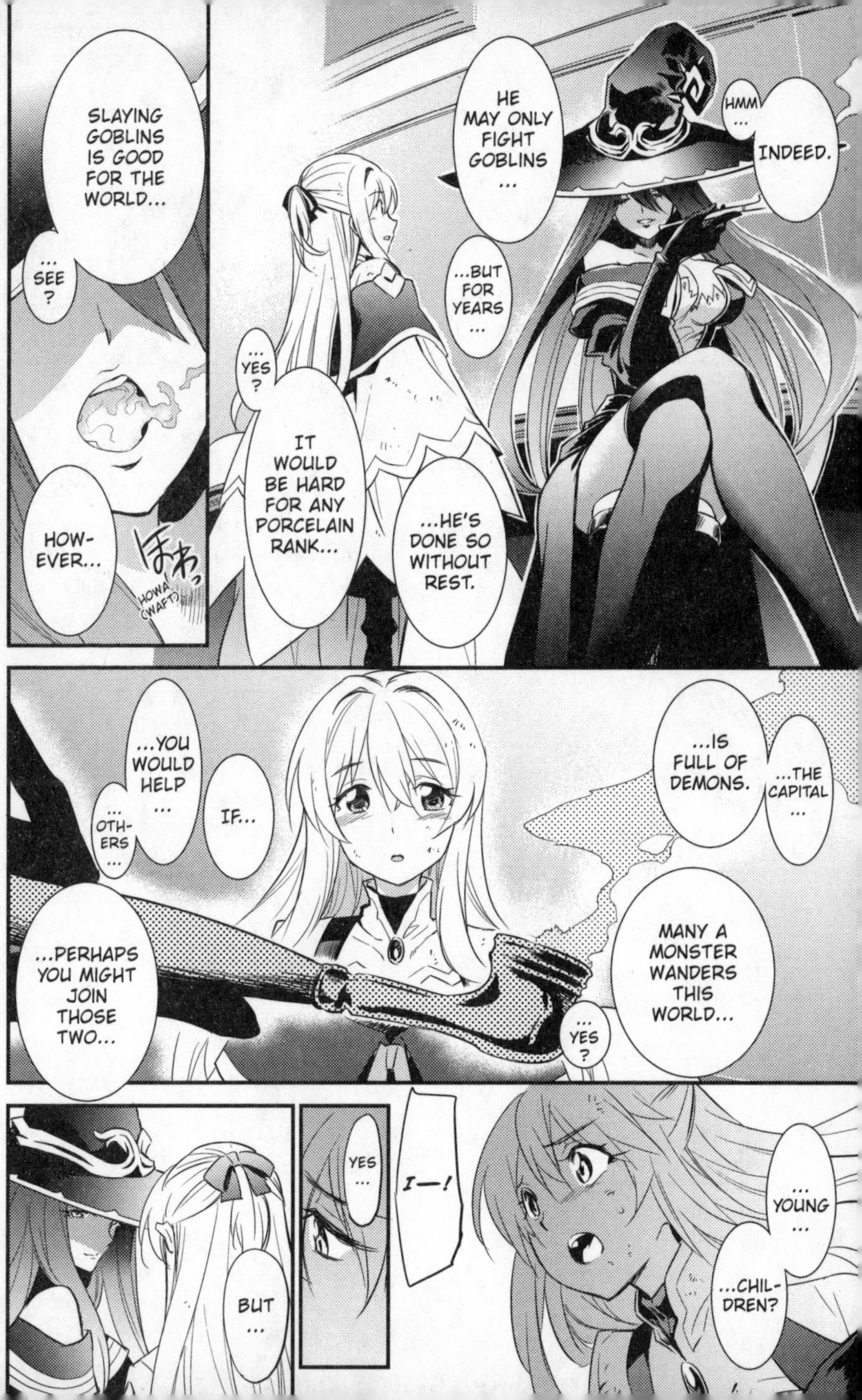
HMM...
INDEED.
HE MAY ONLY FIGHT GOBLINS...
...BUT FOR YEARS...
...YES?
IT WOULD BE HARD FOR ANY PORCELAIN RANK...
...HE'S DONE SO WITHOUT REST.
SLAYING GOBLINS IS GOOD FOR THE WORLD...
...SEE?
HOW-EVER...
ほわっ
HOWA (WAFT)
...THE CAPITAL...
...IS FULL OF DEMONS.
MANY A MONSTER WANDERS THIS WORLD...
...YES?
IF...
...YOU WOULD HELP...
...OTHERS...
...PERHAPS YOU MIGHT JOIN THOSE TWO...
...YOUNG...
...CHIL-DREN?
I—!
YES...
BUT...

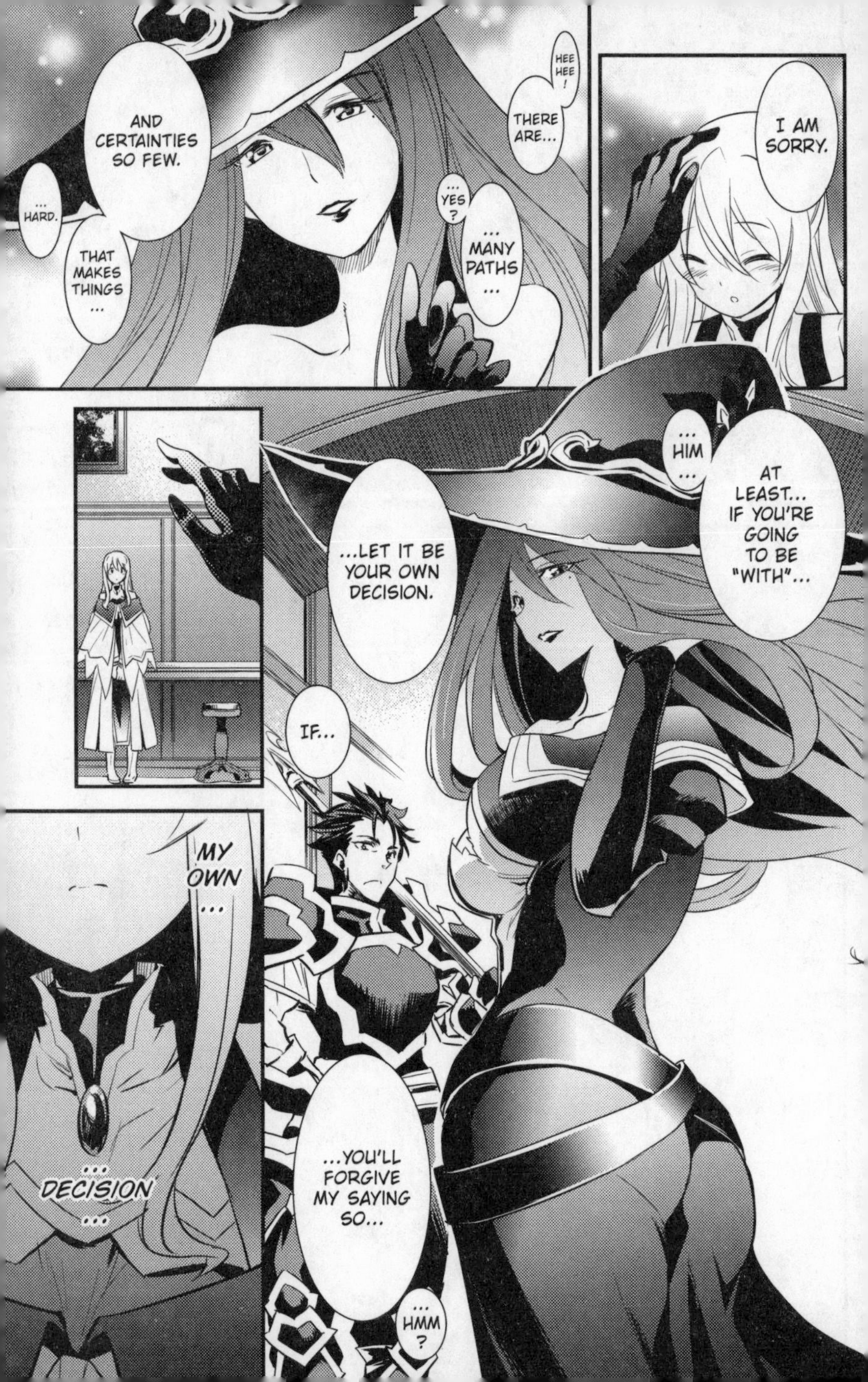
I AM SORRY.
HEE HEE!
THERE ARE...
...YES?
...MANY PATHS...
AND CERTAINTIES SO FEW.
THAT MAKES THINGS...
...HARD.
...HIM...
AT LEAST... IF YOU'RE GOING TO BE "WITH"...
...LET IT BE YOUR OWN DECISION.
IF...
...YOU'LL FORGIVE MY SAYING SO...
...HMM?
MY OWN...
...DECISION...

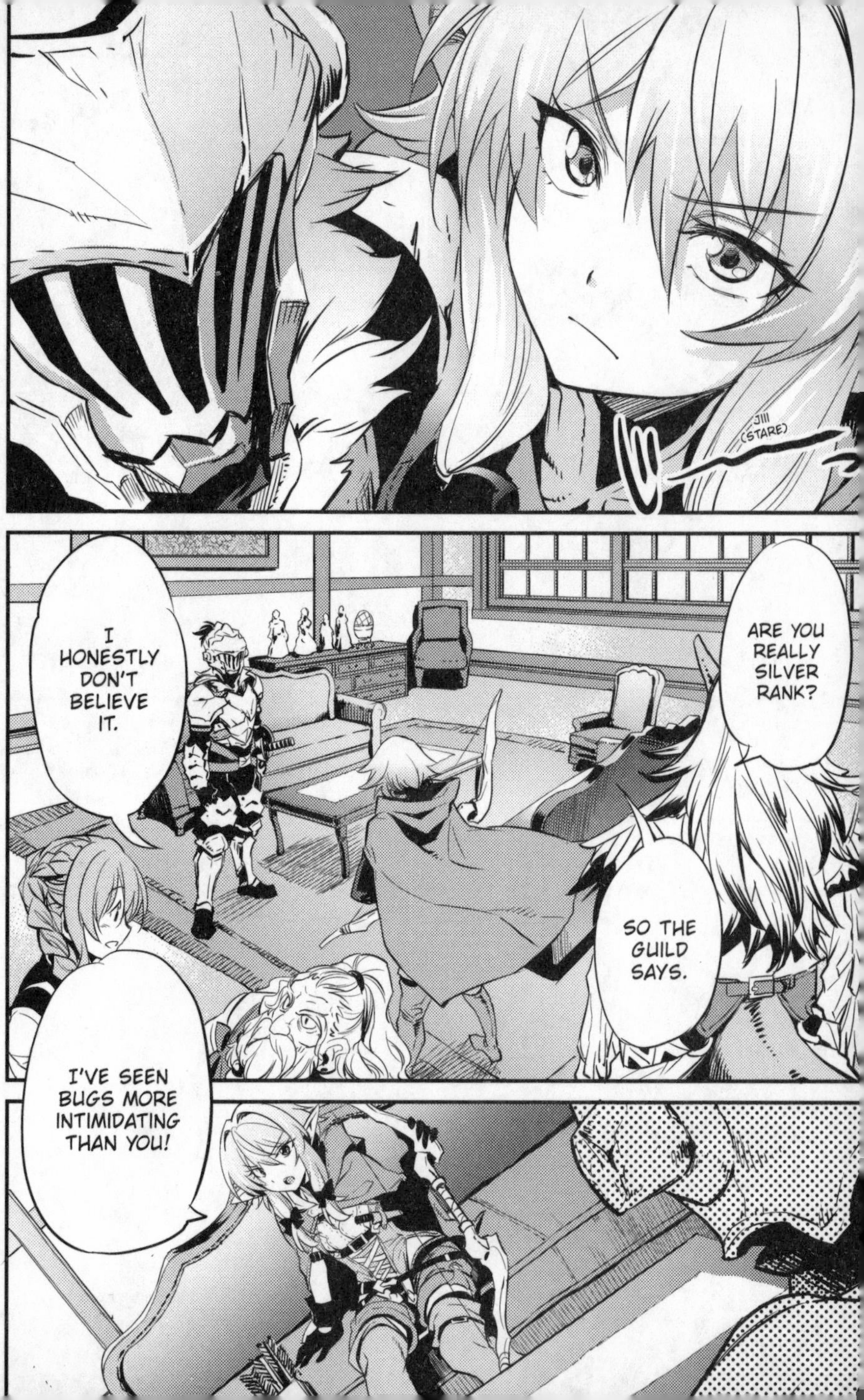
JIII
(STARE)
ARE YOU REALLY SILVER RANK?
SO THE GUILD SAYS.
I HONESTLY DON'T BELIEVE IT.
I'VE SEEN BUGS MORE INTIMIDATING THAN YOU!

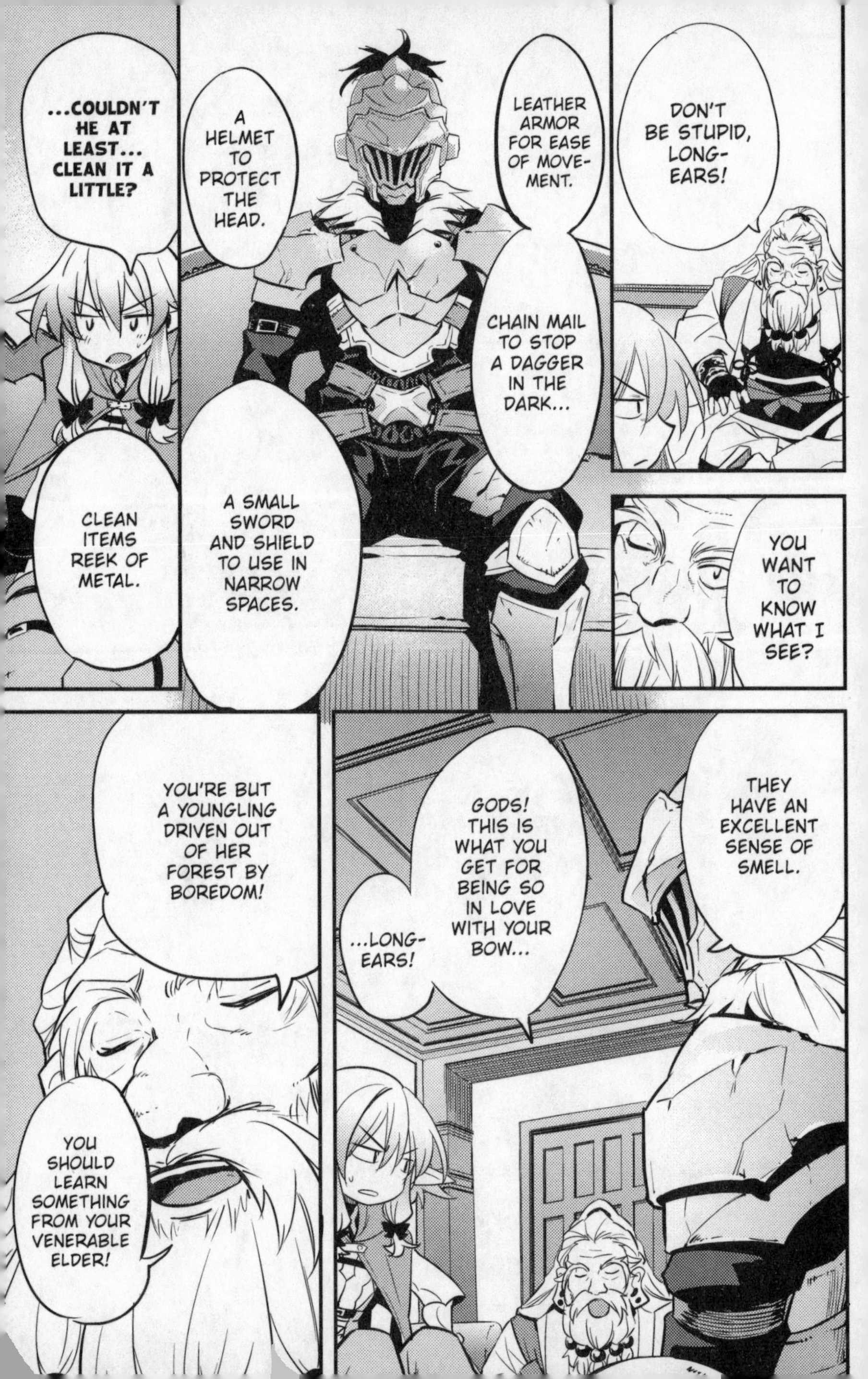
DON'T BE STUPID, LONG-EARS!
YOU WANT TO KNOW WHAT I SEE?
LEATHER ARMOR FOR EASE OF MOVE-MENT.
A HELMET TO PROTECT THE HEAD.
CHAIN MAIL TO STOP A DAGGER IN THE DARK...
A SMALL SWORD AND SHIELD TO USE IN NARROW SPACES.
...COULDN'T HE AT LEAST... CLEAN IT A LITTLE?
CLEAN ITEMS REEK OF METAL.
THEY HAVE AN EXCELLENT SENSE OF SMELL.
GODS! THIS IS WHAT YOU GET FOR BEING SO IN LOVE WITH YOUR BOW...
...LONG-EARS!
YOU'RE BUT A YOUNGLING DRIVEN OUT OF HER FOREST BY BOREDOM!
YOU SHOULD LEARN SOMETHING FROM YOUR VENERABLE ELDER!

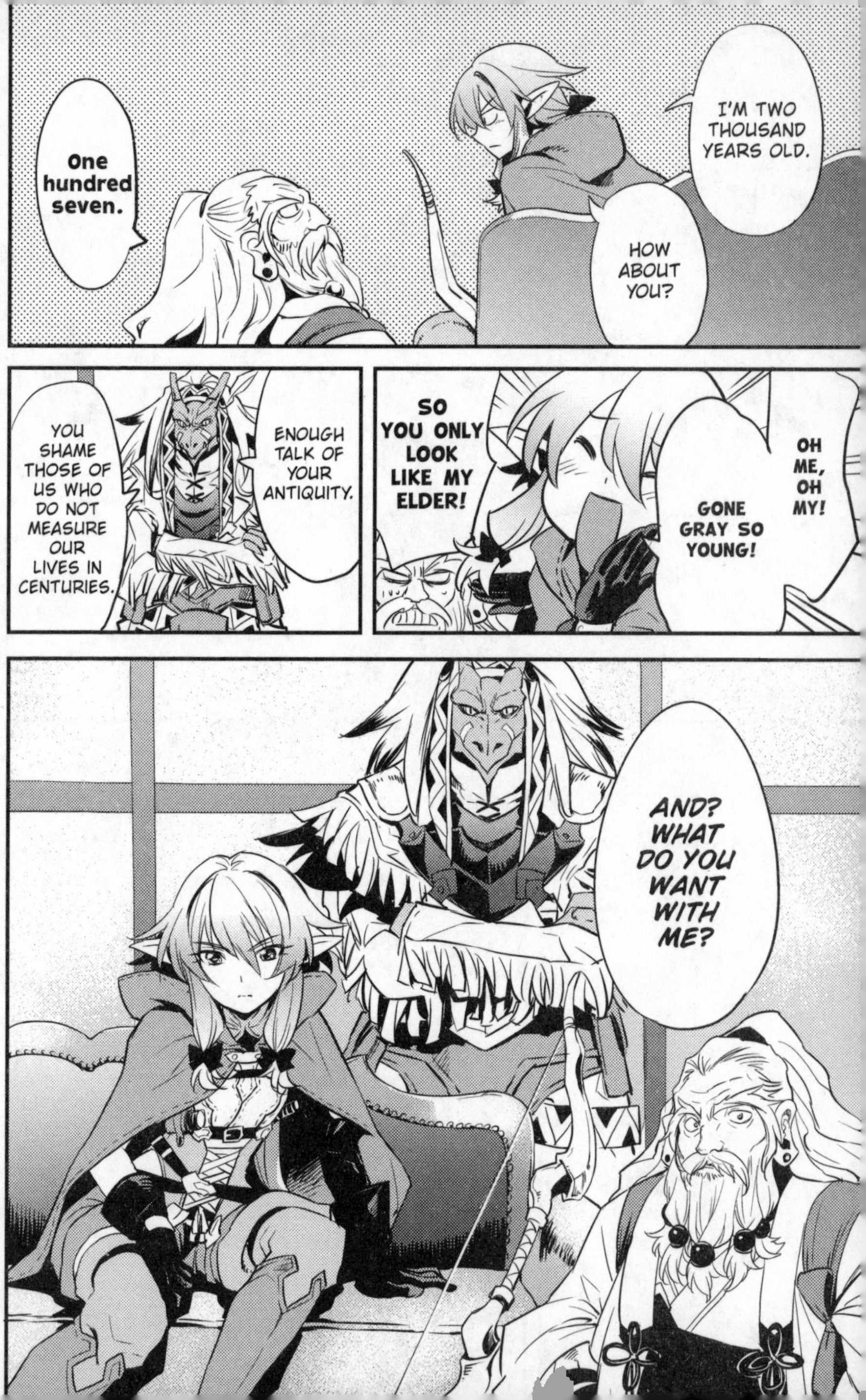
I'M TWO THOUSAND YEARS OLD.
HOW ABOUT YOU?
One hundred seven.
OH ME, OH MY!
GONE GRAY SO YOUNG!
SO YOU ONLY LOOK LIKE MY ELDER!
ENOUGH TALK OF YOUR ANTIQUITY.
YOU SHAME THOSE OF US WHO DO NOT MEASURE OUR LIVES IN CENTURIES.
AND? WHAT DO YOU WANT WITH ME?

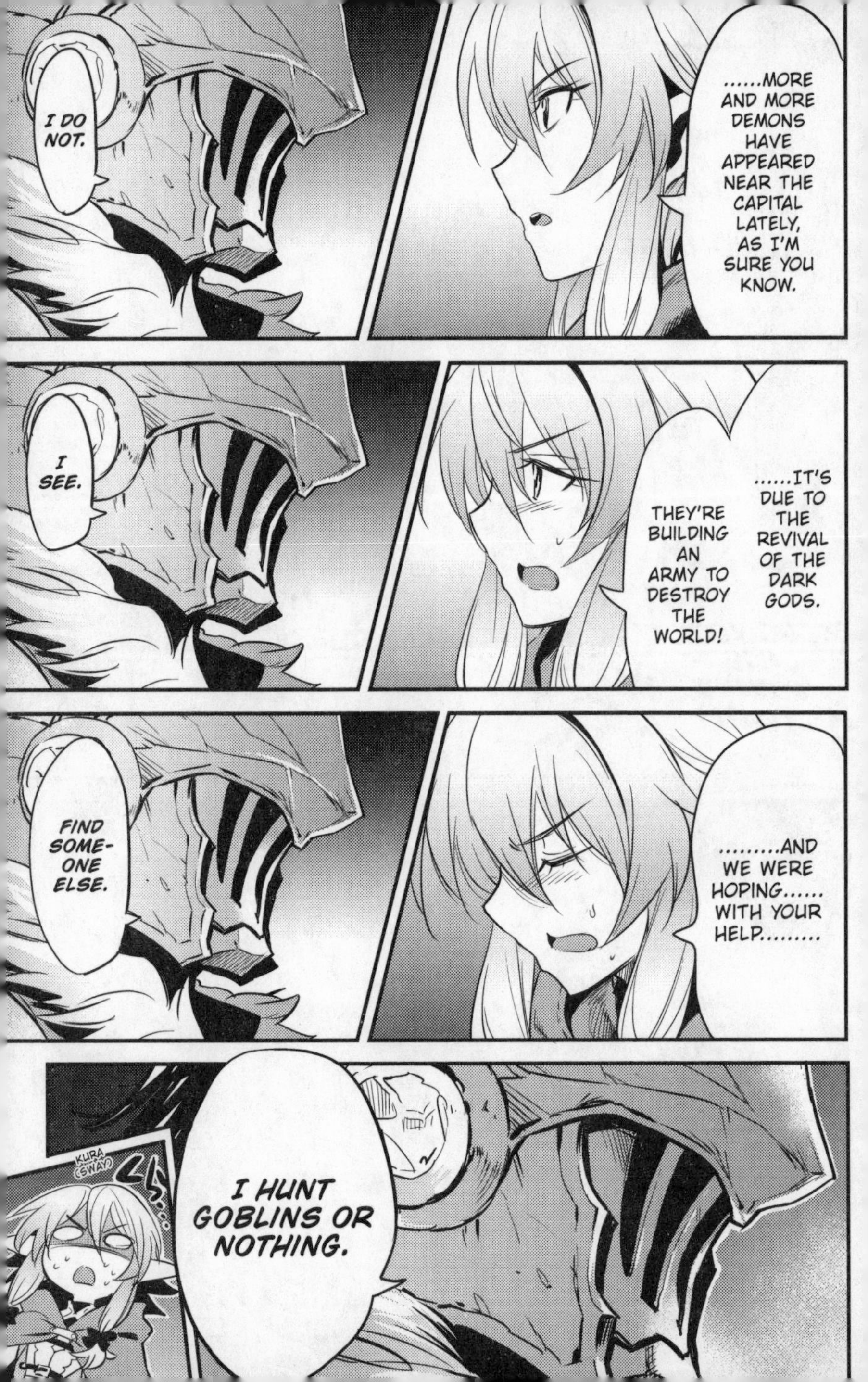
......MORE AND MORE DEMONS HAVE APPEARED NEAR THE CAPITAL LATELY, AS I'M SURE YOU KNOW.
I DO NOT.
......IT'S DUE TO THE REVIVAL OF THE DARK GODS.
THEY'RE BUILDING AN ARMY TO DESTROY THE WORLD!
I SEE.
.........AND WE WERE HOPING...... WITH YOUR HELP.........
FIND SOME-ONE ELSE.
I HUNT GOBLINS OR NOTHING.
KURA (SWAY)

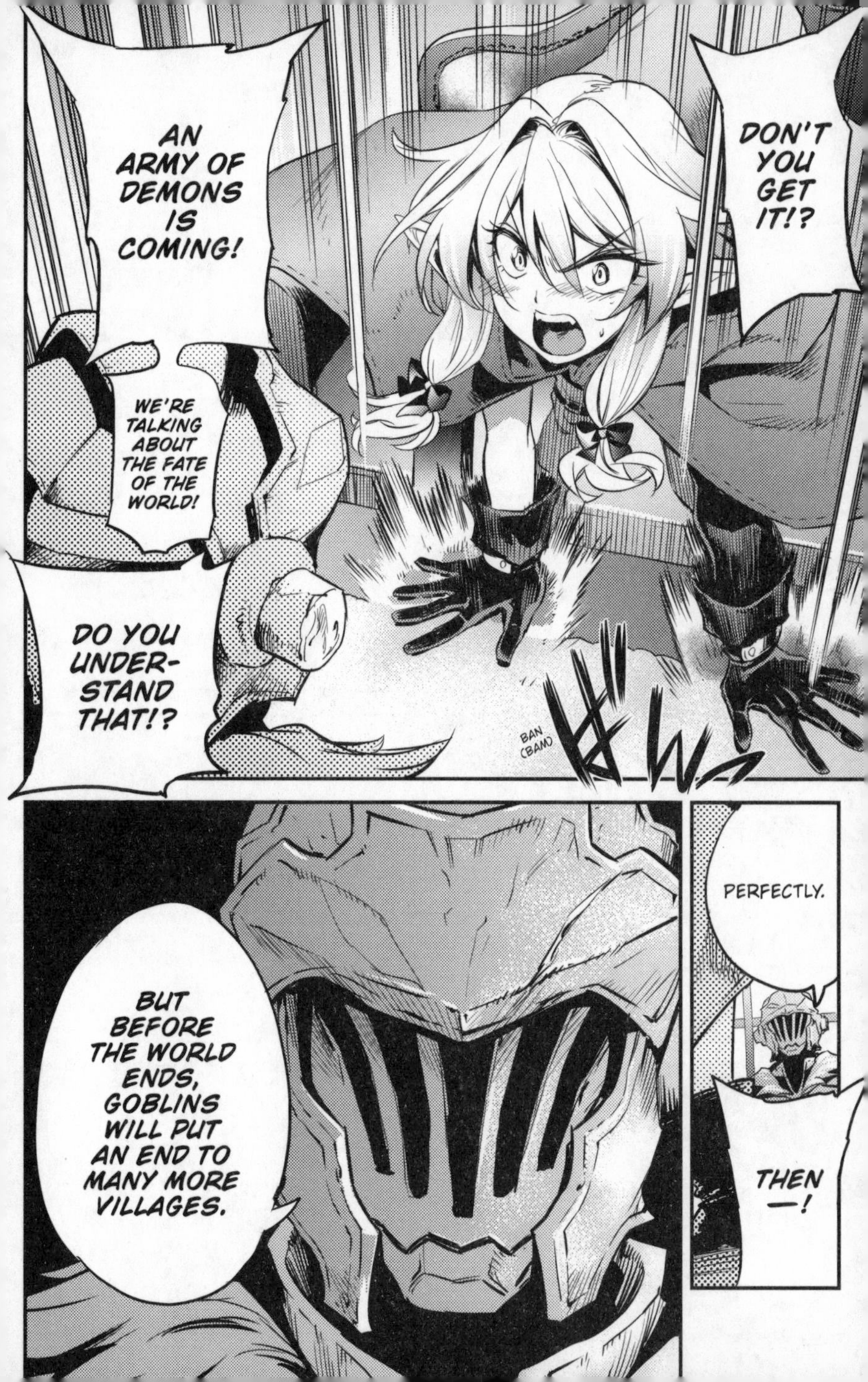
DON'T YOU GET IT!?
AN ARMY OF DEMONS IS COMING!
WE'RE TALKING ABOUT THE FATE OF THE WORLD!
BAN (BAM)
DO YOU UNDER-STAND THAT!?
PERFECTLY.
THEN—!
BUT BEFORE THE WORLD ENDS, GOBLINS WILL PUT AN END TO MANY MORE VILLAGES.

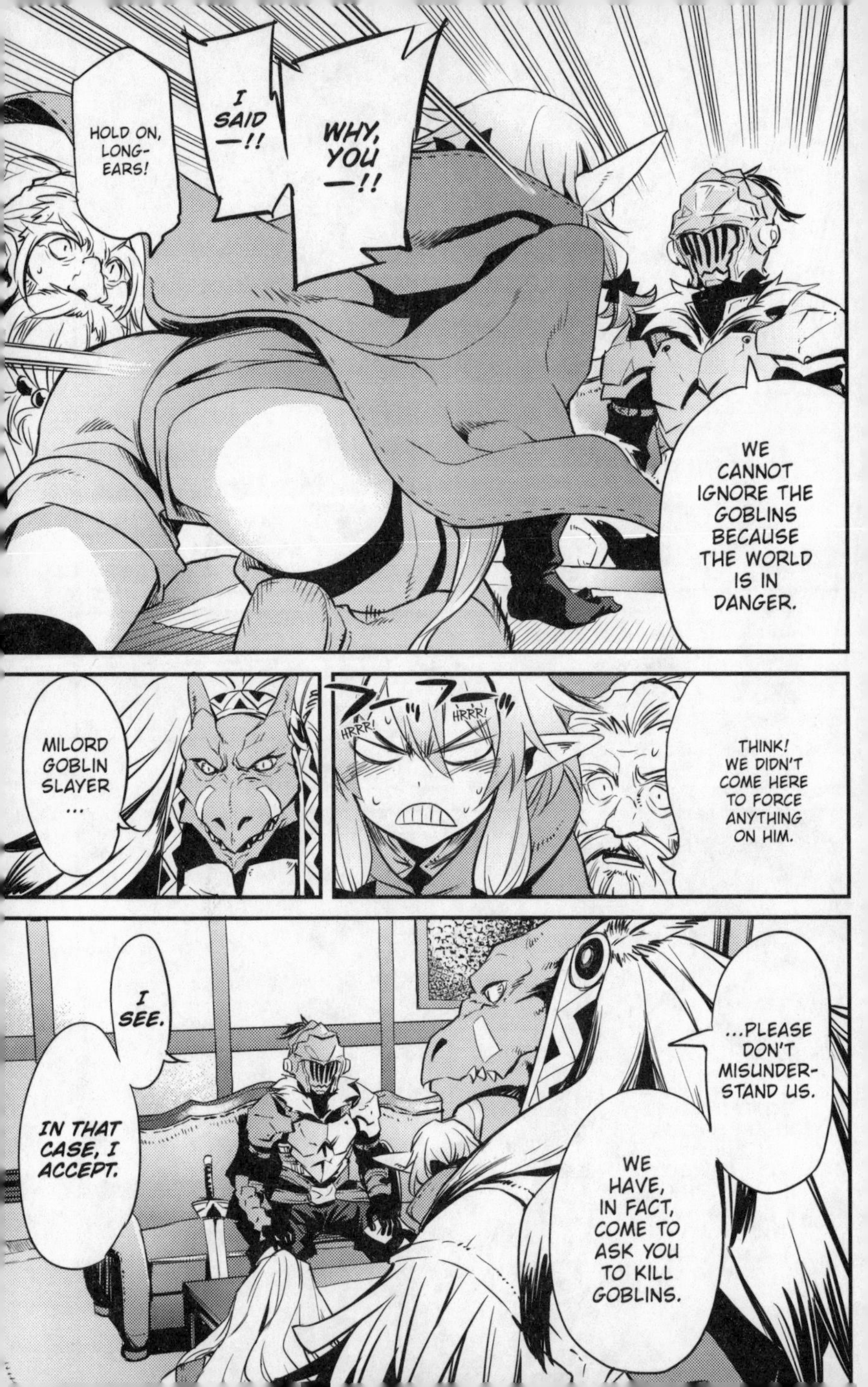
WE CANNOT IGNORE THE GOBLINS BECAUSE THE WORLD IS IN DANGER.
WHY, YOU—!!
I SAID—!!
HOLD ON, LONG-EARS!
THINK! WE DIDN'T COME HERE TO FORCE ANYTHING ON HIM.
HRRR!
HRRR!
MILORD GOBLIN SLAYER...
...PLEASE DON'T MISUNDER-STAND US.
WE HAVE, IN FACT, COME TO ASK YOU TO KILL GOBLINS.
I SEE.
IN THAT CASE, I ACCEPT.

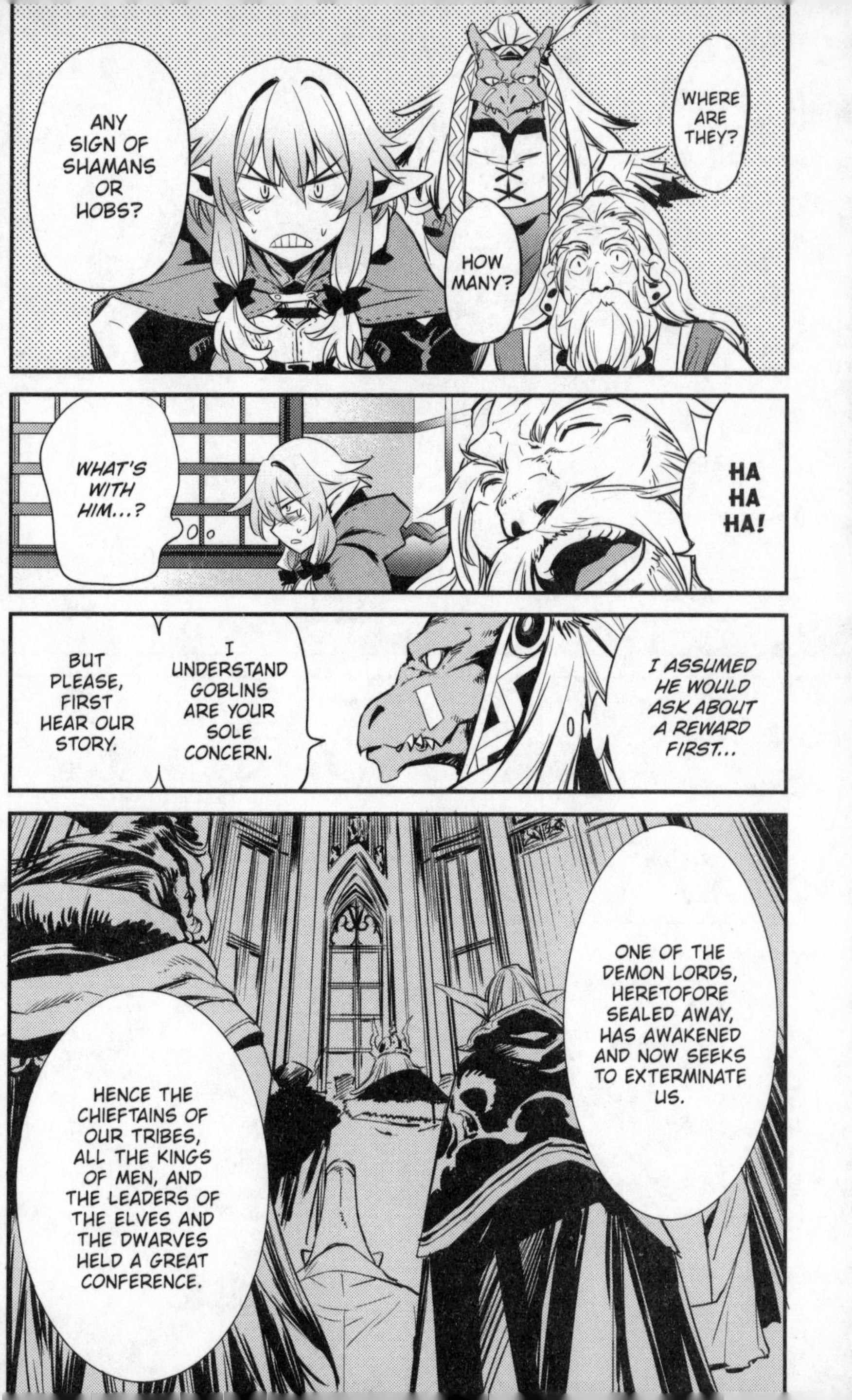
WHERE ARE THEY?
HOW MANY?
ANY SIGN OF SHAMANS OR HOBS?
HA HA HA!
WHAT'S WITH HIM...?
I ASSUMED HE WOULD ASK ABOUT A REWARD FIRST...
I UNDERSTAND GOBLINS ARE YOUR SOLE CONCERN.
BUT PLEASE, FIRST HEAR OUR STORY.
ONE OF THE DEMON LORDS, HERETOFORE SEALED AWAY, HAS AWAKENED AND NOW SEEKS TO EXTERMINATE US.
HENCE THE CHIEFTAINS OF OUR TRIBES, ALL THE KINGS OF MEN, AND THE LEADERS OF THE ELVES AND THE DWARVES HELD A GREAT CONFERENCE.

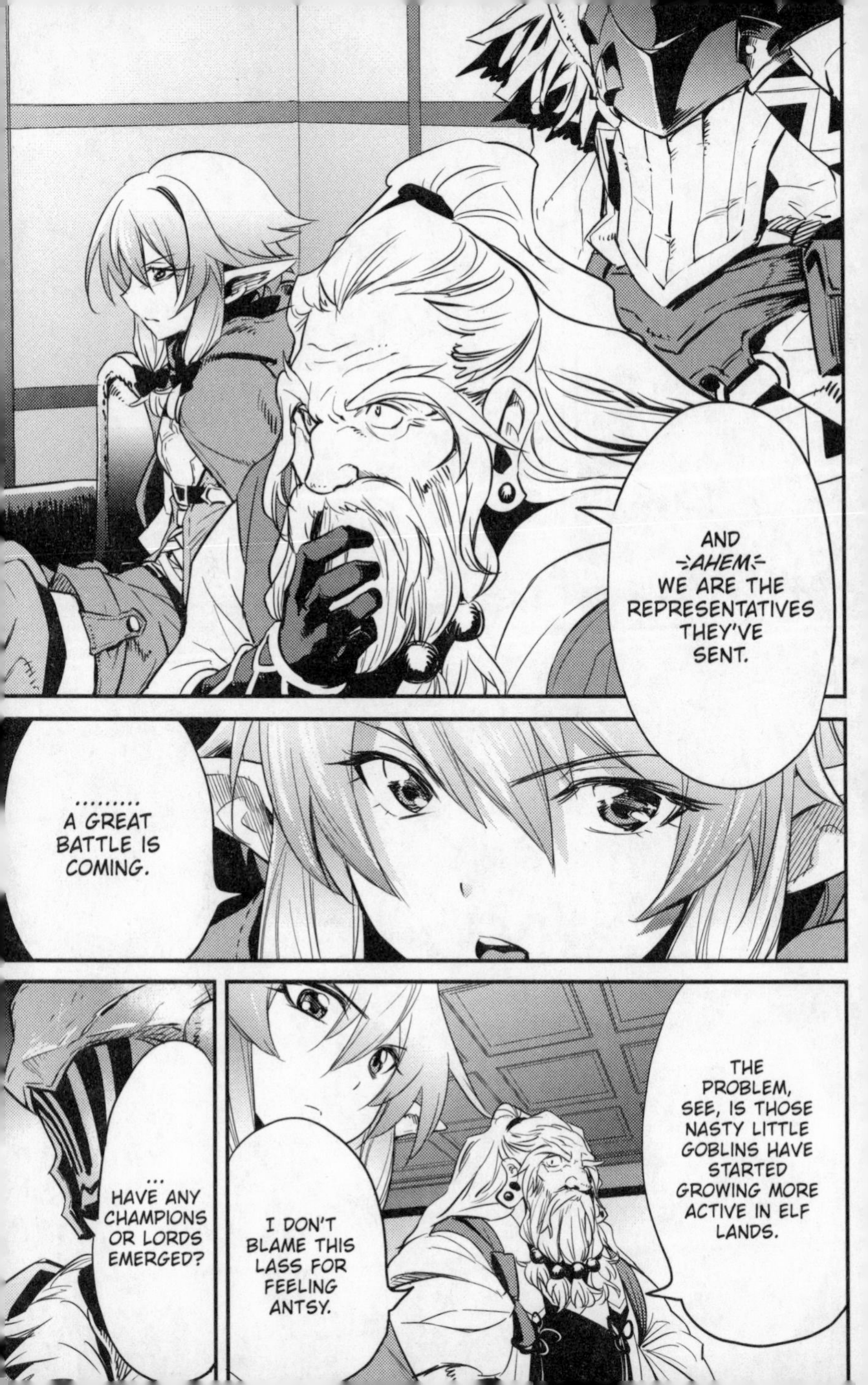
AND -AHEM- WE ARE THE REPRESENTATIVES THEY'VE SENT.
.... A GREAT BATTLE IS COMING.
THE PROBLEM, SEE, IS THOSE NASTY LITTLE GOBLINS HAVE STARTED GROWING MORE ACTIVE IN ELF LANDS.
I DON'T BLAME THIS LASS FOR FEELING ANTSY.
... HAVE ANY CHAMPIONS OR LORDS EMERGED?

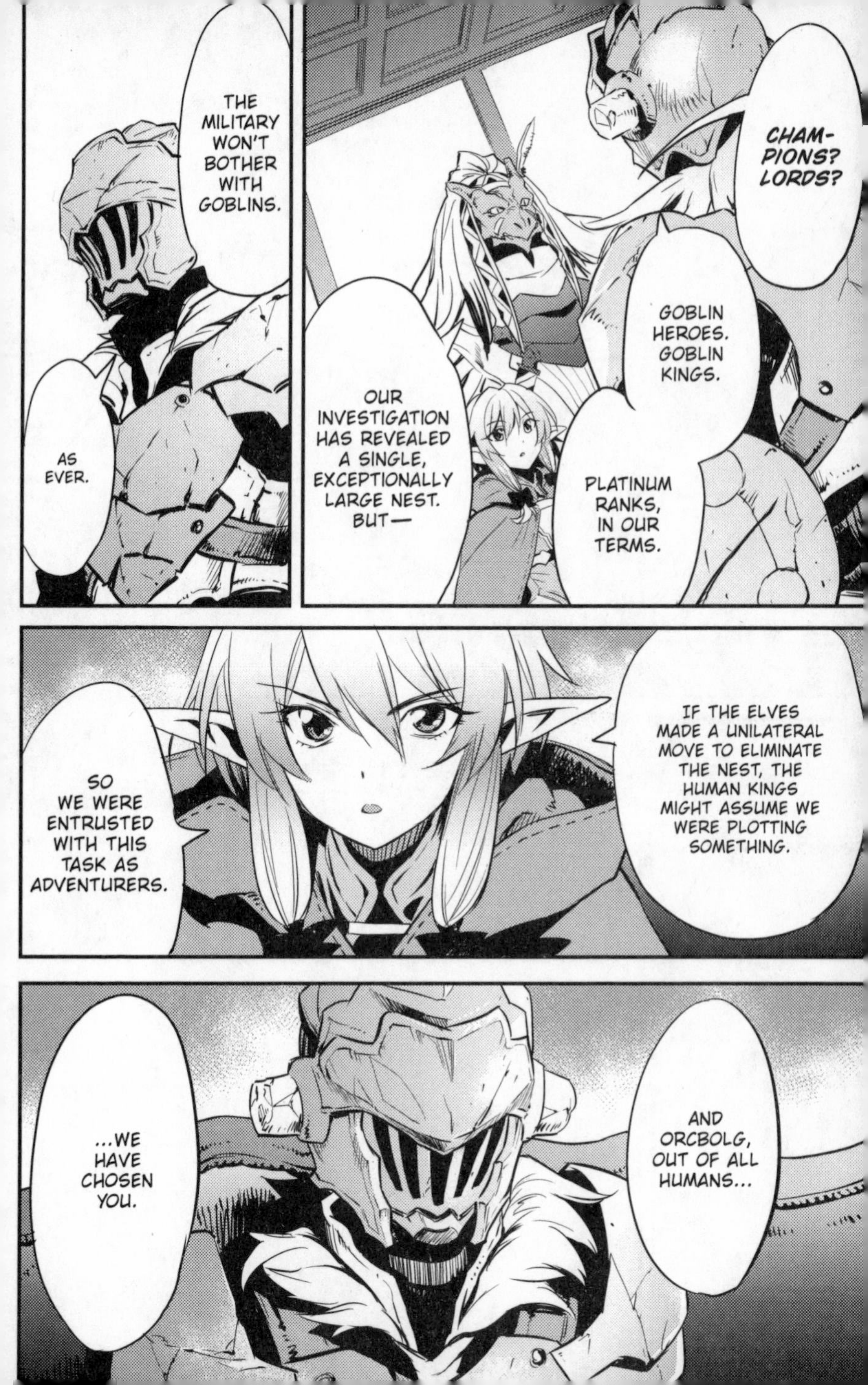
CHAMPIONS? LORDS?
GOBLIN HEROES. GOBLIN KINGS.
PLATINUM RANKS, IN OUR TERMS.
OUR INVESTIGATION HAS REVEALED A SINGLE, EXCEPTIONALLY LARGE NEST. BUT—
THE MILITARY WON'T BOTHER WITH GOBLINS.
AS EVER.
IF THE ELVES MADE A UNILATERAL MOVE TO ELIMINATE THE NEST, THE HUMAN KINGS MIGHT ASSUME WE WERE PLOTTING SOMETHING.
SO WE WERE ENTRUSTED WITH THIS TASK AS ADVENTURERS.
AND ORCBOLG, OUT OF ALL HUMANS...
...WE HAVE CHOSEN YOU.

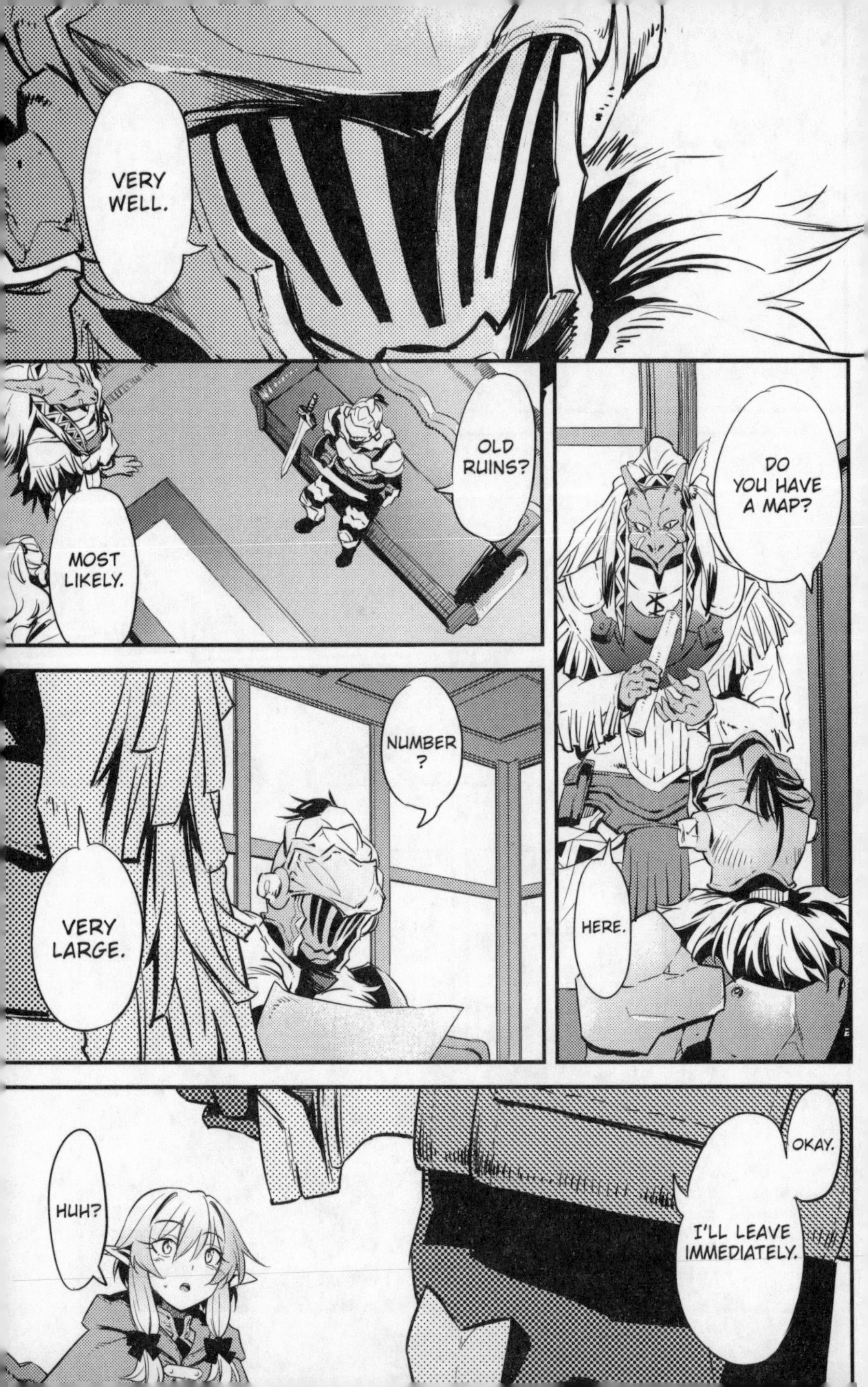

VERY WELL.
DO YOU HAVE A MAP?
HERE.
OLD RUINS?
MOST LIKELY.
NUMBER?
VERY LARGE.
OKAY.
I'LL LEAVE IMMEDIATELY.
HUH?

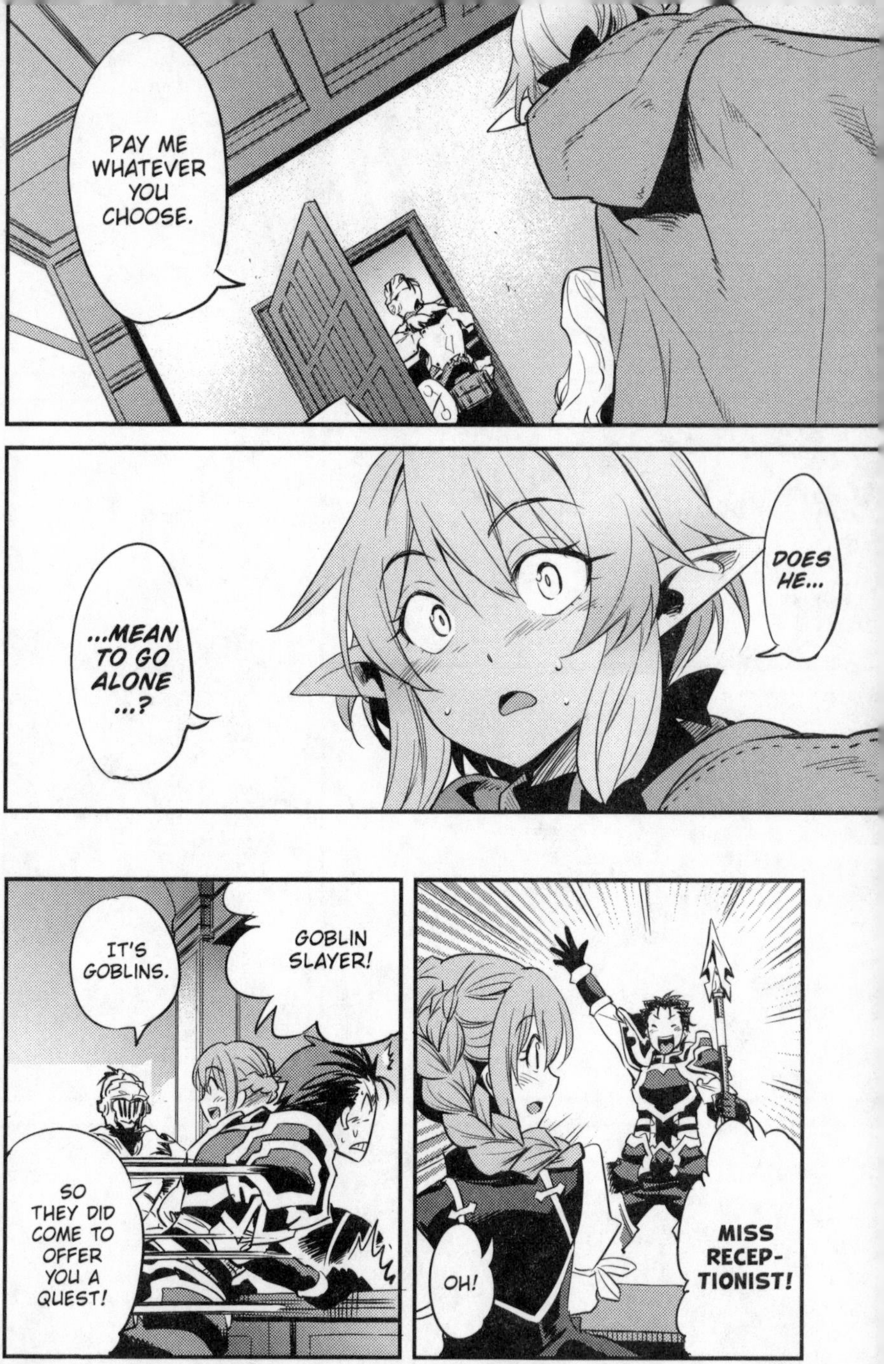
PAY ME WHATEVER YOU CHOOSE.
DOES HE...
...MEAN TO GO ALONE ...?
MISS RECEP-TIONIST!
OH!
GOBLIN SLAYER!
IT'S GOBLINS.
SO THEY DID COME TO OFFER YOU A QUEST!

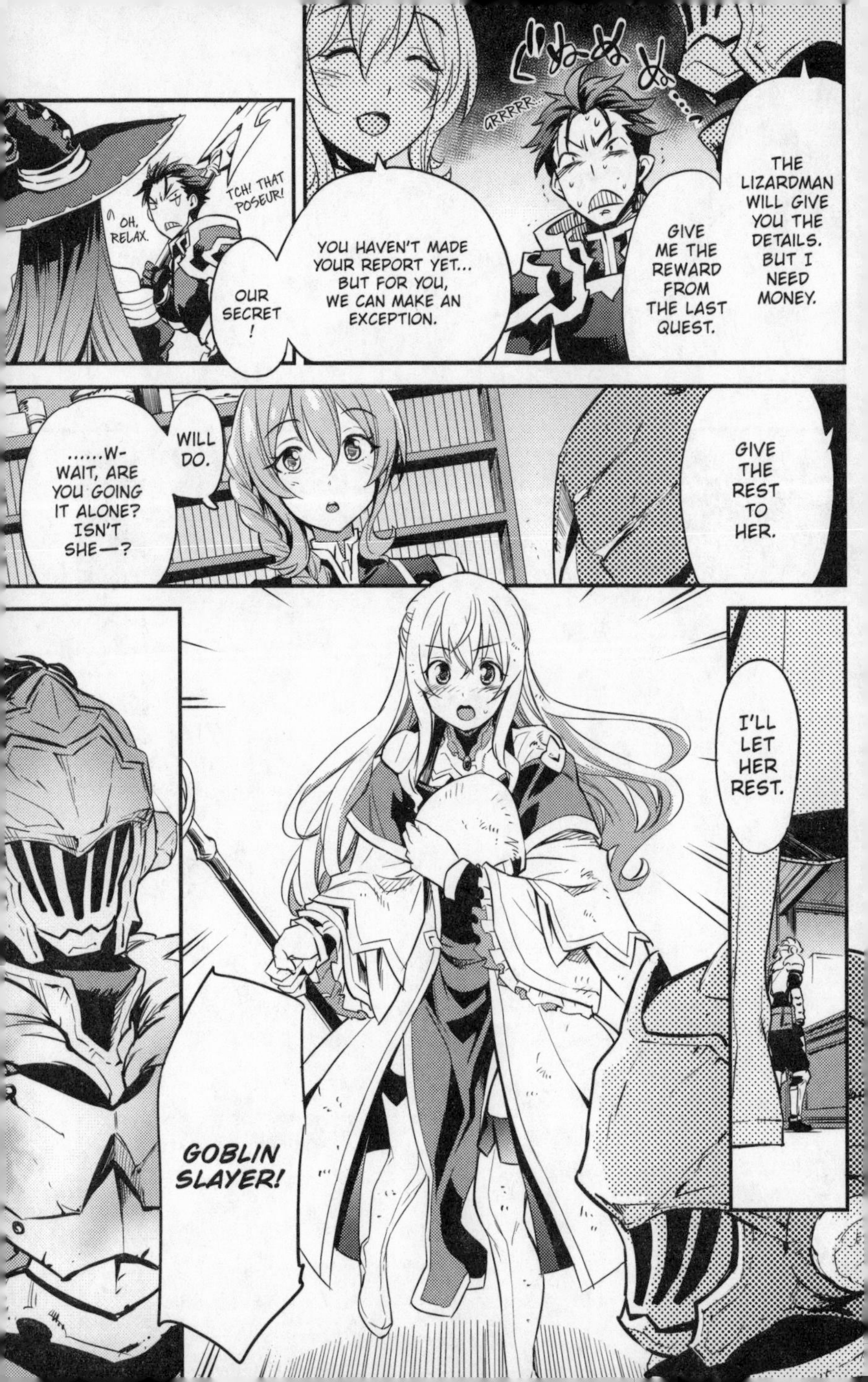
THE LIZARDMAN WILL GIVE YOU THE DETAILS. BUT I NEED MONEY.
GIVE ME THE REWARD FROM THE LAST QUEST.
GRRRRR...
YOU HAVEN'T MADE YOUR REPORT YET... BUT FOR YOU, WE CAN MAKE AN EXCEPTION.
OUR SECRET!
TCH! THAT POSEUR!
OH, RELAX.
GIVE THE REST TO HER.
WILL DO.
......W-WAIT, ARE YOU GOING IT ALONE? ISN'T SHE—?
I'LL LET HER REST.
GOBLIN SLAYER!

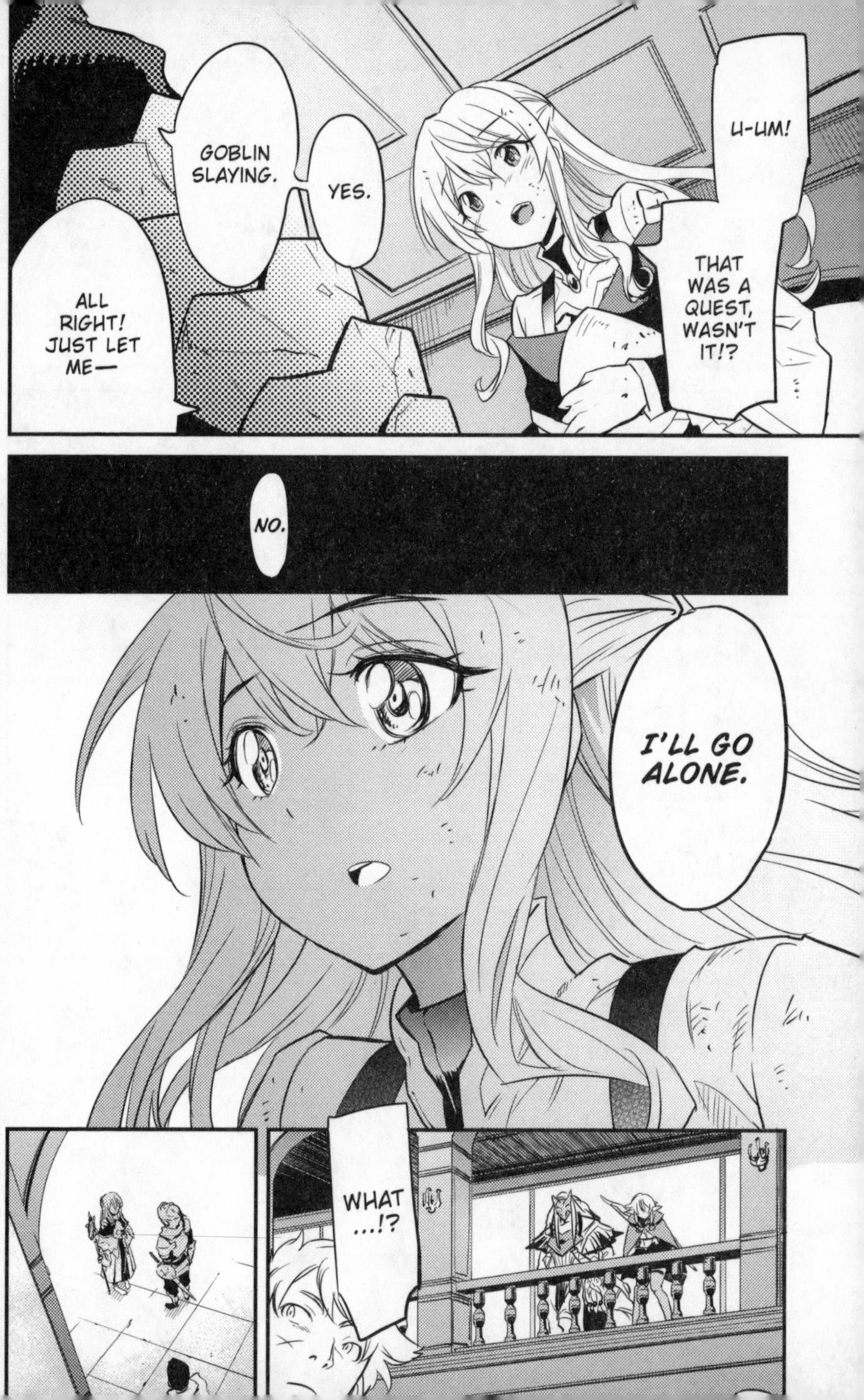
U-UM!
THAT WAS A QUEST, WASN'T IT!?
YES.
GOBLIN SLAYING.
ALL RIGHT! JUST LET ME—
NO.
I'LL GO ALONE.
WHAT ...!?

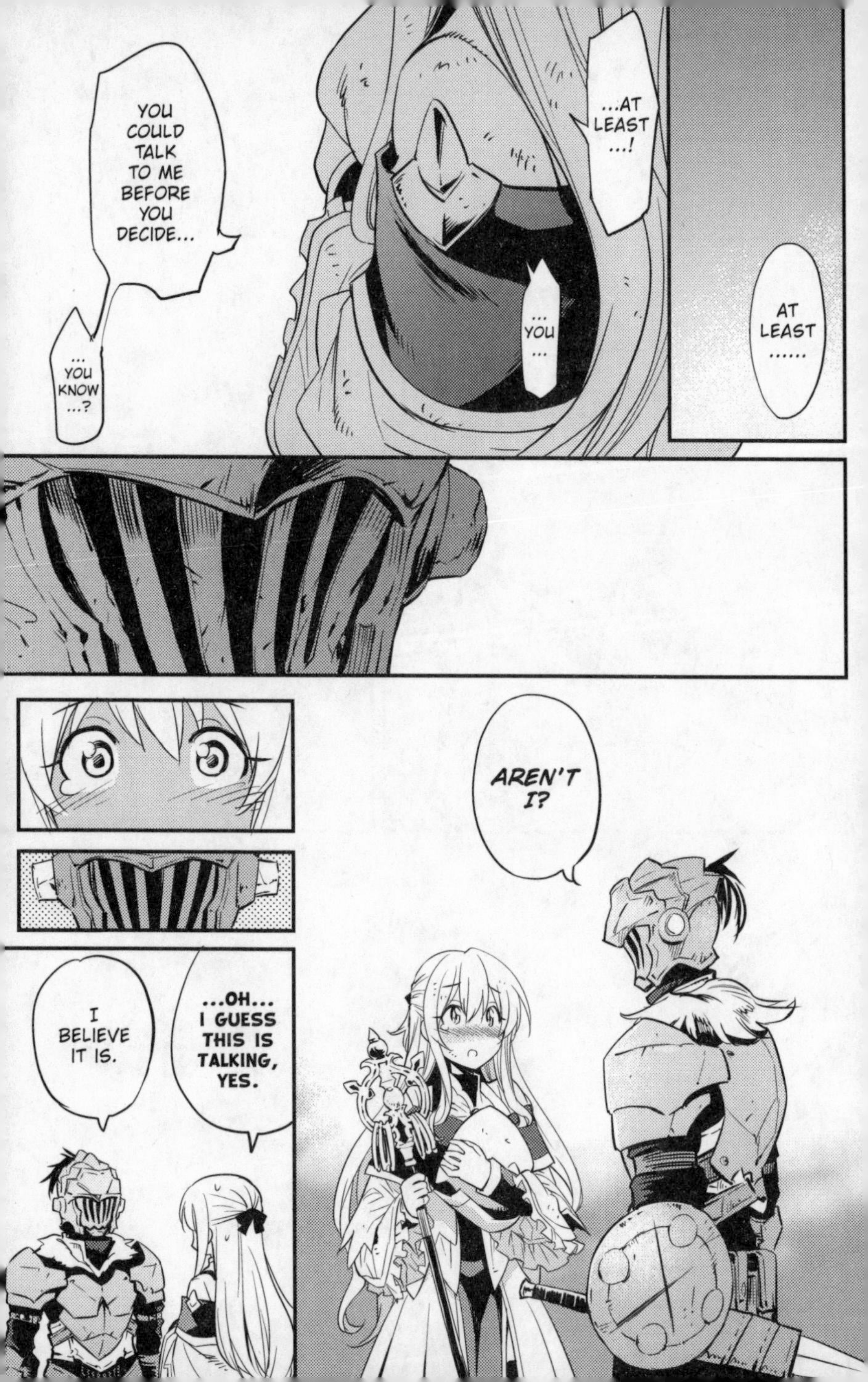
AT LEAST......
...AT LEAST...!
...YOU...
YOU COULD TALK TO ME BEFORE YOU DECIDE...
...YOU KNOW...?
AREN'T I?
...OH... I GUESS THIS IS TALKING, YES.
I BELIEVE IT IS.

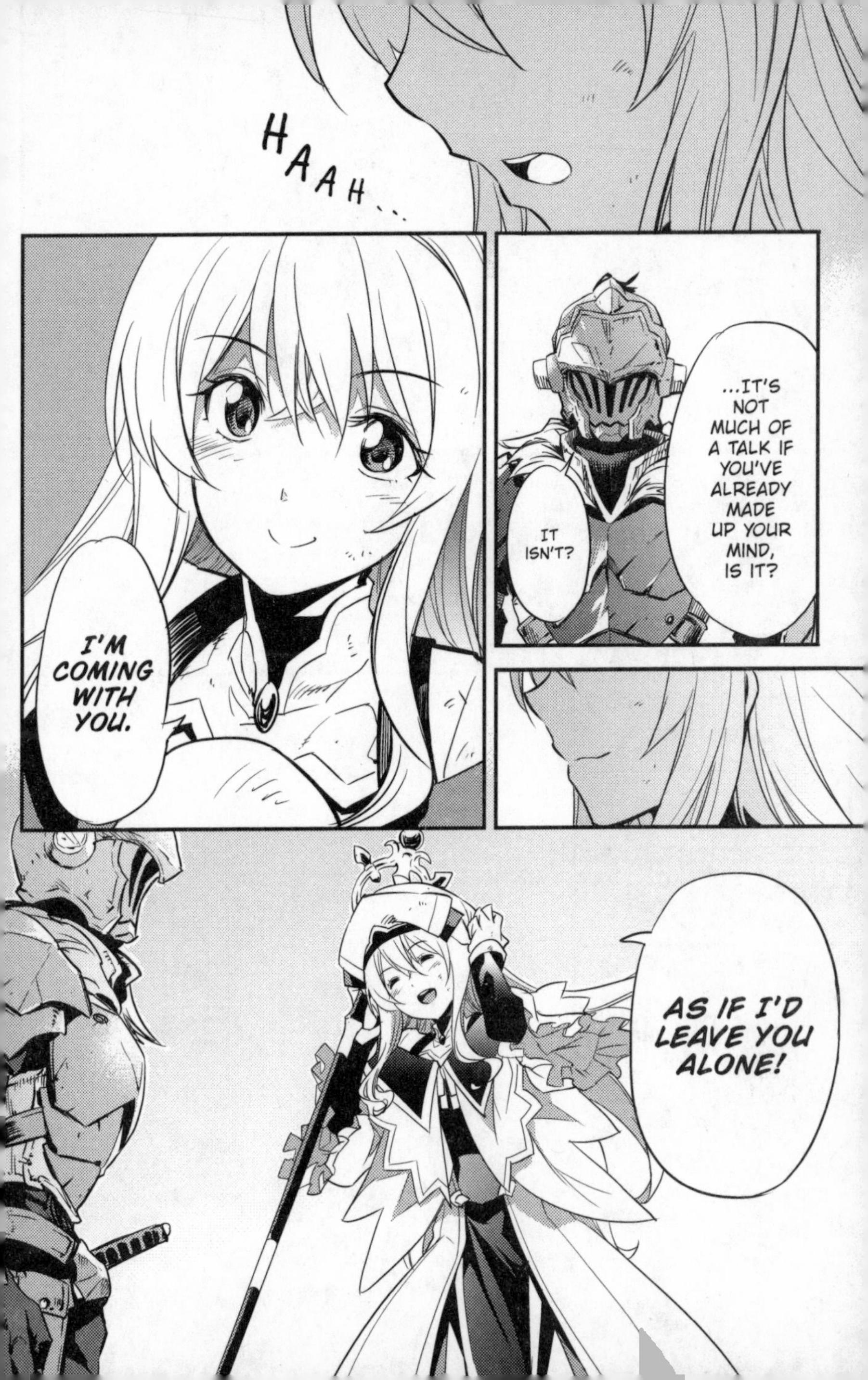
HAAH...
...IT'S NOT MUCH OF A TALK IF YOU'VE ALREADY MADE UP YOUR MIND, IS IT?
IT ISN'T?
I'M COMING WITH YOU.
AS IF I'D LEAVE YOU ALONE!

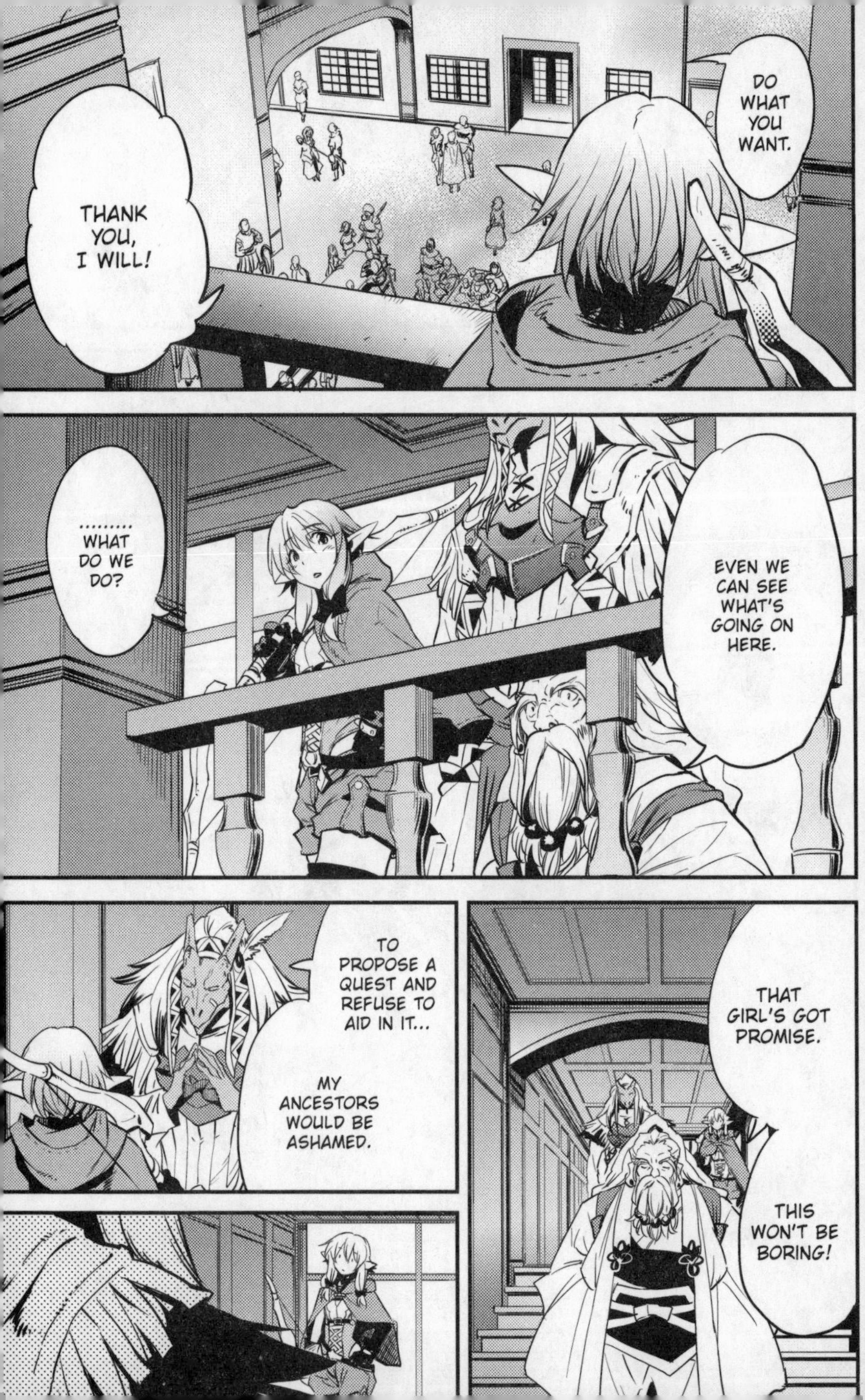
DO WHAT YOU WANT.
THANK YOU, I WILL!
EVEN WE CAN SEE WHAT'S GOING ON HERE.
.........WHAT DO WE DO?
THAT GIRL'S GOT PROMISE.
THIS WON'T BE BORING!
TO PROPOSE A QUEST AND REFUSE TO AID IN IT...
MY ANCESTORS WOULD BE ASHAMED.

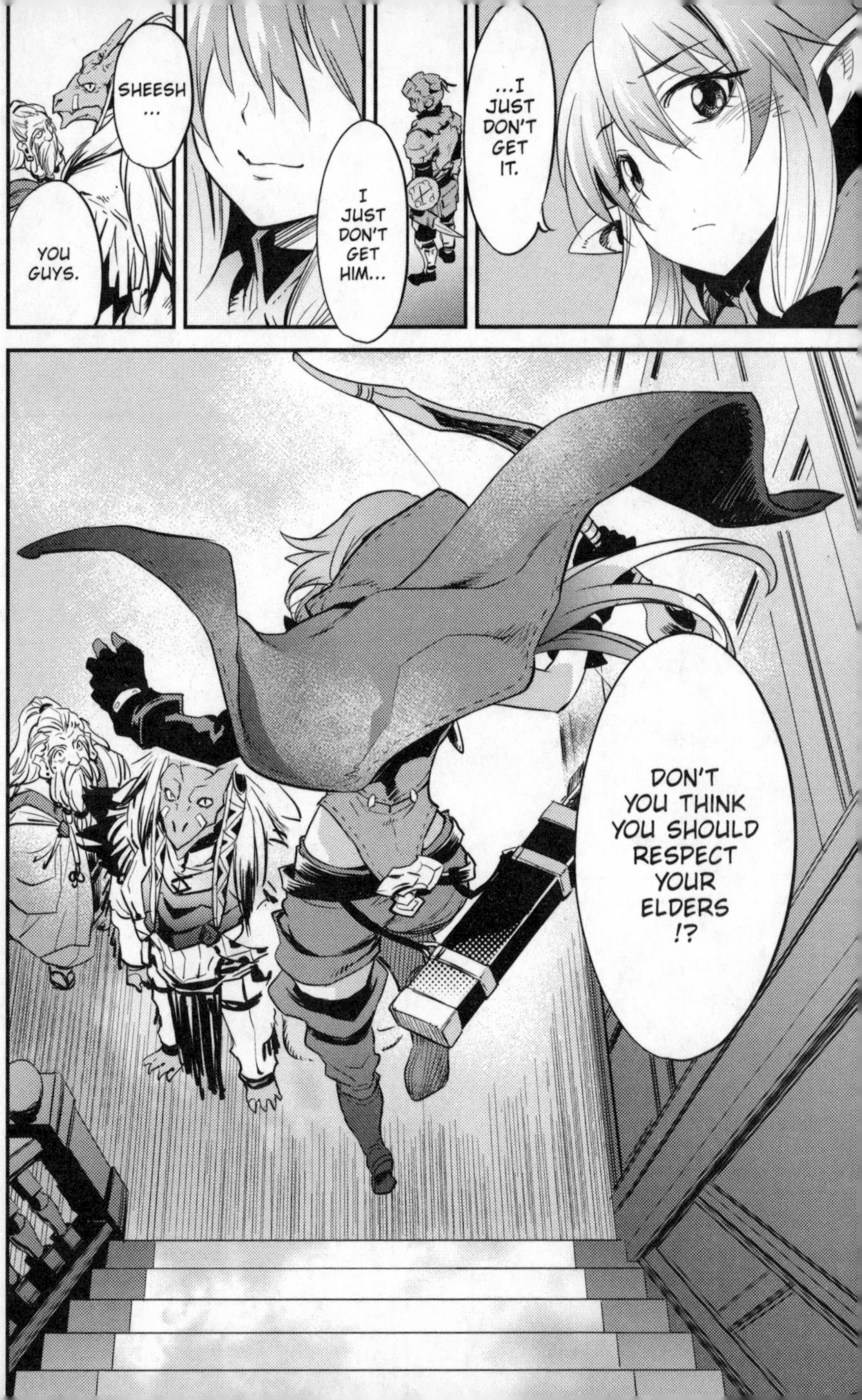
...I JUST DON'T GET IT.
I JUST DON'T GET HIM...
SHEESH ...
YOU GUYS.
DON'T YOU THINK YOU SHOULD RESPECT YOUR ELDERS !?

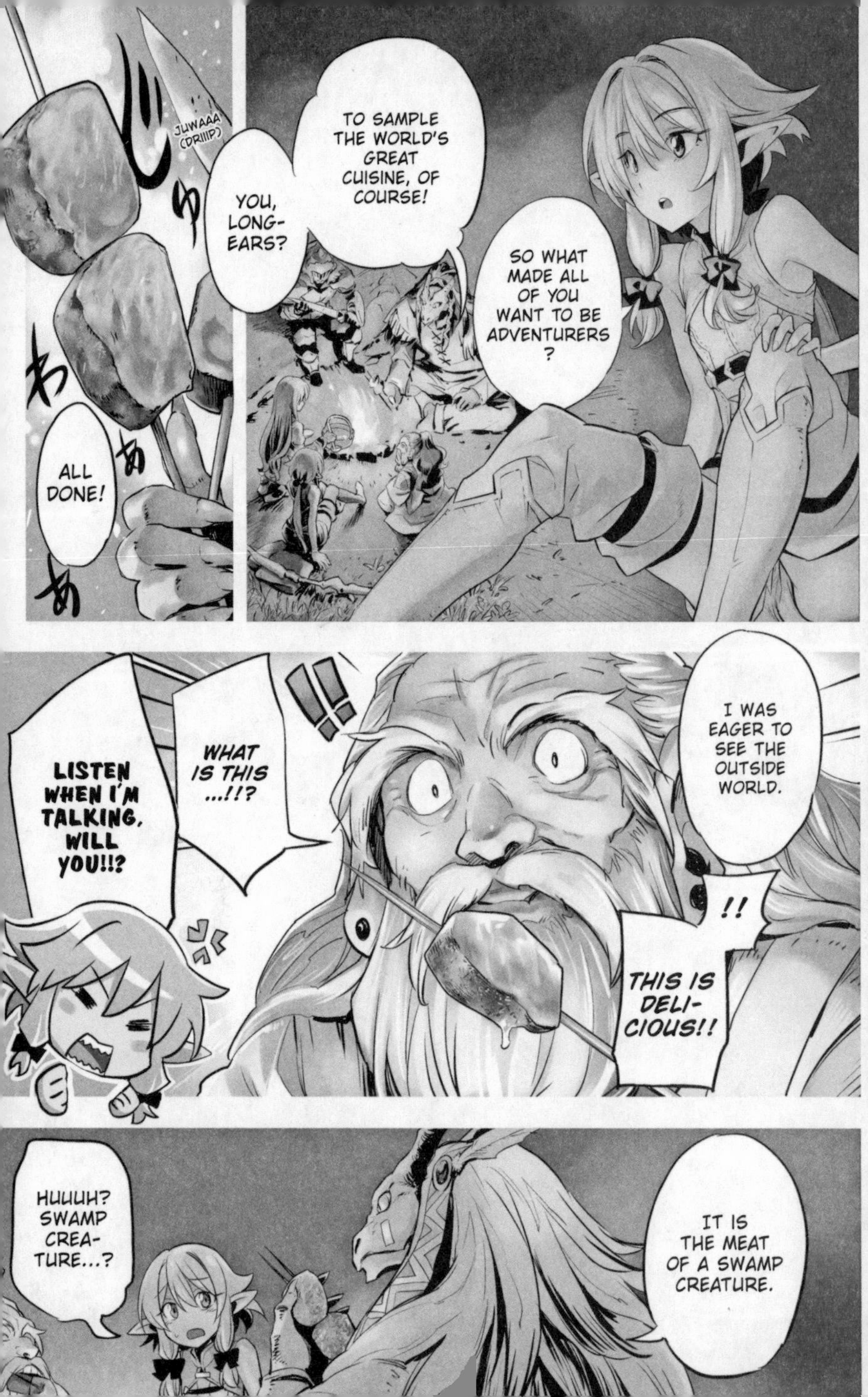
SO WHAT MADE ALL OF YOU WANT TO BE ADVENTURERS ?
TO SAMPLE THE WORLD'S GREAT CUISINE, OF COURSE!
YOU, LONG-EARS?
JUWAAA (DRIIIP)
ALL DONE!
I WAS EAGER TO SEE THE OUTSIDE WORLD.
!!
THIS IS DELI-CIOUS!!
WHAT IS THIS ...!!?
LISTEN WHEN I'M TALKING, WILL YOU!!?
IT IS THE MEAT OF A SWAMP CREATURE.
HUUUH? SWAMP CREA-TURE...?

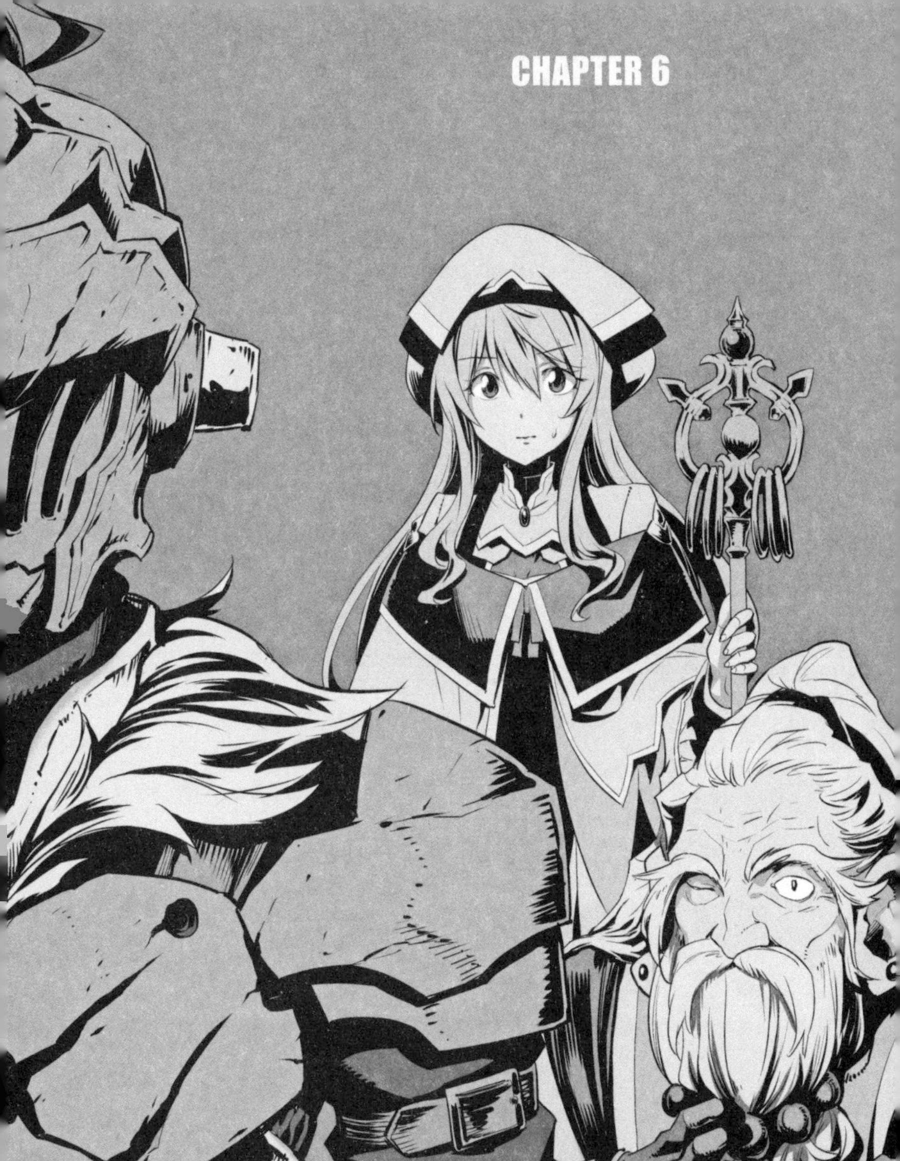
CHAPTER 6

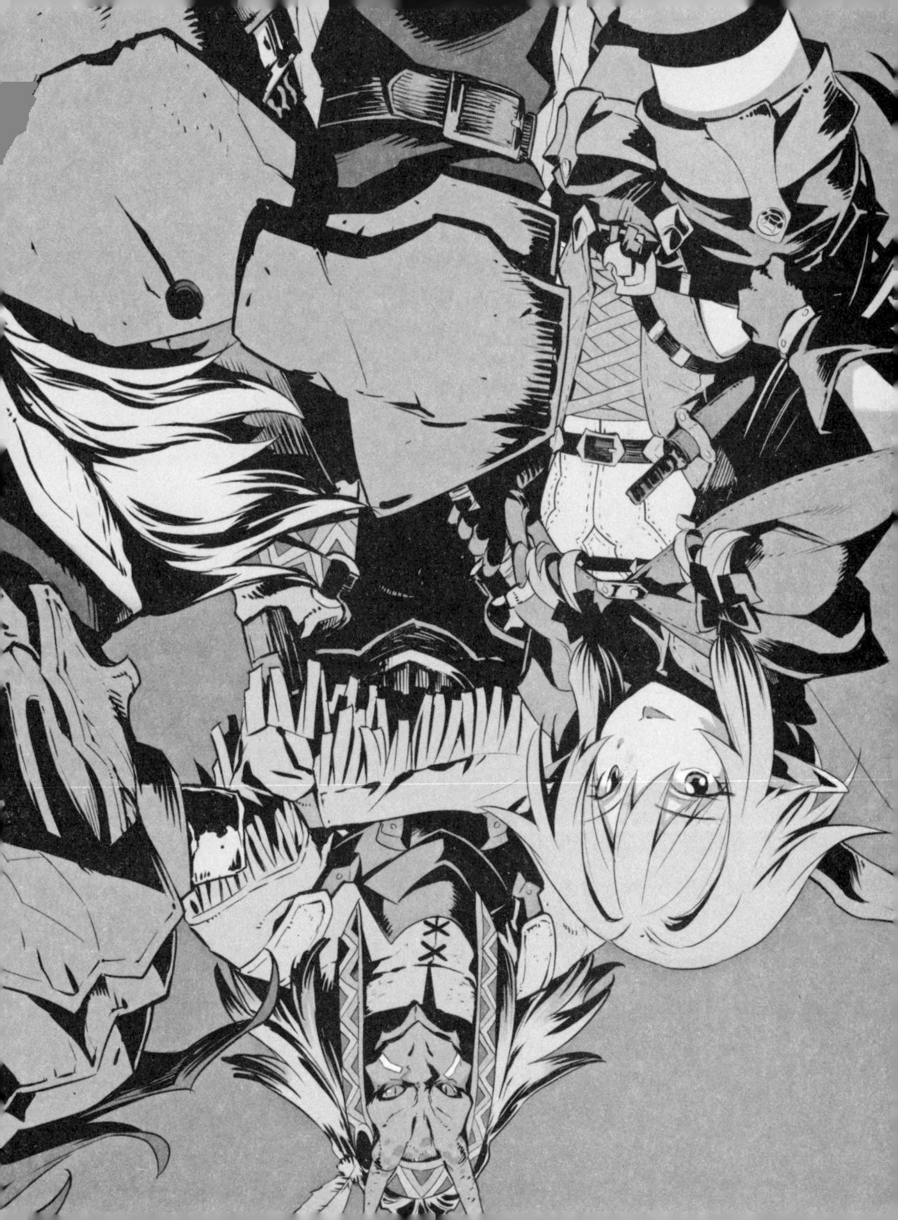

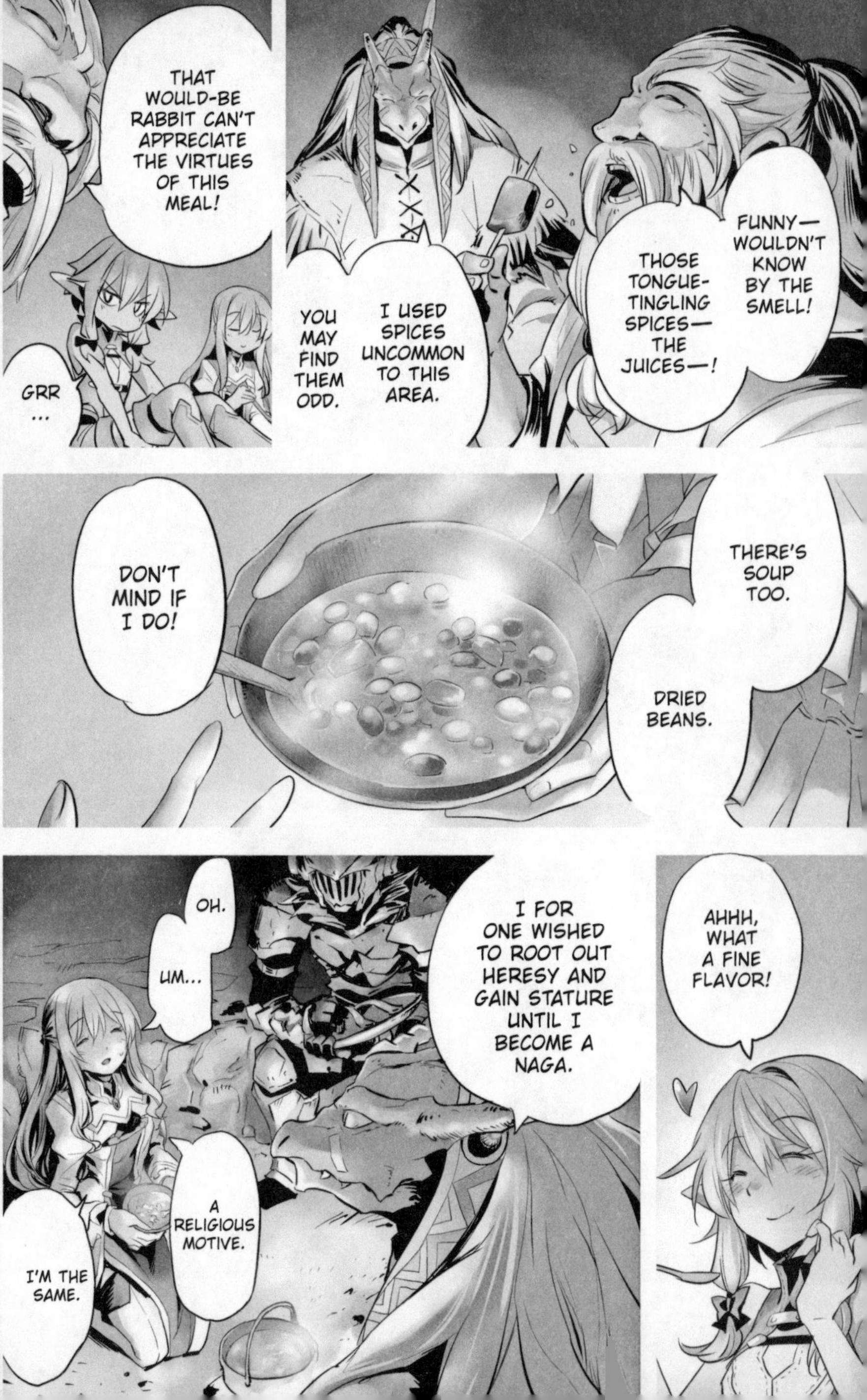
FUNNY—WOULDN'T KNOW BY THE SMELL!
THOSE TONGUE-TINGLING SPICES—THE JUICES—!
I USED SPICES UNCOMMON TO THIS AREA.
YOU MAY FIND THEM ODD.
THAT WOULD-BE RABBIT CAN'T APPRECIATE THE VIRTUES OF THIS MEAL!
GRR...
THERE'S SOUP TOO.
DRIED BEANS.
DON'T MIND IF I DO!
AHHH, WHAT A FINE FLAVOR!
I FOR ONE WISHED TO ROOT OUT HERESY AND GAIN STATURE UNTIL I BECOME A NAGA.
OH.
UM...
A RELIGIOUS MOTIVE.
I'M THE SAME.

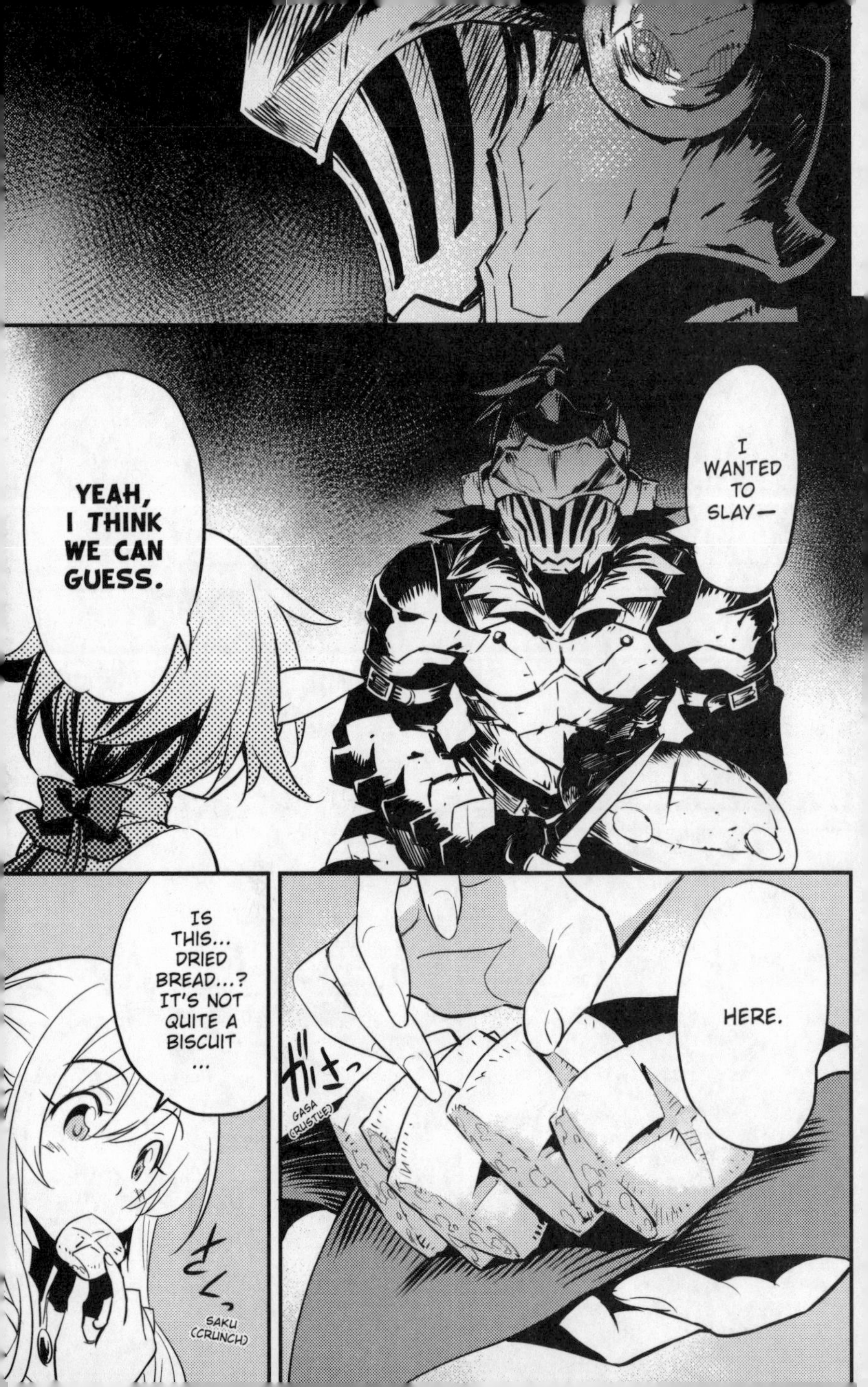
I WANTED TO SLAY—
YEAH, I THINK WE CAN GUESS.
HERE.
GASA (RUSTLE)
IS THIS... DRIED BREAD...? IT'S NOT QUITE A BISCUIT ...
SAKU (CRUNCH)

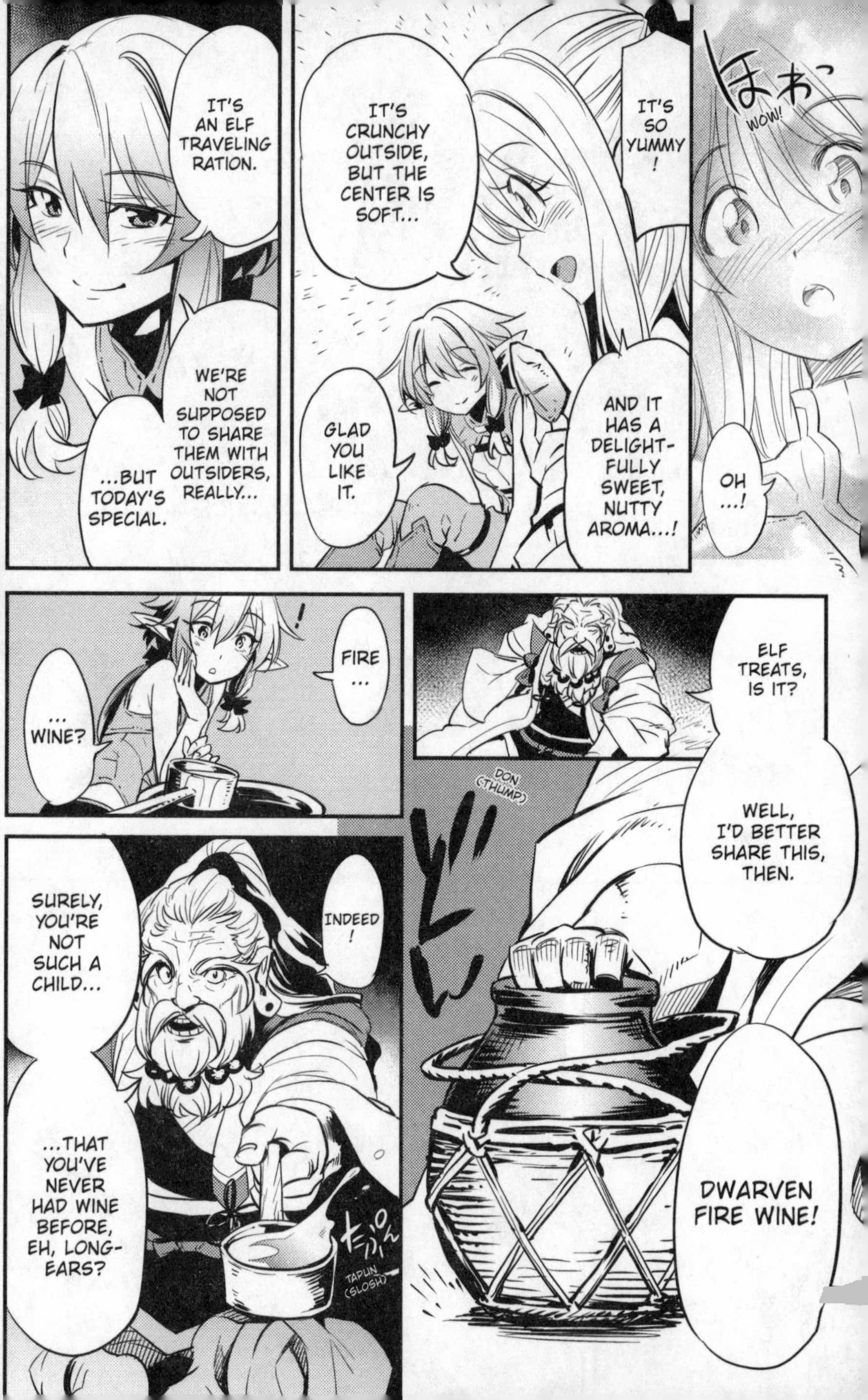
ほわっ
WOW!
OH ...!
IT'S SO YUMMY!
AND IT HAS A DELIGHT-FULLY SWEET, NUTTY AROMA...!
IT'S CRUNCHY OUTSIDE, BUT THE CENTER IS SOFT...
GLAD YOU LIKE IT.
IT'S AN ELF TRAVELING RATION.
WE'RE NOT SUPPOSED TO SHARE THEM WITH OUTSIDERS, REALLY...
...BUT TODAY'S SPECIAL.
ELF TREATS, IS IT?
!
FIRE ...
... WINE?
WELL, I'D BETTER SHARE THIS, THEN.
DON (THUMP)
DWARVEN FIRE WINE!
SURELY, YOU'RE NOT SUCH A CHILD...
INDEED!
...THAT YOU'VE NEVER HAD WINE BEFORE, EH, LONG-EARS?
たぷん
TAPUN (SLOSH)

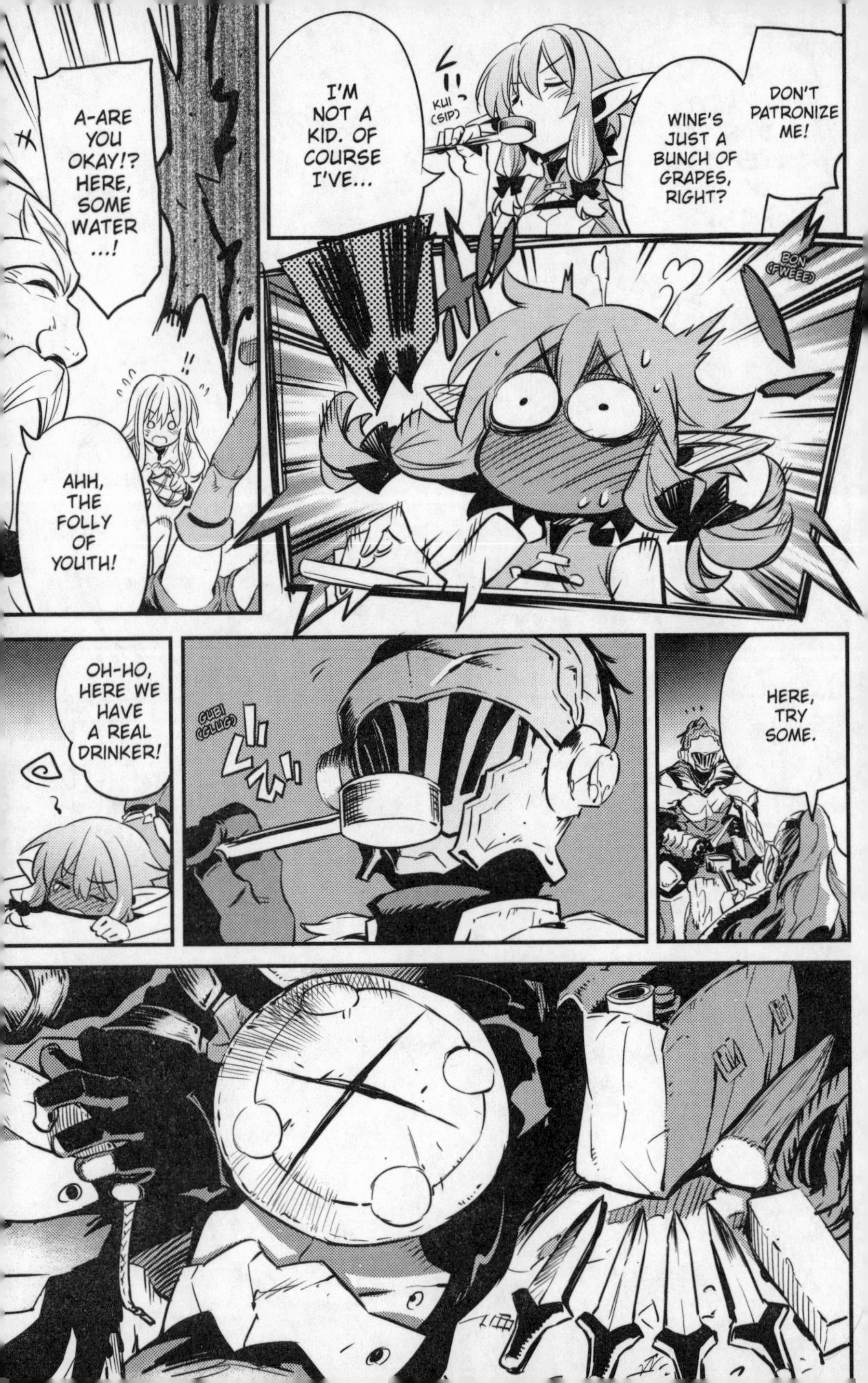
DON'T PATRONIZE ME!
WINE'S JUST A BUNCH OF GRAPES, RIGHT?
KUI (SIP)
I'M NOT A KID. OF COURSE I'VE...
A-ARE YOU OKAY!? HERE, SOME WATER ...!
BON (FWEEE)
AHH, THE FOLLY OF YOUTH!
HERE, TRY SOME.
GUBI (GLUG)
OH-HO, HERE WE HAVE A REAL DRINKER!

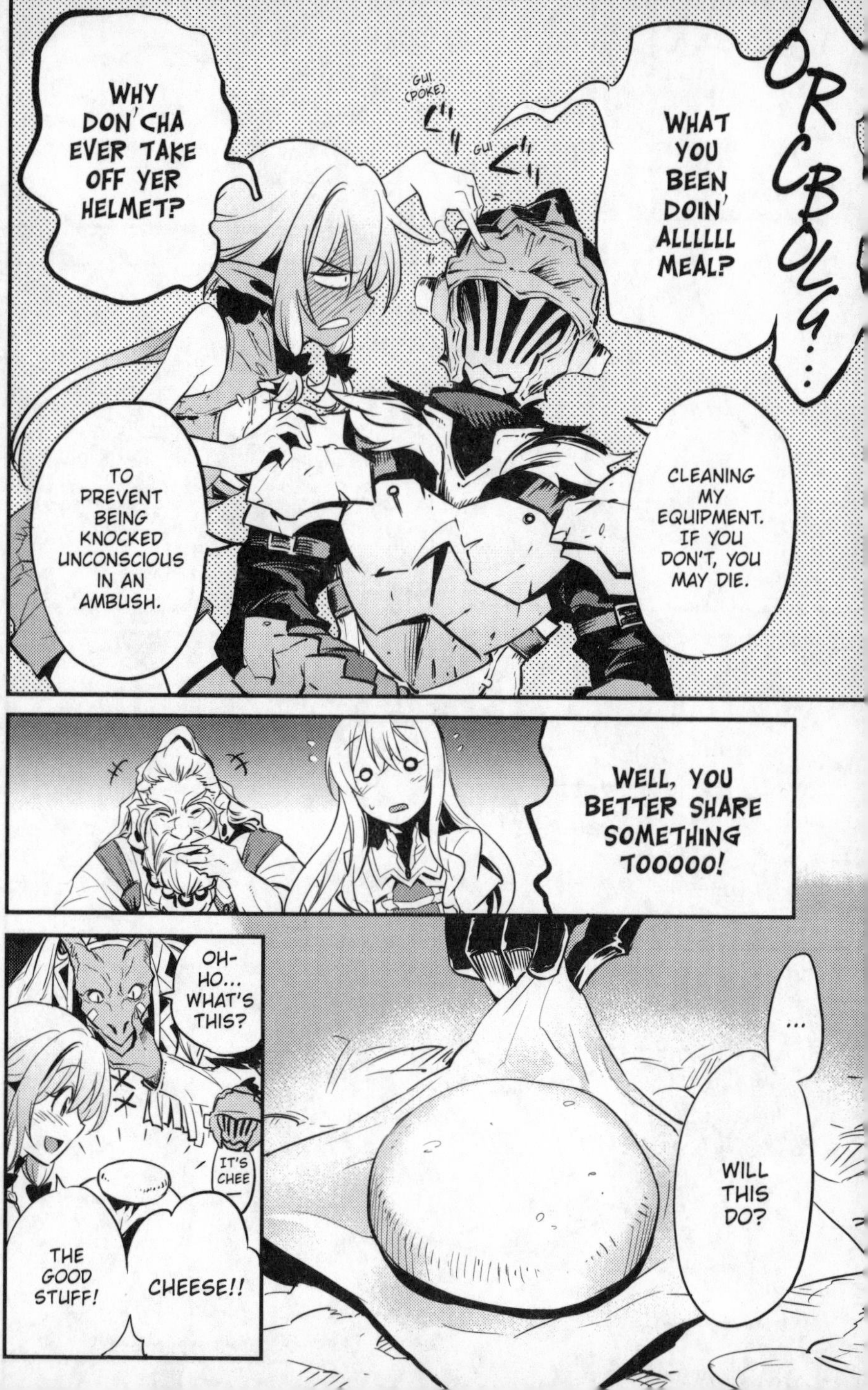
ORCBOLG...
WHAT YOU BEEN DOIN' ALLLLLL MEAL?
GUI (POKE)
GUI
WHY DON'CHA EVER TAKE OFF YER HELMET?
CLEANING MY EQUIPMENT. IF YOU DON'T, YOU MAY DIE.
TO PREVENT BEING KNOCKED UNCONSCIOUS IN AN AMBUSH.
WELL, YOU BETTER SHARE SOMETHING TOOOOO!
...
WILL THIS DO?
OH-HO... WHAT'S THIS?
IT'S CHEE—
THE GOOD STUFF!
CHEESE!!

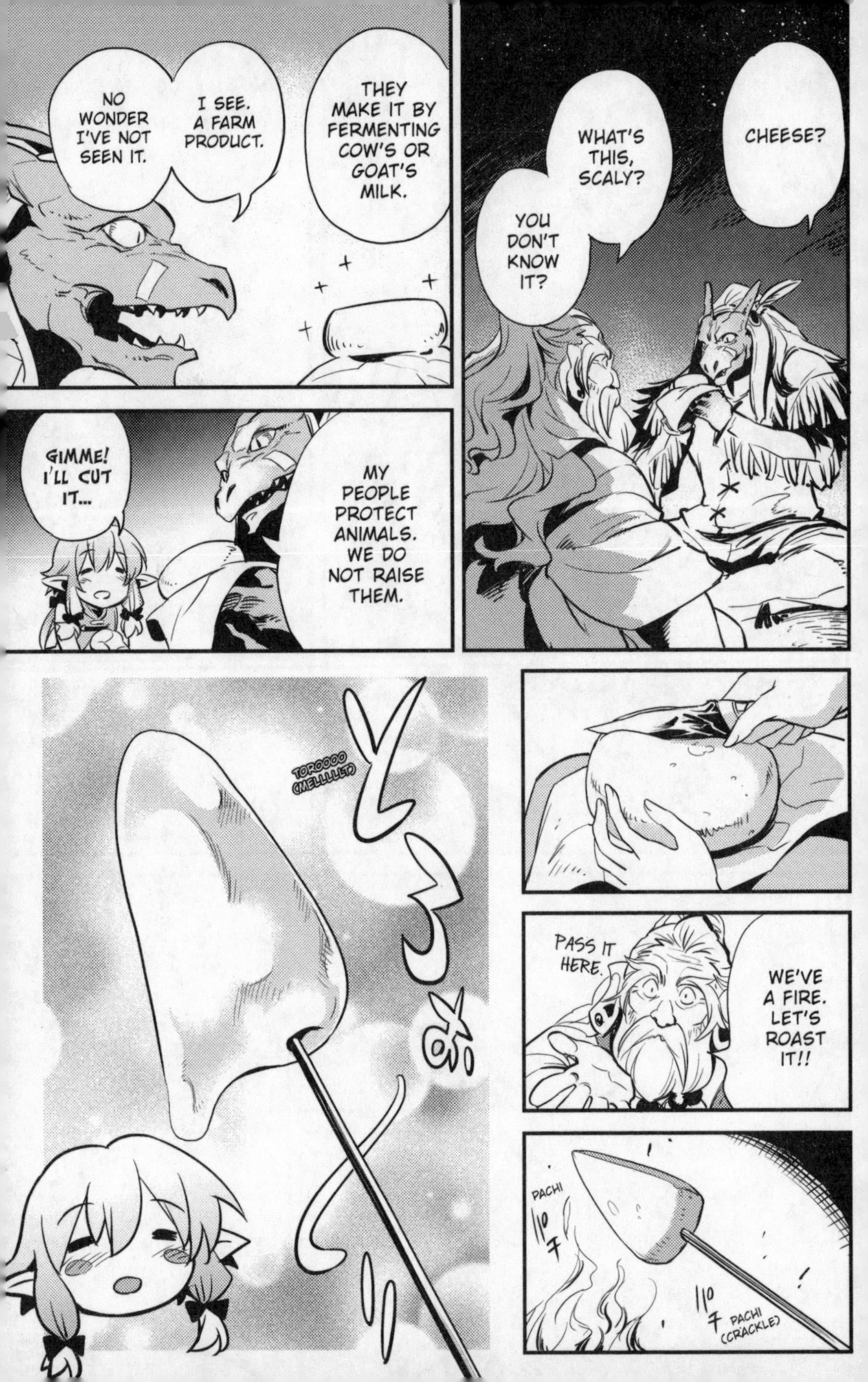
CHEESE?
WHAT'S THIS, SCALY?
YOU DON'T KNOW IT?
THEY MAKE IT BY FERMENTING COW'S OR GOAT'S MILK.
I SEE. A FARM PRODUCT.
NO WONDER I'VE NOT SEEN IT.
MY PEOPLE PROTECT ANIMALS. WE DO NOT RAISE THEM.
GIMME! I'LL CUT IT...
WE'VE A FIRE. LET'S ROAST IT!!
PASS IT HERE.
PACHI
PACHI (CRACKLE)
TOROOOO (MELLLLLT)

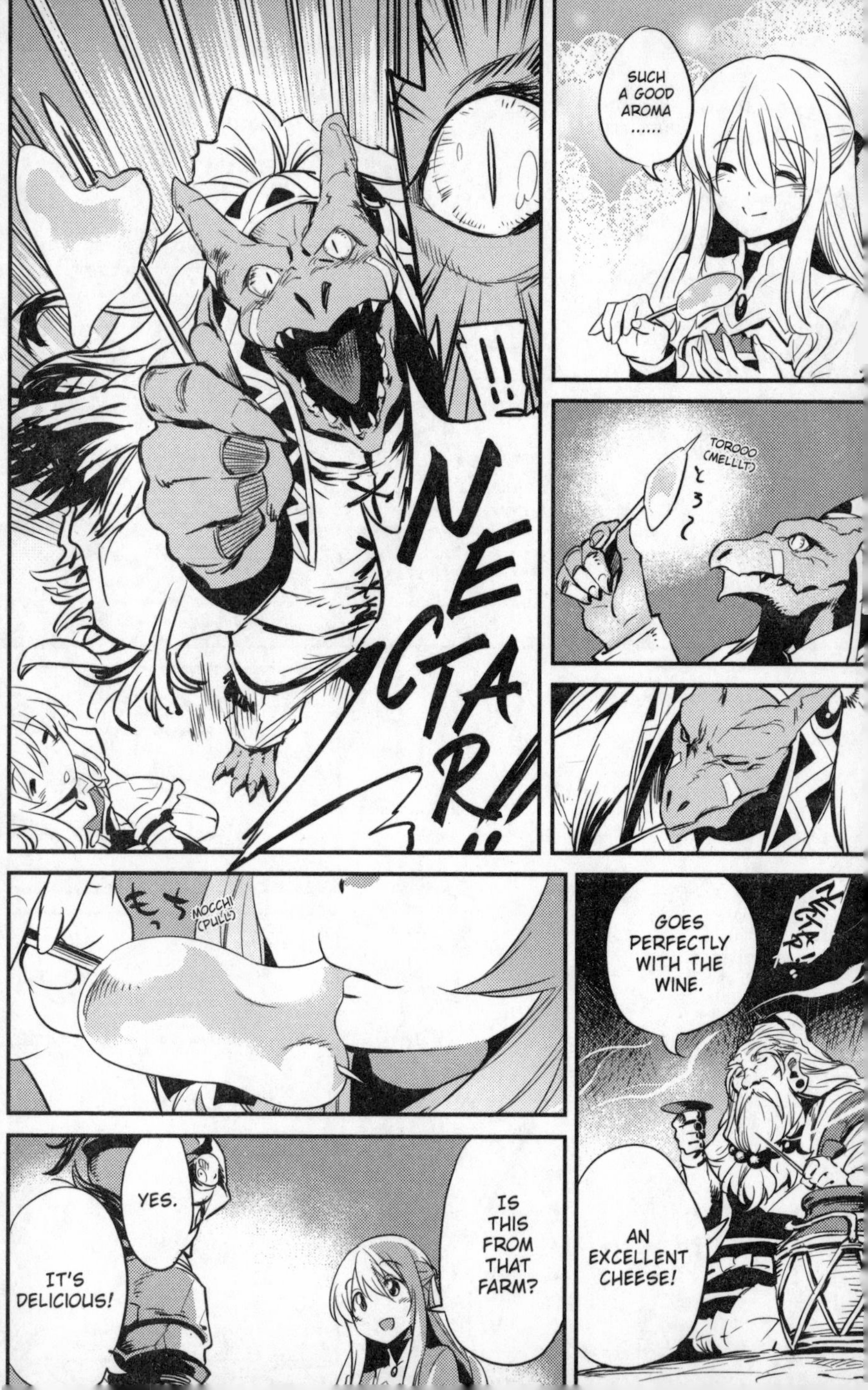
SUCH A GOOD AROMA ......
TOROOO (MELLLT)
NECTAR!!
!!!
GOES PERFECTLY WITH THE WINE.
MOCCHI (PULL)
AN EXCELLENT CHEESE!
IS THIS FROM THAT FARM?
YES.
IT'S DELICIOUS!

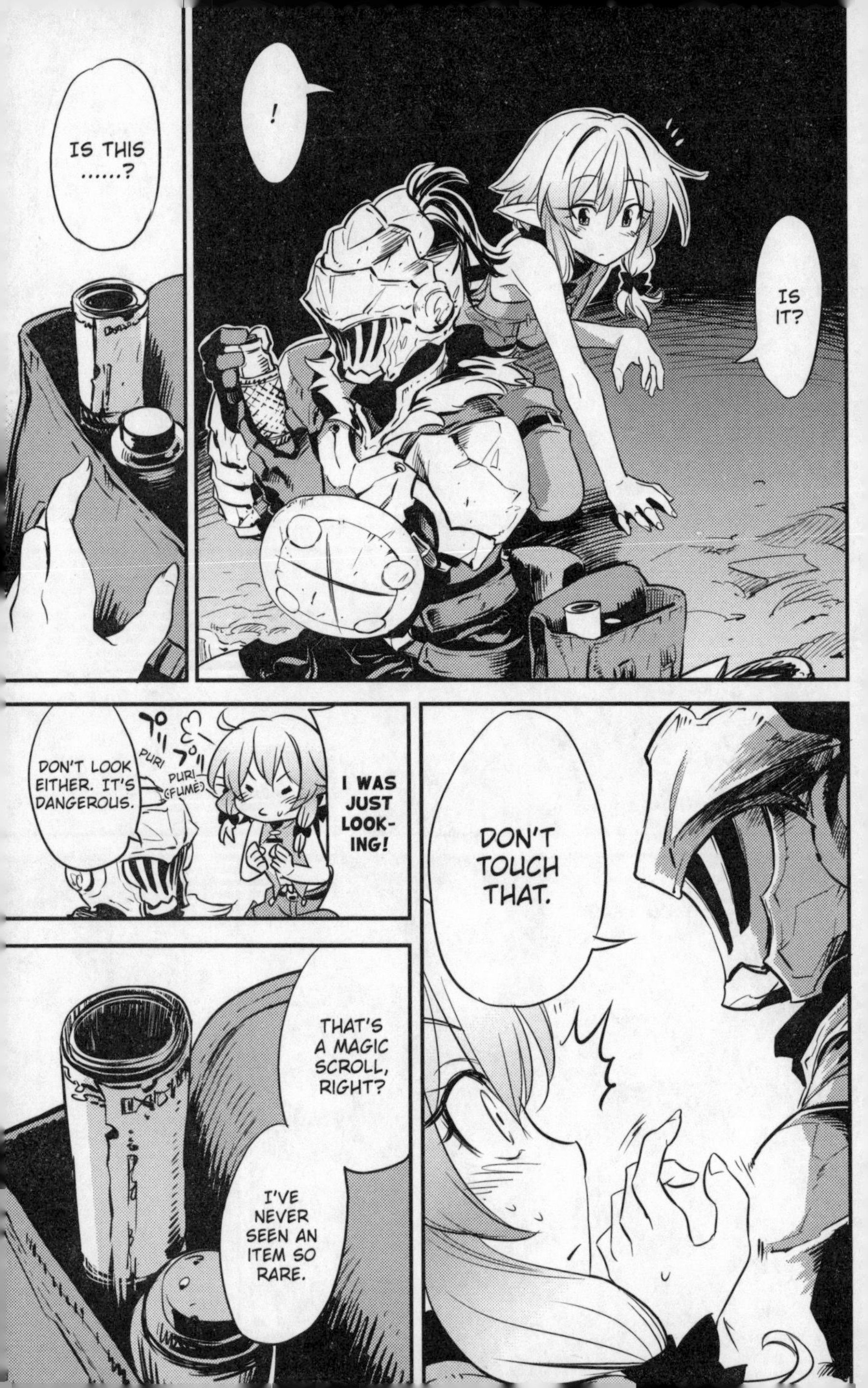
!
IS IT?
IS THIS ......?
DON'T TOUCH THAT.
I WAS JUST LOOKING!
PURI PURI (FUME)
DON'T LOOK EITHER. IT'S DANGEROUS.
THAT'S A MAGIC SCROLL, RIGHT?
I'VE NEVER SEEN AN ITEM SO RARE.

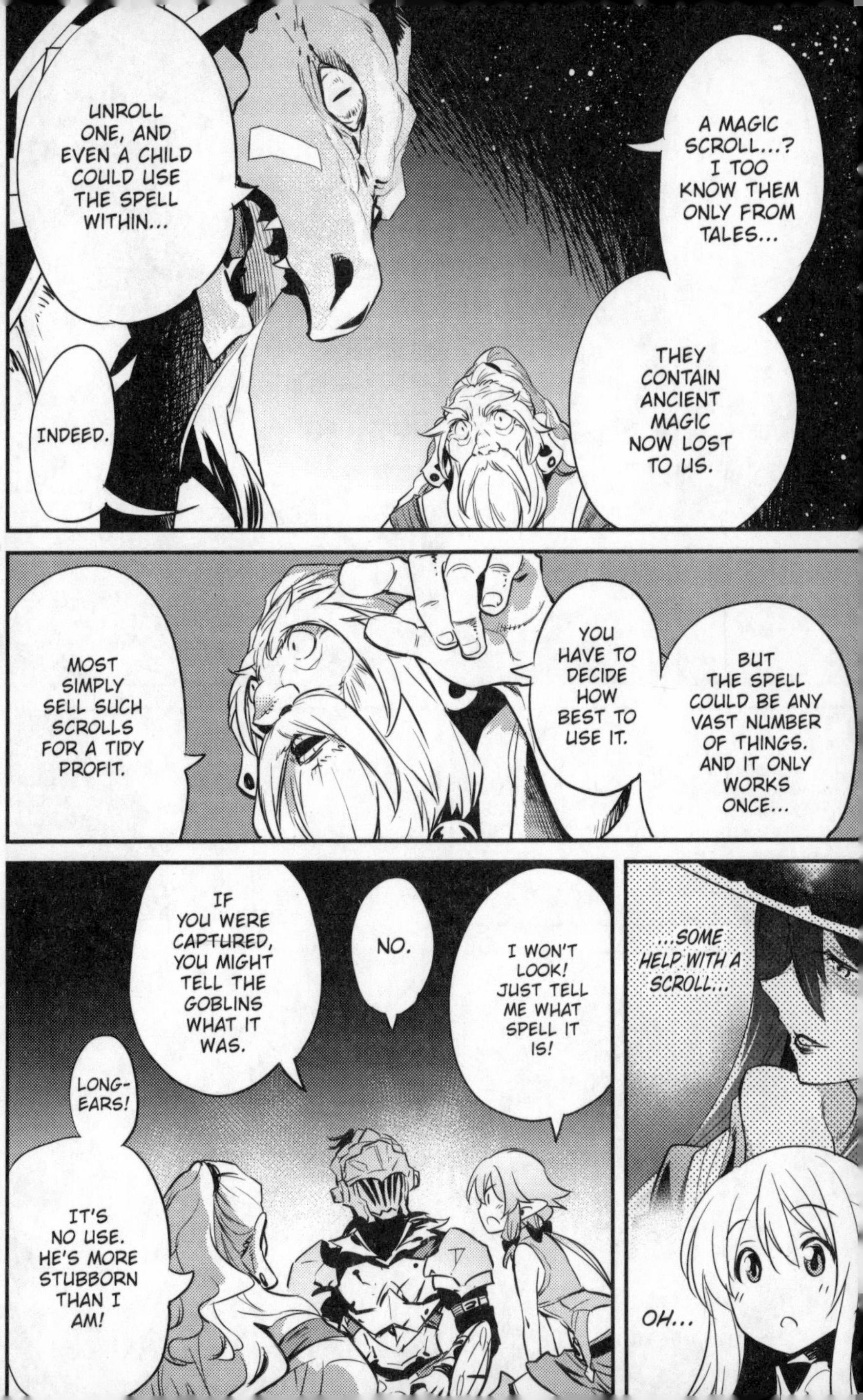
A MAGIC SCROLL...? I TOO KNOW THEM ONLY FROM TALES...
THEY CONTAIN ANCIENT MAGIC NOW LOST TO US.
UNROLL ONE, AND EVEN A CHILD COULD USE THE SPELL WITHIN...
INDEED.
BUT THE SPELL COULD BE ANY VAST NUMBER OF THINGS. AND IT ONLY WORKS ONCE...
YOU HAVE TO DECIDE HOW BEST TO USE IT.
MOST SIMPLY SELL SUCH SCROLLS FOR A TIDY PROFIT.
...SOME HELP WITH A SCROLL...
OH...
I WON'T LOOK! JUST TELL ME WHAT SPELL IT IS!
NO.
IF YOU WERE CAPTURED, YOU MIGHT TELL THE GOBLINS WHAT IT WAS.
LONG-EARS!
IT'S NO USE. HE'S MORE STUBBORN THAN I AM!

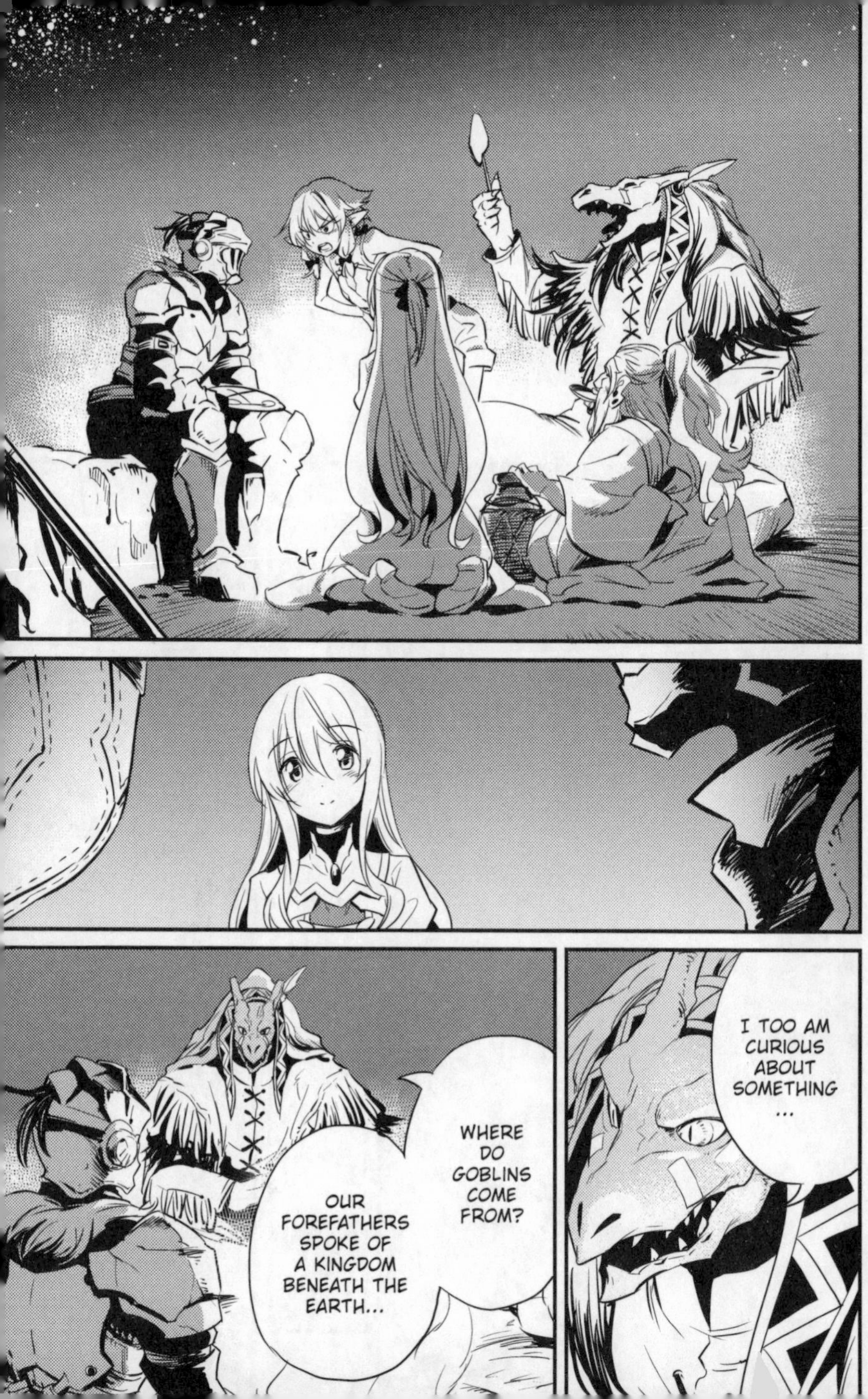
I TOO AM CURIOUS ABOUT SOMETHING ...
WHERE DO GOBLINS COME FROM?
OUR FOREFATHERS SPOKE OF A KINGDOM BENEATH THE EARTH...

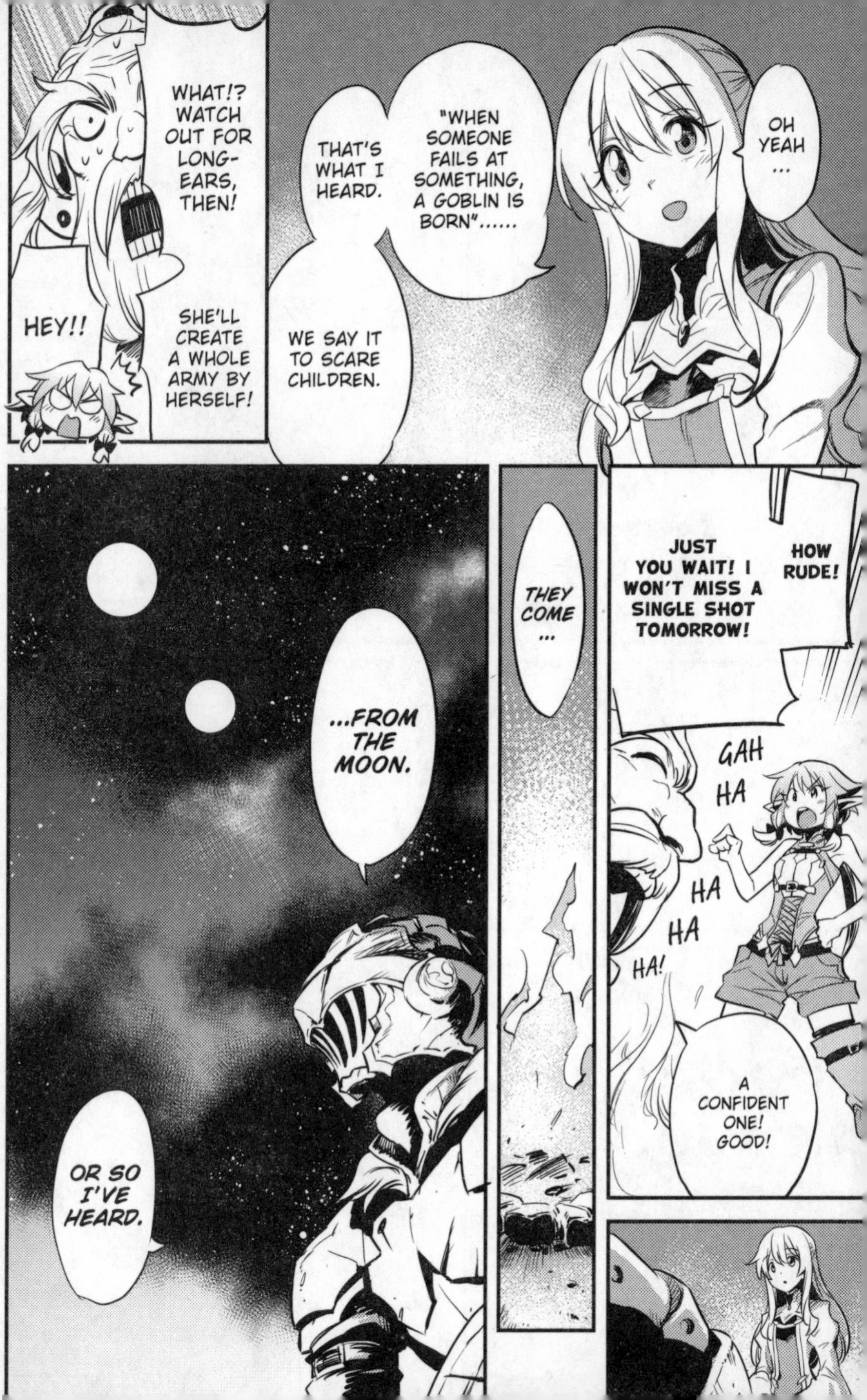
OH YEAH ...
"WHEN SOMEONE FAILS AT SOMETHING, A GOBLIN IS BORN"......
THAT'S WHAT I HEARD.
WE SAY IT TO SCARE CHILDREN.
WHAT!? WATCH OUT FOR LONG-EARS, THEN!
SHE'LL CREATE A WHOLE ARMY BY HERSELF!
HEY!!
HOW RUDE!
JUST YOU WAIT! I WON'T MISS A SINGLE SHOT TOMORROW!
GAH HA HA HA HA!
A CONFIDENT ONE! GOOD!
THEY COME ...
...FROM THE MOON.
OR SO I'VE HEARD.

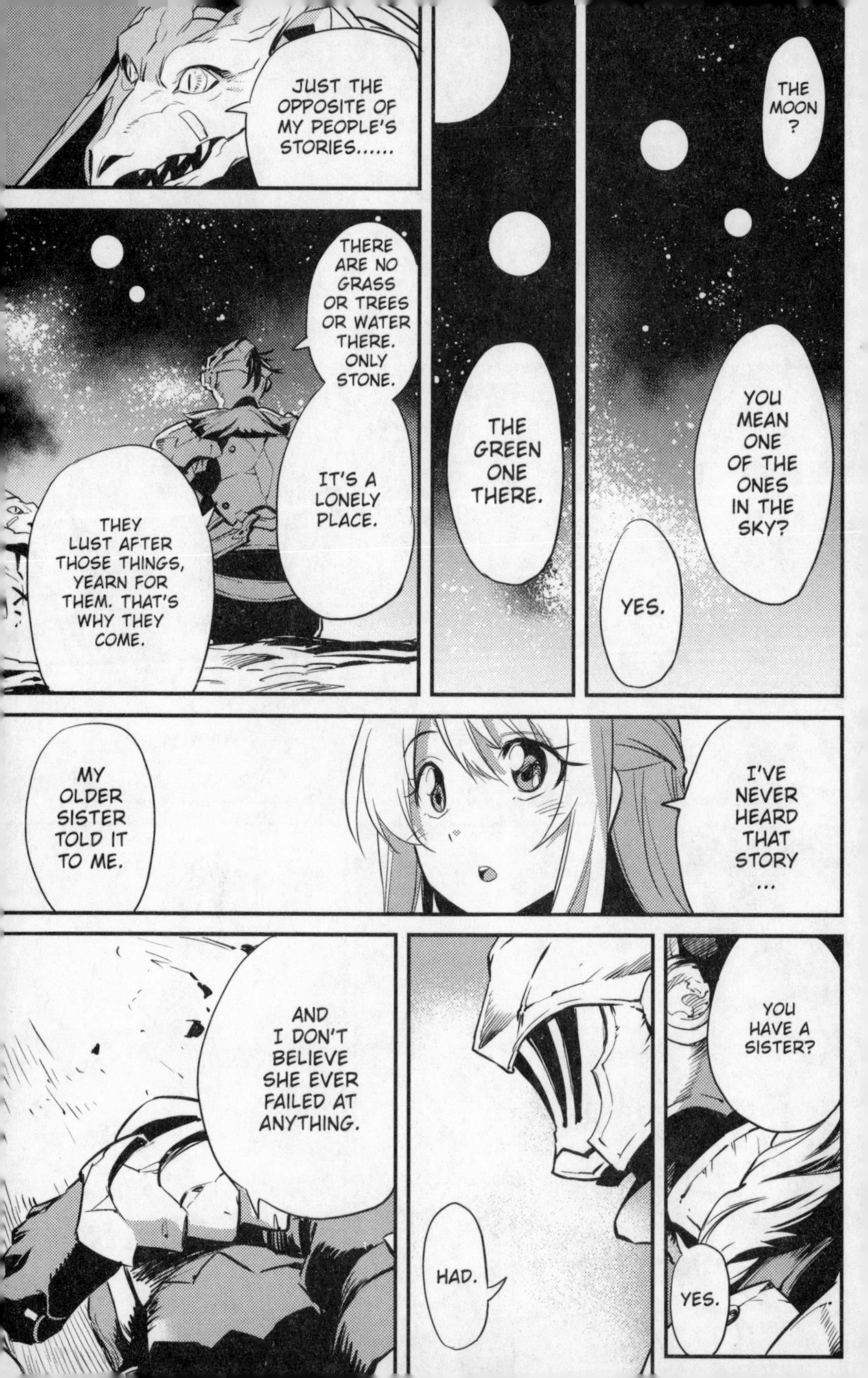
THE MOON ?
YOU MEAN ONE OF THE ONES IN THE SKY?
YES.
THE GREEN ONE THERE.
JUST THE OPPOSITE OF MY PEOPLE'S STORIES......
THERE ARE NO GRASS OR TREES OR WATER THERE. ONLY STONE.
IT'S A LONELY PLACE.
THEY LUST AFTER THOSE THINGS, YEARN FOR THEM. THAT'S WHY THEY COME.
I'VE NEVER HEARD THAT STORY ...
MY OLDER SISTER TOLD IT TO ME.
YOU HAVE A SISTER?
YES.
HAD.
AND I DON'T BELIEVE SHE EVER FAILED AT ANYTHING.

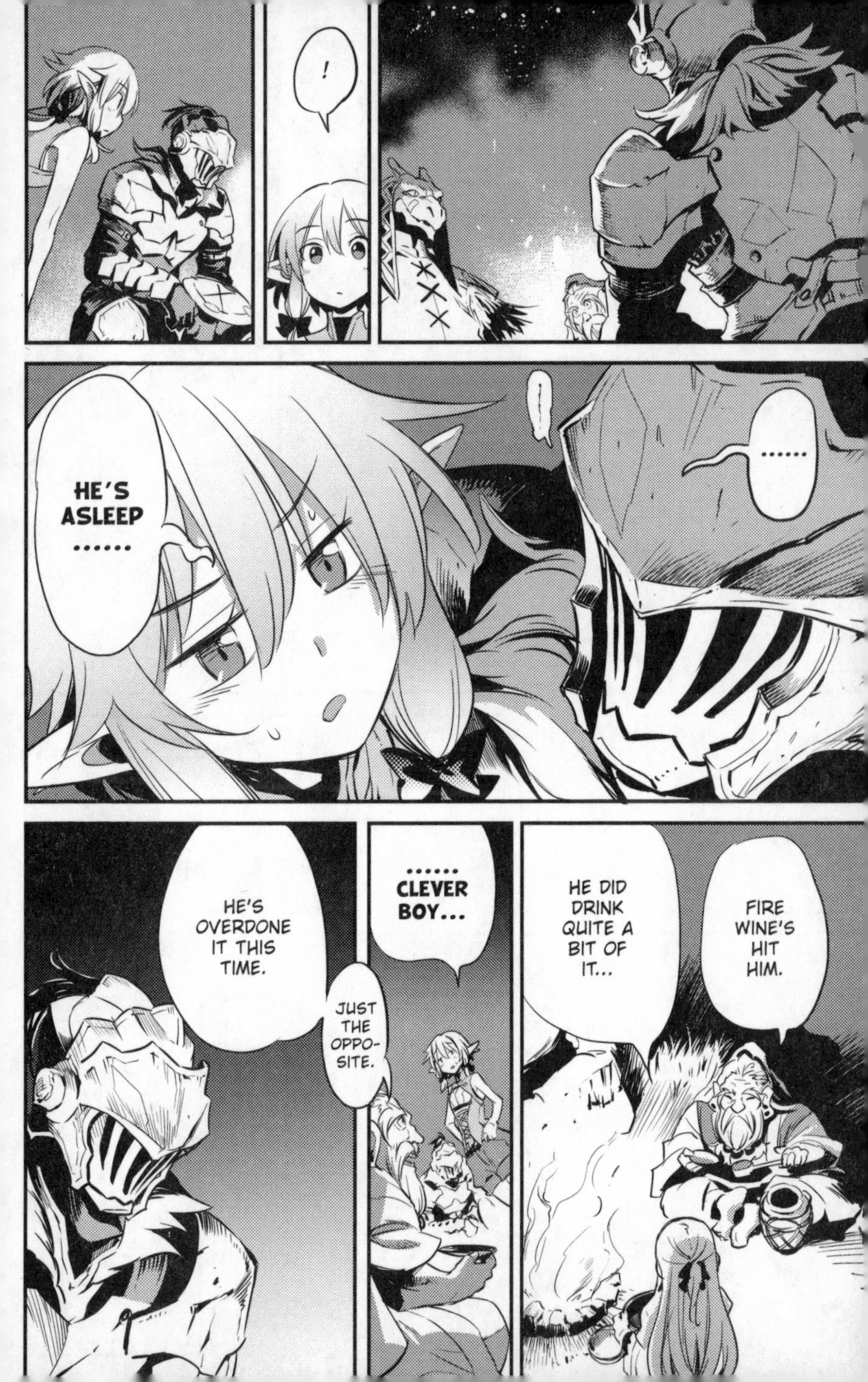
!
......
!
HE'S ASLEEP ......
FIRE WINE'S HIT HIM.
HE DID DRINK QUITE A BIT OF IT...
......CLEVER BOY...
JUST THE OPPO-SITE.
HE'S OVERDONE IT THIS TIME.

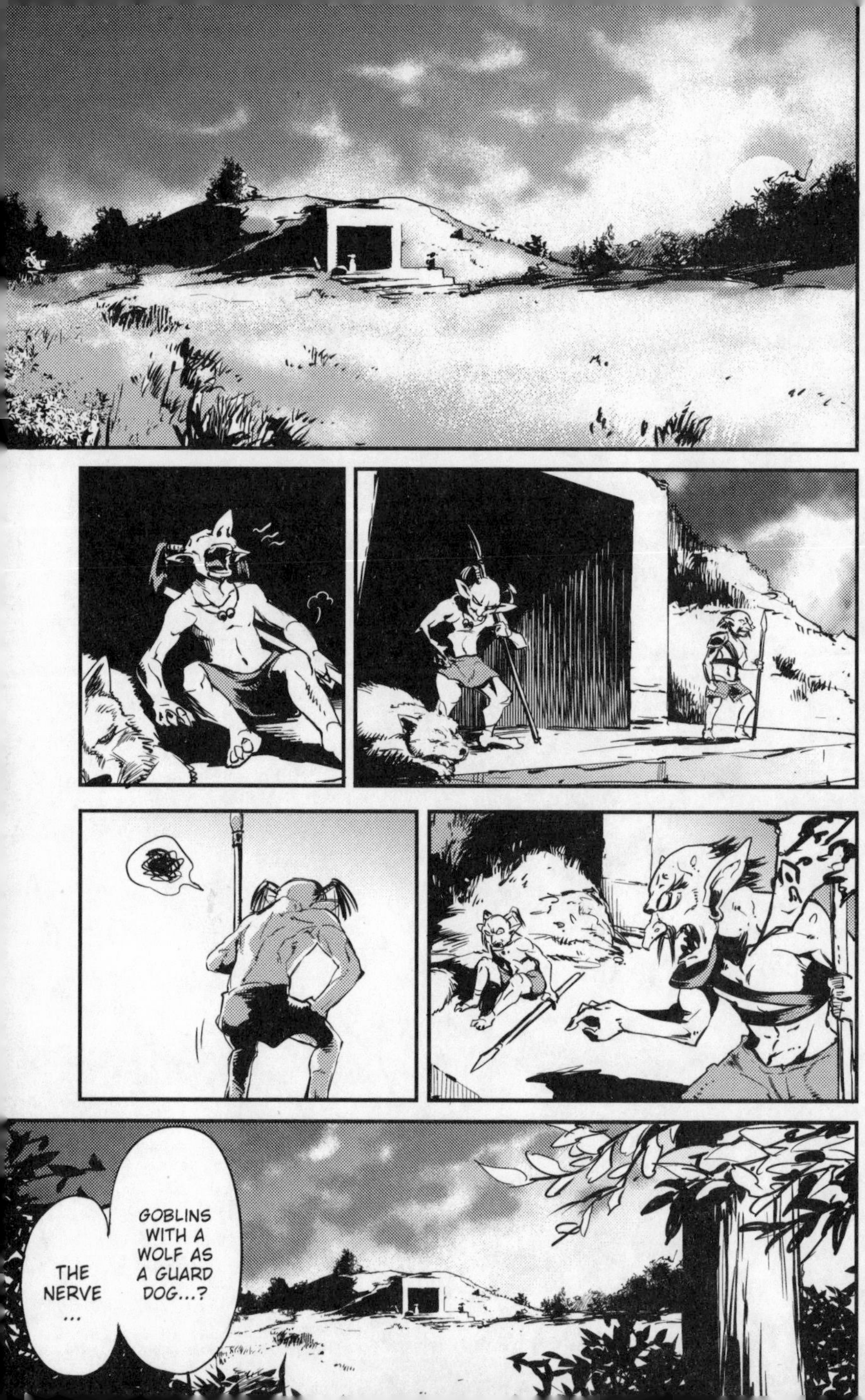
GOBLINS WITH A WOLF AS A GUARD DOG...?
THE NERVE ...

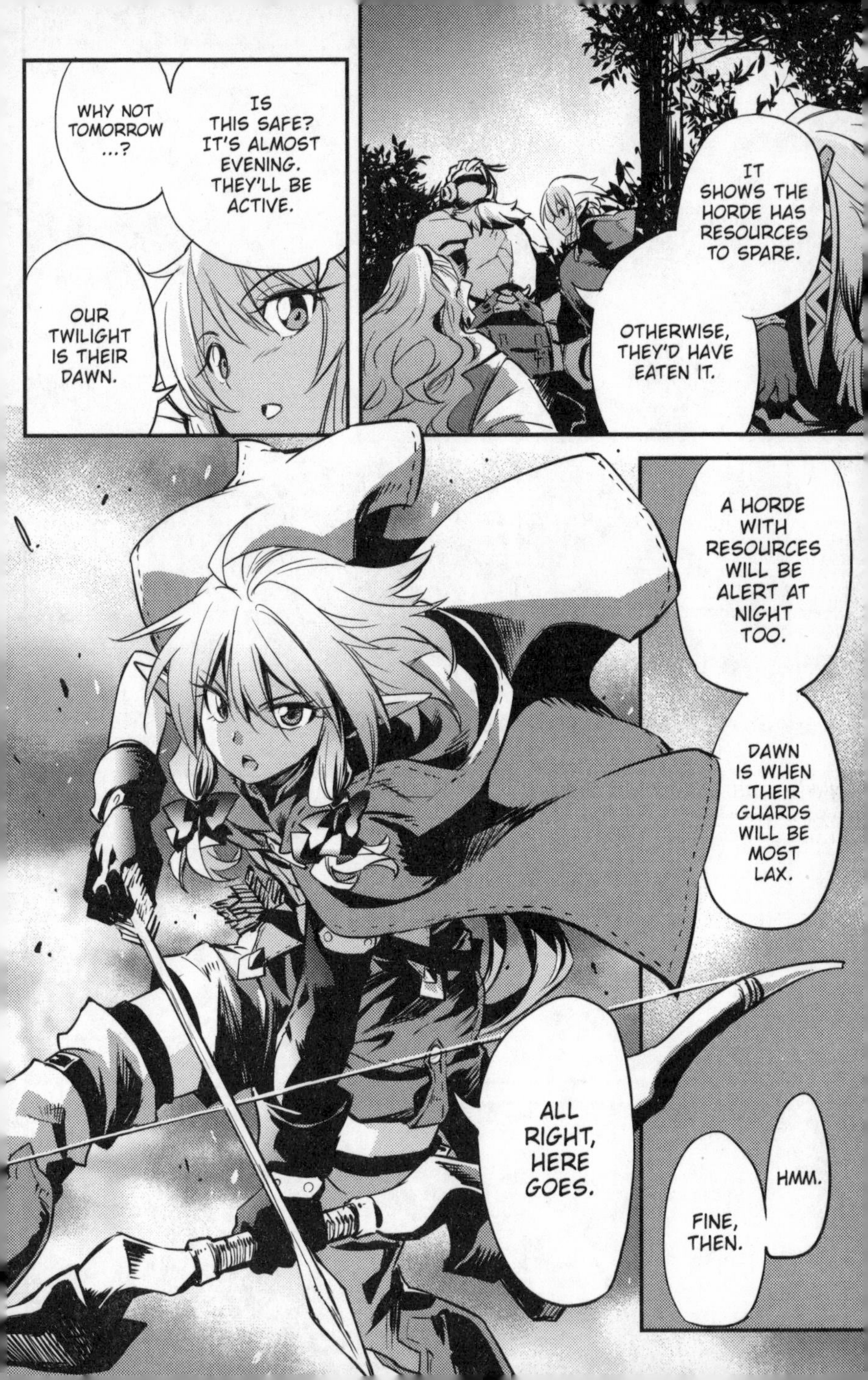
IT SHOWS THE HORDE HAS RESOURCES TO SPARE.
OTHERWISE, THEY'D HAVE EATEN IT.
IS THIS SAFE? IT'S ALMOST EVENING. THEY'LL BE ACTIVE.
WHY NOT TOMORROW ...?
OUR TWILIGHT IS THEIR DAWN.
A HORDE WITH RESOURCES WILL BE ALERT AT NIGHT TOO.
DAWN IS WHEN THEIR GUARDS WILL BE MOST LAX.
HMM.
FINE, THEN.
ALL RIGHT, HERE GOES.

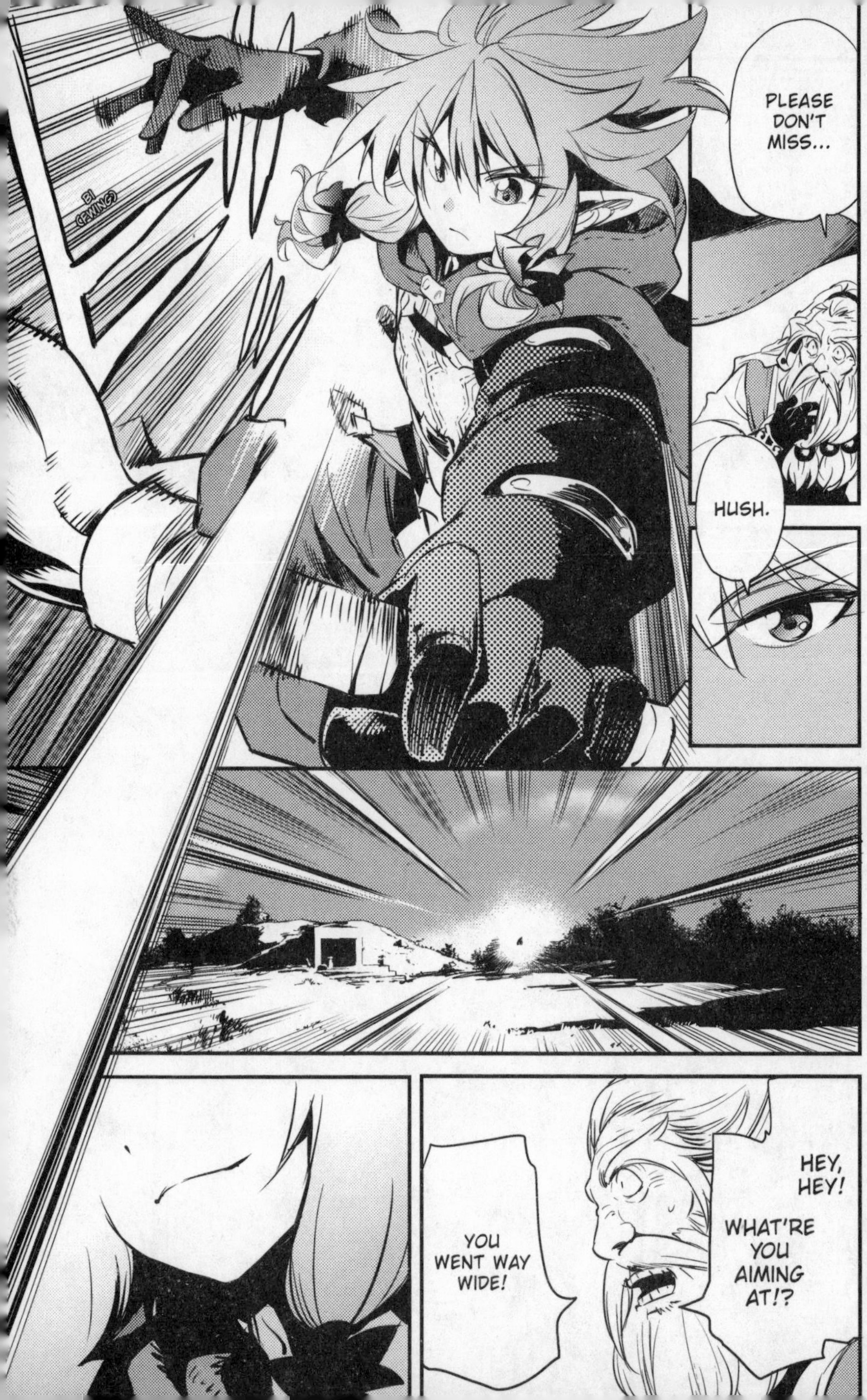
PLEASE DON'T MISS…
BI (FWING)
HUSH.
HEY, HEY!
WHAT'RE YOU AIMING AT!?
YOU WENT WAY WIDE!

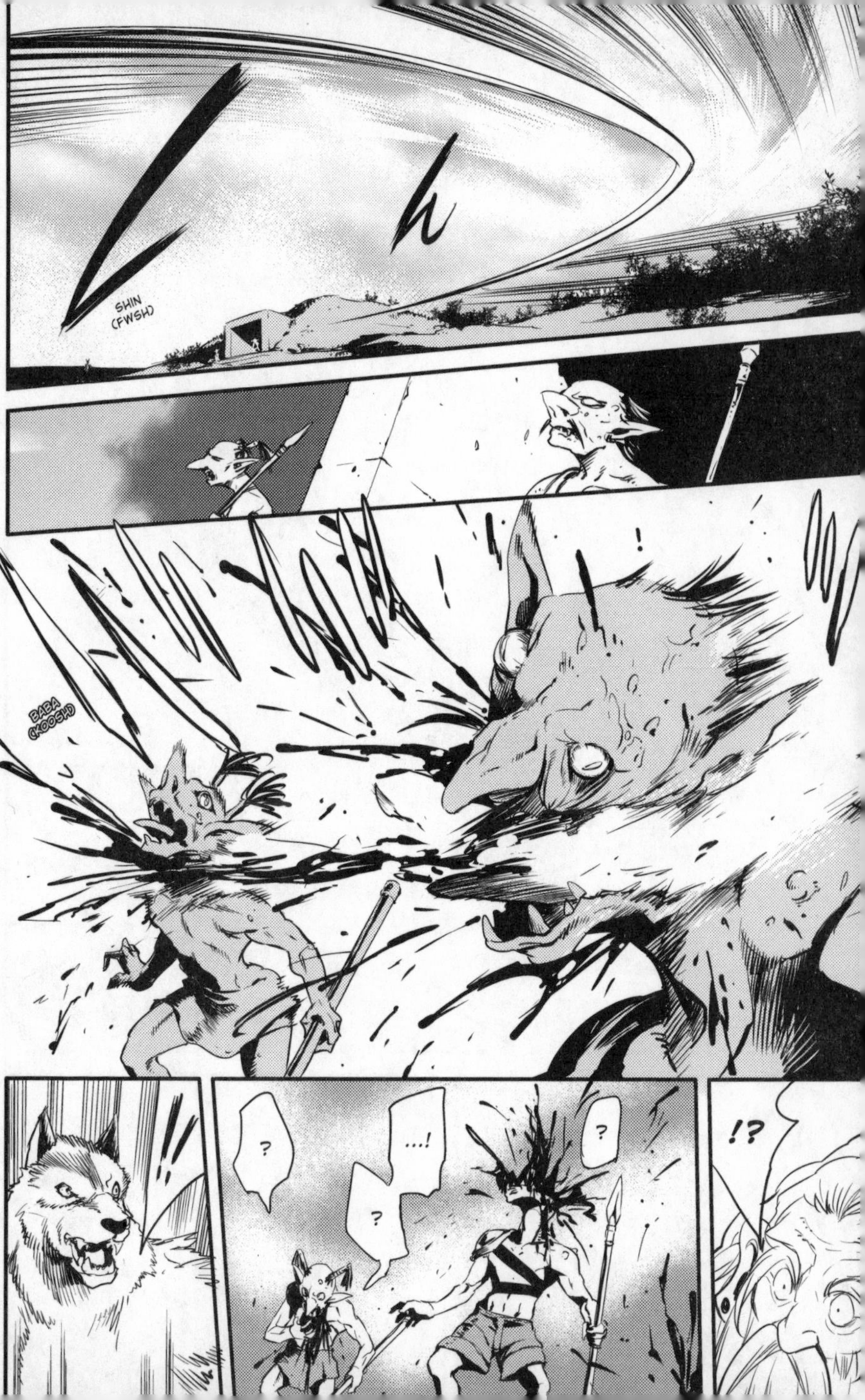
SHIN
(FWSH)
BABA
(KOOSH)
!?
?
...!
?
?
!!

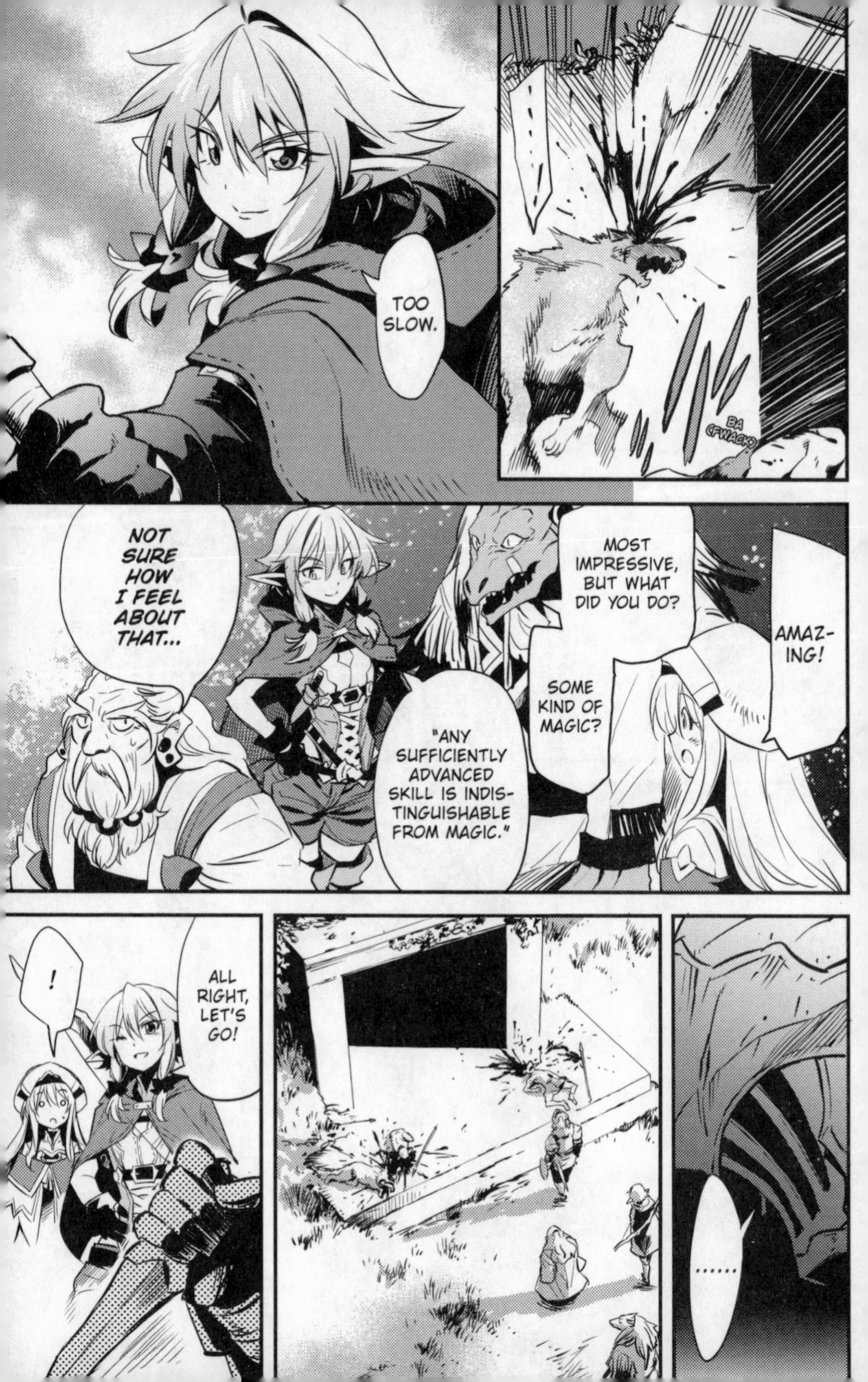
BA
(FWACK)
TOO SLOW.
AMAZ-ING!
MOST IMPRESSIVE, BUT WHAT DID YOU DO?
SOME KIND OF MAGIC?
"ANY SUFFICIENTLY ADVANCED SKILL IS INDIS-TINGUISHABLE FROM MAGIC."
NOT SURE HOW I FEEL ABOUT THAT...
......
ALL RIGHT, LET'S GO!
!

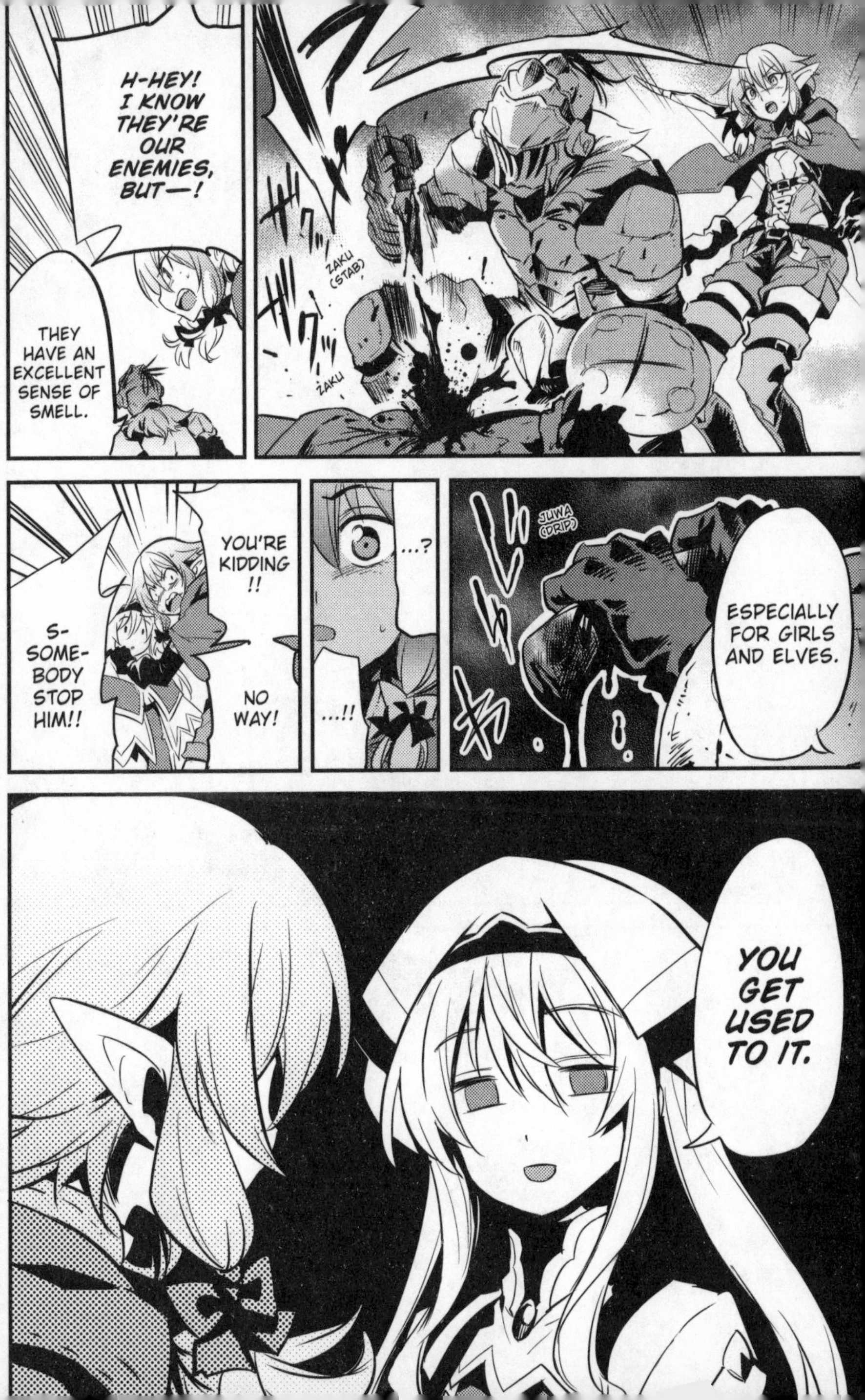
ZAKU (STAB)
ZAKU
H-HEY! I KNOW THEY'RE OUR ENEMIES, BUT—!
THEY HAVE AN EXCELLENT SENSE OF SMELL.
JUWA (DRIP)
ESPECIALLY FOR GIRLS AND ELVES.
...?
...!!
YOU'RE KIDDING !!
NO WAY!
S-SOME-BODY STOP HIM!!
YOU GET USED TO IT.

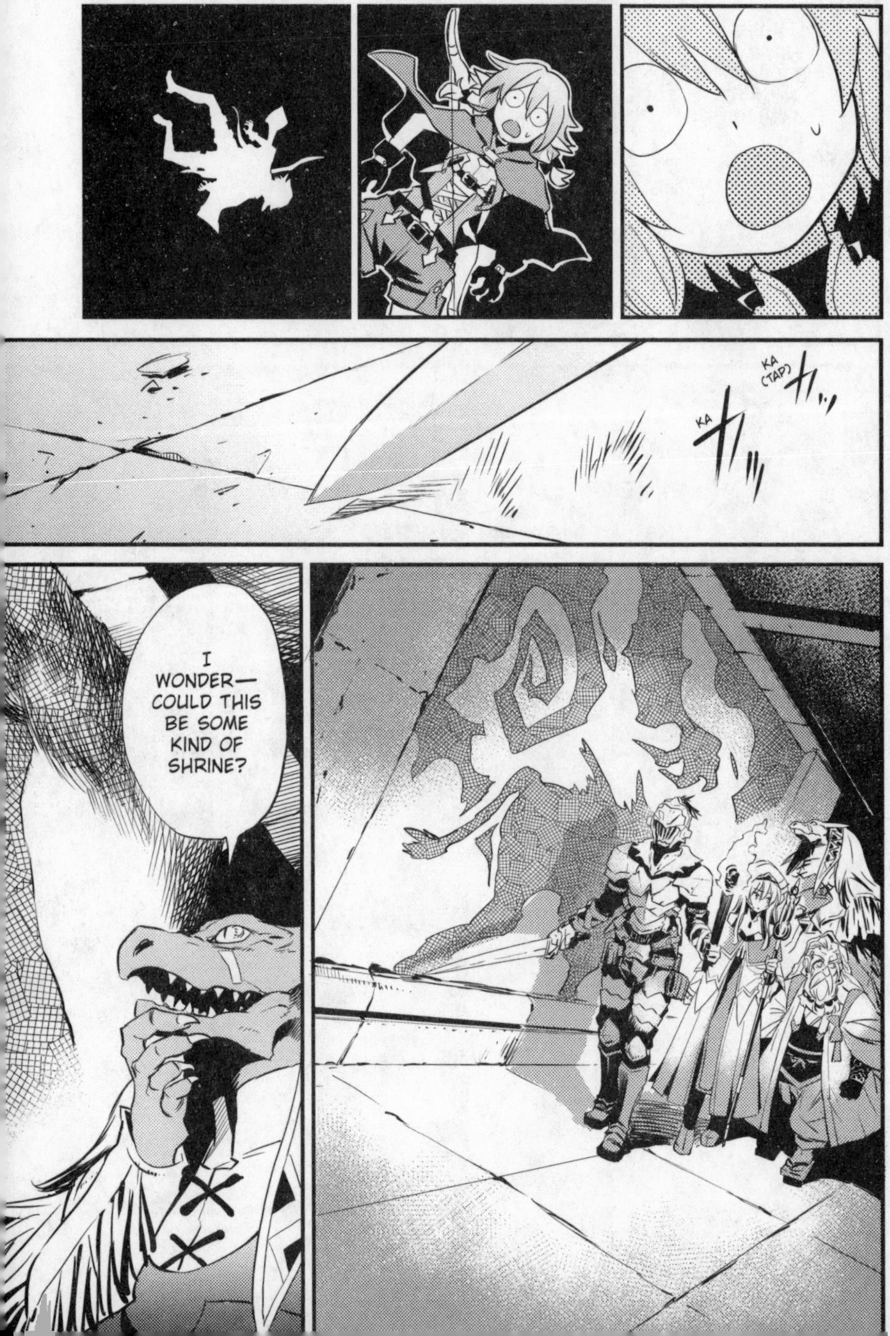
KA
KA (TAP)
I WONDER—COULD THIS BE SOME KIND OF SHRINE?

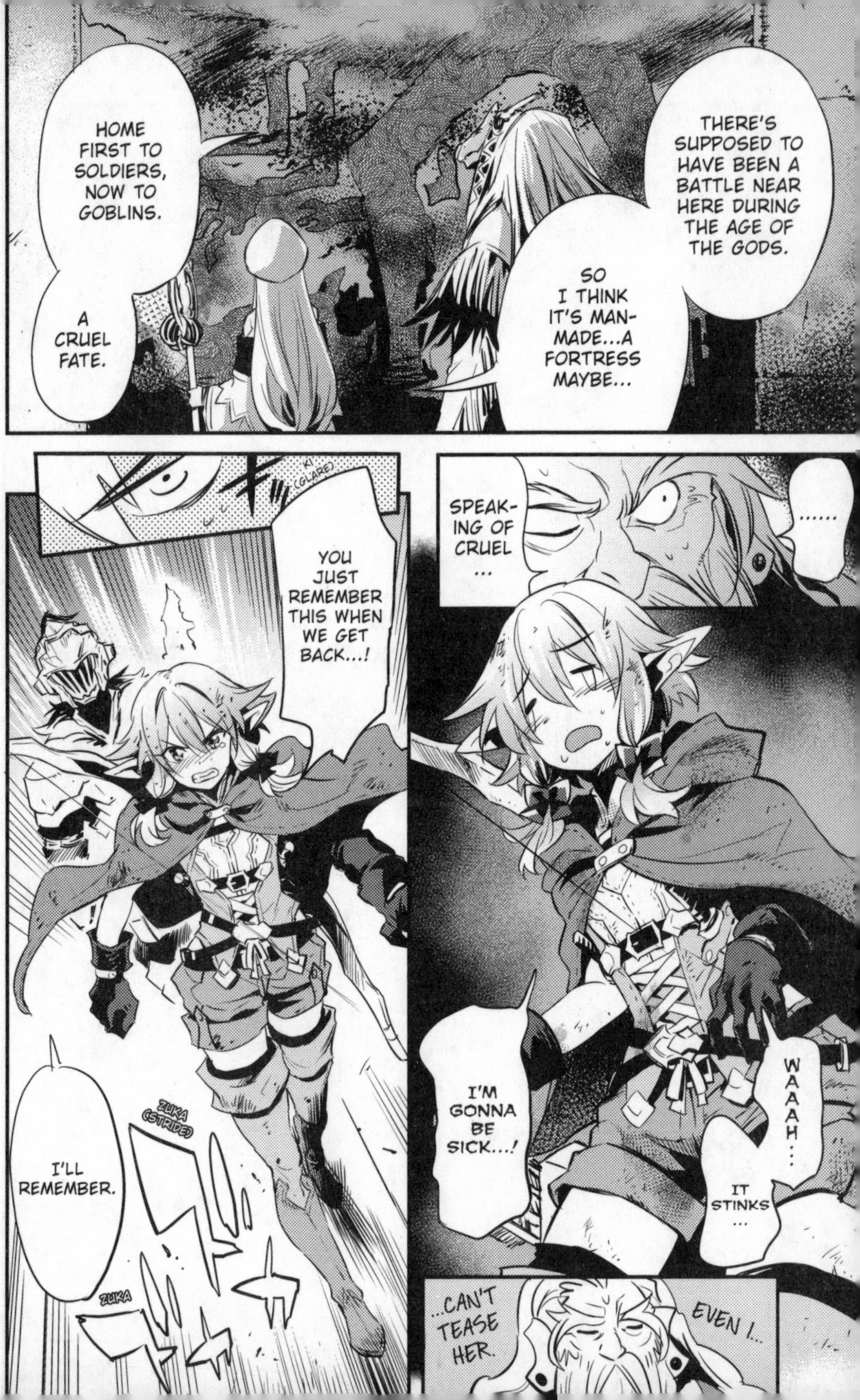
THERE'S SUPPOSED TO HAVE BEEN A BATTLE NEAR HERE DURING THE AGE OF THE GODS.
SO I THINK IT'S MAN-MADE...A FORTRESS MAYBE...
HOME FIRST TO SOLDIERS, NOW TO GOBLINS.
A CRUEL FATE.
......
SPEAK-ING OF CRUEL ...
WAAAH...
IT STINKS ...
I'M GONNA BE SICK...!
EVEN I...
...CAN'T TEASE HER.
KI (GLARE)
YOU JUST REMEMBER THIS WHEN WE GET BACK...!
ZUKA (STRIDE)
I'LL REMEMBER.
ZUKA

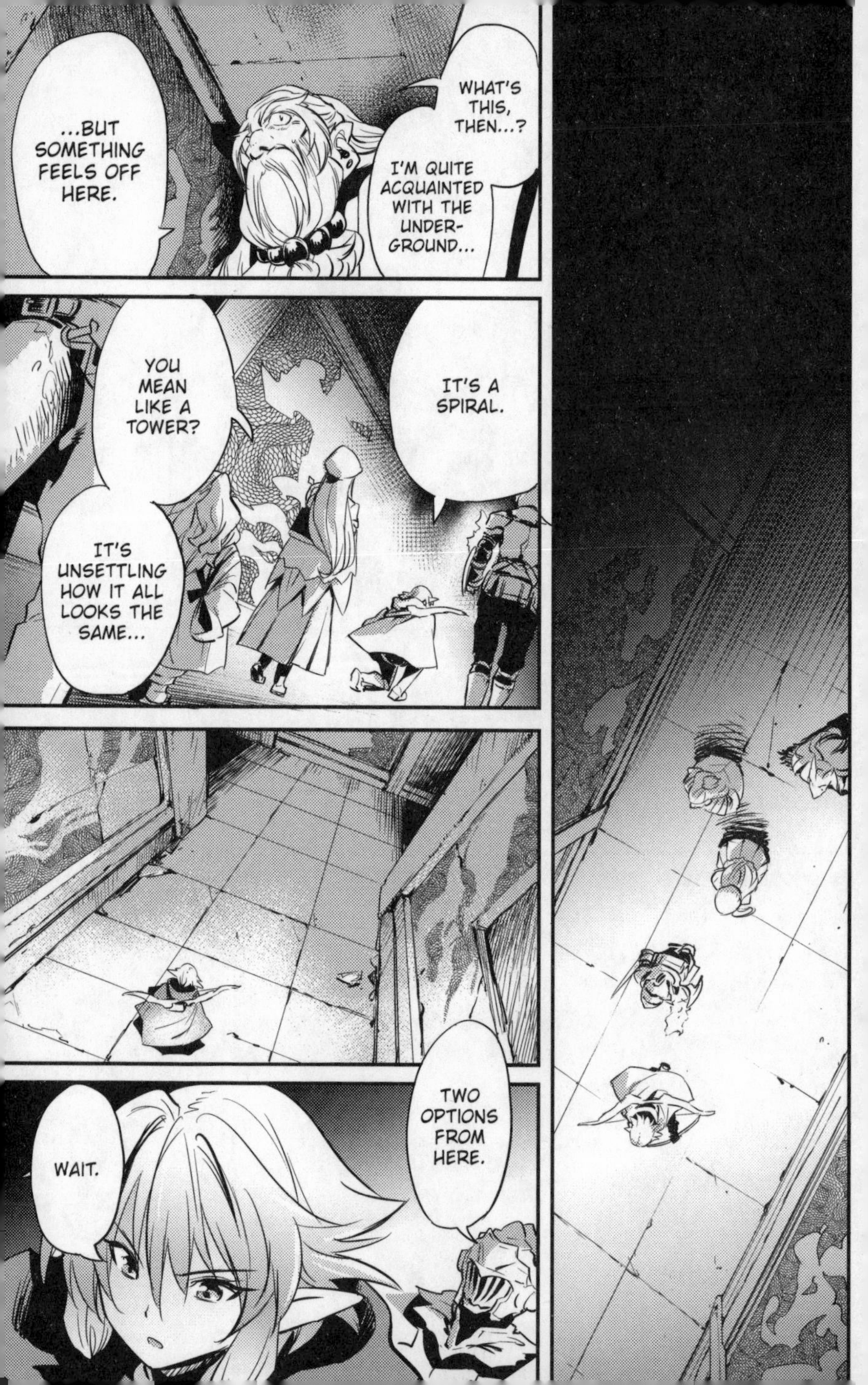
WHAT'S THIS, THEN...?
I'M QUITE ACQUAINTED WITH THE UNDER-GROUND...
...BUT SOMETHING FEELS OFF HERE.
IT'S A SPIRAL.
YOU MEAN LIKE A TOWER?
IT'S UNSETTLING HOW IT ALL LOOKS THE SAME...
TWO OPTIONS FROM HERE.
WAIT.

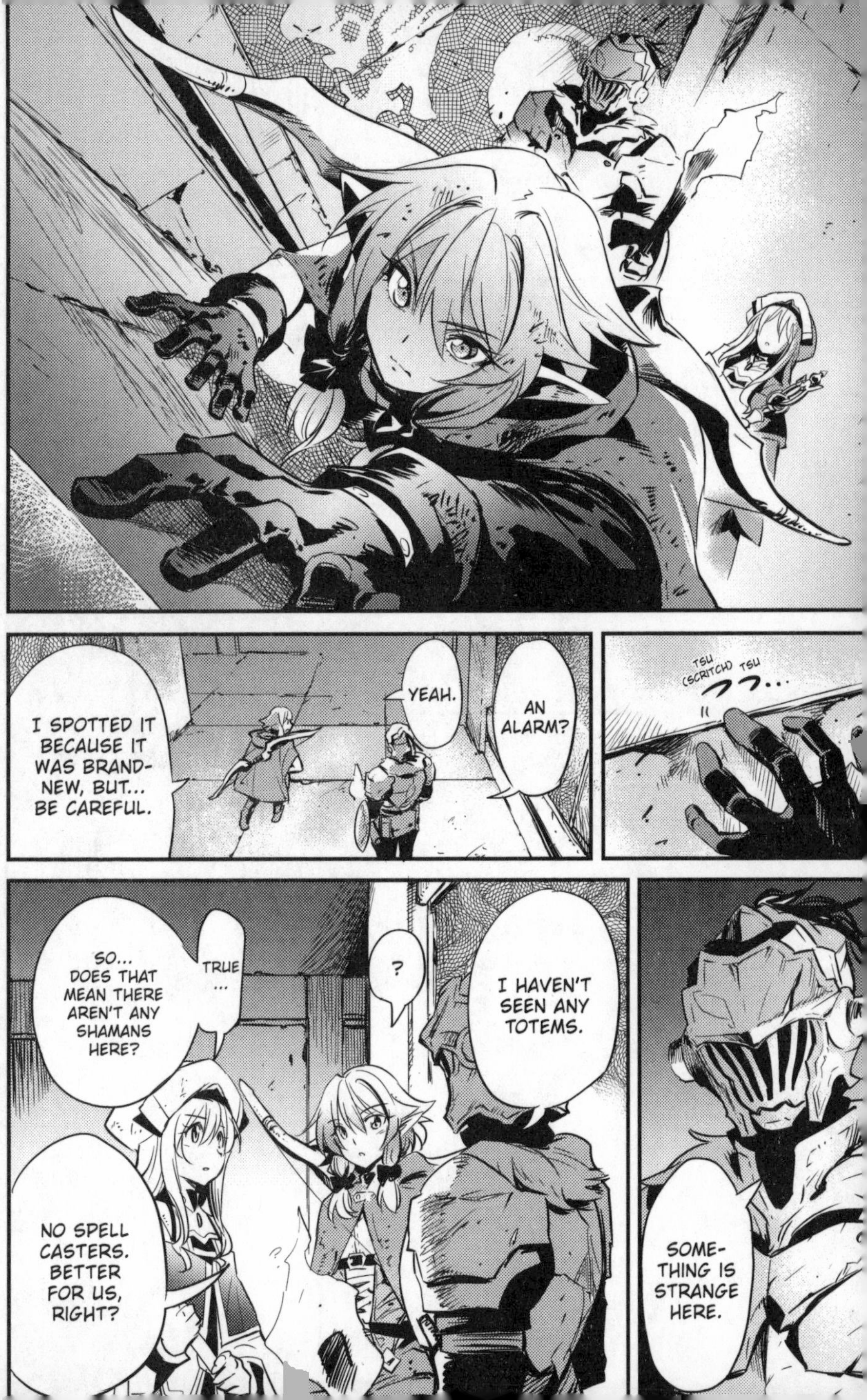
TSU (SCRITCH) TSU
ツツ…
AN ALARM?
YEAH.
I SPOTTED IT BECAUSE IT WAS BRAND-NEW, BUT... BE CAREFUL.
SOME-THING IS STRANGE HERE.
I HAVEN'T SEEN ANY TOTEMS.
?
SO... DOES THAT MEAN THERE AREN'T ANY SHAMANS HERE?
TRUE...
NO SPELL CASTERS. BETTER FOR US, RIGHT?

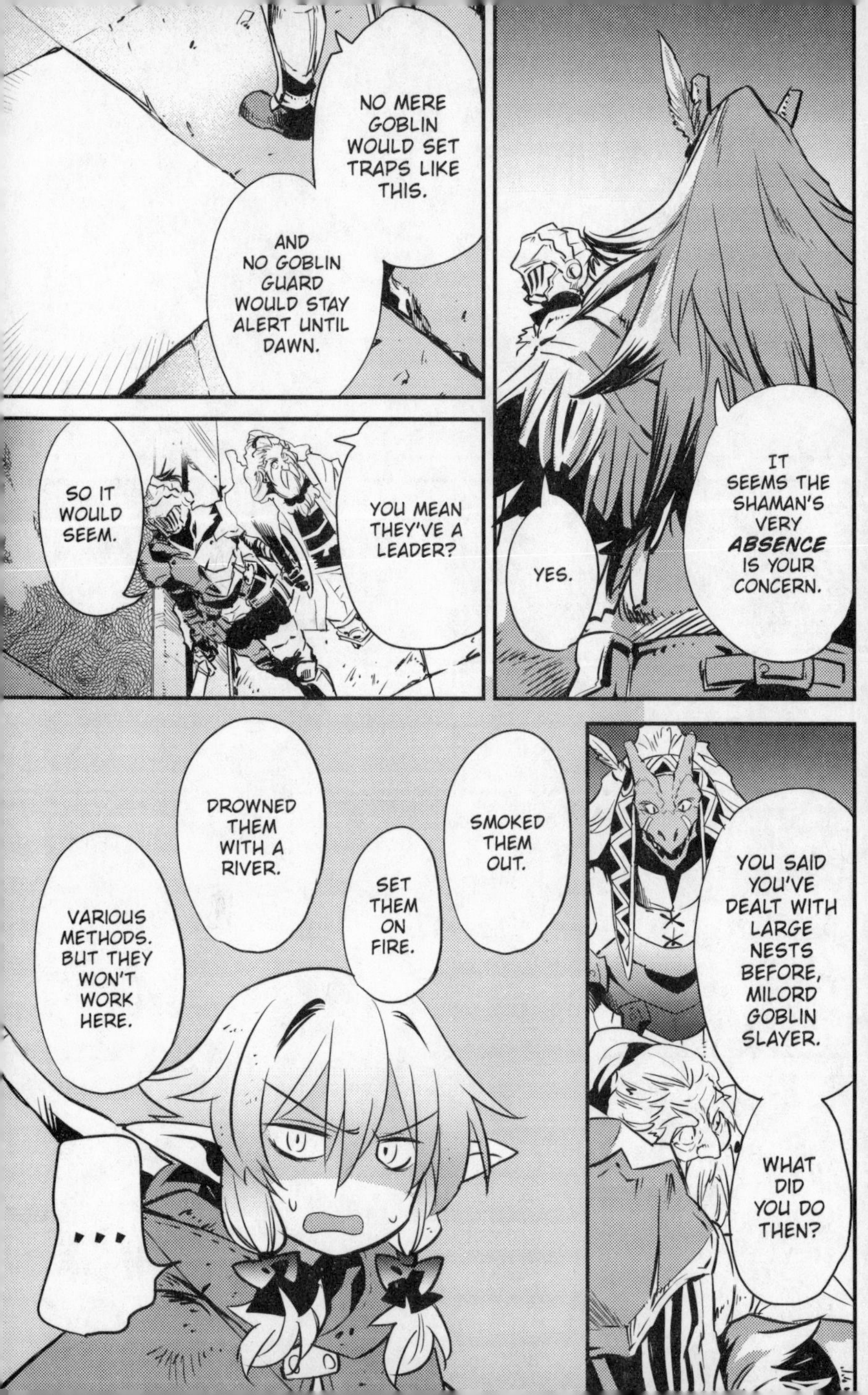
IT SEEMS THE SHAMAN'S VERY ***ABSENCE*** IS YOUR CONCERN.
YES.
NO MERE GOBLIN WOULD SET TRAPS LIKE THIS.
AND NO GOBLIN GUARD WOULD STAY ALERT UNTIL DAWN.
YOU MEAN THEY'VE A LEADER?
SO IT WOULD SEEM.
YOU SAID YOU'VE DEALT WITH LARGE NESTS BEFORE, MILORD GOBLIN SLAYER.
WHAT DID YOU DO THEN?
SMOKED THEM OUT.
SET THEM ON FIRE.
DROWNED THEM WITH A RIVER.
VARIOUS METHODS. BUT THEY WON'T WORK HERE.
...

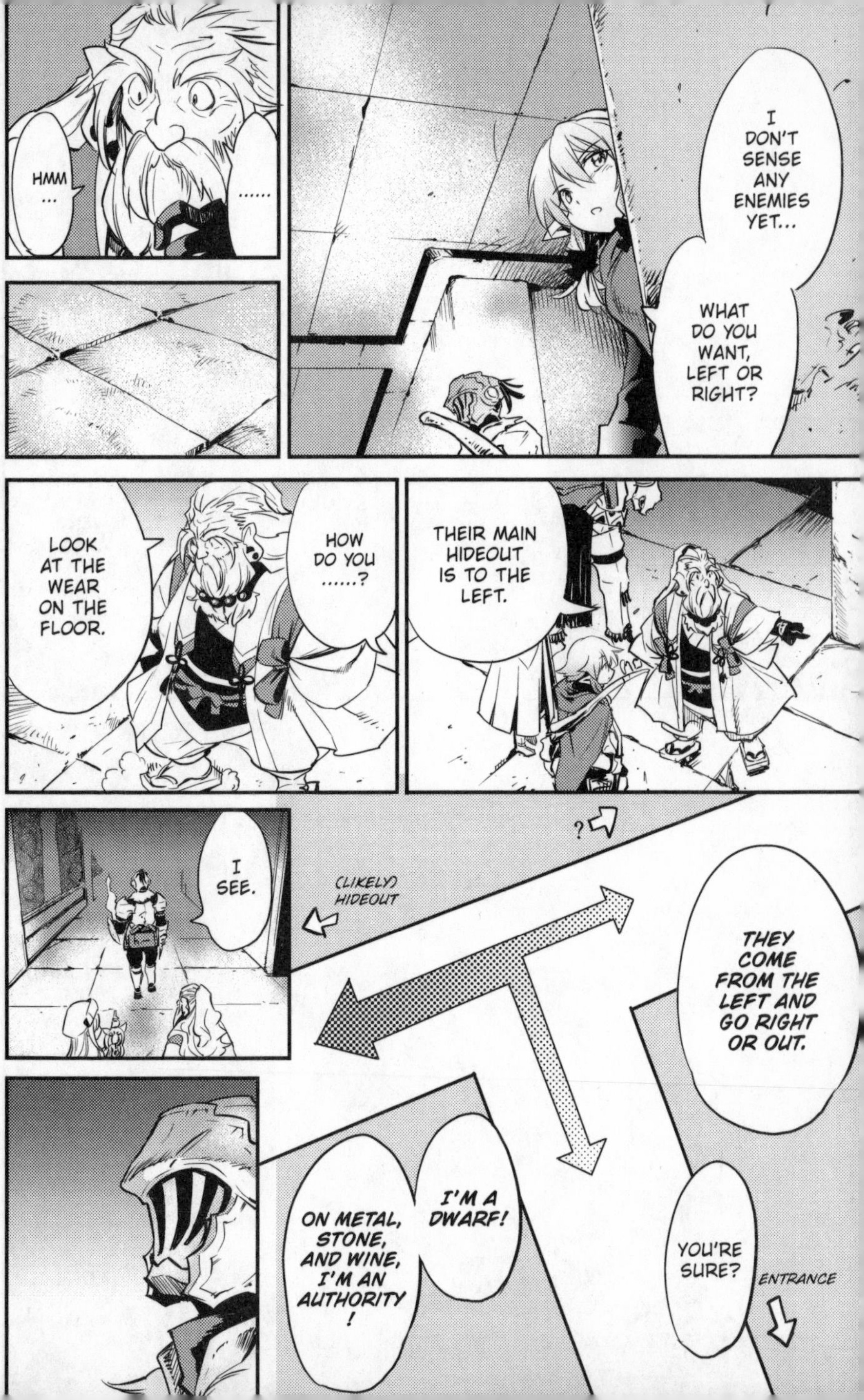
I DON'T SENSE ANY ENEMIES YET...
WHAT DO YOU WANT, LEFT OR RIGHT?
HMM...
......
THEIR MAIN HIDEOUT IS TO THE LEFT.
HOW DO YOU ......?
LOOK AT THE WEAR ON THE FLOOR.
?
(LIKELY) HIDEOUT
THEY COME FROM THE LEFT AND GO RIGHT OR OUT.
I SEE.
ENTRANCE
YOU'RE SURE?
I'M A DWARF!
ON METAL, STONE, AND WINE, I'M AN AUTHORITY!

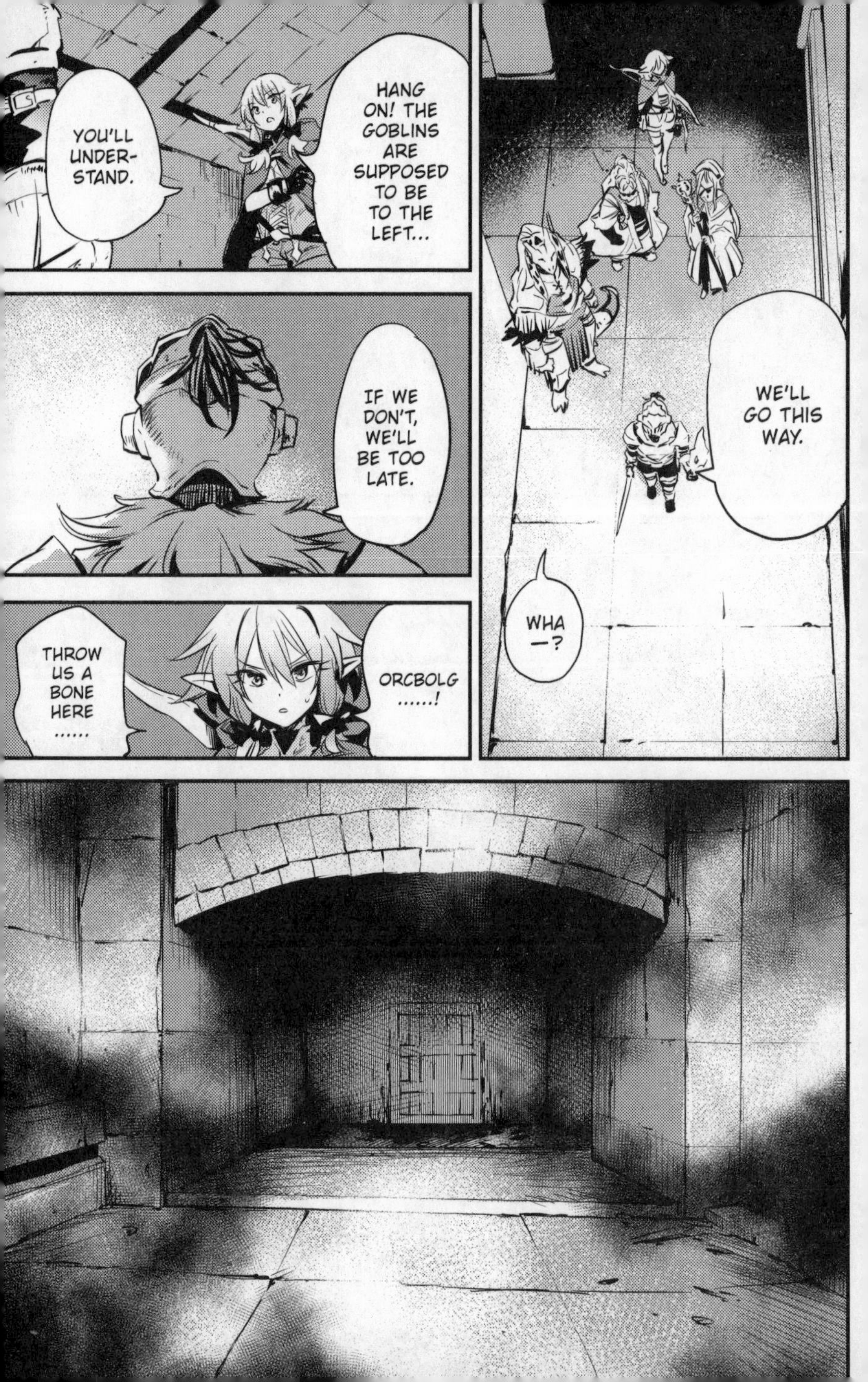
WE'LL GO THIS WAY.
WHA—?
HANG ON! THE GOBLINS ARE SUPPOSED TO BE TO THE LEFT...
YOU'LL UNDER-STAND.
IF WE DON'T, WE'LL BE TOO LATE.
ORCBOLG ......!
THROW US A BONE HERE ......

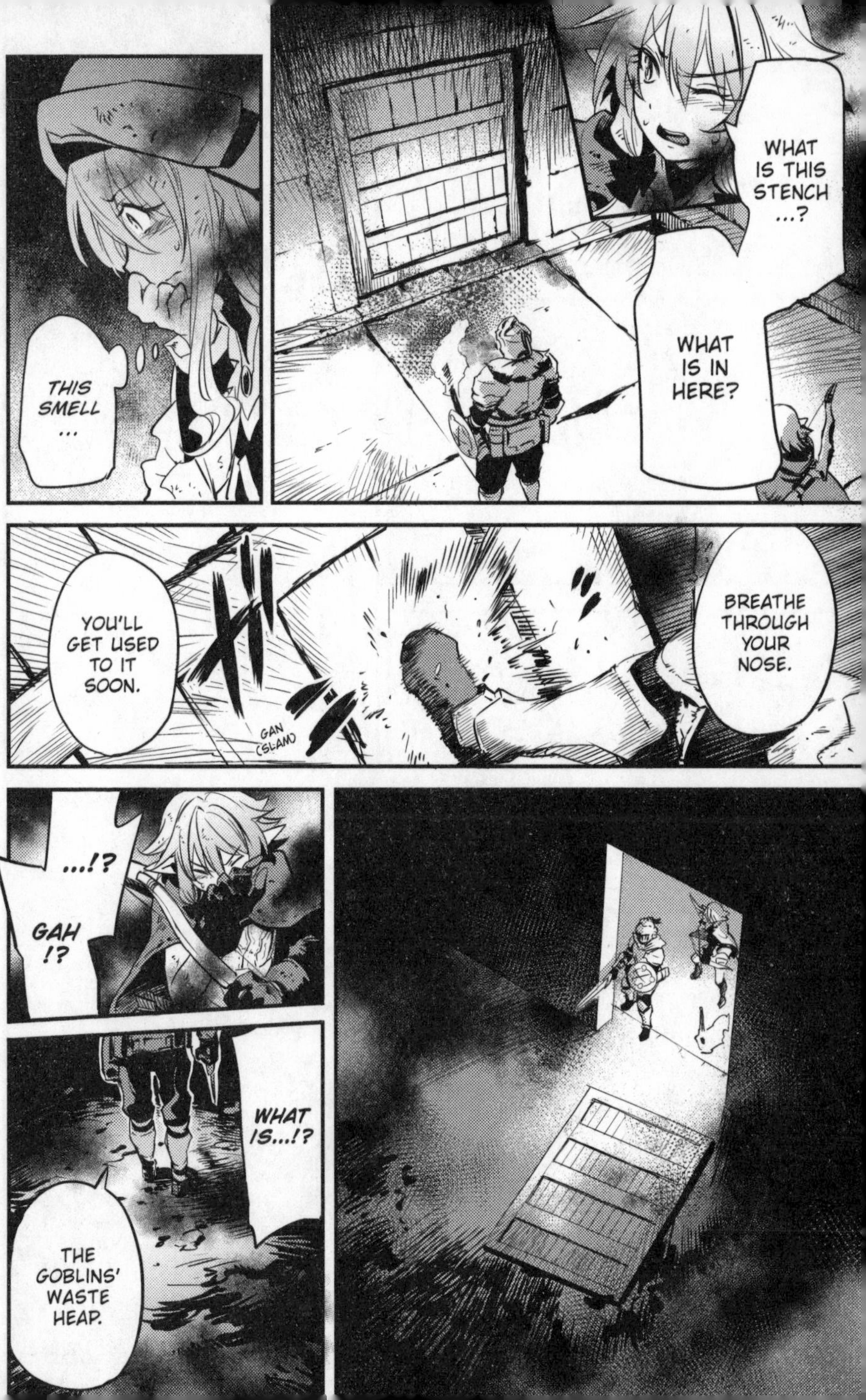
WHAT IS THIS STENCH ...?
WHAT IS IN HERE?
THIS SMELL ...
BREATHE THROUGH YOUR NOSE.
GAN (SLAM)
YOU'LL GET USED TO IT SOON.
...!?
GAH !?
WHAT IS...!?
THE GOBLINS' WASTE HEAP.

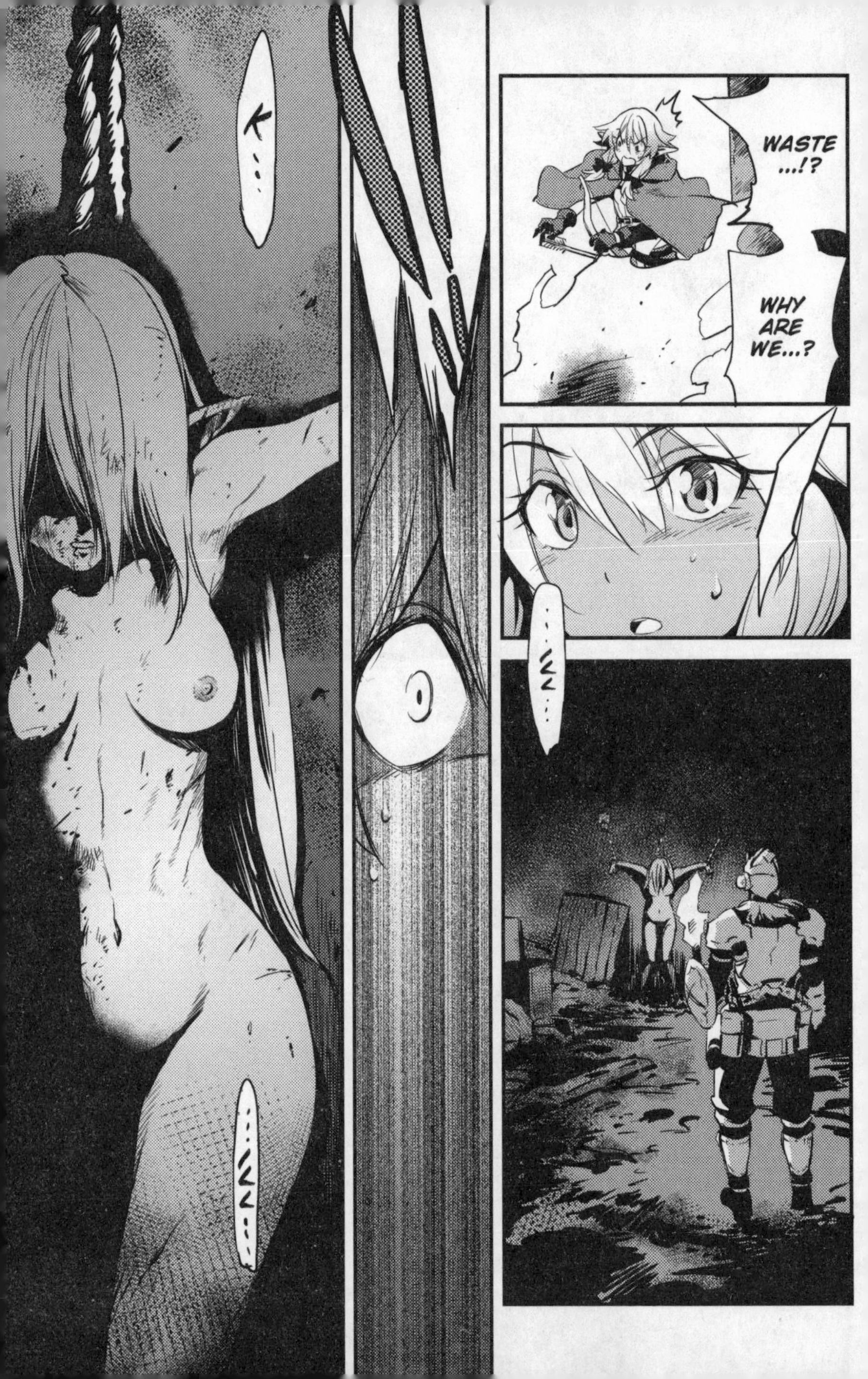
WASTE ...!?
WHY ARE WE...?

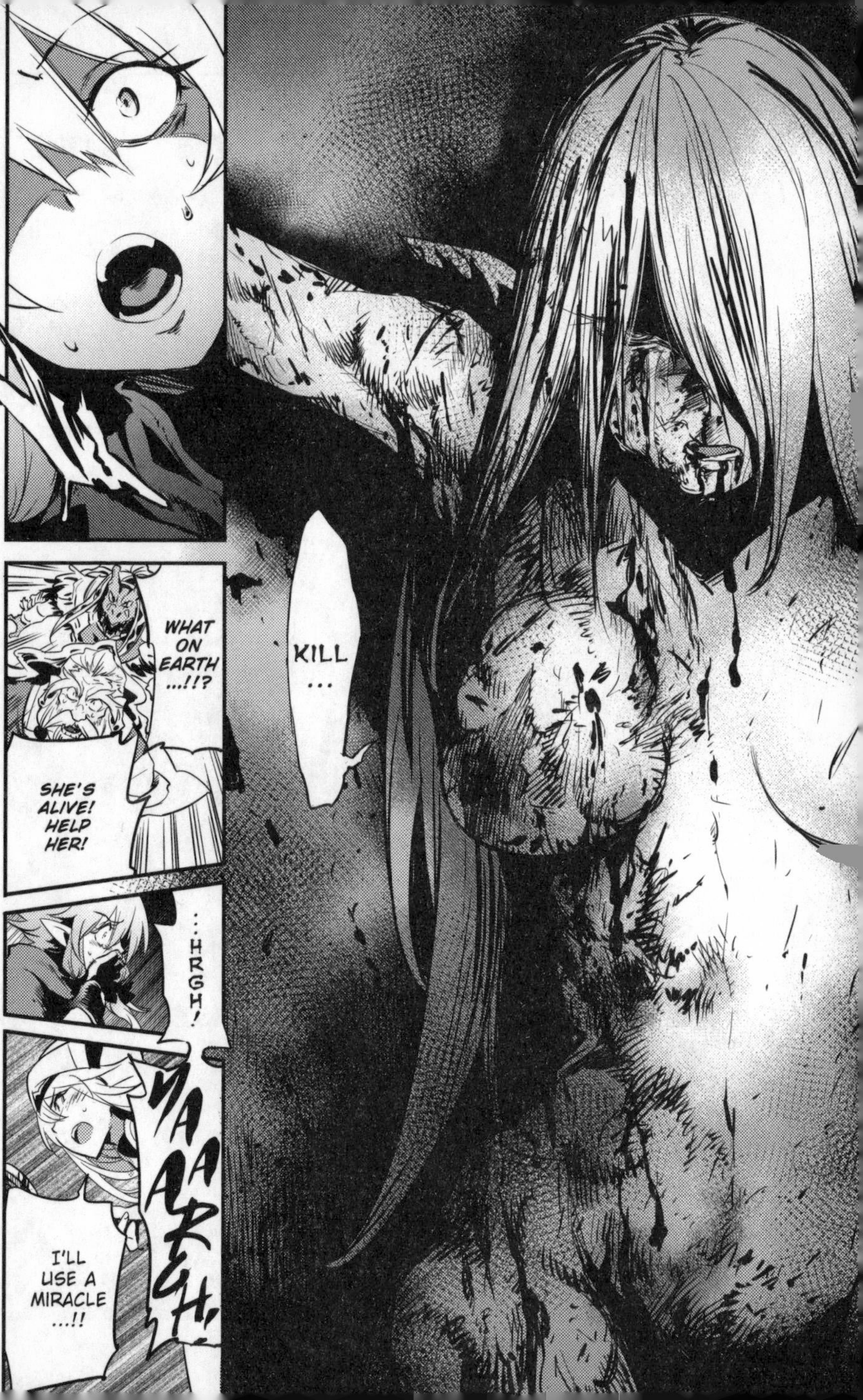
KILL ...
WHAT ON EARTH ...!!?
SHE'S ALIVE! HELP HER!
...HRGH!
VAAAARGH!
I'LL USE A MIRACLE ...!!

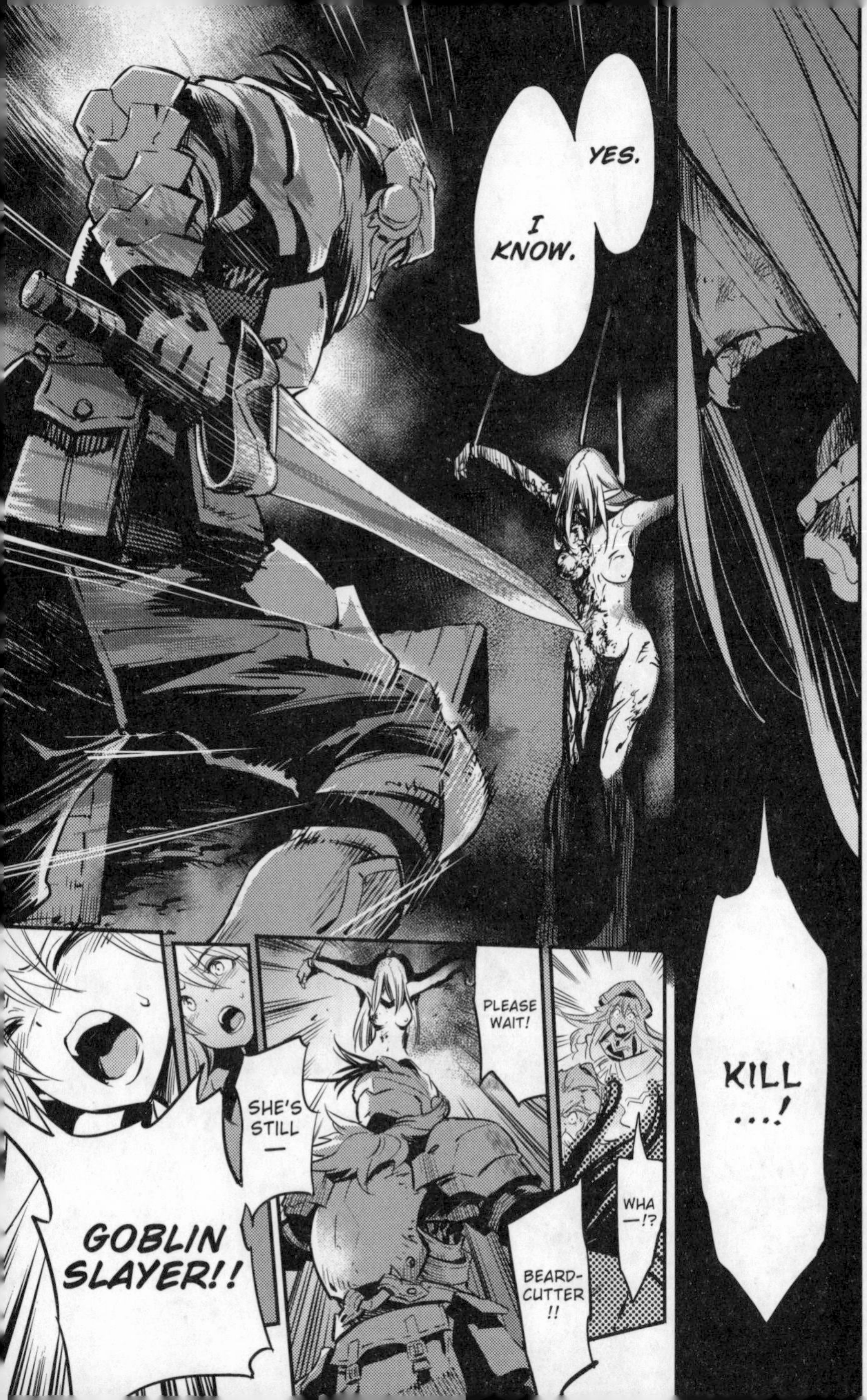
KILL ...!
YES.
I KNOW.
WHA—!?
BEARD-CUTTER!!
PLEASE WAIT!
SHE'S STILL—
GOBLIN SLAYER!!

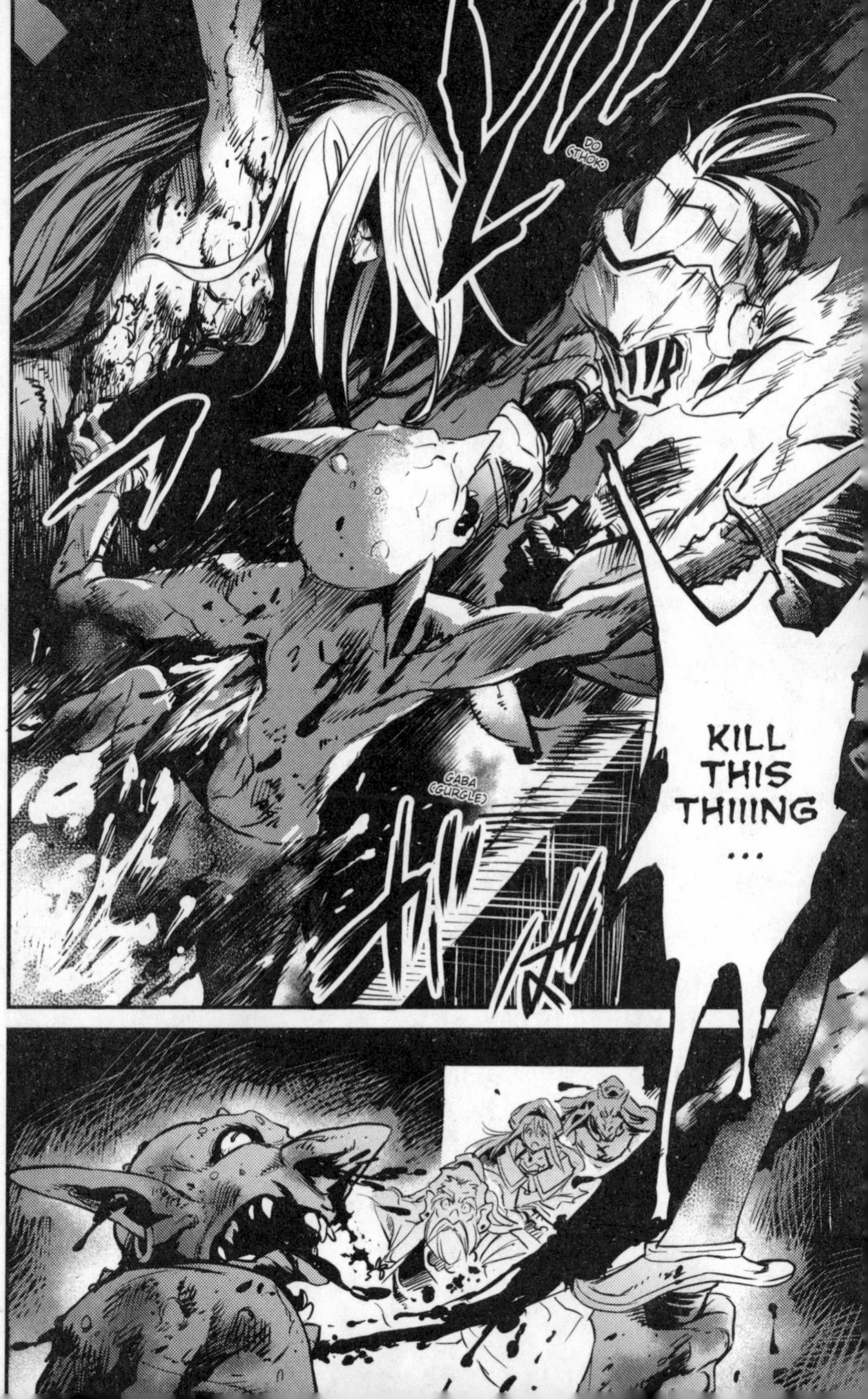
DO (THOK)
KILL THIS THIIING ...
GABA (GURGLE)
!

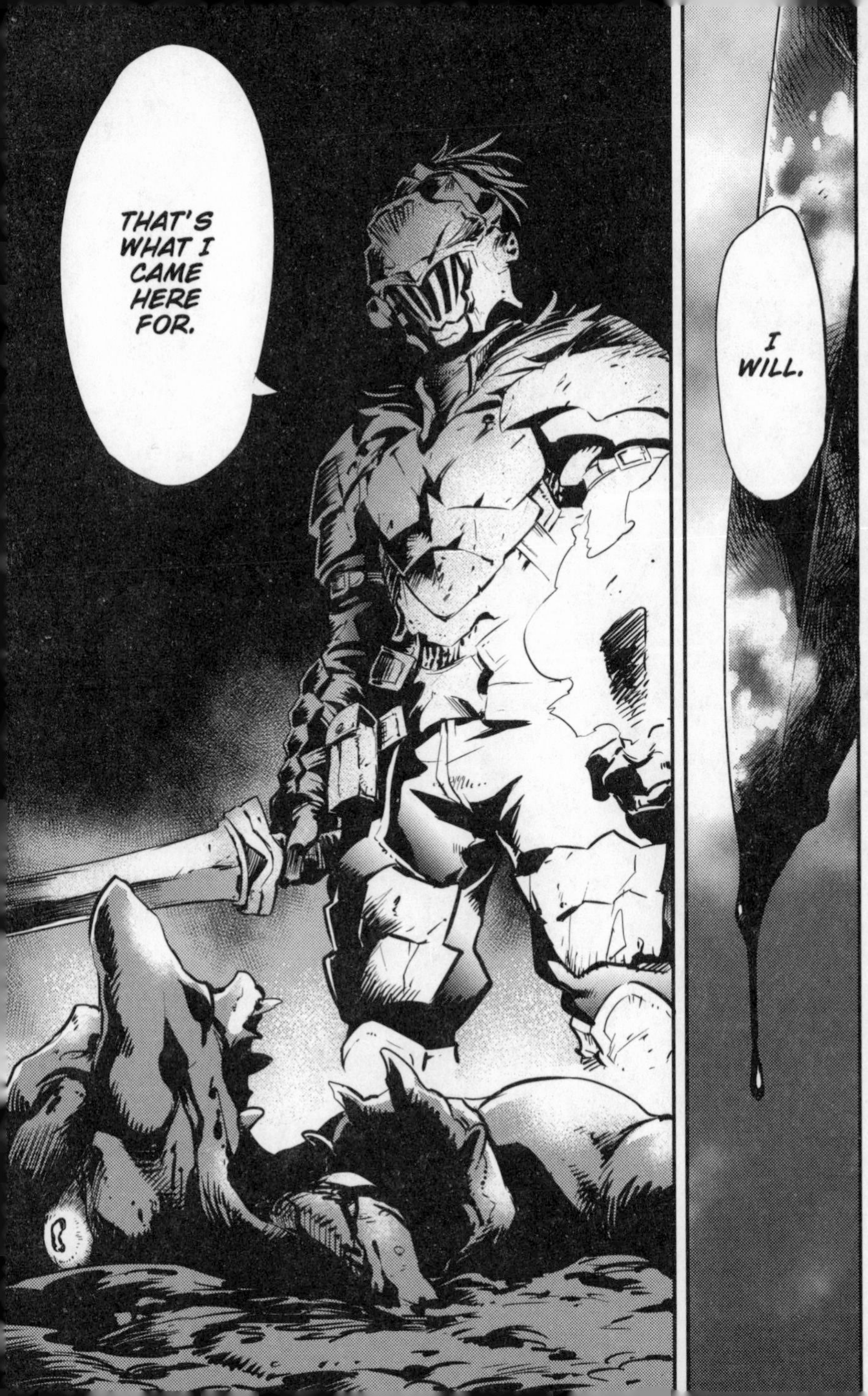
I WILL.
THAT'S WHAT I CAME HERE FOR.

GOBLIN SLAYER

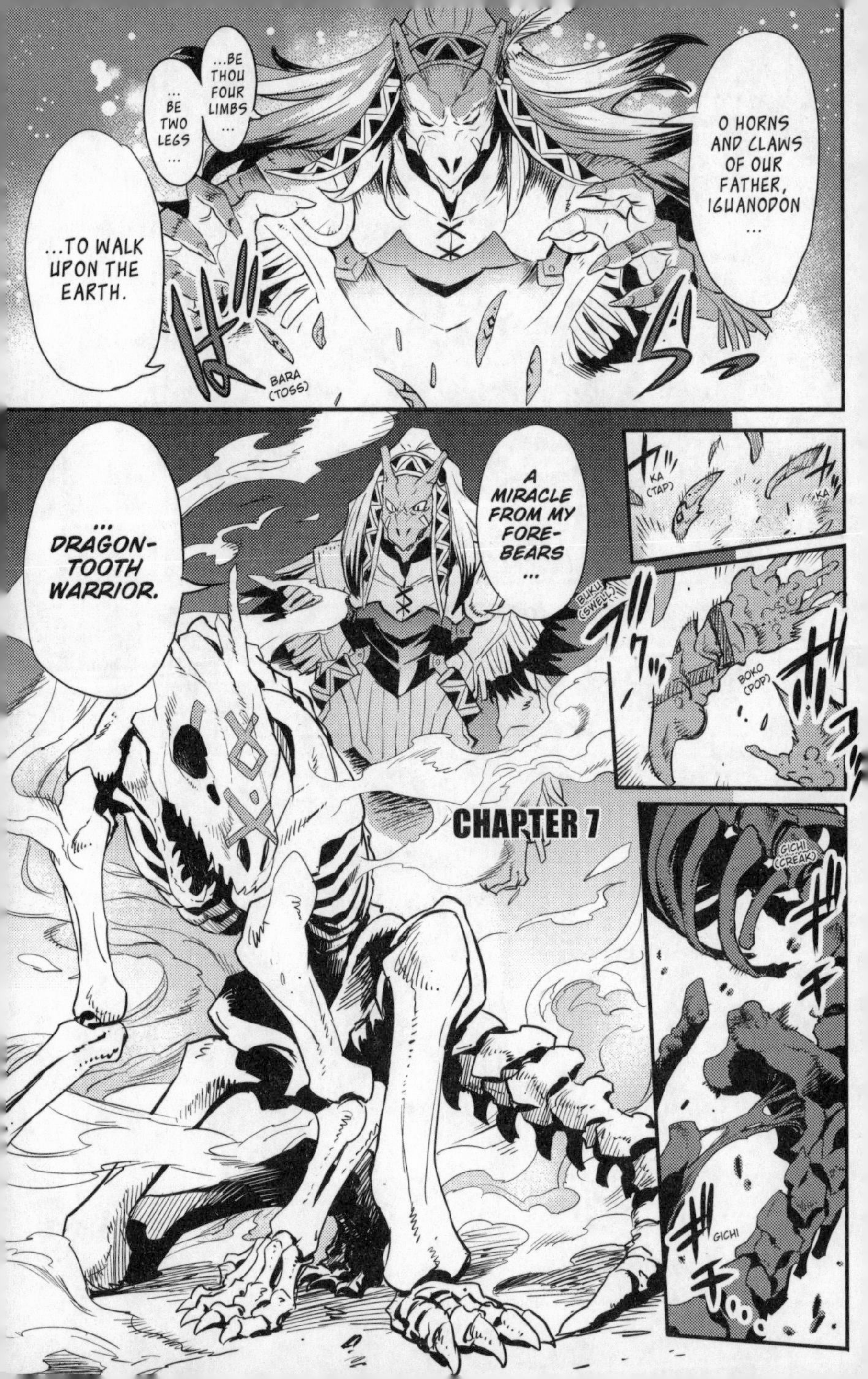
O HORNS AND CLAWS OF OUR FATHER, IGUANODON ...
...BE THOU FOUR LIMBS ...
... BE TWO LEGS ...
...TO WALK UPON THE EARTH.
BARA (TOSS)
KA (TAP)
KA
BUKU (SWELL)
BOKO (POP)
GICHI (CREAK)
GICHI
A MIRACLE FROM MY FORE-BEARS ...
... DRAGON-TOOTH WARRIOR.
CHAPTER 7

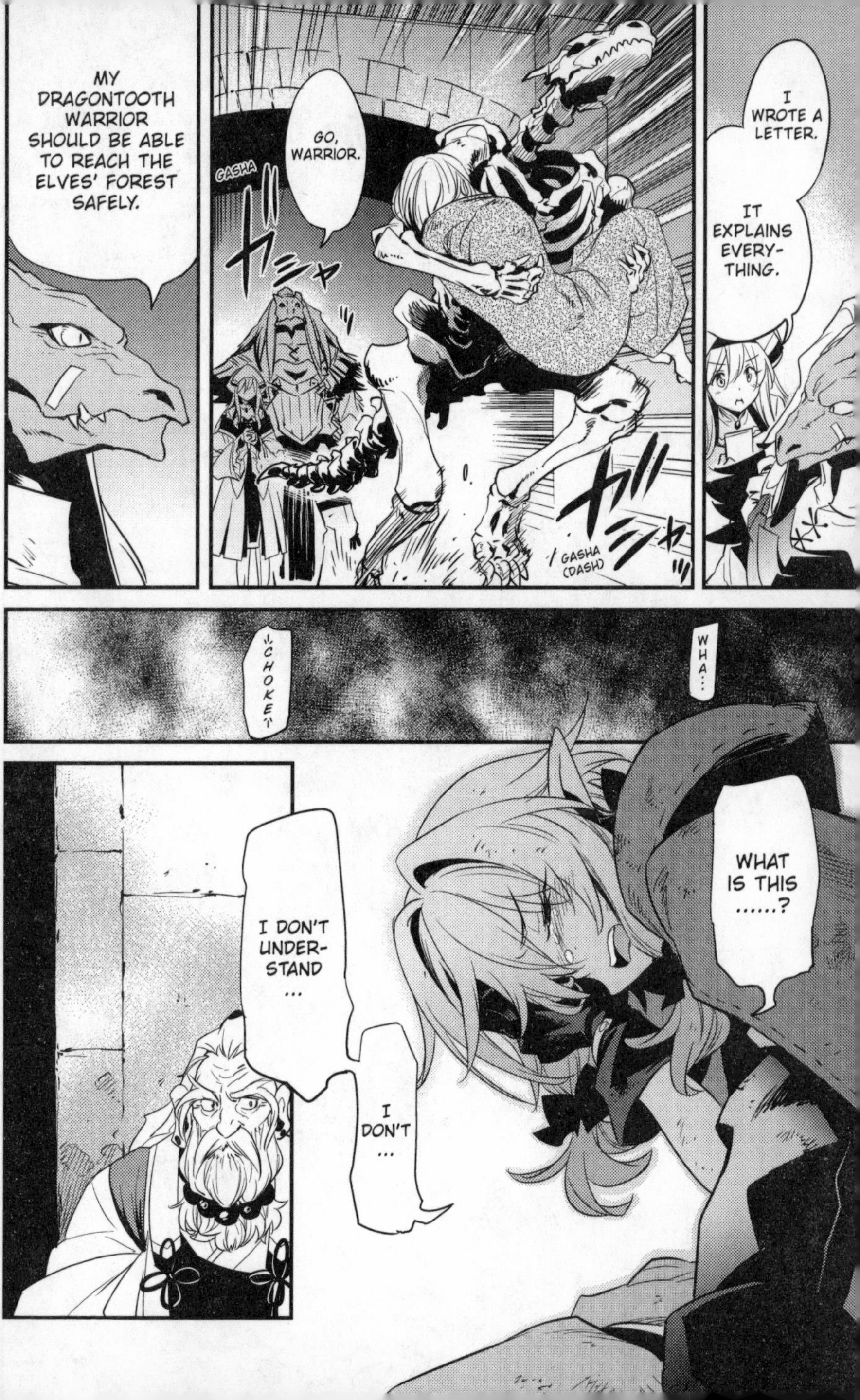
I WROTE A LETTER.
IT EXPLAINS EVERY-THING.
GASHA (DASH)
GO, WARRIOR.
GASHA
MY DRAGONTOOTH WARRIOR SHOULD BE ABLE TO REACH THE ELVES' FOREST SAFELY.
WHA...
CHOKE
WHAT IS THIS ......?
I DON'T UNDER-STAND ...
I DON'T ...

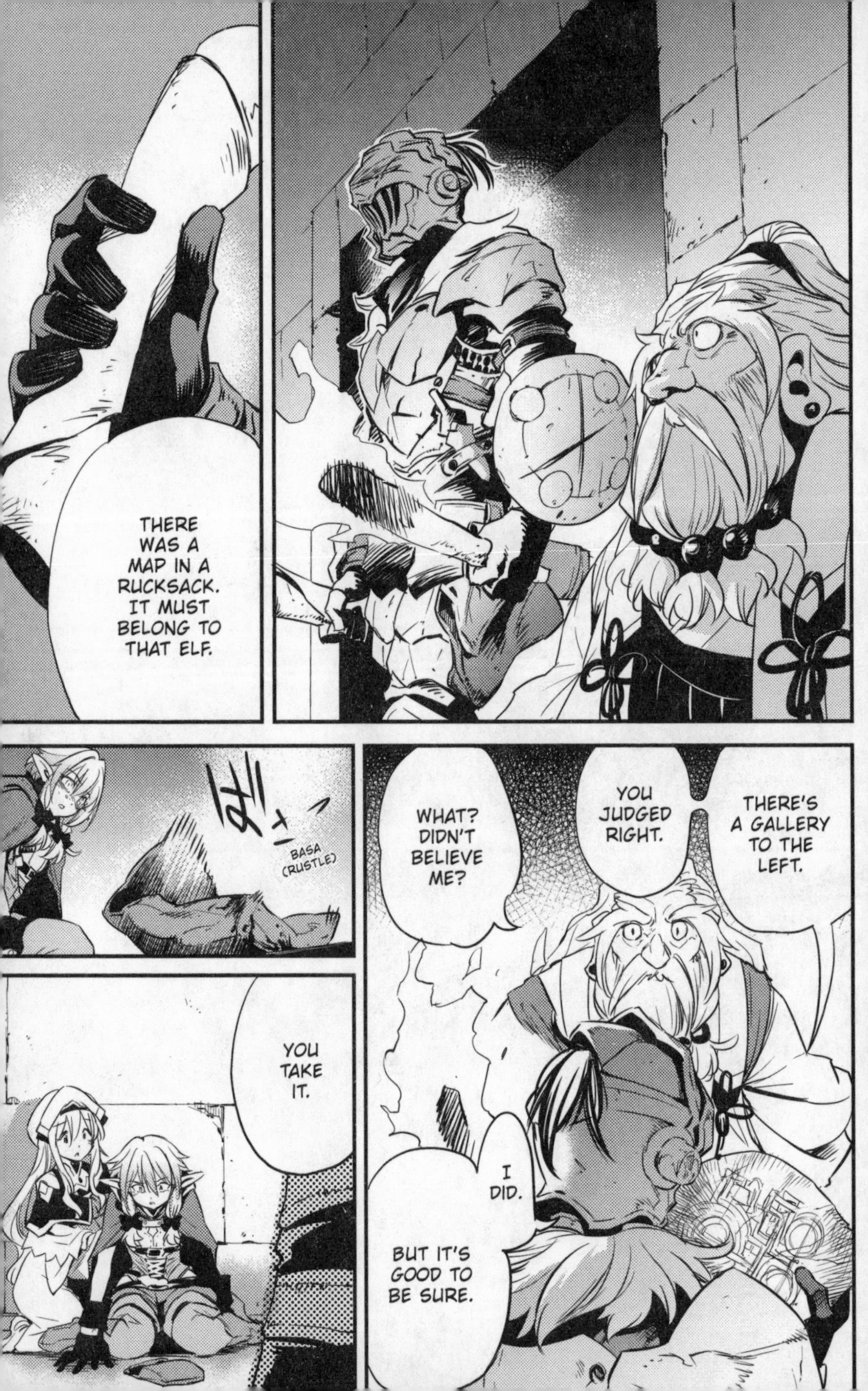
THERE WAS A MAP IN A RUCKSACK. IT MUST BELONG TO THAT ELF.
THERE'S A GALLERY TO THE LEFT.
YOU JUDGED RIGHT.
WHAT? DIDN'T BELIEVE ME?
I DID.
BUT IT'S GOOD TO BE SURE.
BASA (RUSTLE)
YOU TAKE IT.

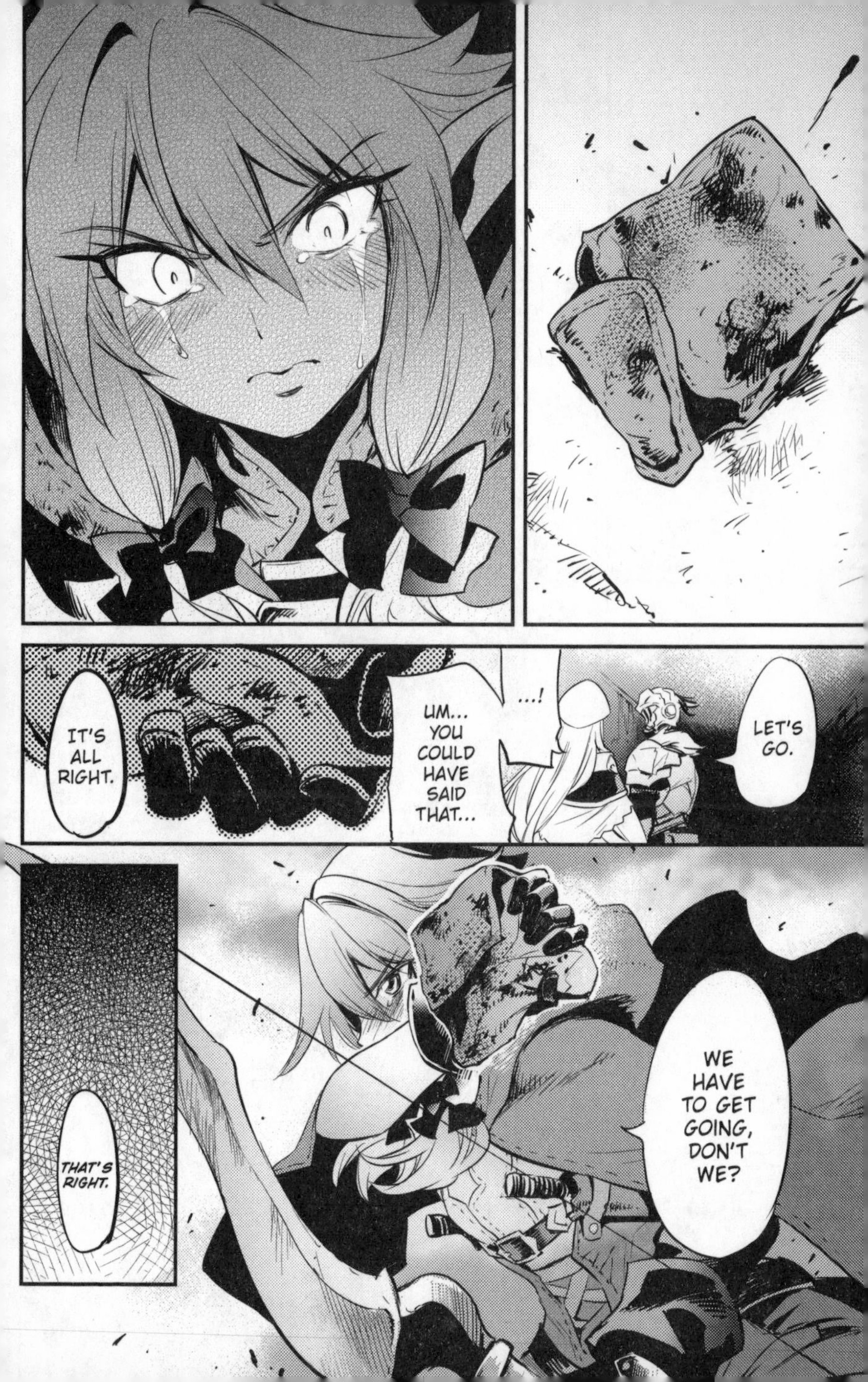
LET'S GO.
...!
UM... YOU COULD HAVE SAID THAT...
IT'S ALL RIGHT.
WE HAVE TO GET GOING, DON'T WE?
THAT'S RIGHT.

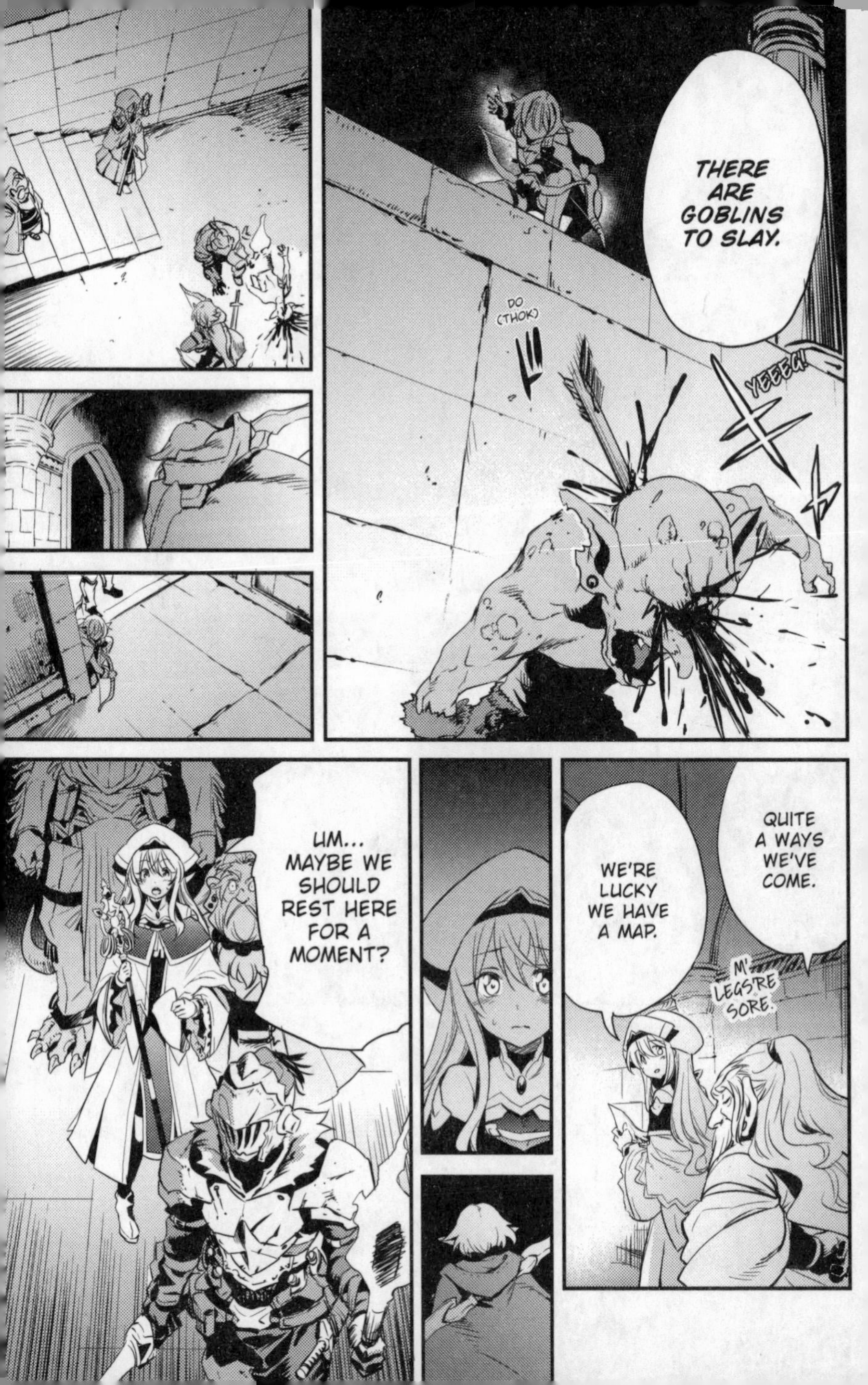
THERE ARE GOBLINS TO SLAY.
DO (THOK)
YEEEG!
QUITE A WAYS WE'VE COME.
M' LEGS'RE SORE.
WE'RE LUCKY WE HAVE A MAP.
UM... MAYBE WE SHOULD REST HERE FOR A MOMENT?

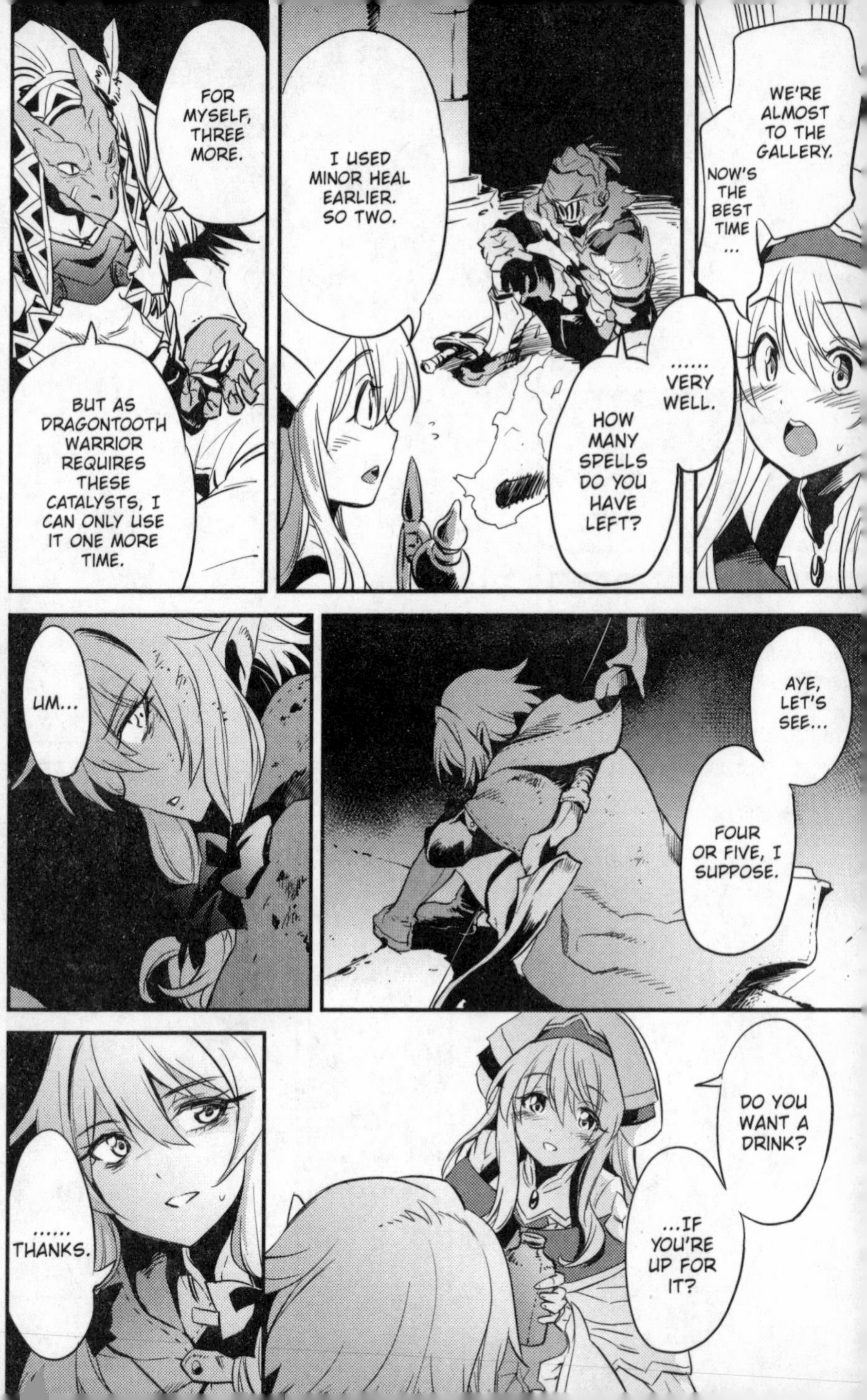
WE'RE ALMOST TO THE GALLERY.
NOW'S THE BEST TIME ...
...... VERY WELL.
HOW MANY SPELLS DO YOU HAVE LEFT?
I USED MINOR HEAL EARLIER. SO TWO.
FOR MYSELF, THREE MORE.
BUT AS DRAGONTOOTH WARRIOR REQUIRES THESE CATALYSTS, I CAN ONLY USE IT ONE MORE TIME.
AYE, LET'S SEE...
FOUR OR FIVE, I SUPPOSE.
UM...
DO YOU WANT A DRINK?
...IF YOU'RE UP FOR IT?
...... THANKS.

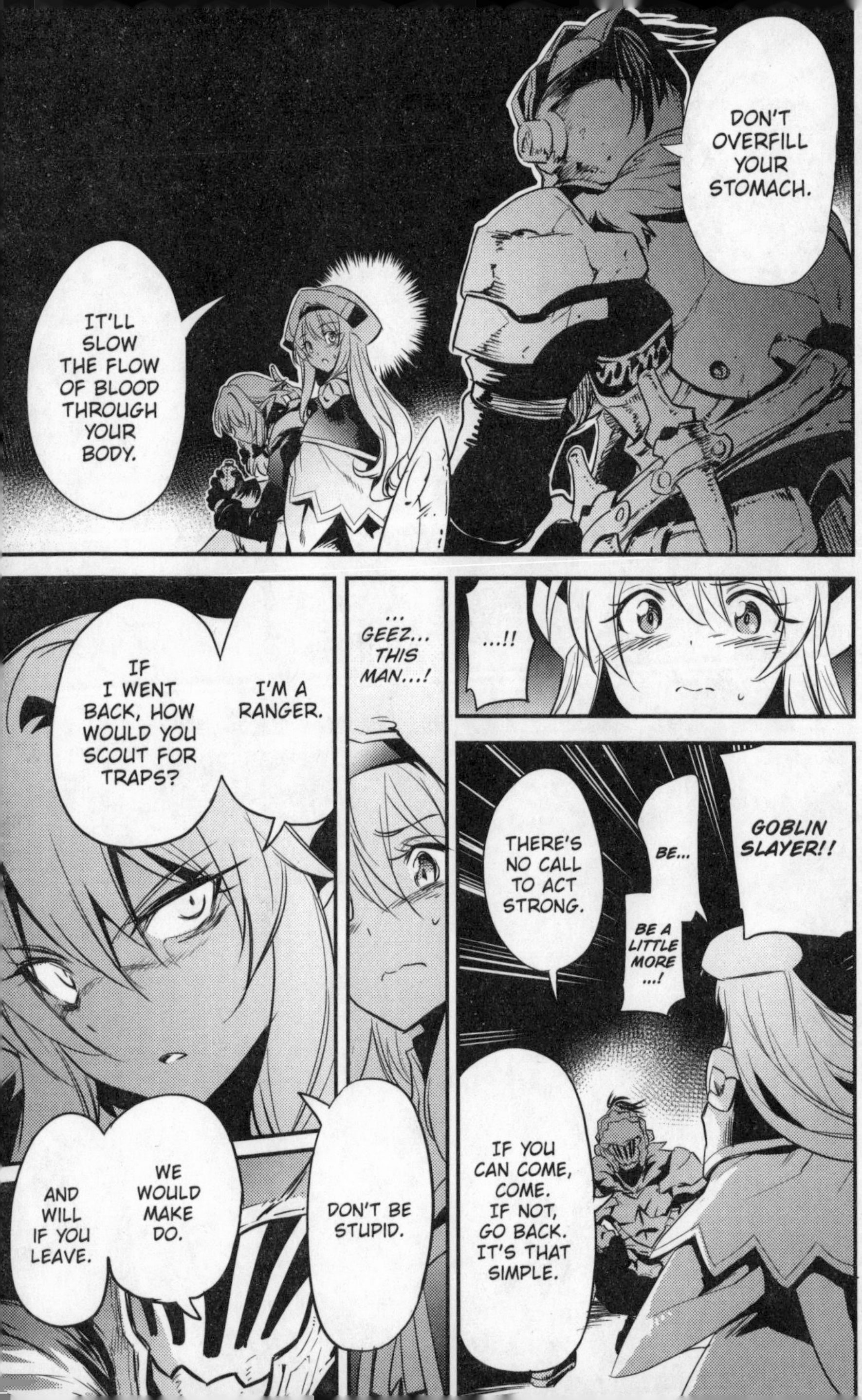
DON'T OVERFILL YOUR STOMACH.
IT'LL SLOW THE FLOW OF BLOOD THROUGH YOUR BODY.
...!!
GOBLIN SLAYER!!
BE...
BE A LITTLE MORE ...!
THERE'S NO CALL TO ACT STRONG.
IF YOU CAN COME, COME. IF NOT, GO BACK. IT'S THAT SIMPLE.
... GEEZ... THIS MAN...!
DON'T BE STUPID.
I'M A RANGER.
IF I WENT BACK, HOW WOULD YOU SCOUT FOR TRAPS?
WE WOULD MAKE DO.
AND WILL IF YOU LEAVE.

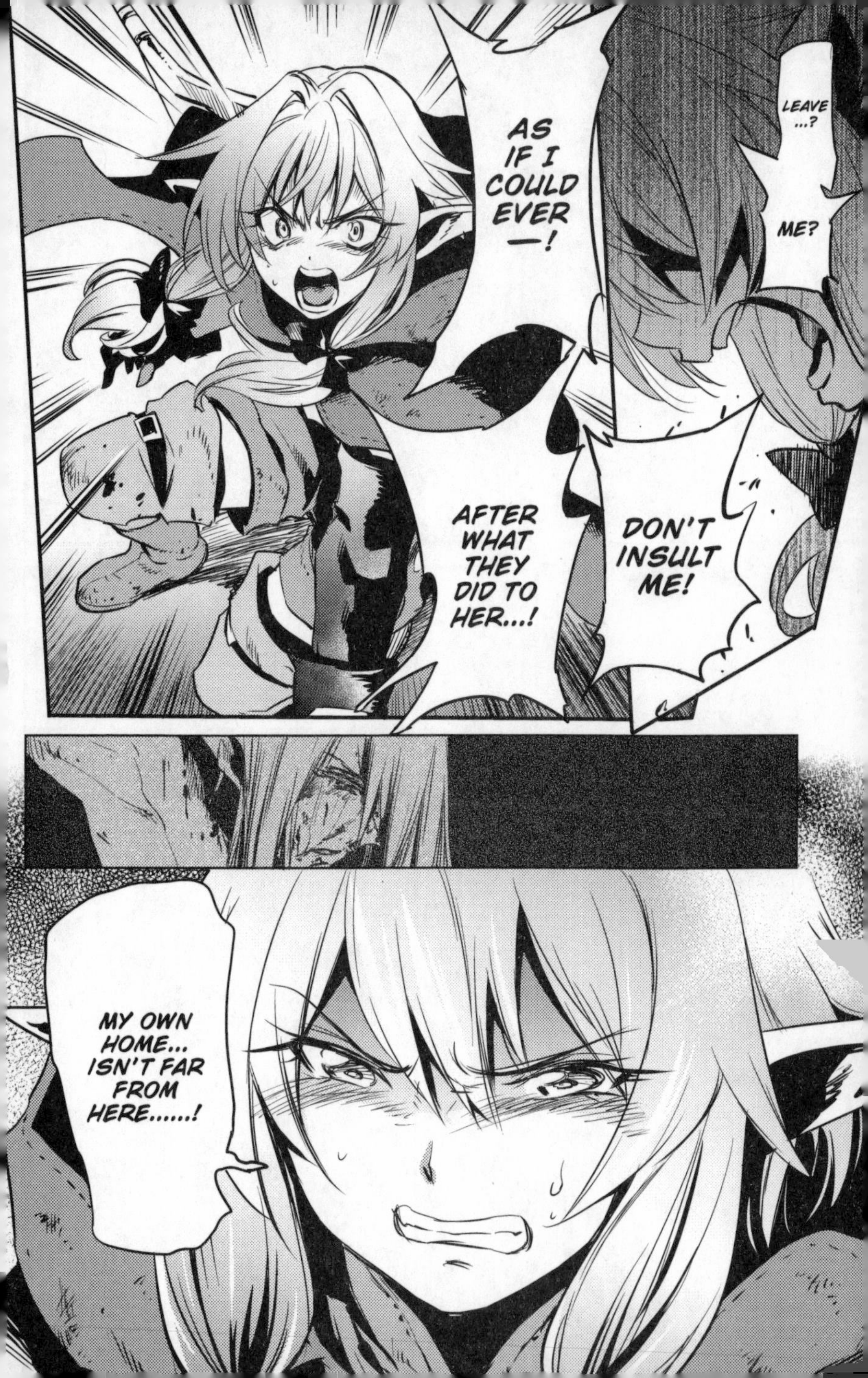
LEAVE ...?
ME?
AS IF I COULD EVER —!
DON'T INSULT ME!
AFTER WHAT THEY DID TO HER...!
MY OWN HOME... ISN'T FAR FROM HERE......!

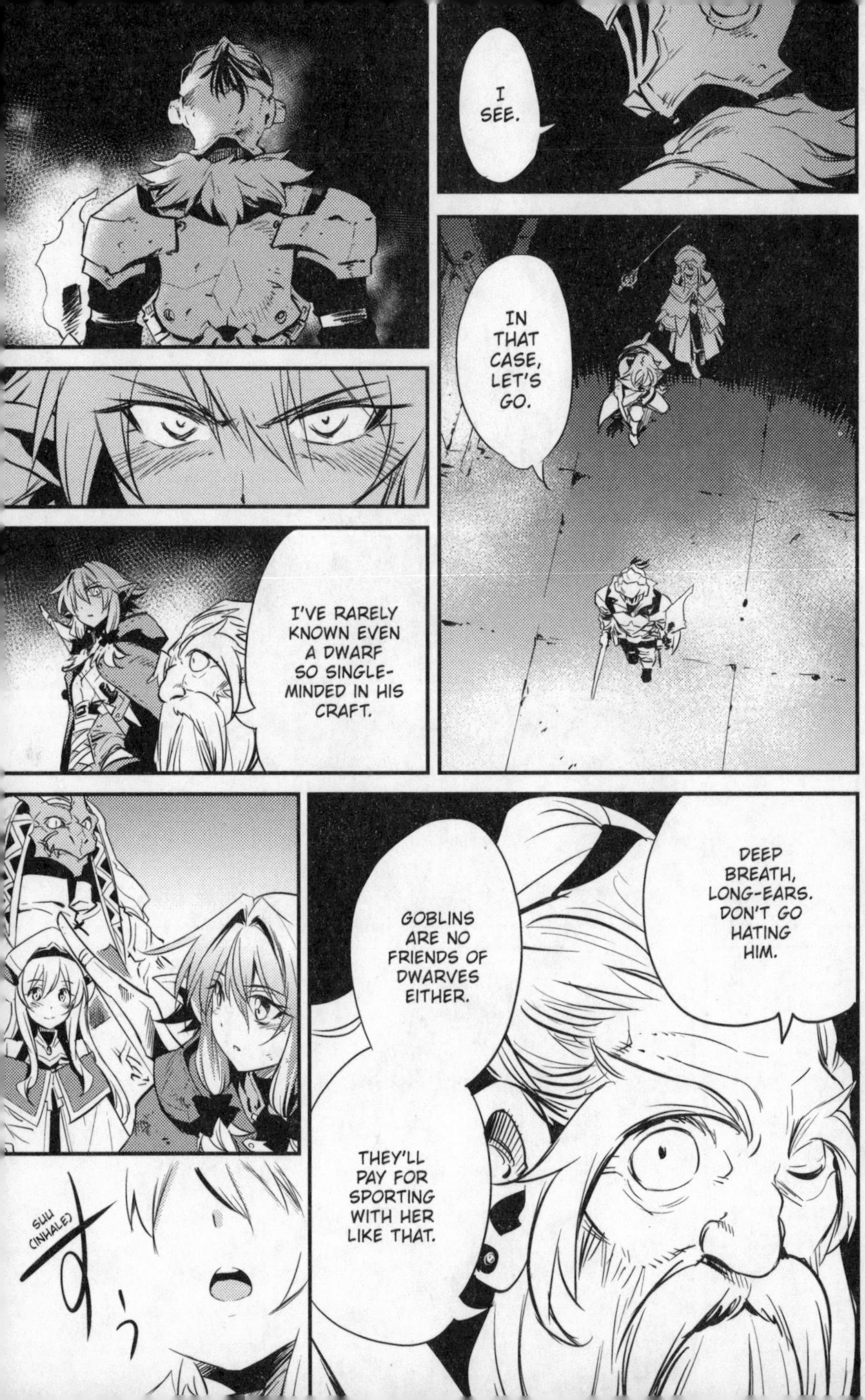
I SEE.
IN THAT CASE, LET'S GO.
I'VE RARELY KNOWN EVEN A DWARF SO SINGLE-MINDED IN HIS CRAFT.
DEEP BREATH, LONG-EARS. DON'T GO HATING HIM.
GOBLINS ARE NO FRIENDS OF DWARVES EITHER.
THEY'LL PAY FOR SPORTING WITH HER LIKE THAT.
SUU (INHALE)

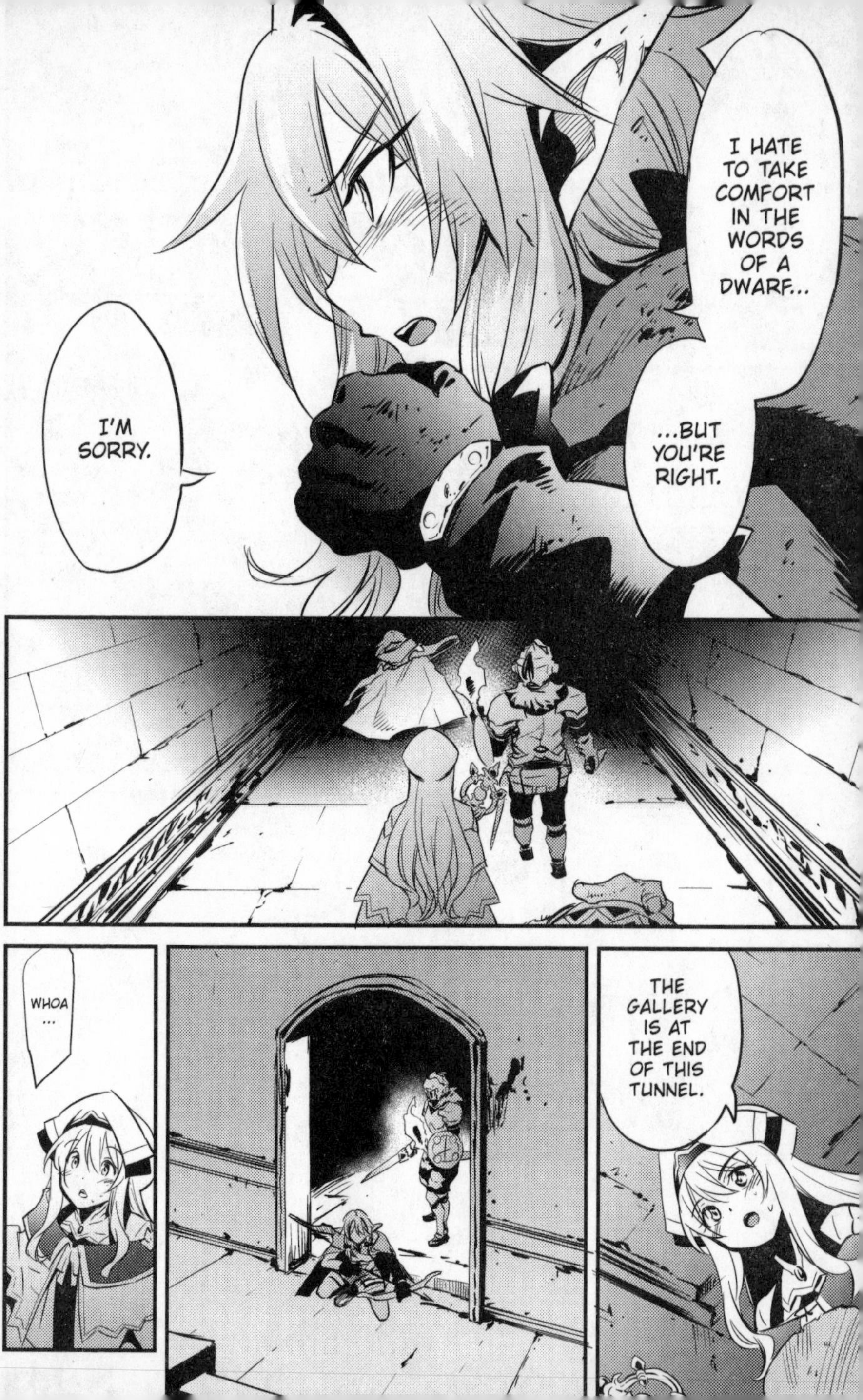
I HATE TO TAKE COMFORT IN THE WORDS OF A DWARF...
...BUT YOU'RE RIGHT.
I'M SORRY.
THE GALLERY IS AT THE END OF THIS TUNNEL.
WHOA ...

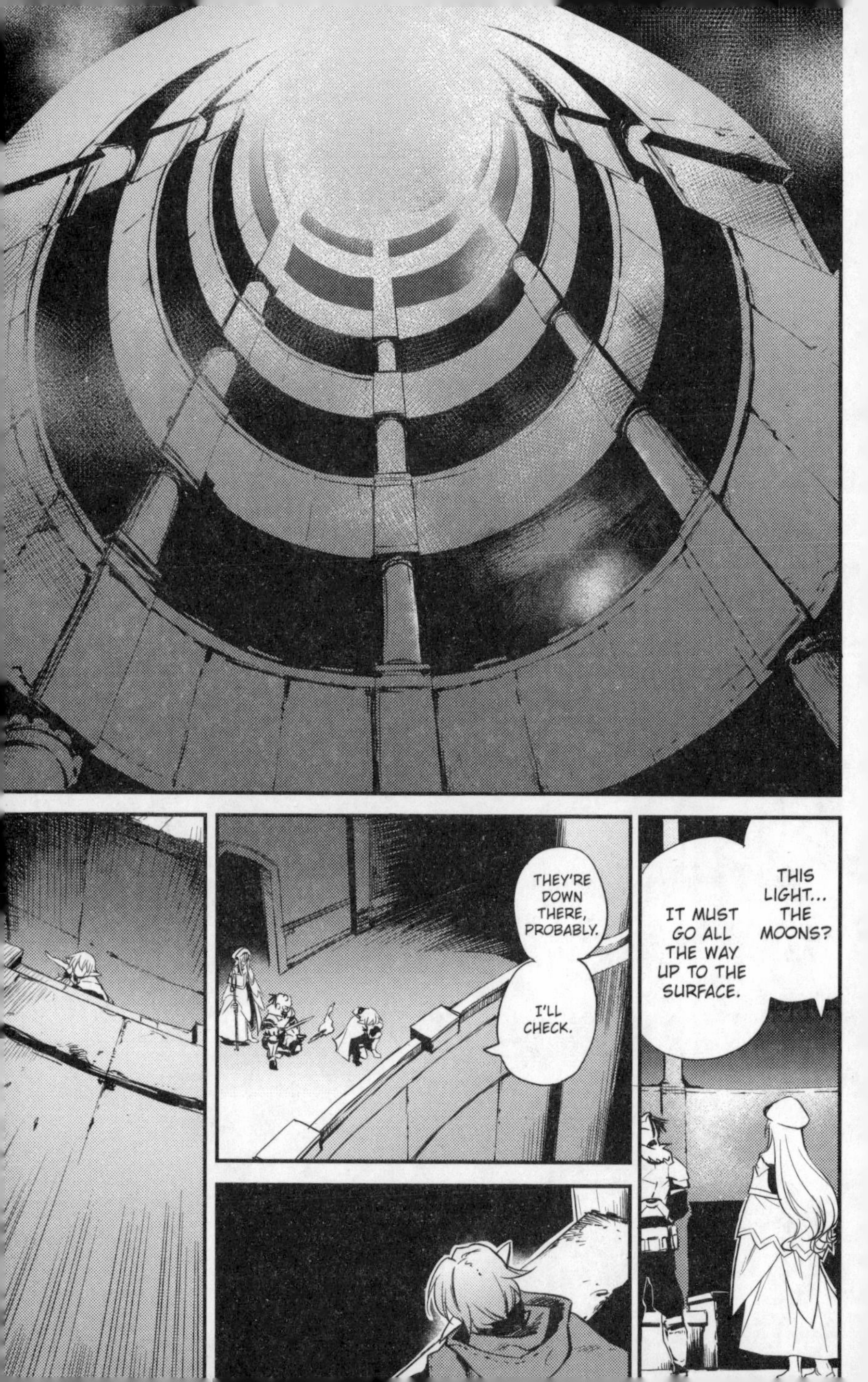
THIS LIGHT... THE MOONS?
IT MUST GO ALL THE WAY UP TO THE SURFACE.
THEY'RE DOWN THERE, PROBABLY.
I'LL CHECK.

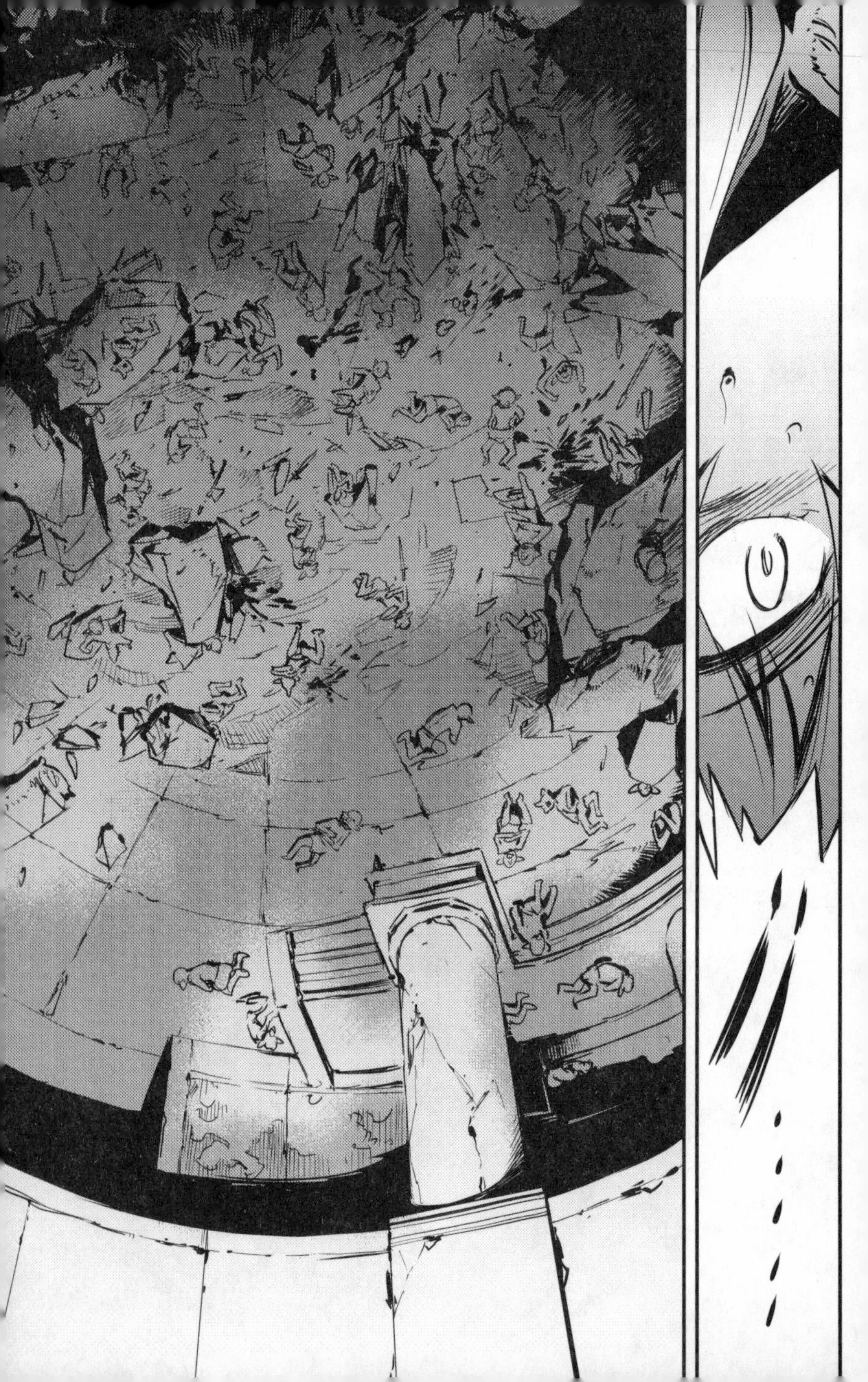

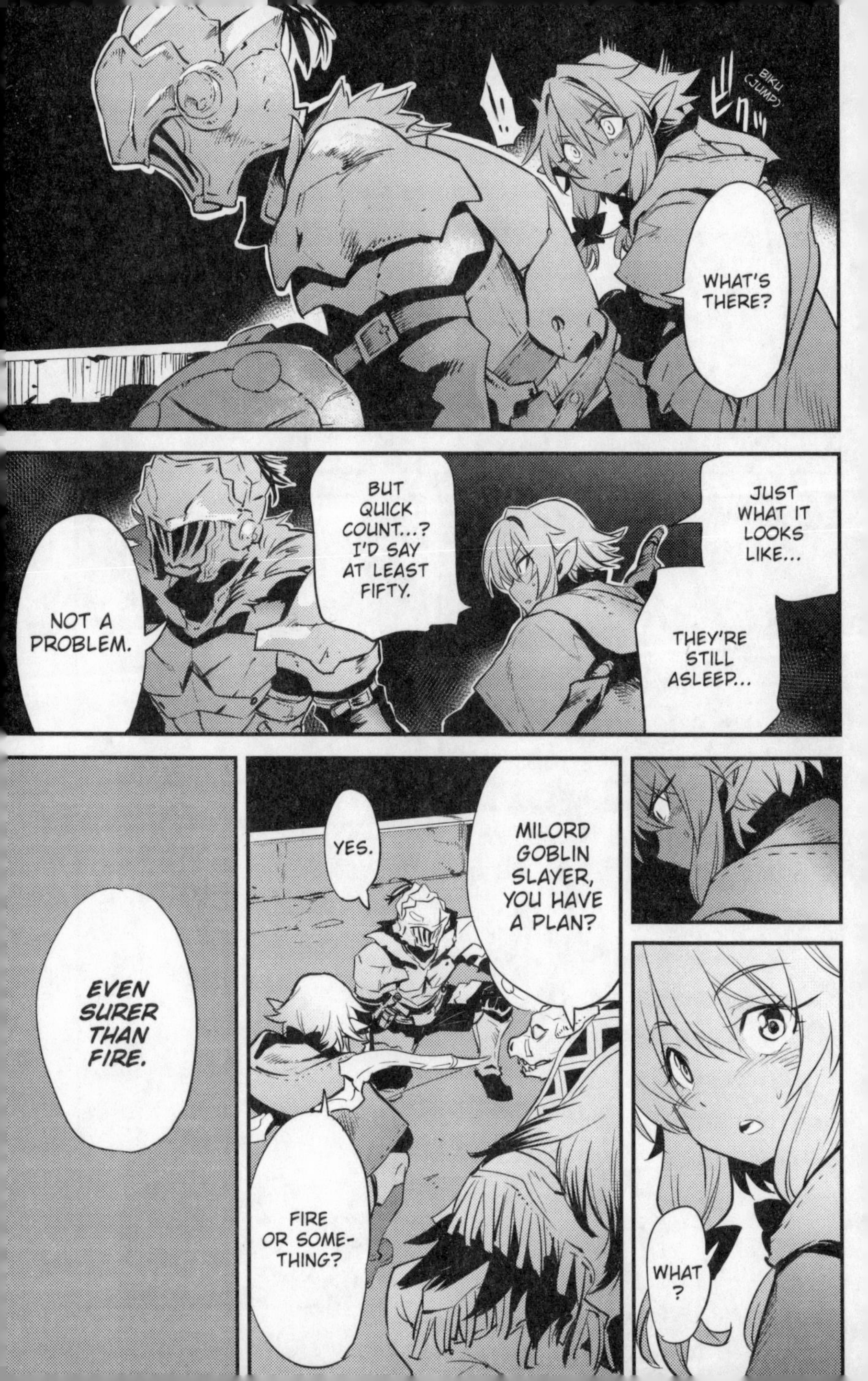
BIKU (JUMP)
WHAT'S THERE?
JUST WHAT IT LOOKS LIKE...
THEY'RE STILL ASLEEP...
BUT QUICK COUNT...? I'D SAY AT LEAST FIFTY.
NOT A PROBLEM.
WHAT?
MILORD GOBLIN SLAYER, YOU HAVE A PLAN?
YES.
FIRE OR SOME-THING?
EVEN SURER THAN FIRE.

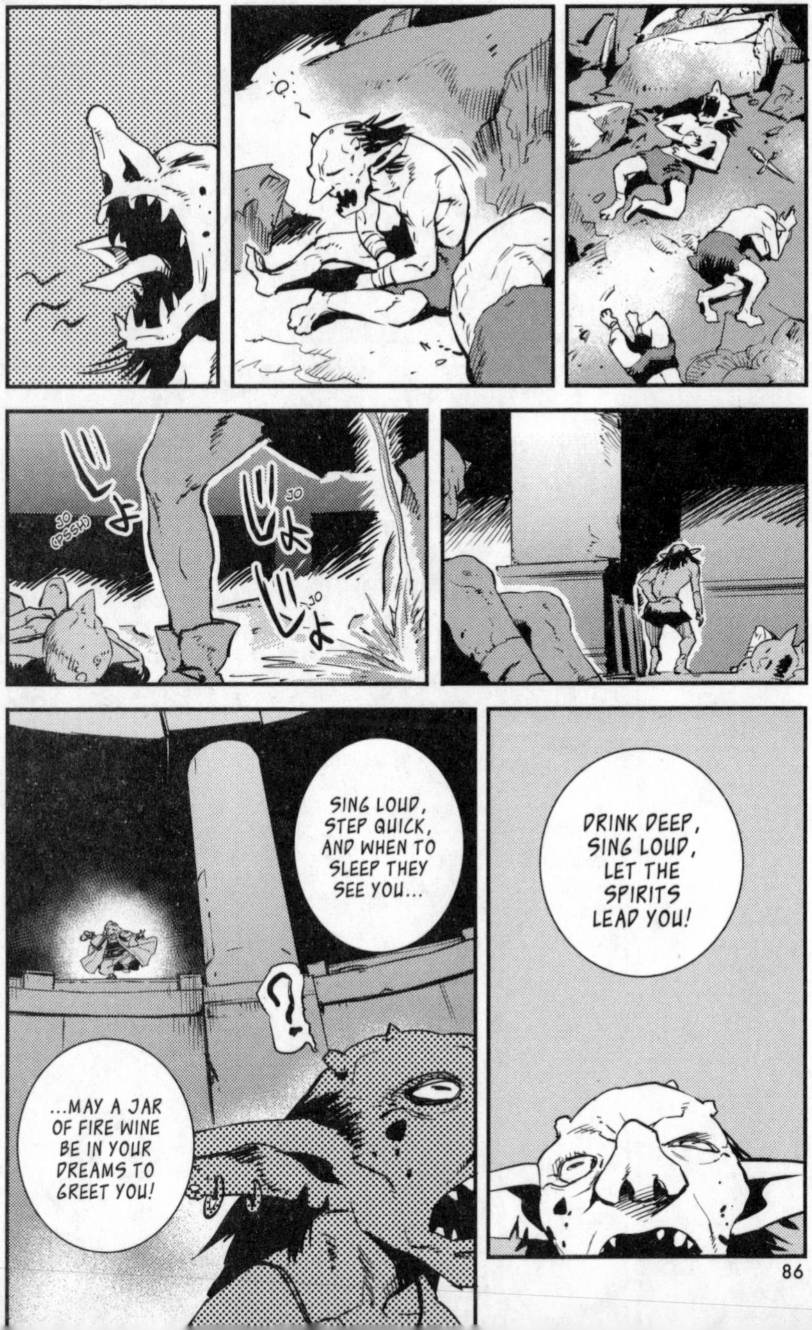
JO JO JO
(PSSH)
DRINK DEEP, SING LOUD, LET THE SPIRITS LEAD YOU!
SING LOUD, STEP QUICK, AND WHEN TO SLEEP THEY SEE YOU...
?
...MAY A JAR OF FIRE WINE BE IN YOUR DREAMS TO GREET YOU!

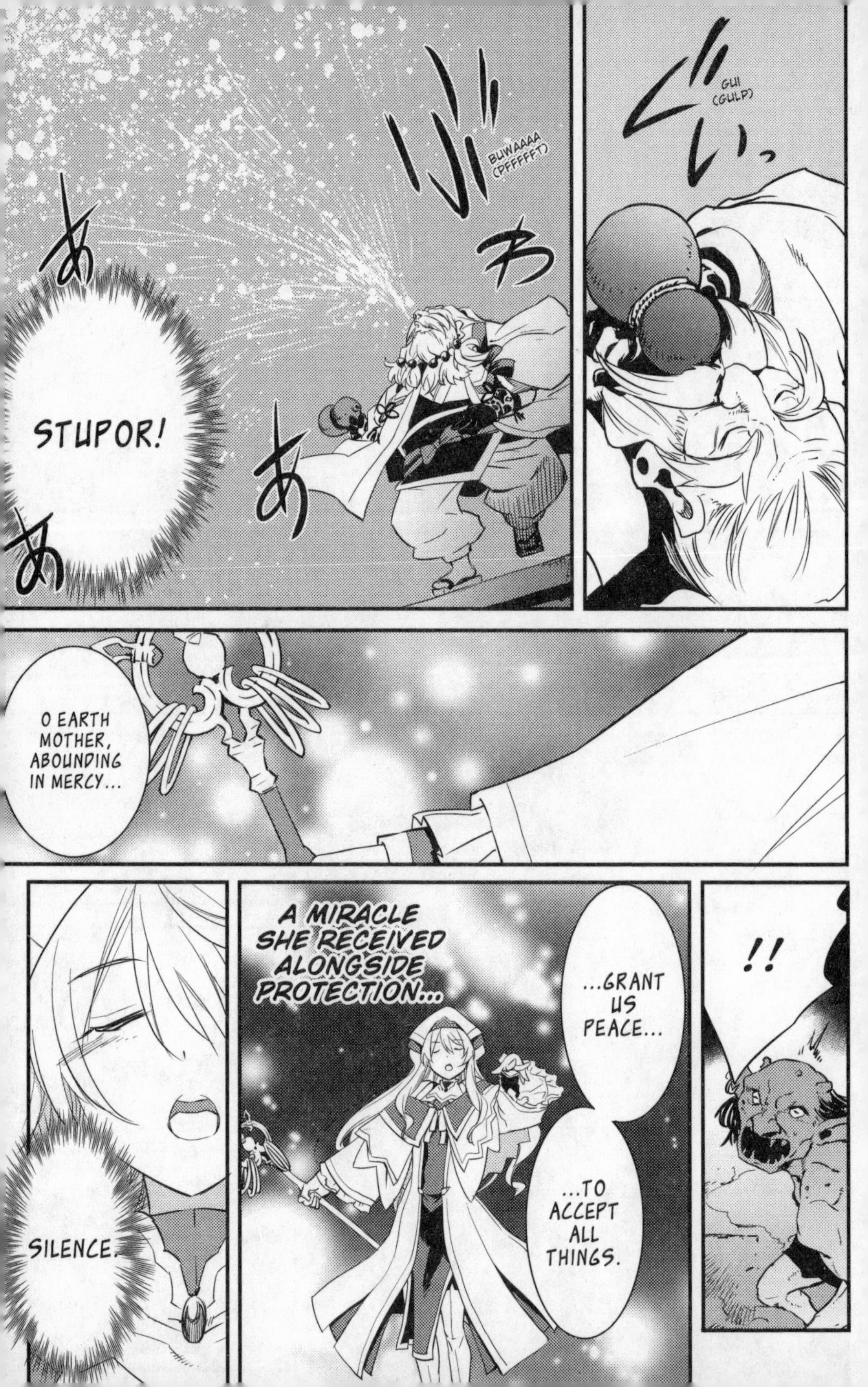
ぐいっ
GUI (GULP)
ぶわ
BUWAAAA (PFFFFFT)
あ
あ
あ
STUPOR!
O EARTH MOTHER, ABOUNDING IN MERCY...
!!
...GRANT US PEACE...
...TO ACCEPT ALL THINGS.
A MIRACLE SHE RECEIVED ALONGSIDE PROTECTION...
SILENCE.

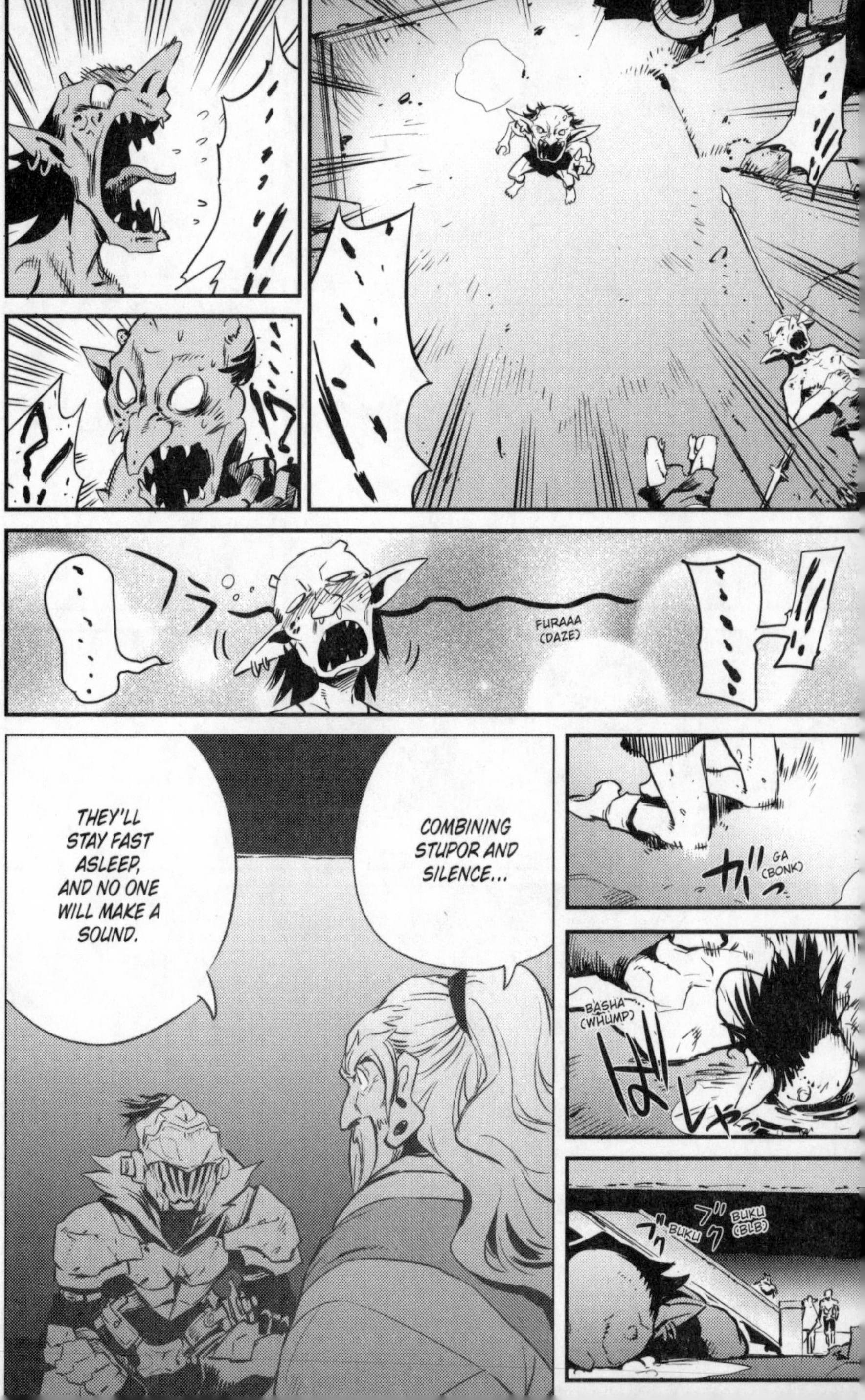
FURAAA (DAZE)
GA (BONK)
BASHA... (WHUMP)
BUKU BUKU (BLB)
COMBINING STUPOR AND SILENCE...
THEY'LL STAY FAST ASLEEP, AND NO ONE WILL MAKE A SOUND.

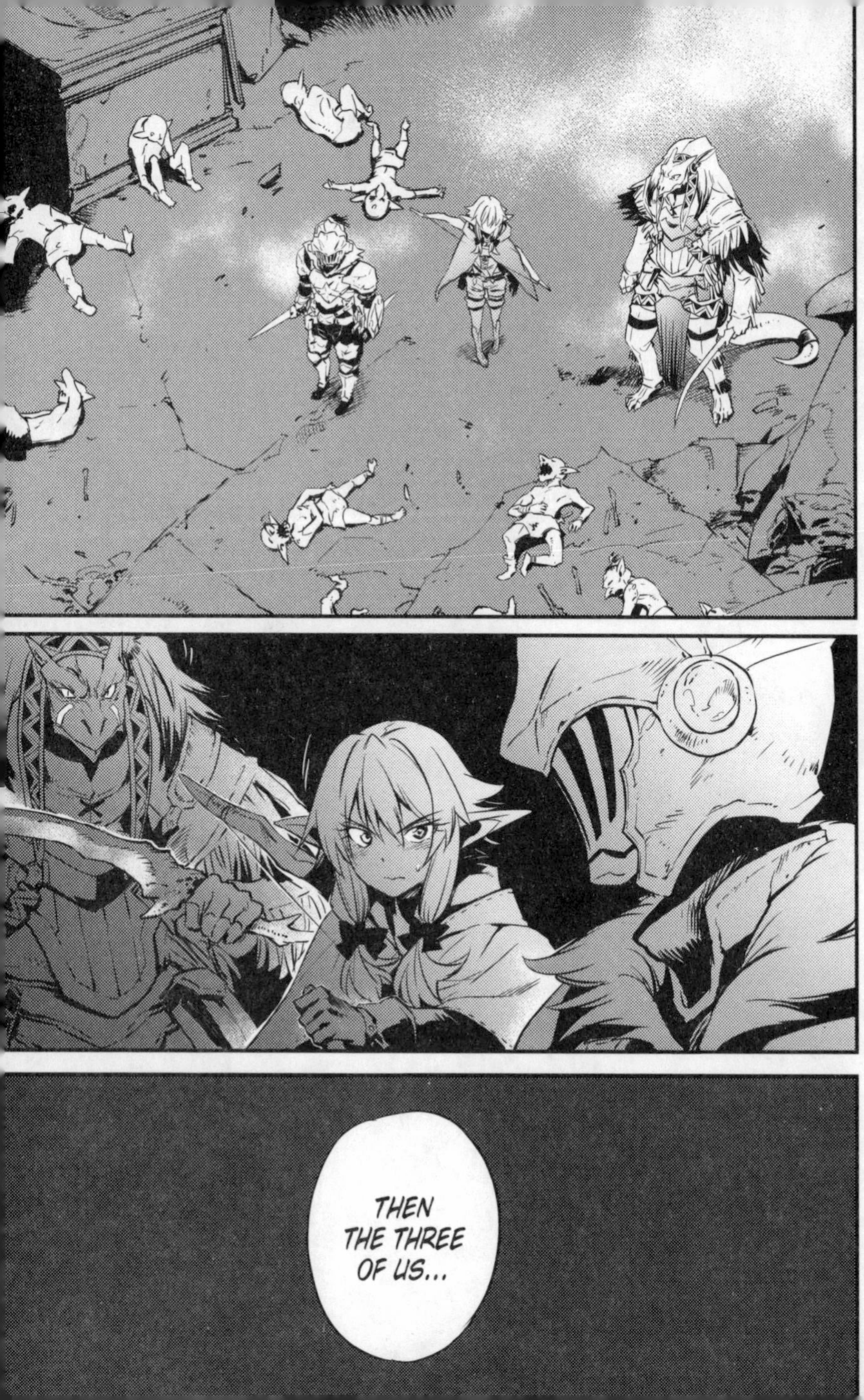
THEN THE THREE OF US...

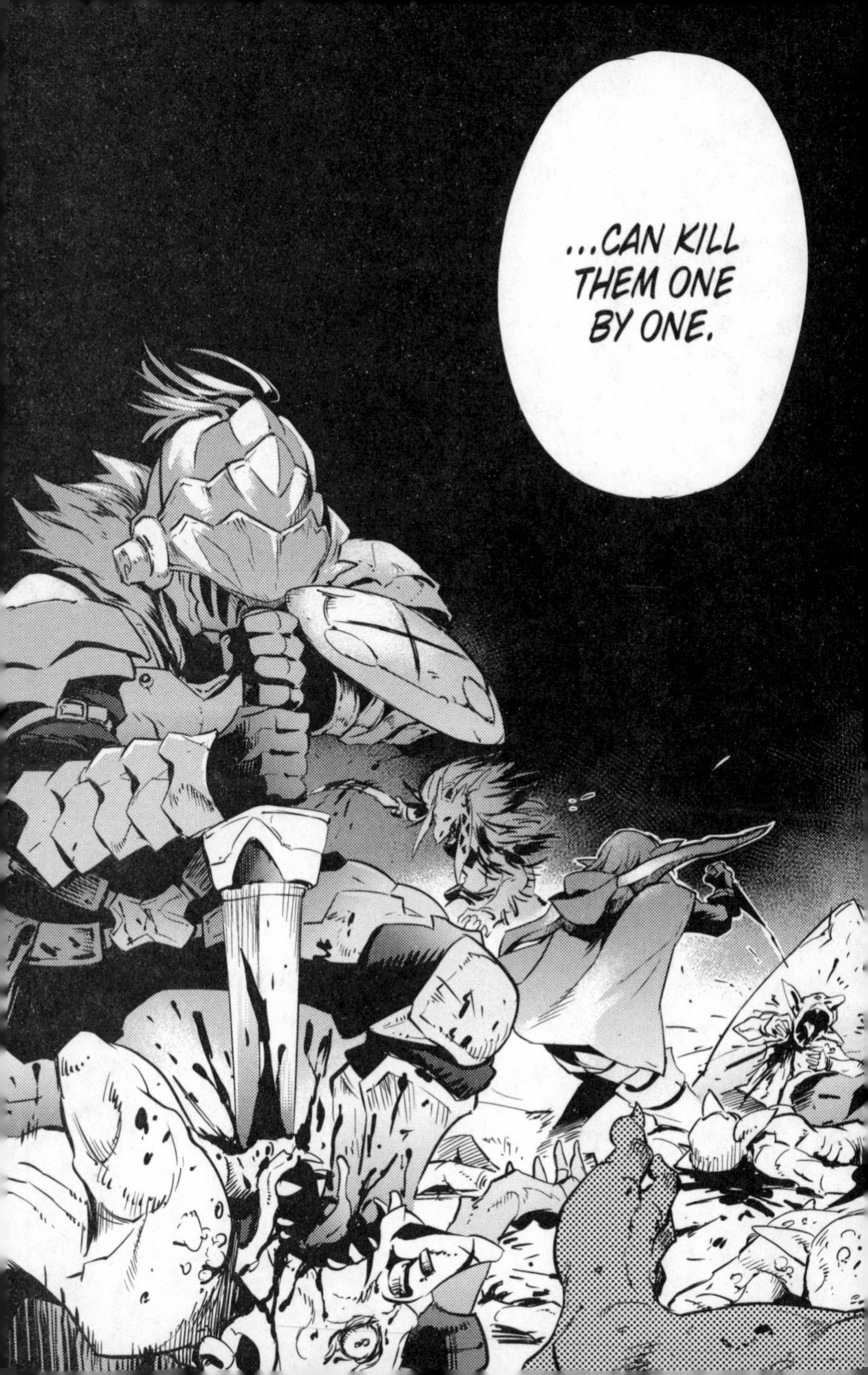
...CAN KILL THEM ONE BY ONE.

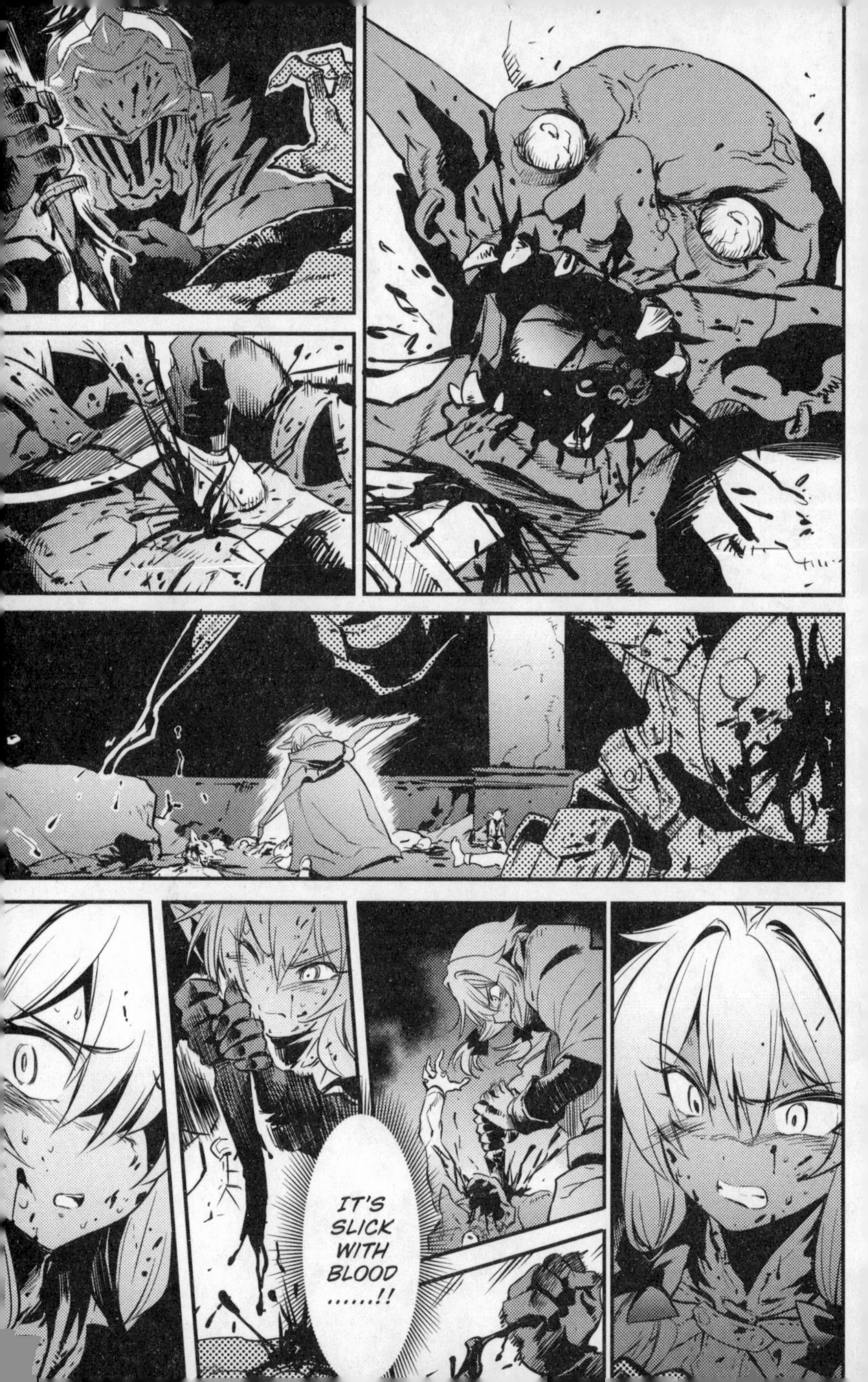
IT'S SLICK WITH BLOOD ......!!

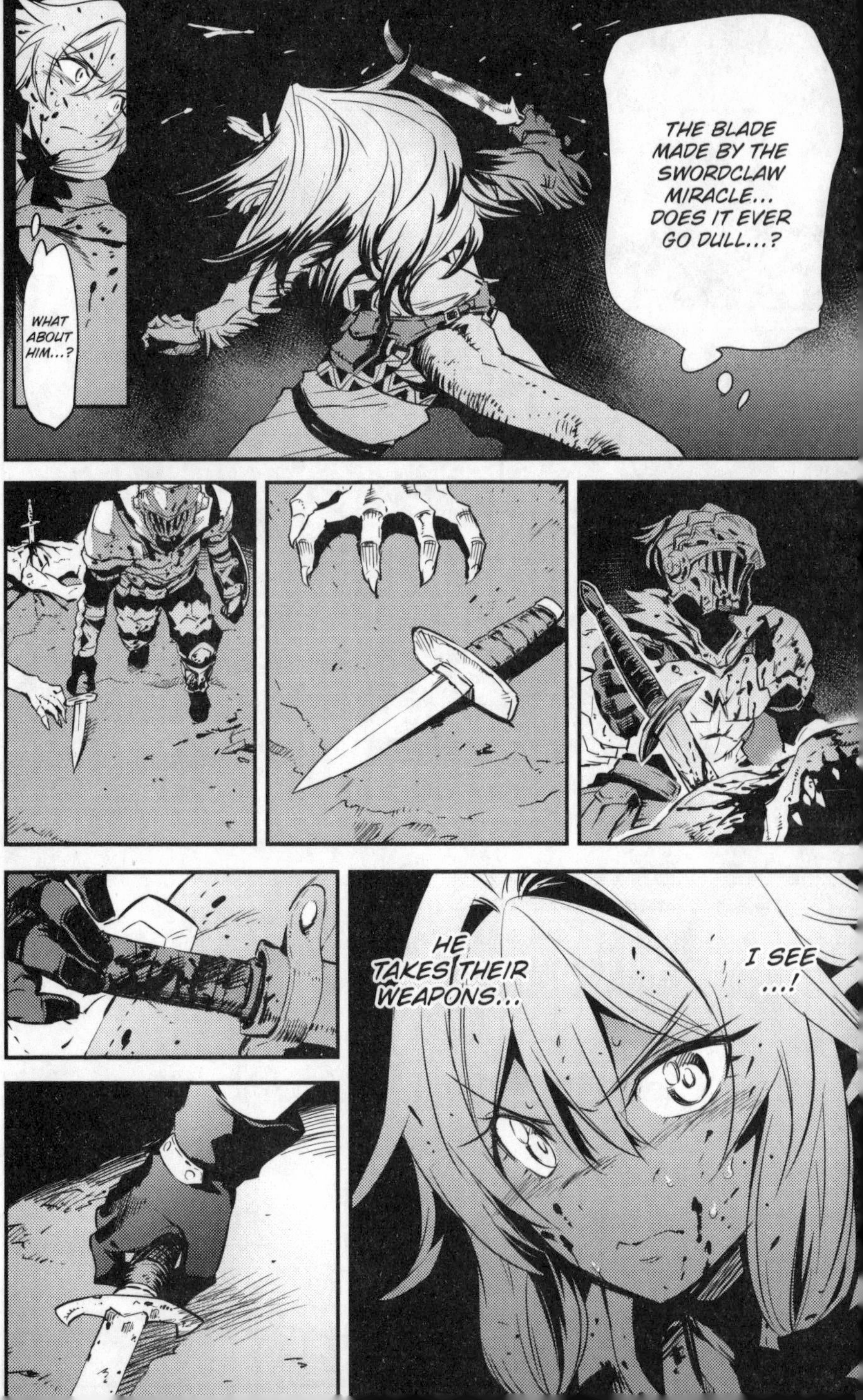
THE BLADE MADE BY THE SWORDCLAW MIRACLE... DOES IT EVER GO DULL...?
WHAT ABOUT HIM...?
I SEE ...!
HE TAKES THEIR WEAPONS...

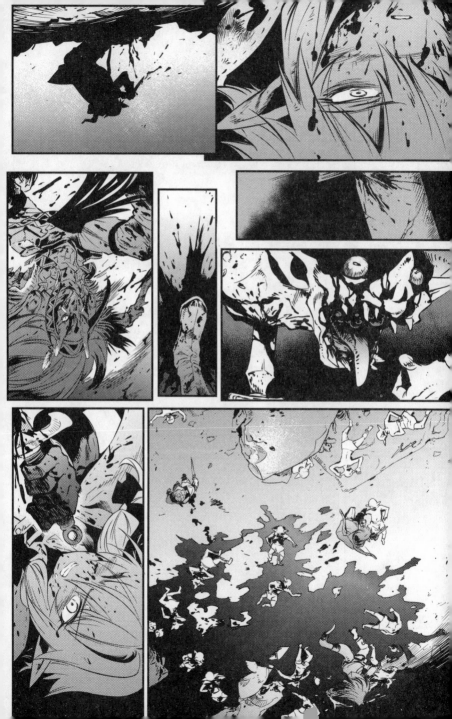

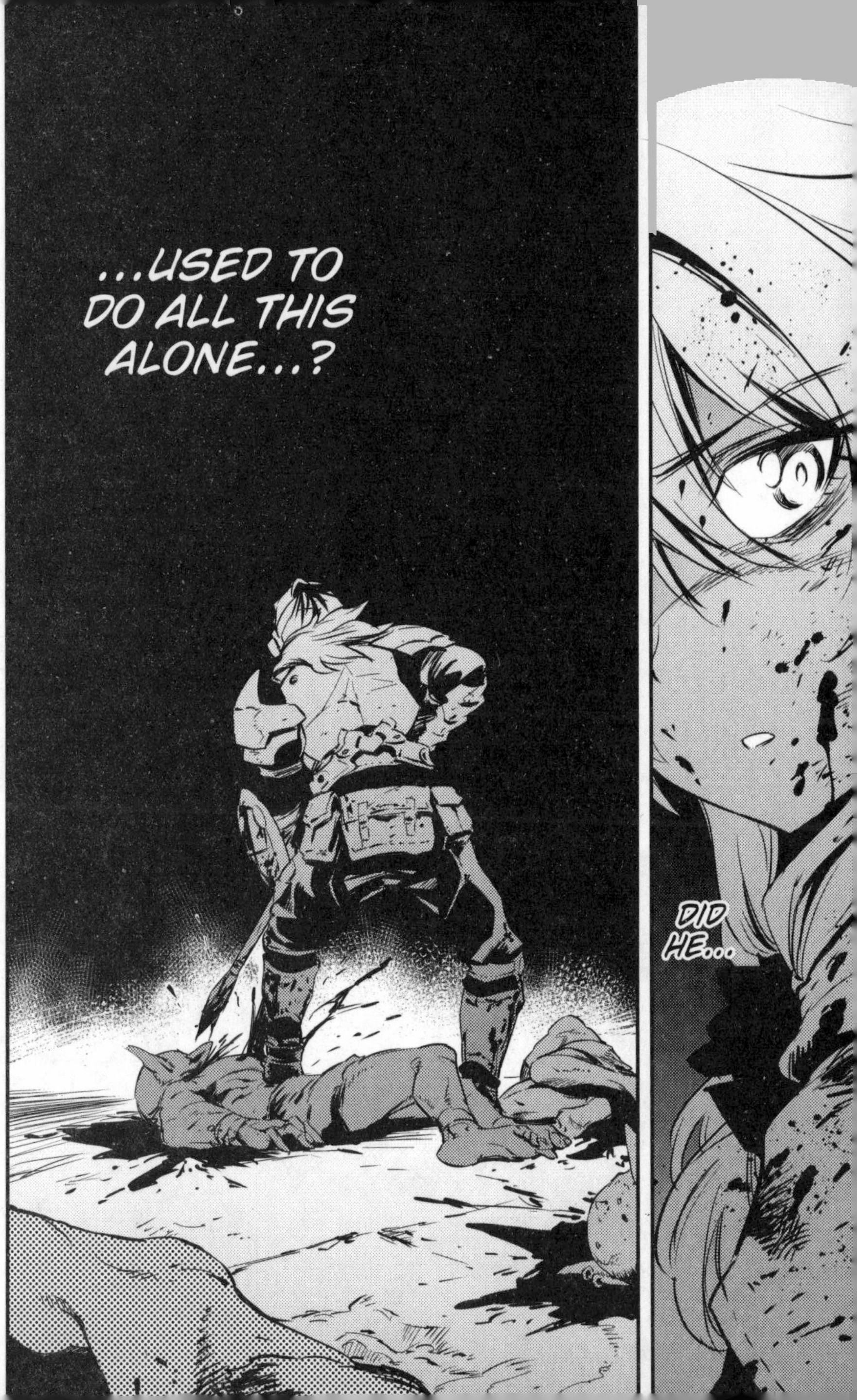
DID HE...
...USED TO DO ALL THIS ALONE...?

ZUGH
(SPLORT)

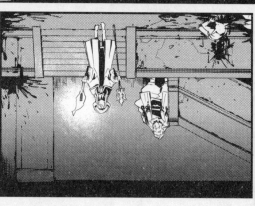

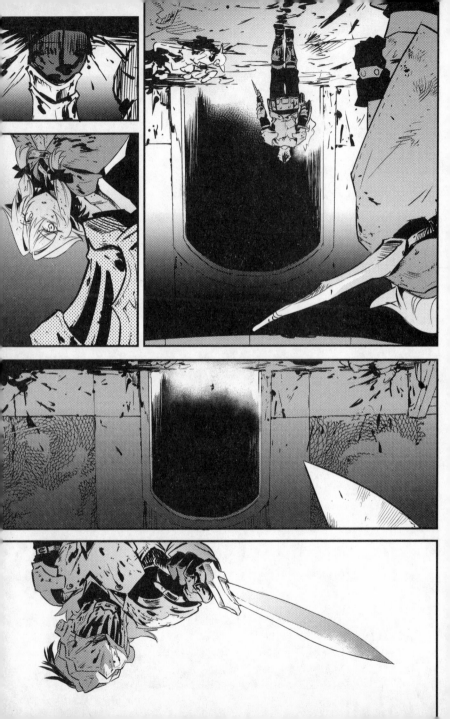

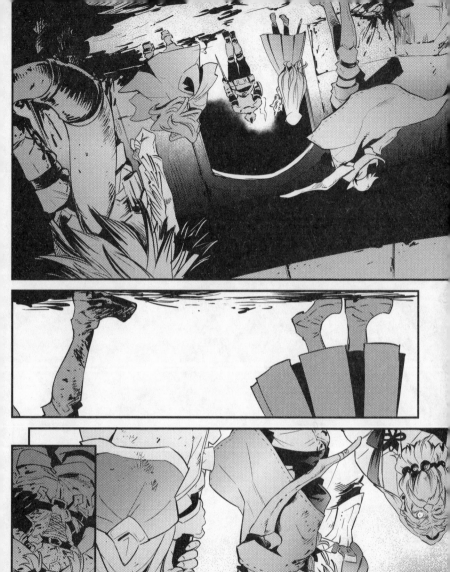

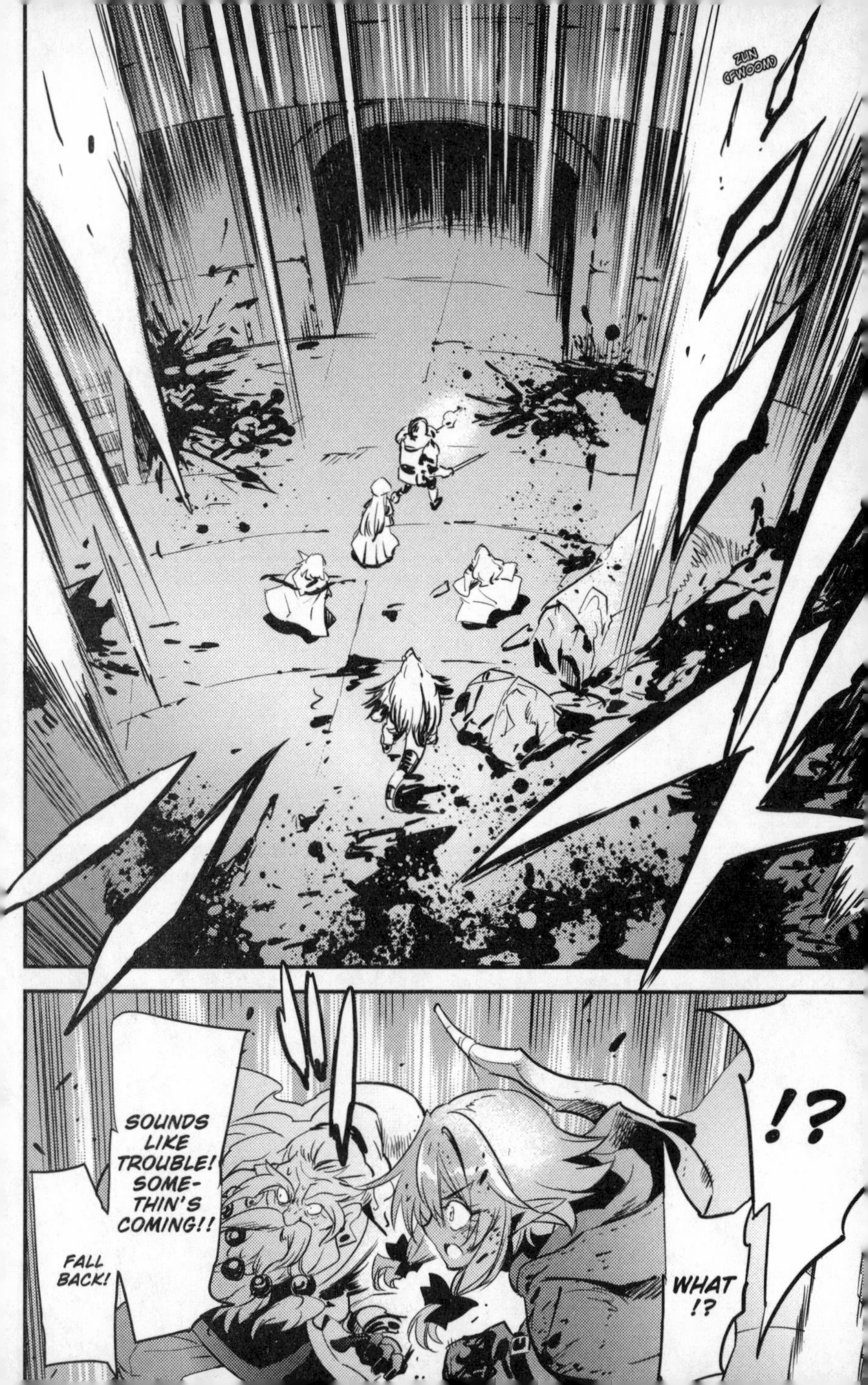
ZUN
(FWOOM)
!?
SOUNDS LIKE TROUBLE! SOME-THIN'S COMING!!
FALL BACK!
WHAT !?

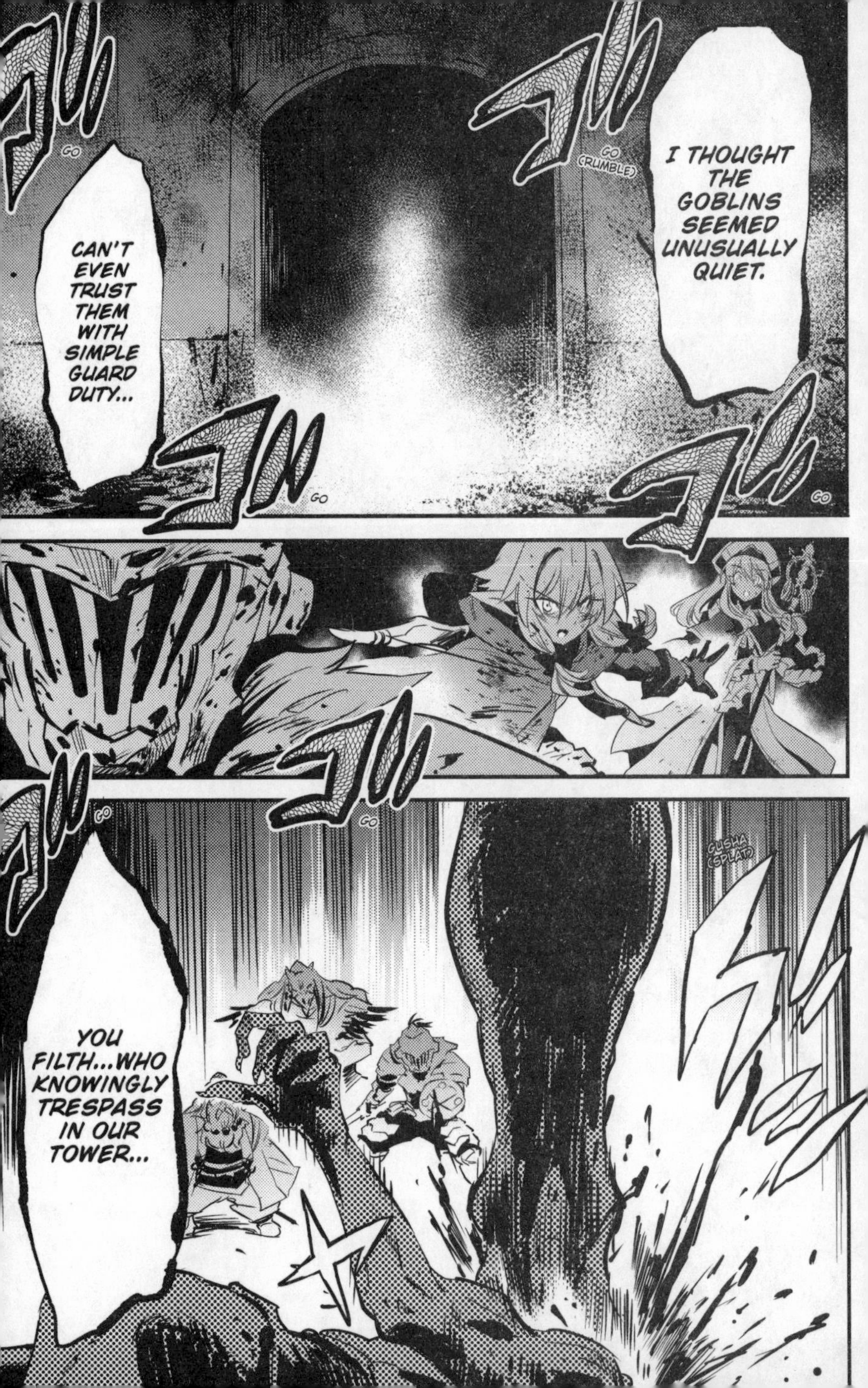
I THOUGHT THE GOBLINS SEEMED UNUSUALLY QUIET.
GO (RUMBLE)
GO
CAN'T EVEN TRUST THEM WITH SIMPLE GUARD DUTY...
GO
GO
GO
GO
GUSHA (SPLAT)
YOU FILTH...WHO KNOWINGLY TRESPASS IN OUR TOWER...

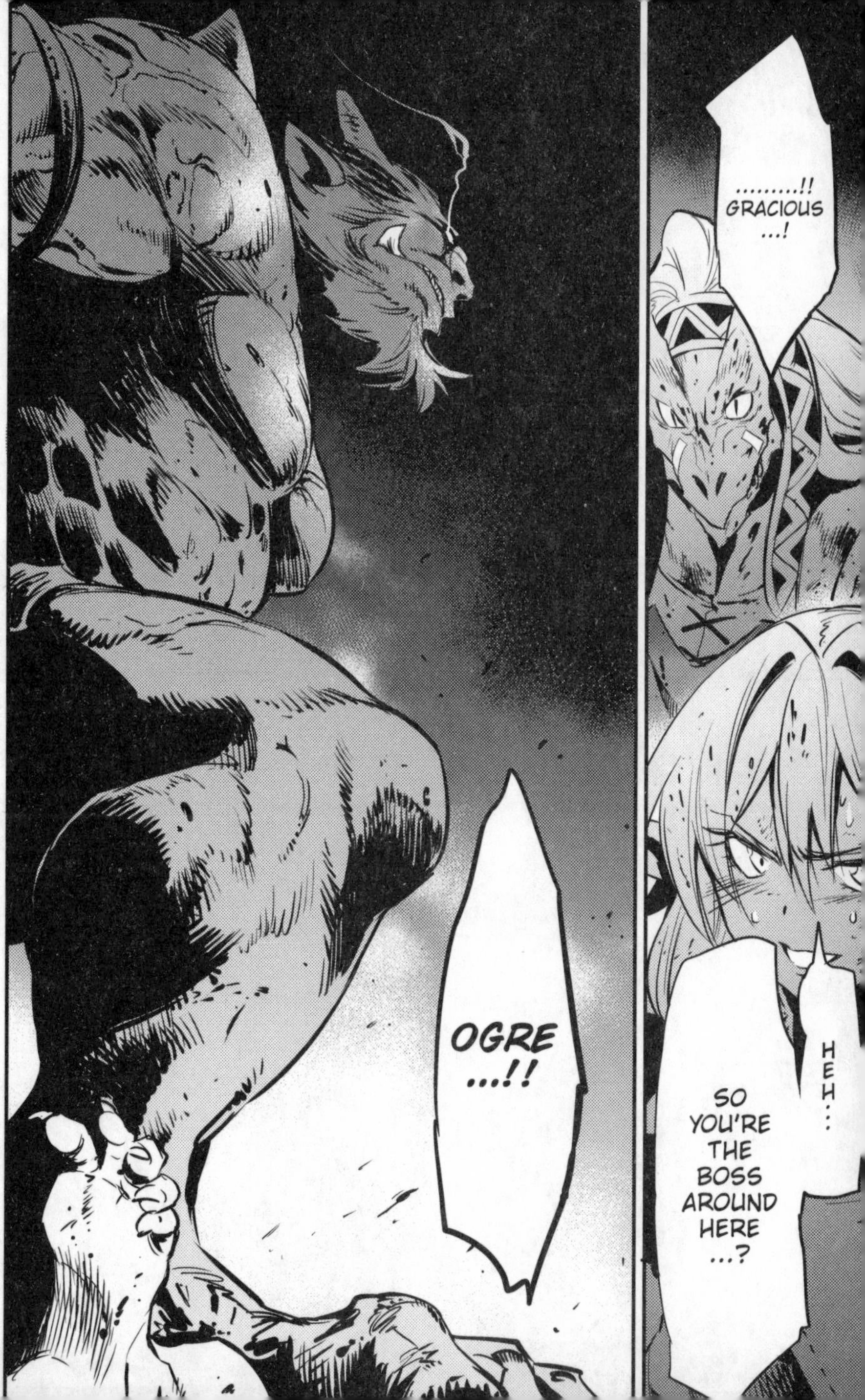
.........!! GRACIOUS ...!
HEH...
SO YOU'RE THE BOSS AROUND HERE ...?
OGRE ...!!

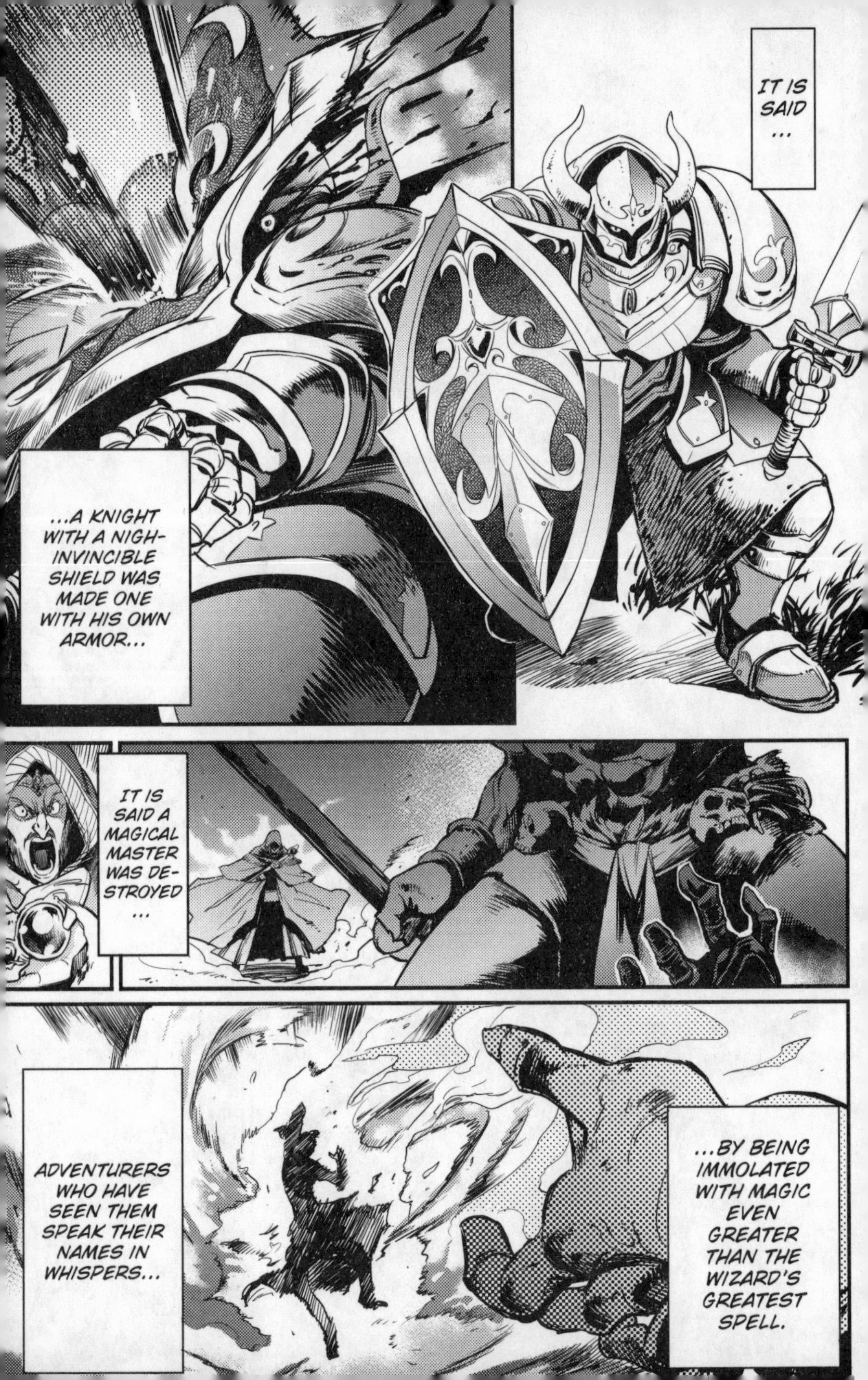
IT IS SAID ...
...A KNIGHT WITH A NIGH-INVINCIBLE SHIELD WAS MADE ONE WITH HIS OWN ARMOR...
IT IS SAID A MAGICAL MASTER WAS DE-STROYED ...
...BY BEING IMMOLATED WITH MAGIC EVEN GREATER THAN THE WIZARD'S GREATEST SPELL.
ADVENTURERS WHO HAVE SEEN THEM SPEAK THEIR NAMES IN WHISPERS...

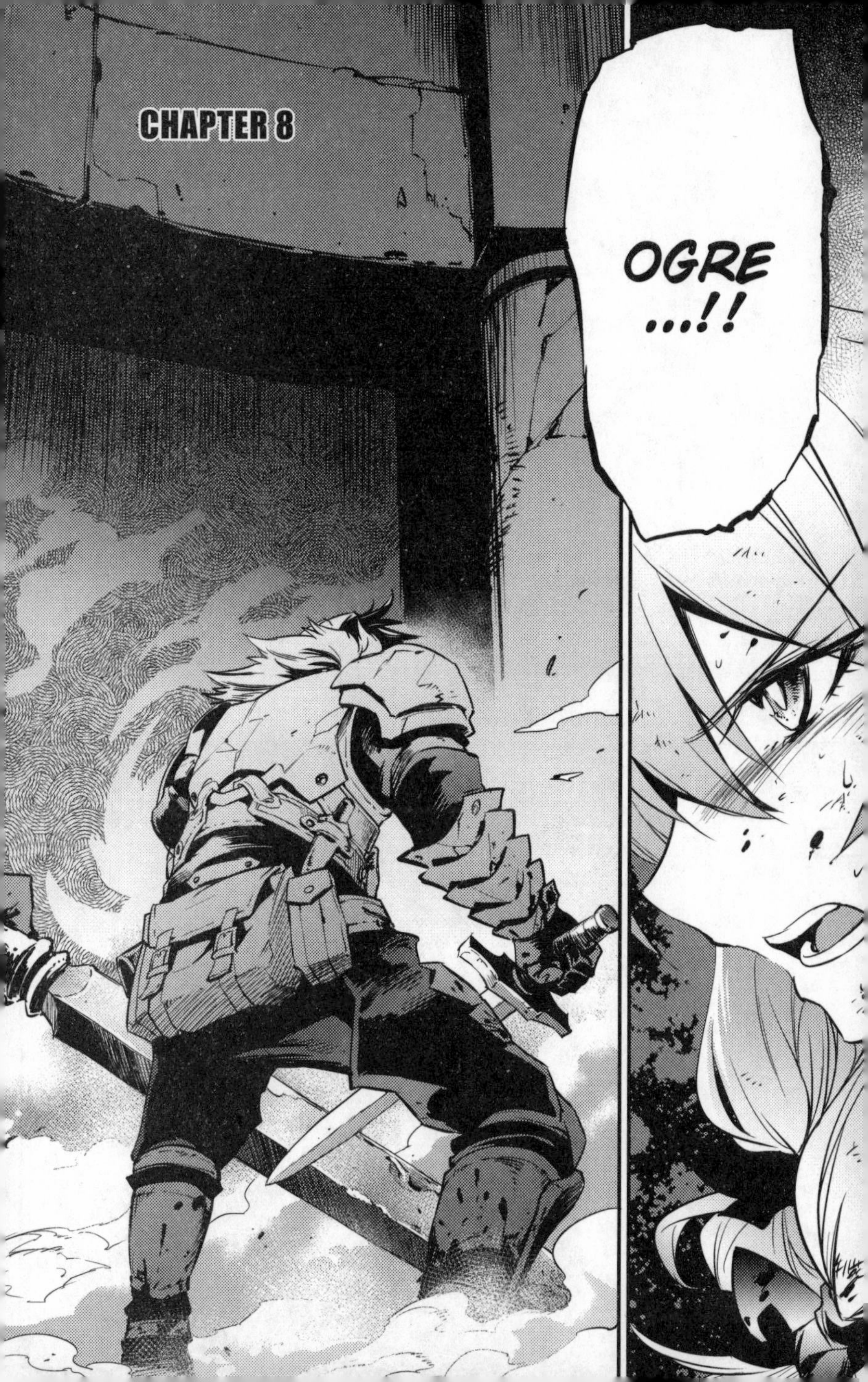
OGRE ...!!
CHAPTER 8

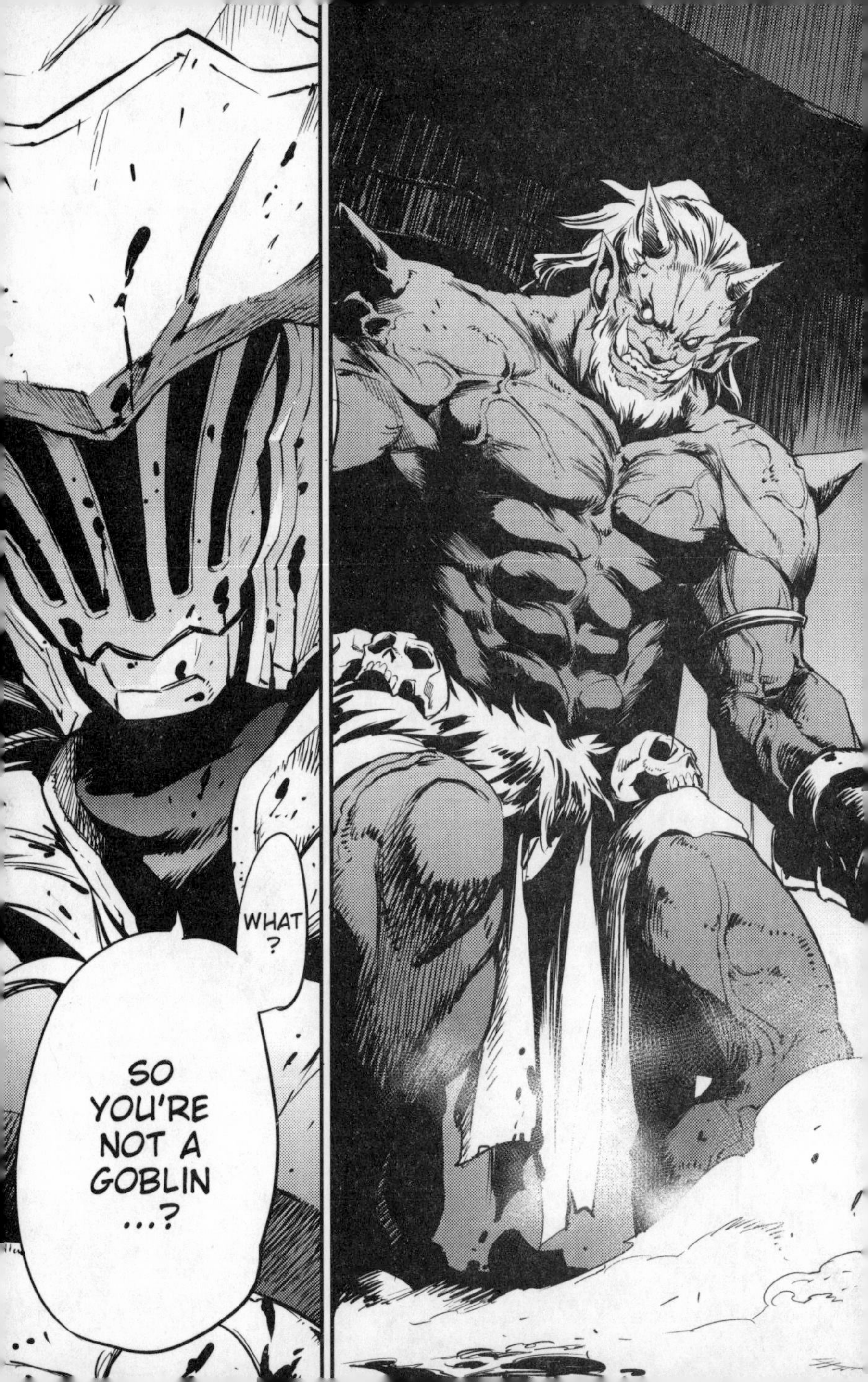
WHAT?
SO YOU'RE NOT A GOBLIN ...?

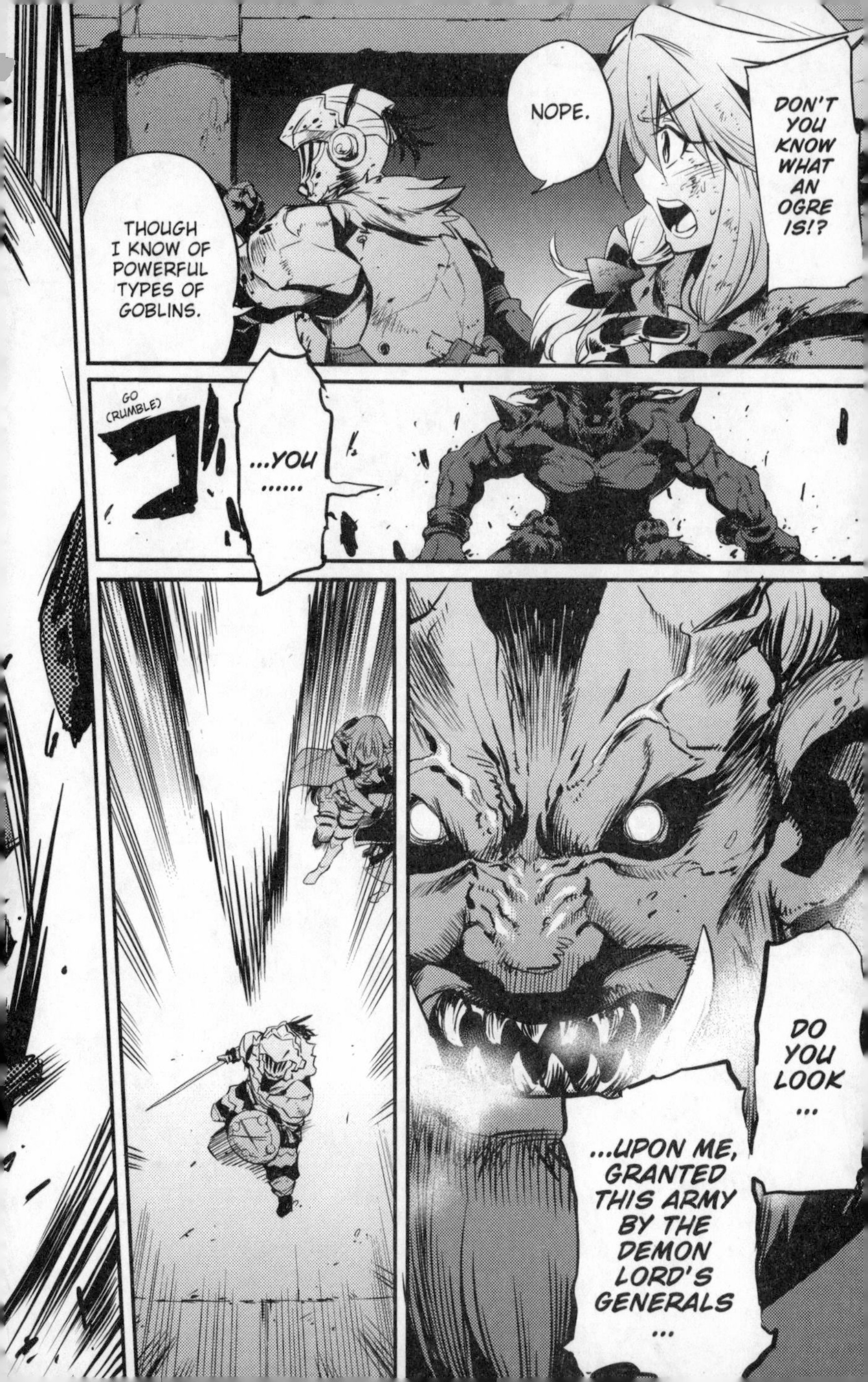
DON'T YOU KNOW WHAT AN OGRE IS!?
NOPE.
THOUGH I KNOW OF POWERFUL TYPES OF GOBLINS.
...YOU ......
GO (RUMBLE)
DO YOU LOOK ...
...UPON ME, GRANTED THIS ARMY BY THE DEMON LORD'S GENERALS ...

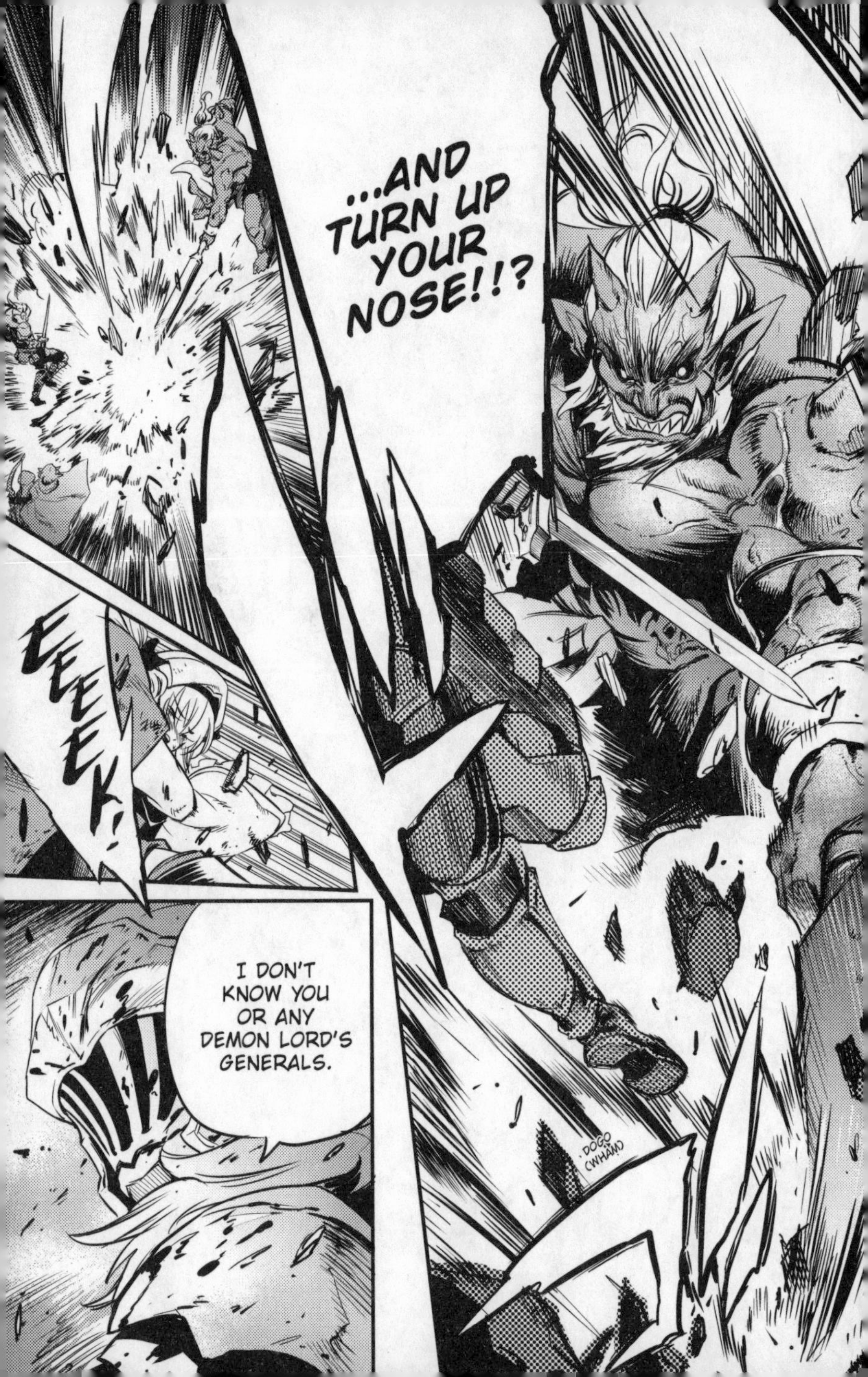
...AND TURN UP YOUR NOSE!!?
EEEEK!
I DON'T KNOW YOU OR ANY DEMON LORD'S GENERALS.
DOGO (WHAM)

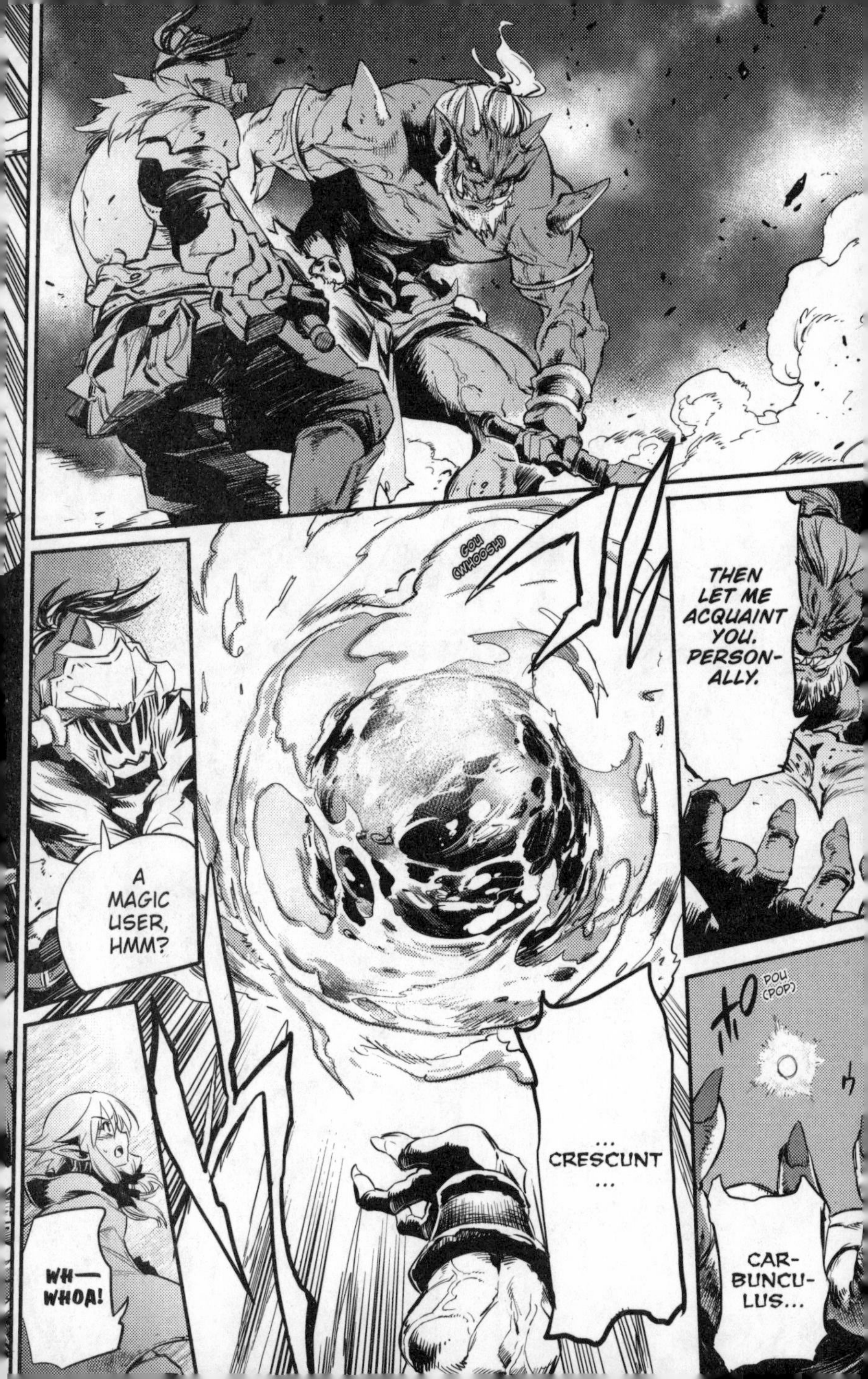
THEN LET ME ACQUAINT YOU. PERSON-ALLY.
GOU (WHOOSH)
A MAGIC USER, HMM?
POU (POP)
CAR-BUNCU-LUS...
... CRESCUNT ...
WH— WHOA!

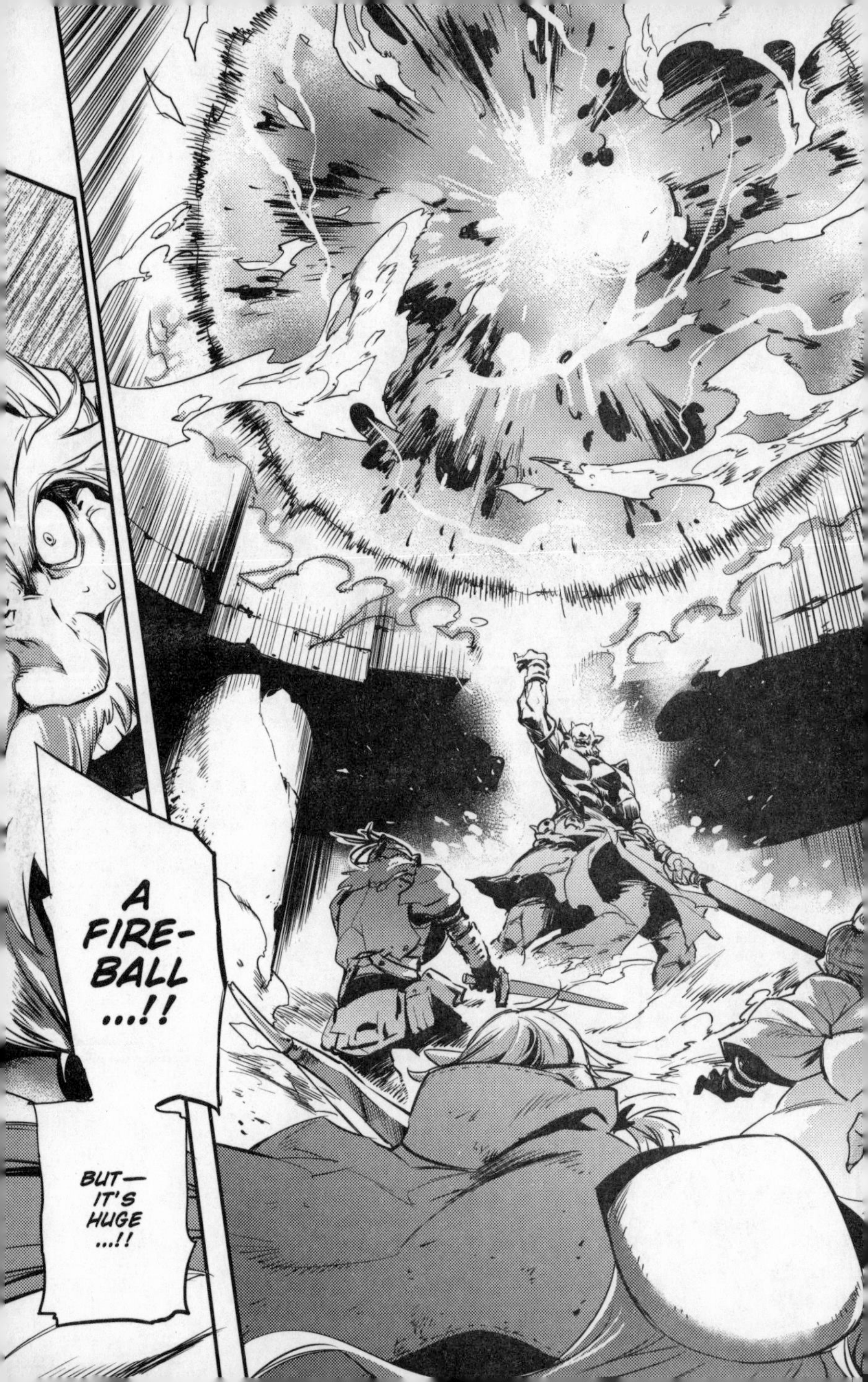
A FIRE-BALL ...!!
BUT— IT'S HUGE ...!!

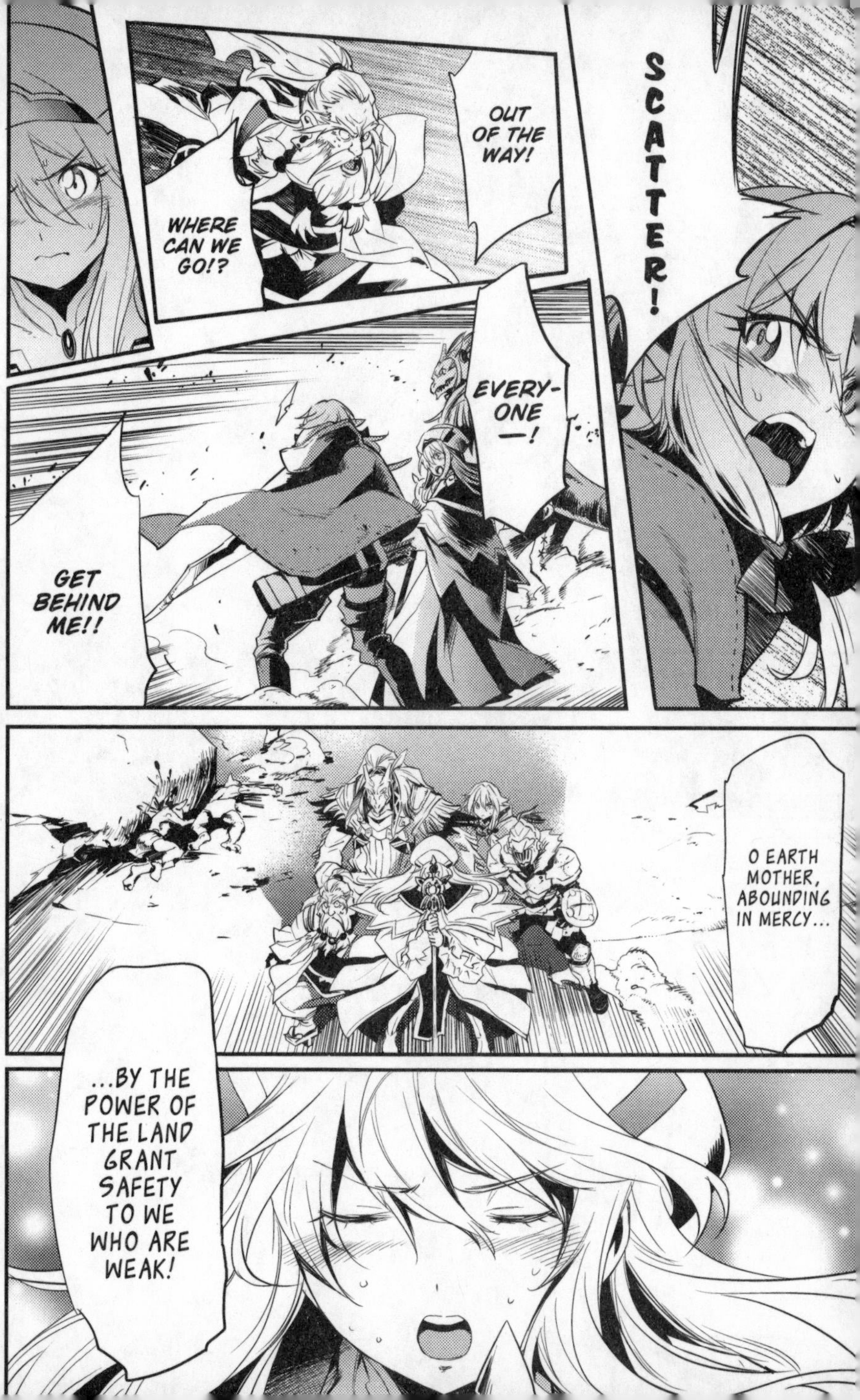
SCATTER!
OUT OF THE WAY!
WHERE CAN WE GO!?
EVERY-ONE —!
GET BEHIND ME!!
O EARTH MOTHER, ABOUNDING IN MERCY...
...BY THE POWER OF THE LAND GRANT SAFETY TO WE WHO ARE WEAK!

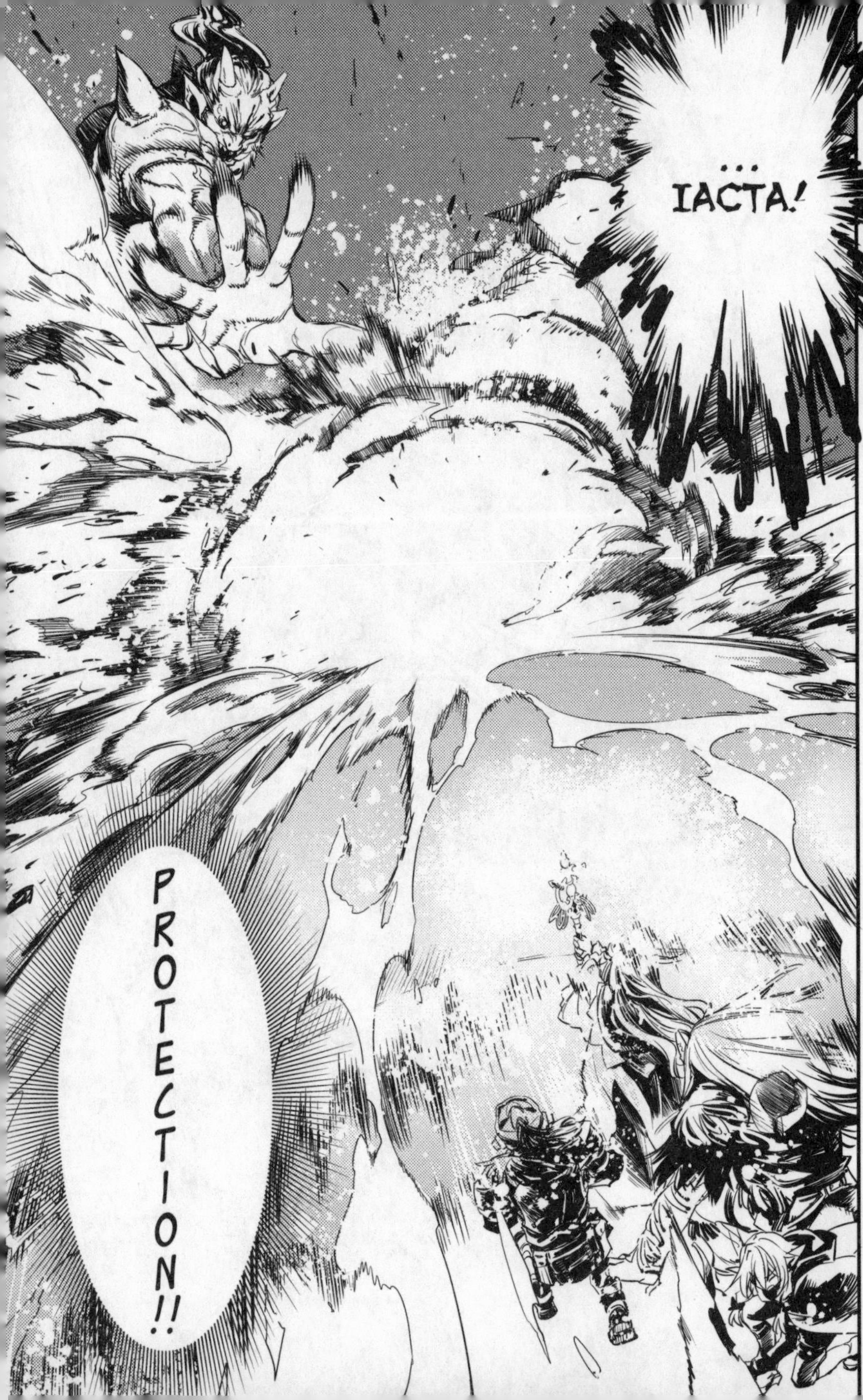
...IACTA!
PROTECTION!!

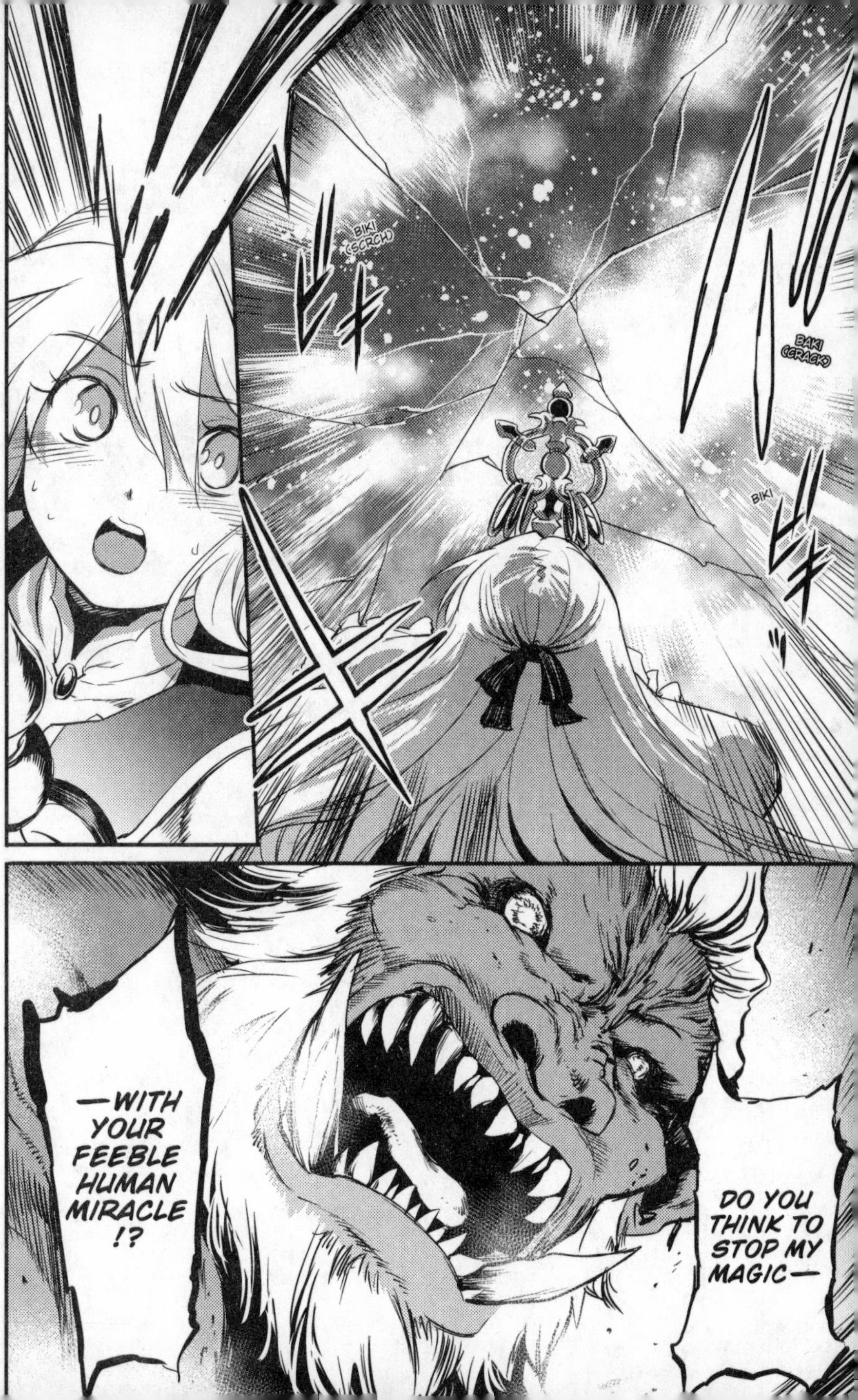
BAKI (CRACK)
BIKI
BIKI (SCRCH)
DO YOU THINK TO STOP MY MAGIC—
—WITH YOUR FEEBLE HUMAN MIRACLE !?

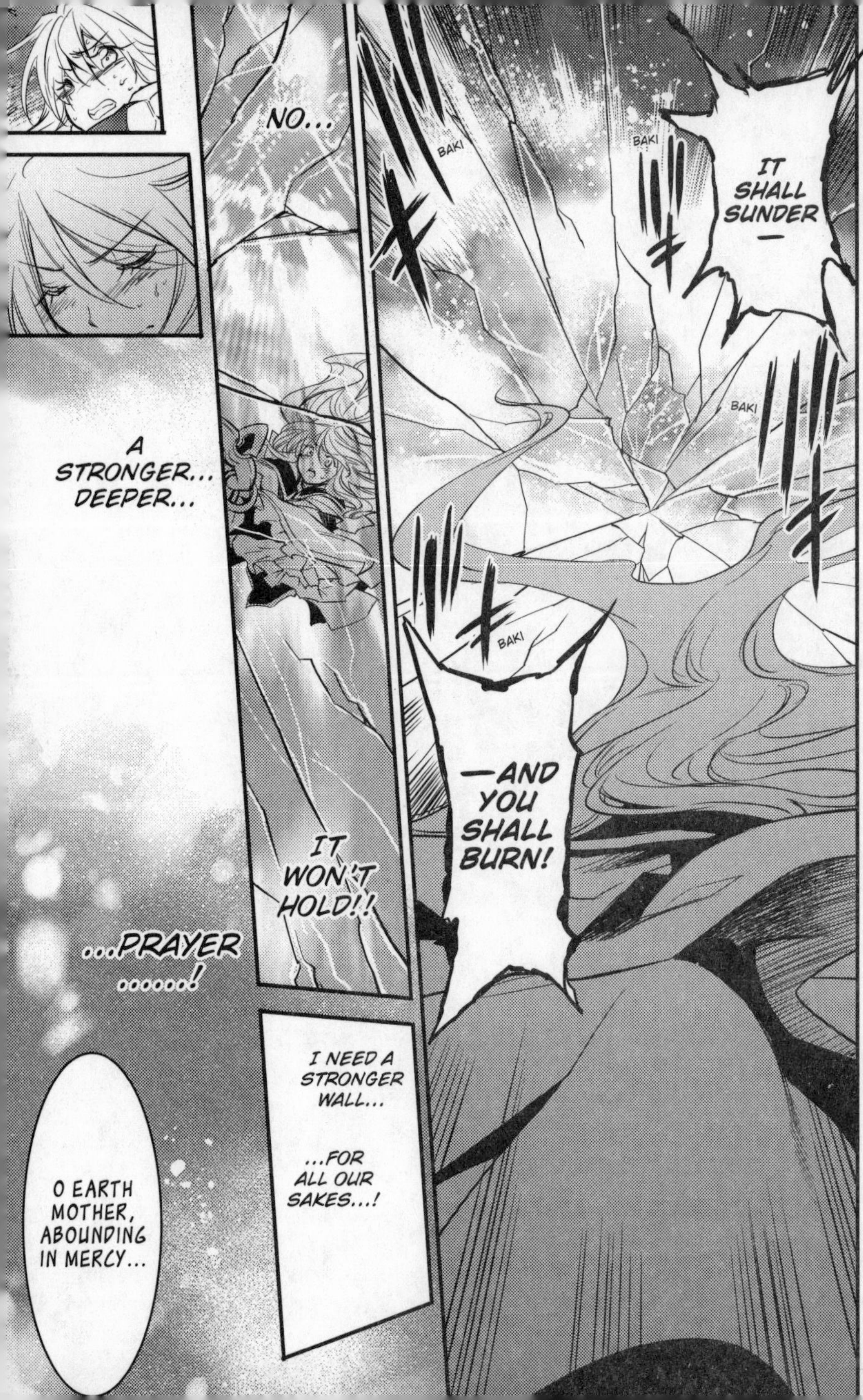
IT SHALL SUNDER —
BAKI
BAKI
BAKI
BAKI
—AND YOU SHALL BURN!
NO...
IT WON'T HOLD!!
I NEED A STRONGER WALL...
...FOR ALL OUR SAKES...!
A STRONGER... DEEPER...
...PRAYER ....!
O EARTH MOTHER, ABOUNDING IN MERCY...

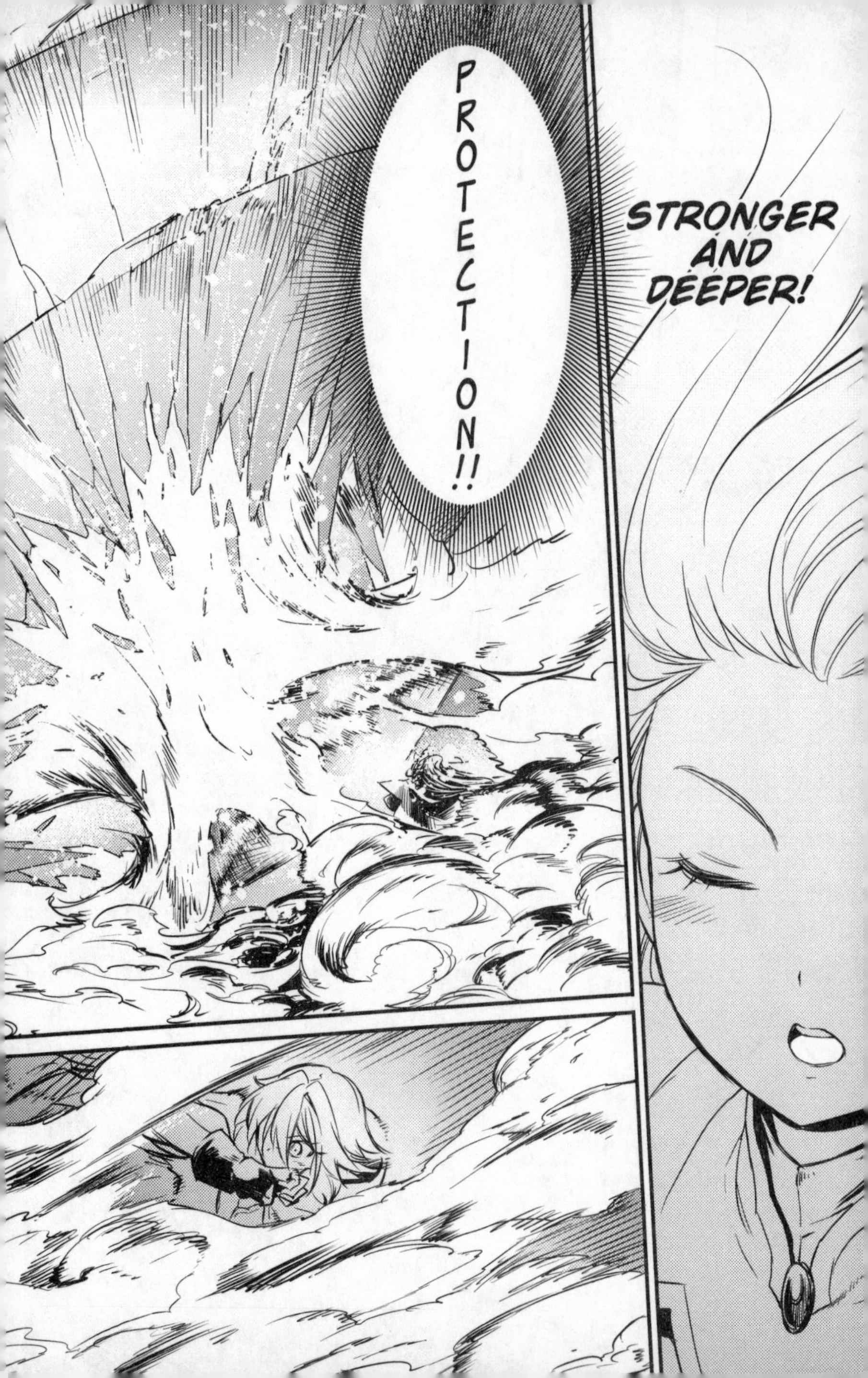
STRONGER AND DEEPER!
PROTECTION!!

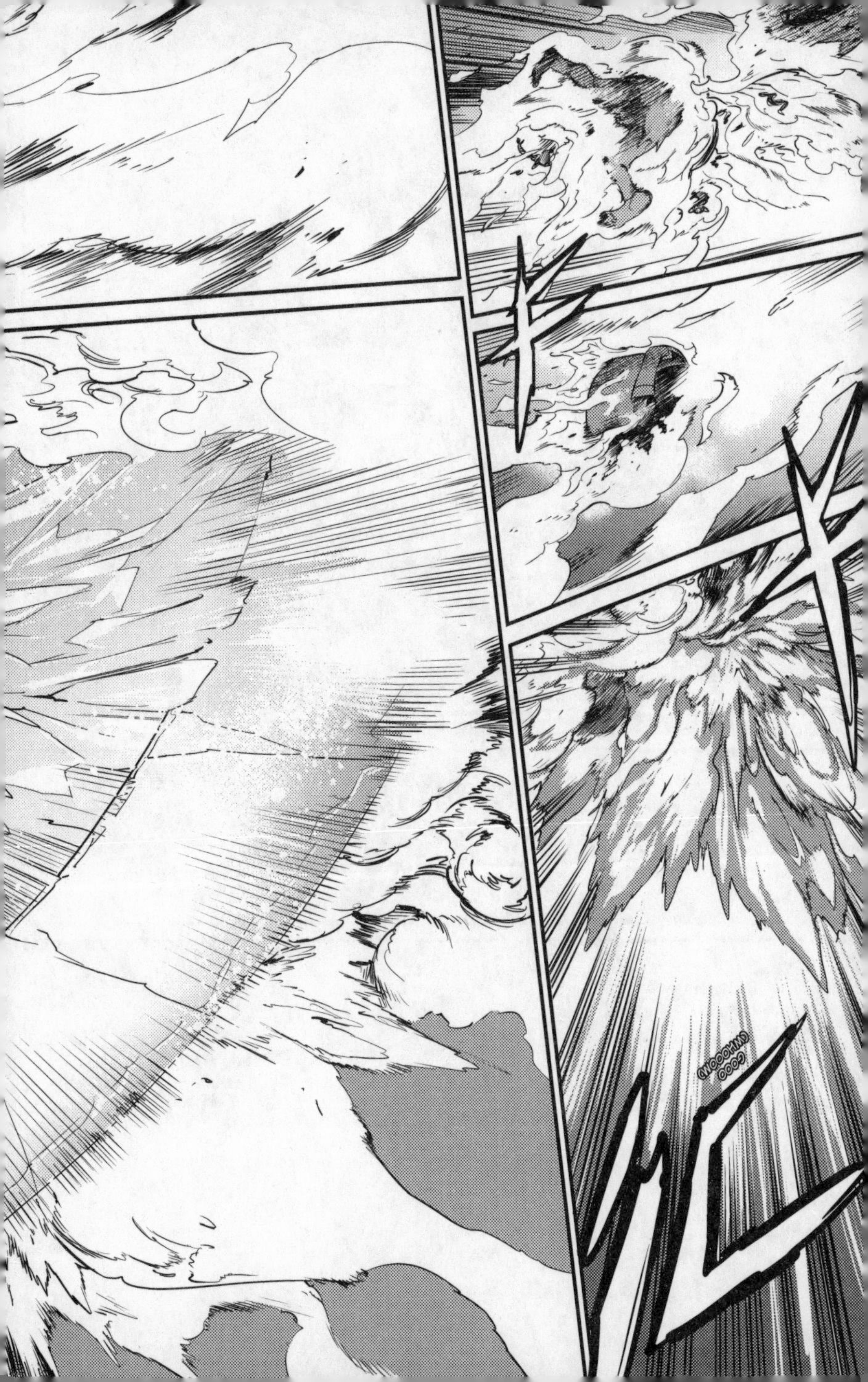
GOOO
(WHOOOM)

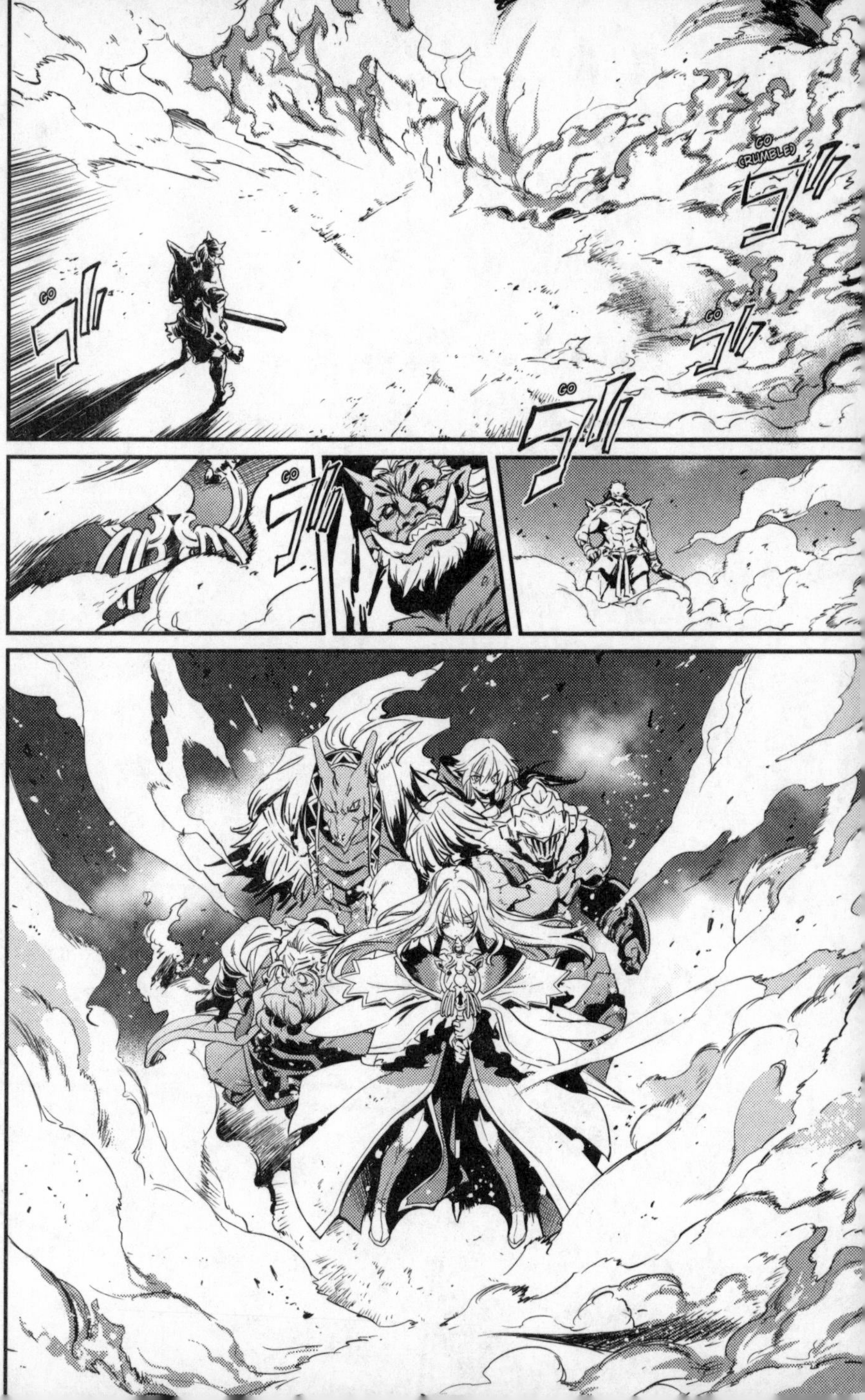
ゴゴ
GO (CRUMBLE)
ゴゴ
GO
ゴゴ
GO
ゴゴ
GO
ゴゴ
GO
ゴゴ
GO

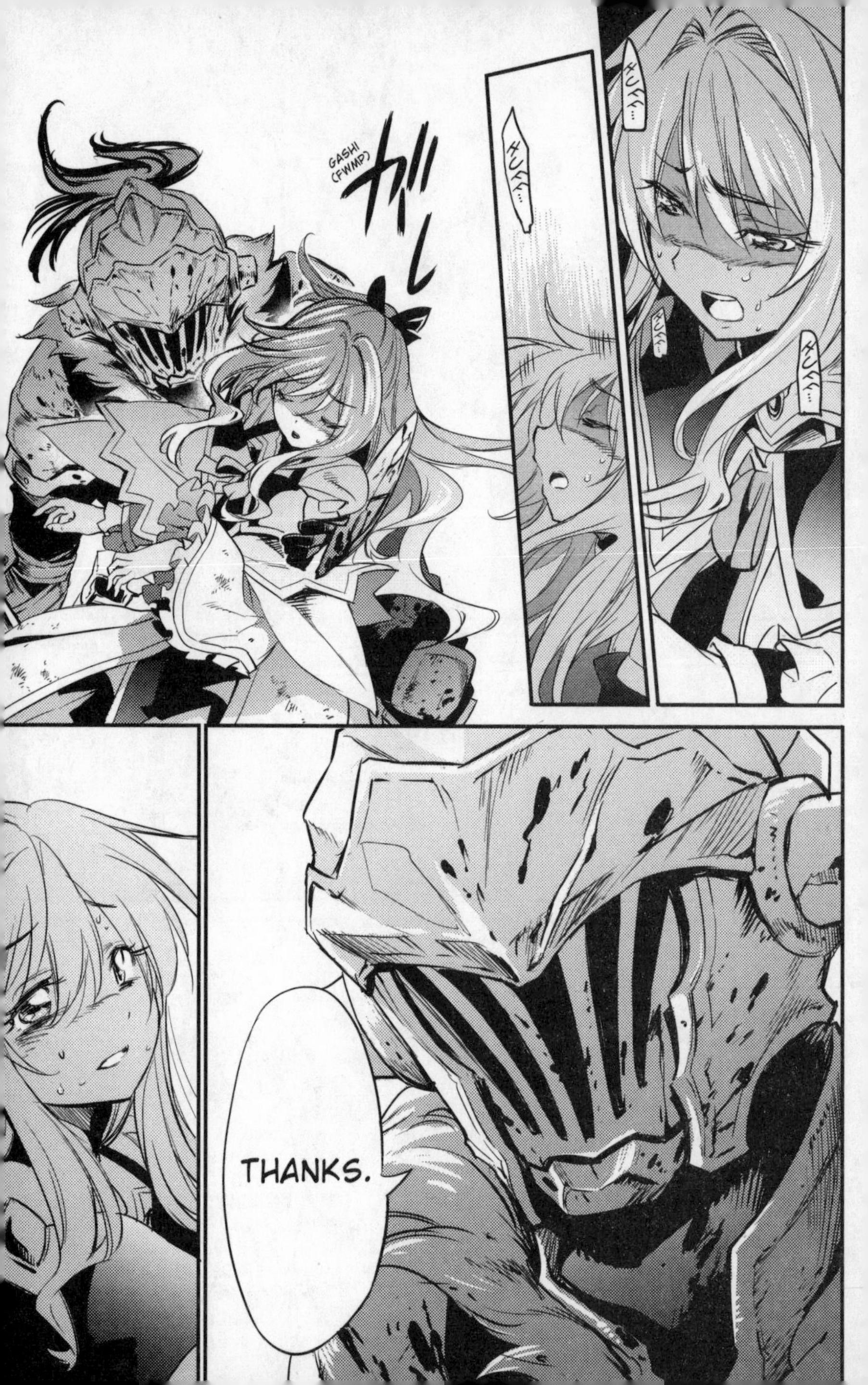
HUFF...
HUFF...
HUFF...
HUFF...
GASHI (FWMP)
THANKS.

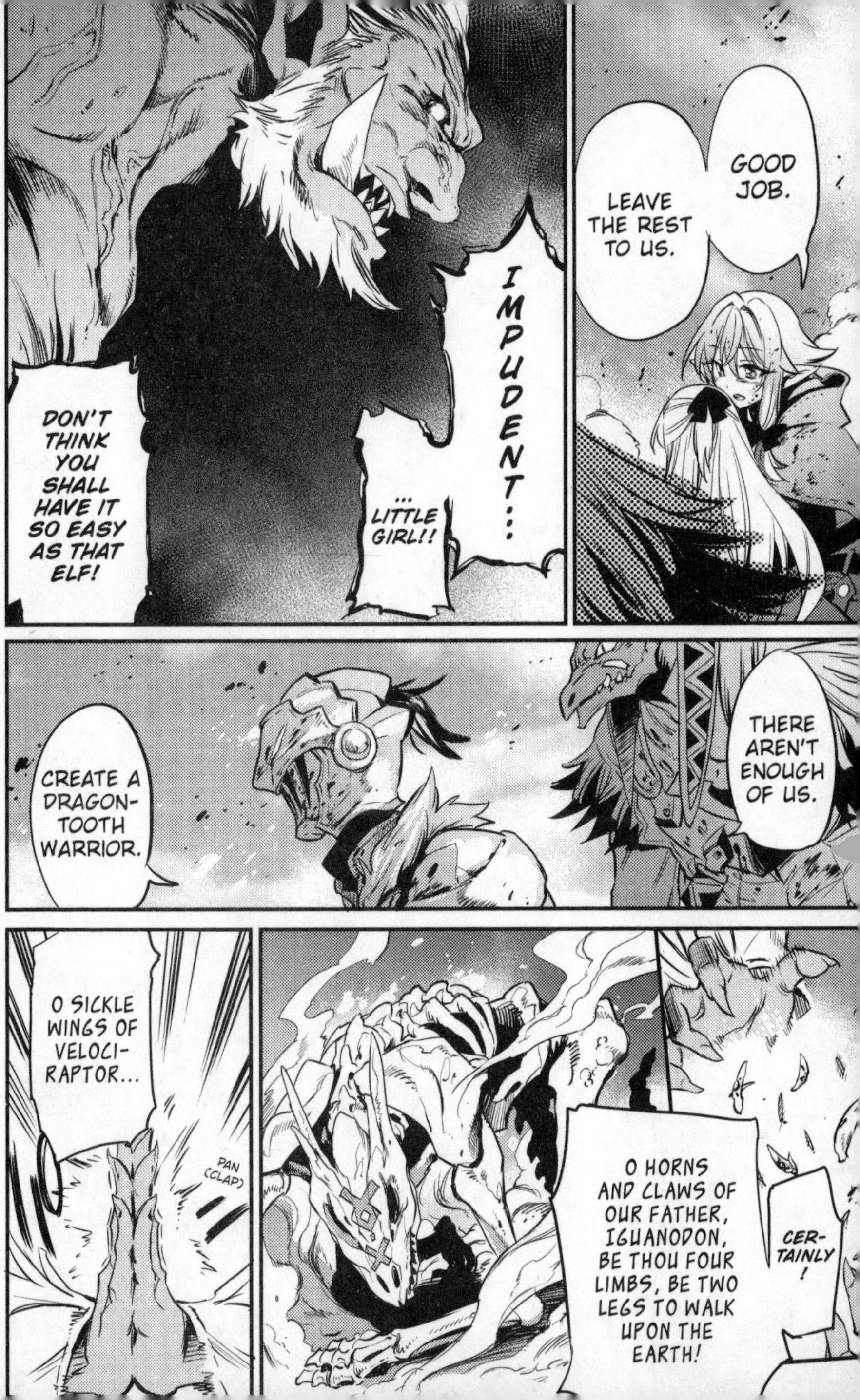
GOOD JOB.
LEAVE THE REST TO US.
IMPUDENT...
...LITTLE GIRL!!
DON'T THINK YOU SHALL HAVE IT SO EASY AS THAT ELF!
THERE AREN'T ENOUGH OF US.
CREATE A DRAGON-TOOTH WARRIOR.
CER-TAINLY!
O HORNS AND CLAWS OF OUR FATHER, IGUANODON, BE THOU FOUR LIMBS, BE TWO LEGS TO WALK UPON THE EARTH!
O SICKLE WINGS OF VELOCI-RAPTOR...
PAN (CLAP)

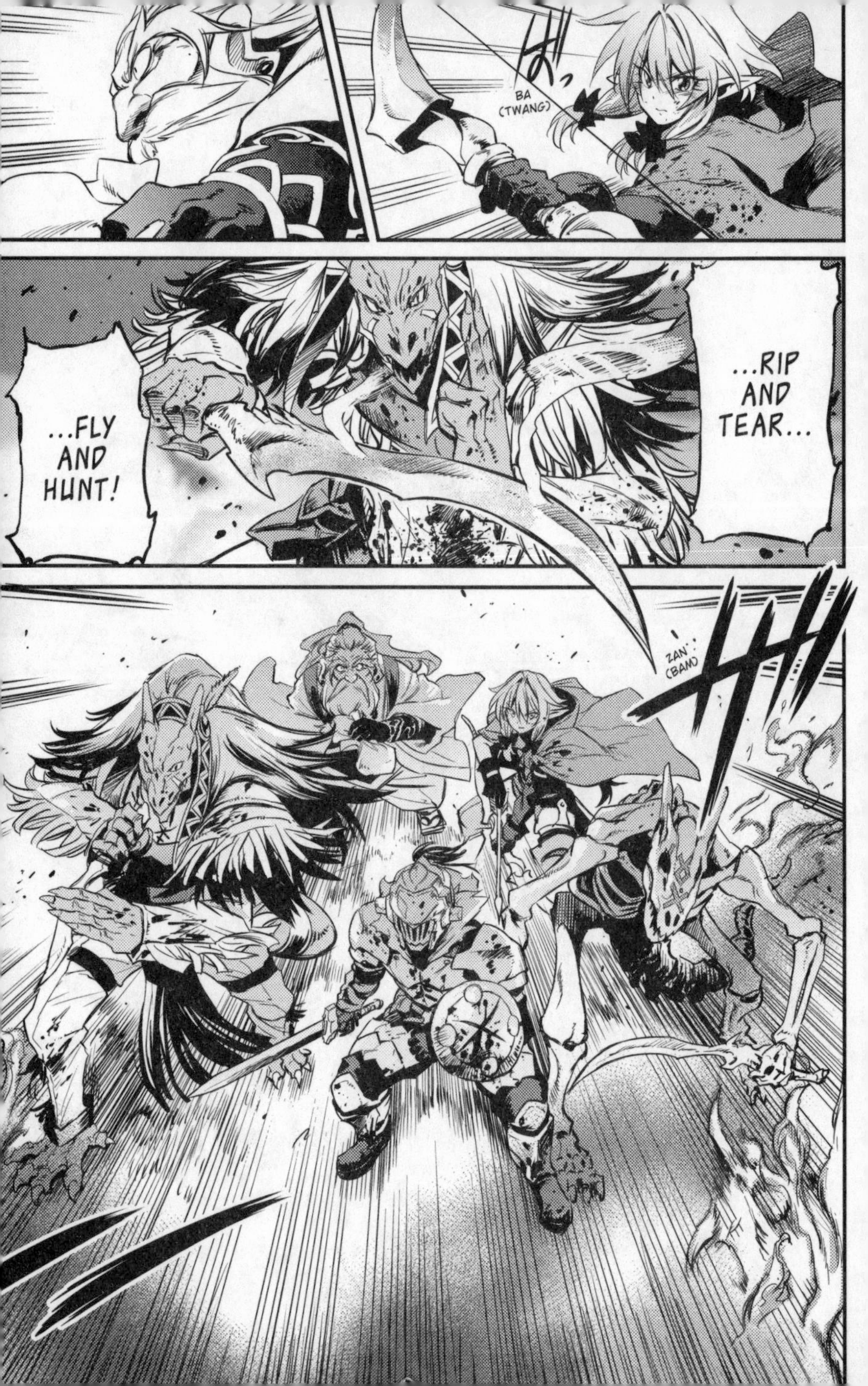
BA (TWANG)
...RIP AND TEAR...
...FLY AND HUNT!
ZAN (BAM)

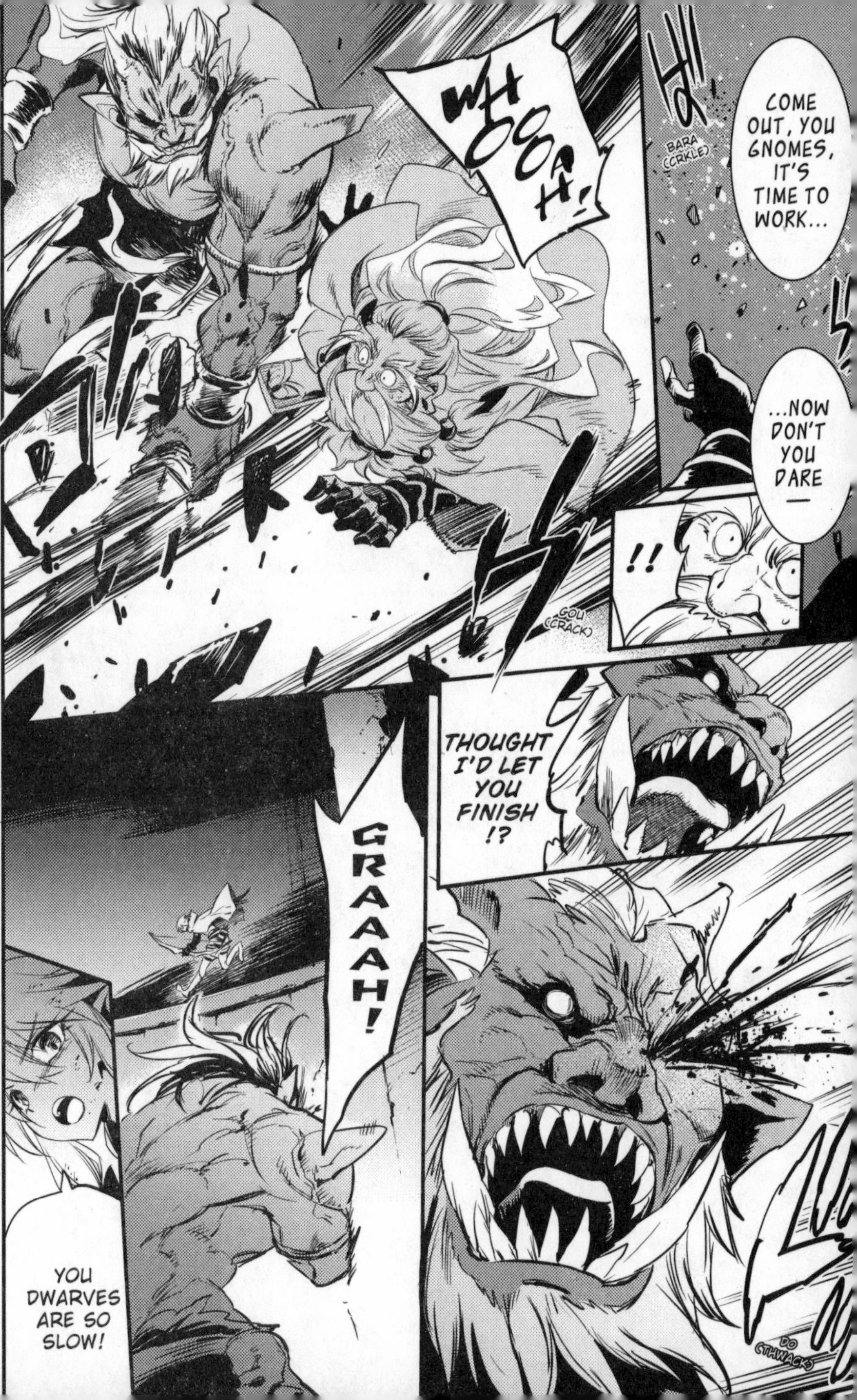
COME OUT, YOU GNOMES, IT'S TIME TO WORK...
BARA (CRKLE)
WHOOOAH!
...NOW DON'T YOU DARE—
!!
GOU (CRACK)
THOUGHT I'D LET YOU FINISH!?
GRAAAH!
DO (THWACK)
YOU DWARVES ARE SO SLOW!

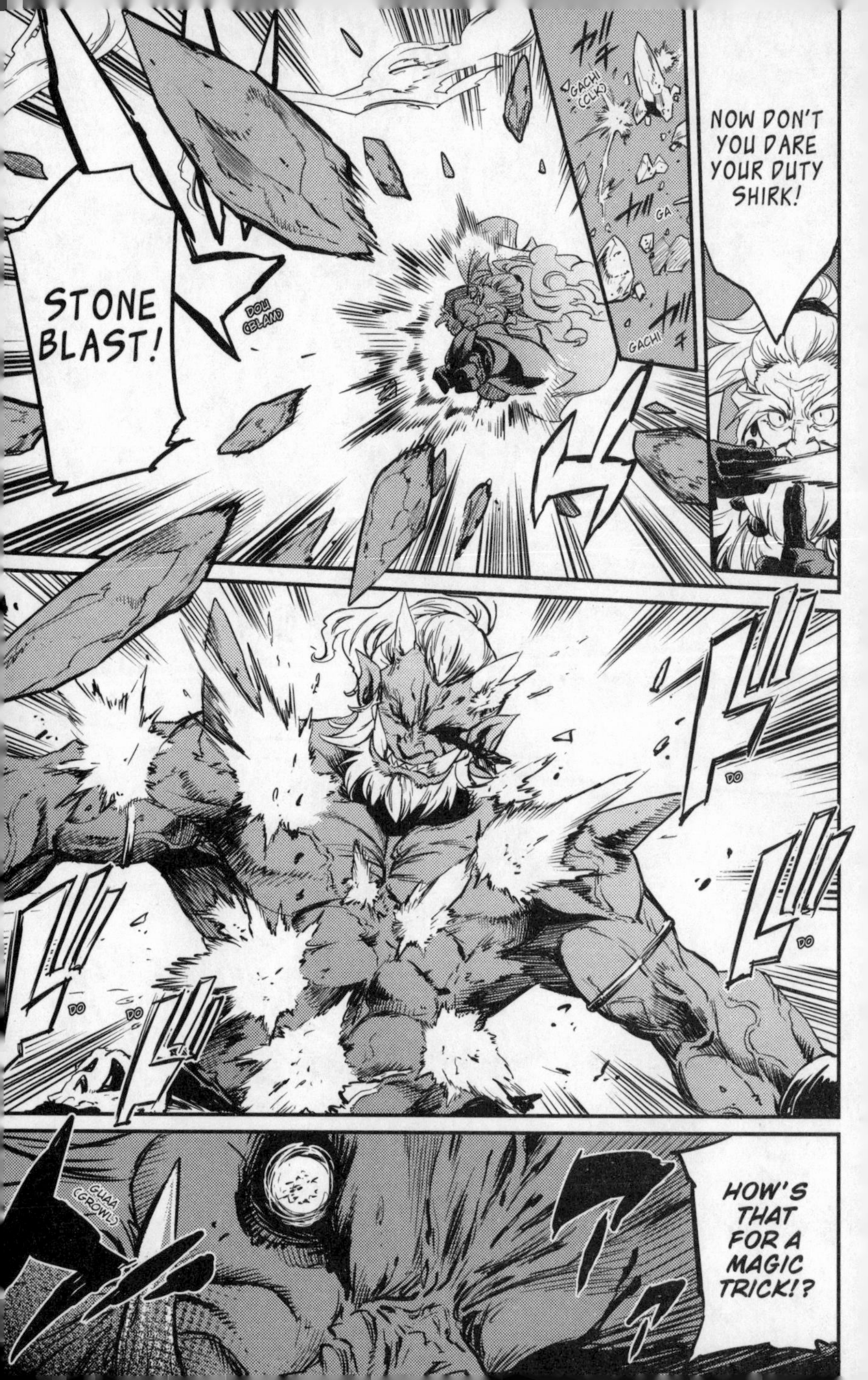
NOW DON'T YOU DARE YOUR DUTY SHIRK!
GACHI (CLK)
GA
GACHI
DOU (BLAM)
STONE BLAST!
DO
DO
DO
DO
HOW'S THAT FOR A MAGIC TRICK!?
GUAA (GROWL)

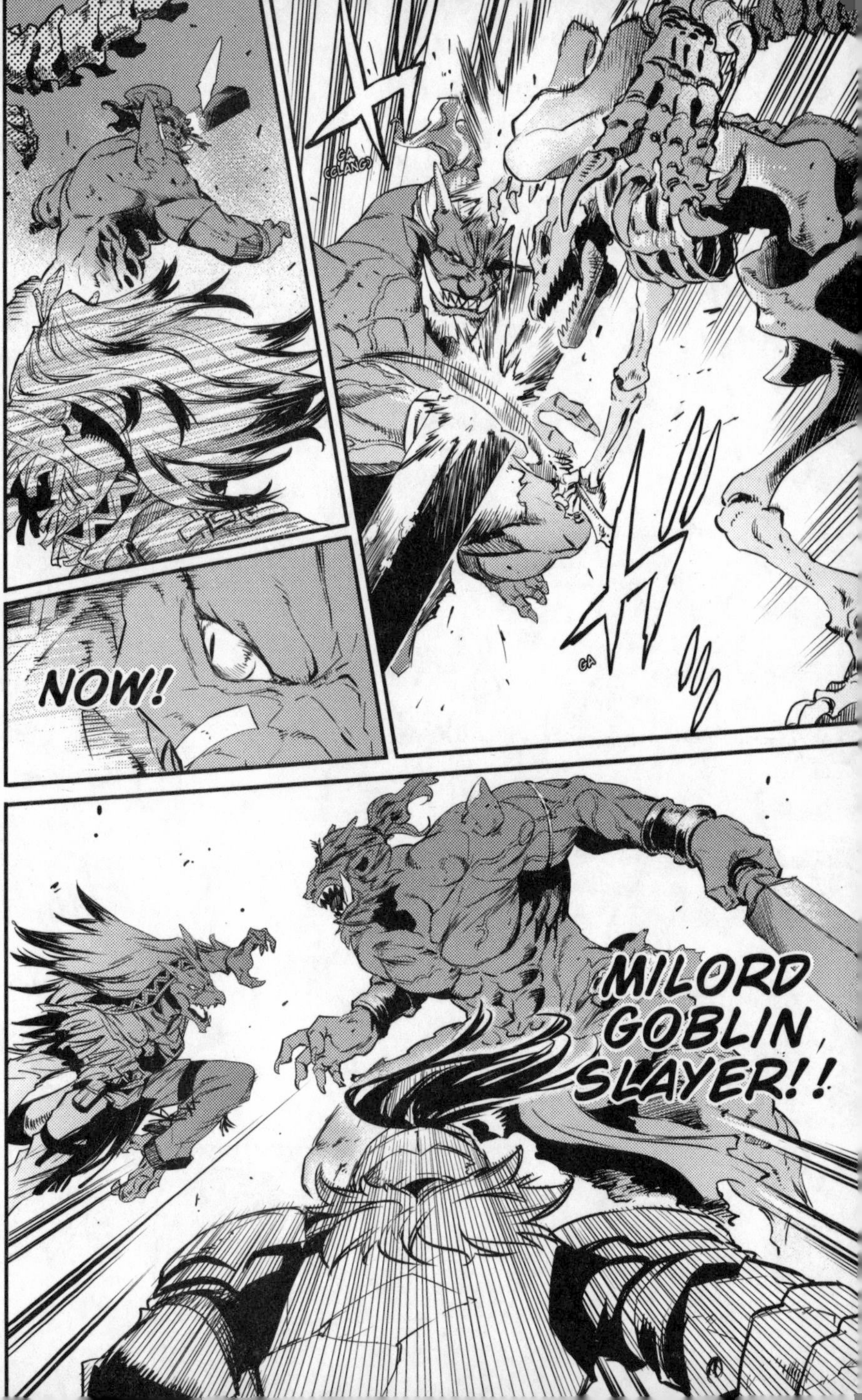
GA (CLANG)
GA
NOW!
MILORD GOBLIN SLAYER!!

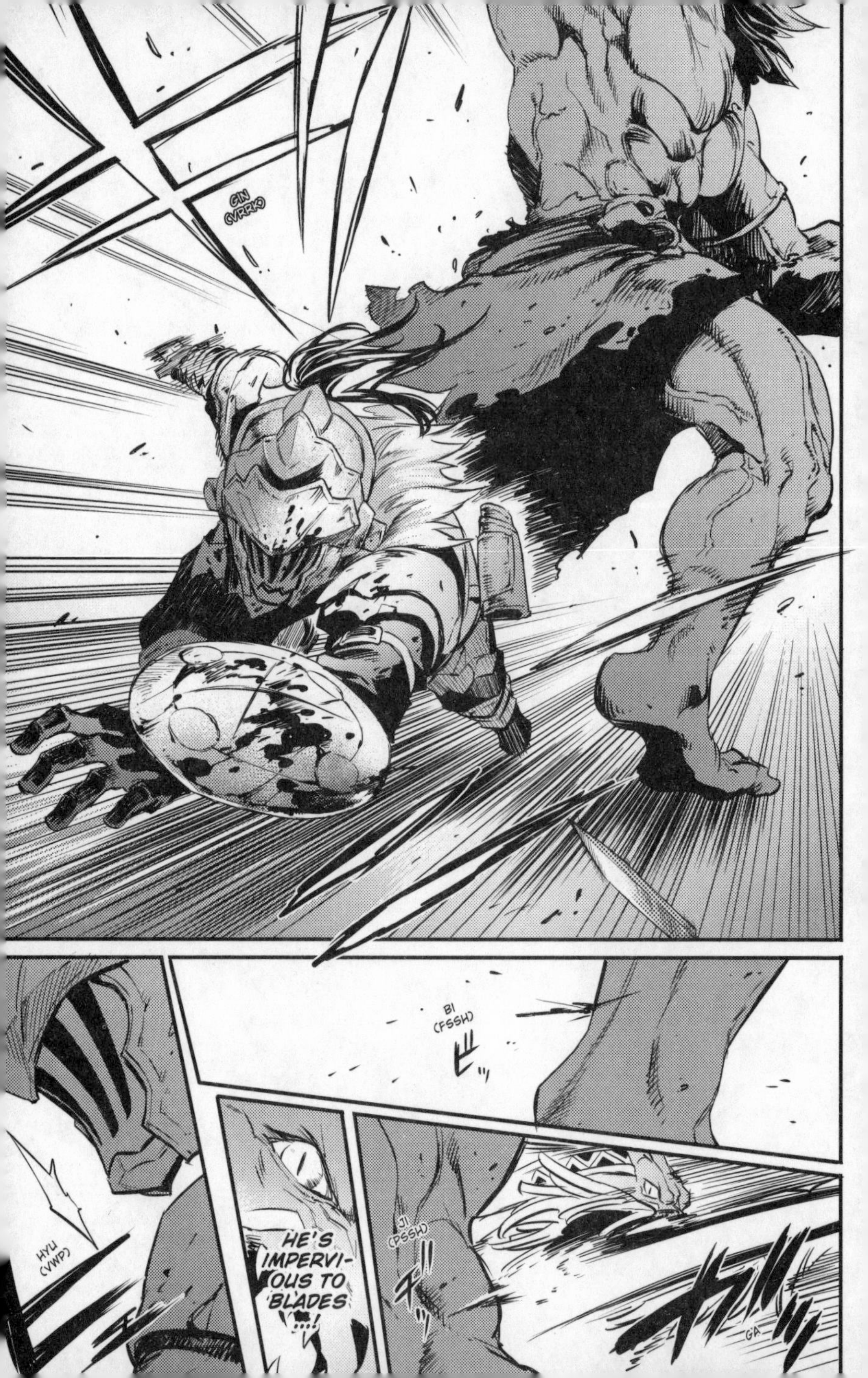
GIN (VRRK)
BI (FSSH)
GA
JI (PSSH)
HE'S IMPERVIOUS TO BLADES...!
HYU (VWP)

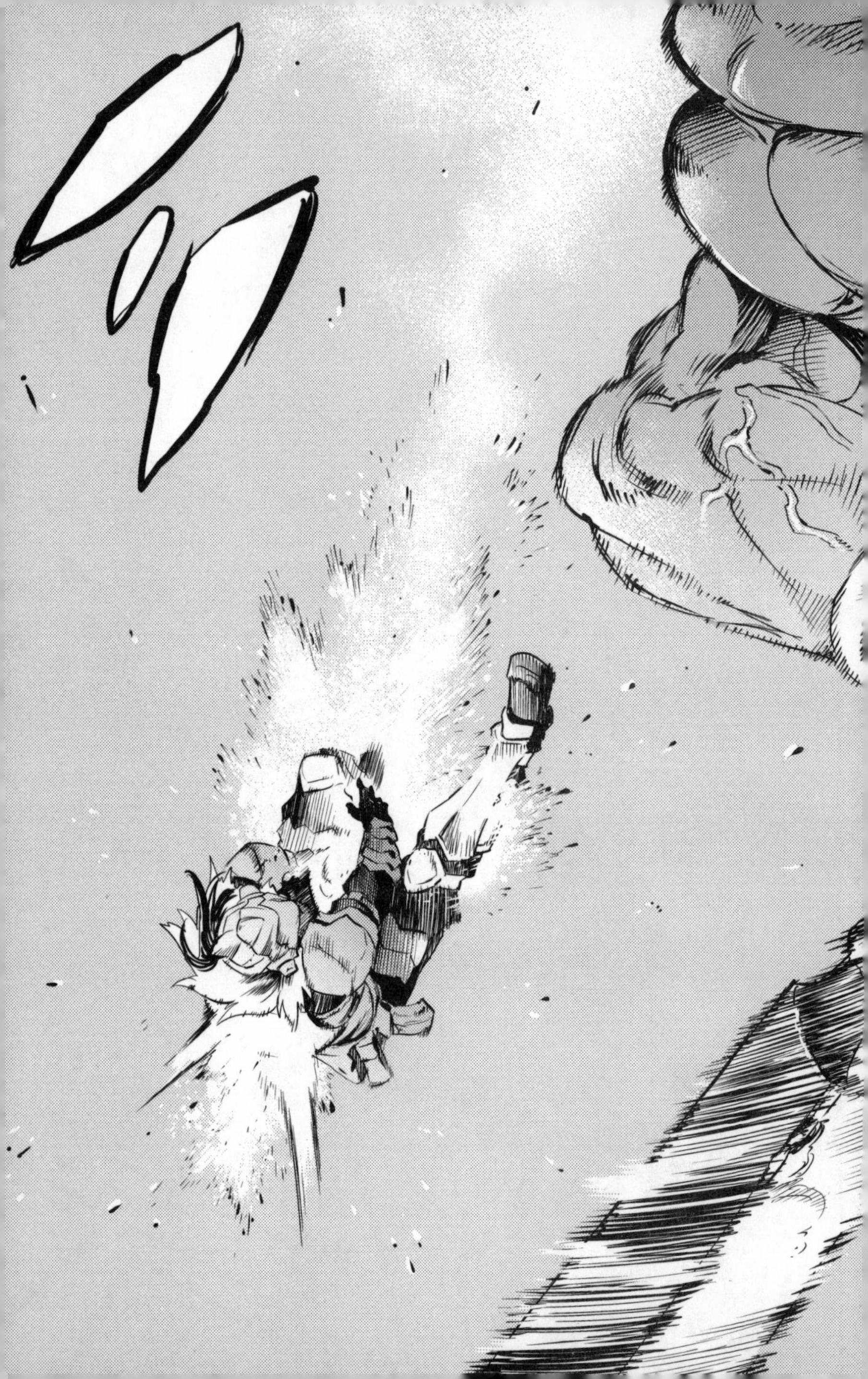

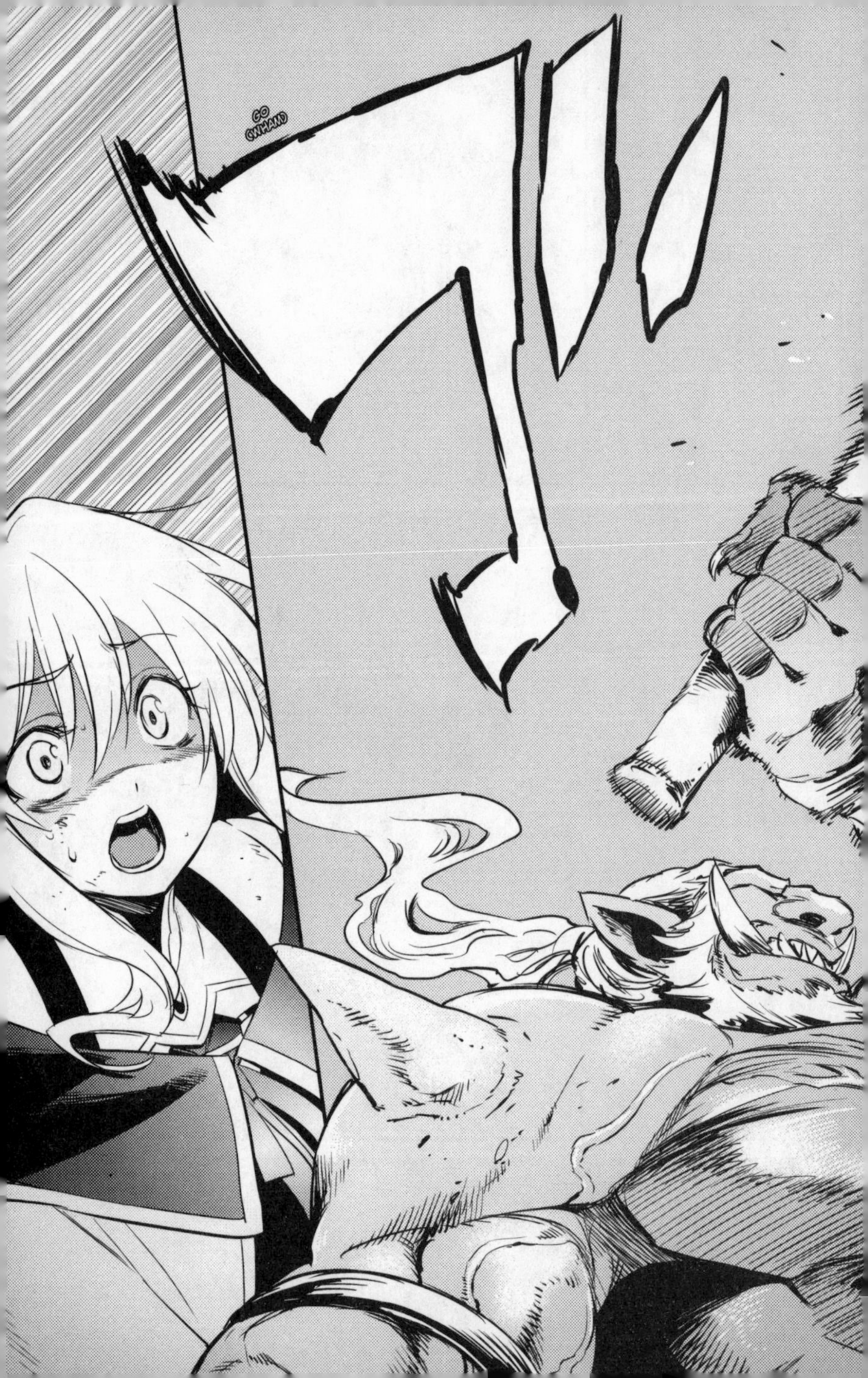
GO
(WHAM)

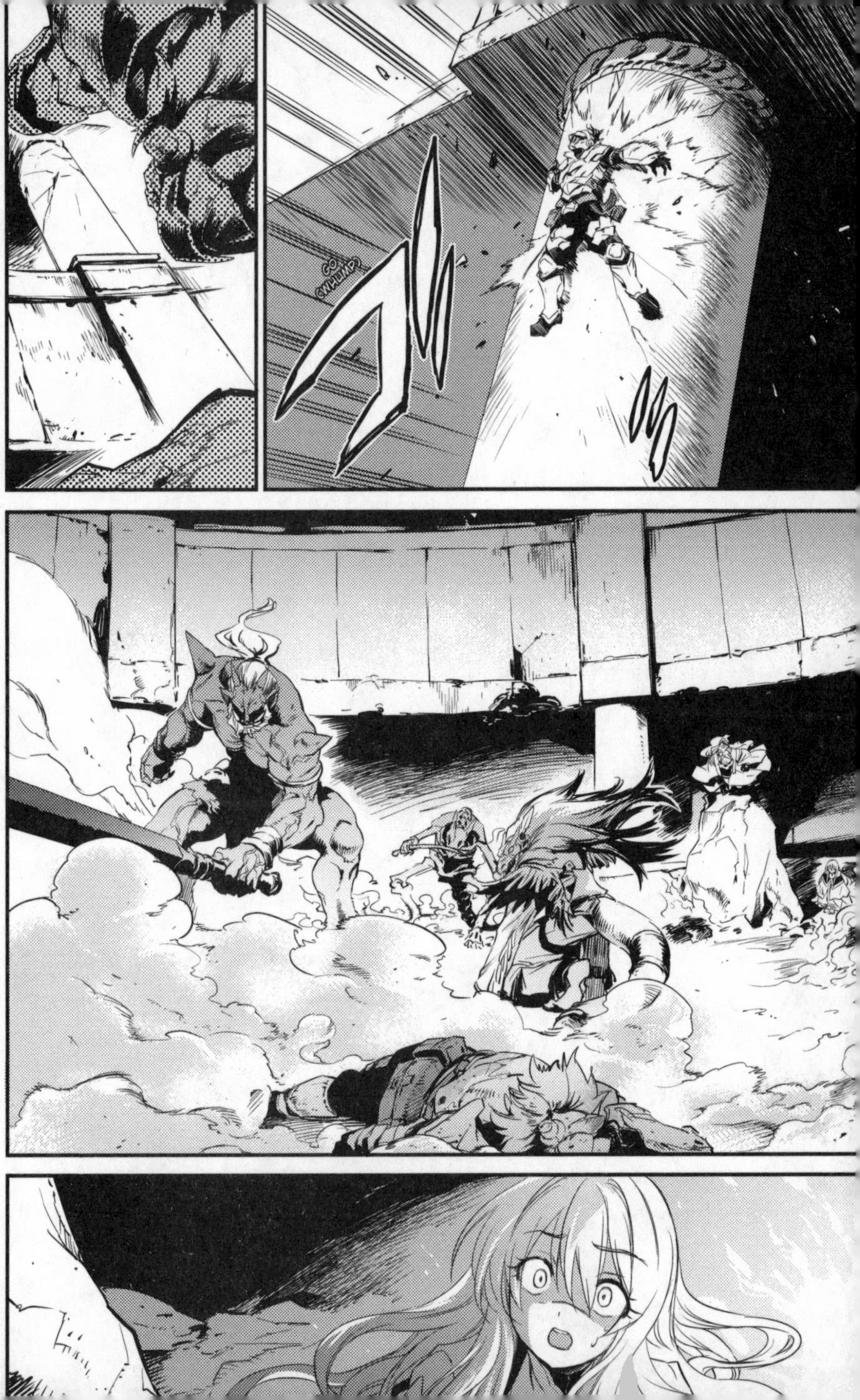
GO
(WHUMP)

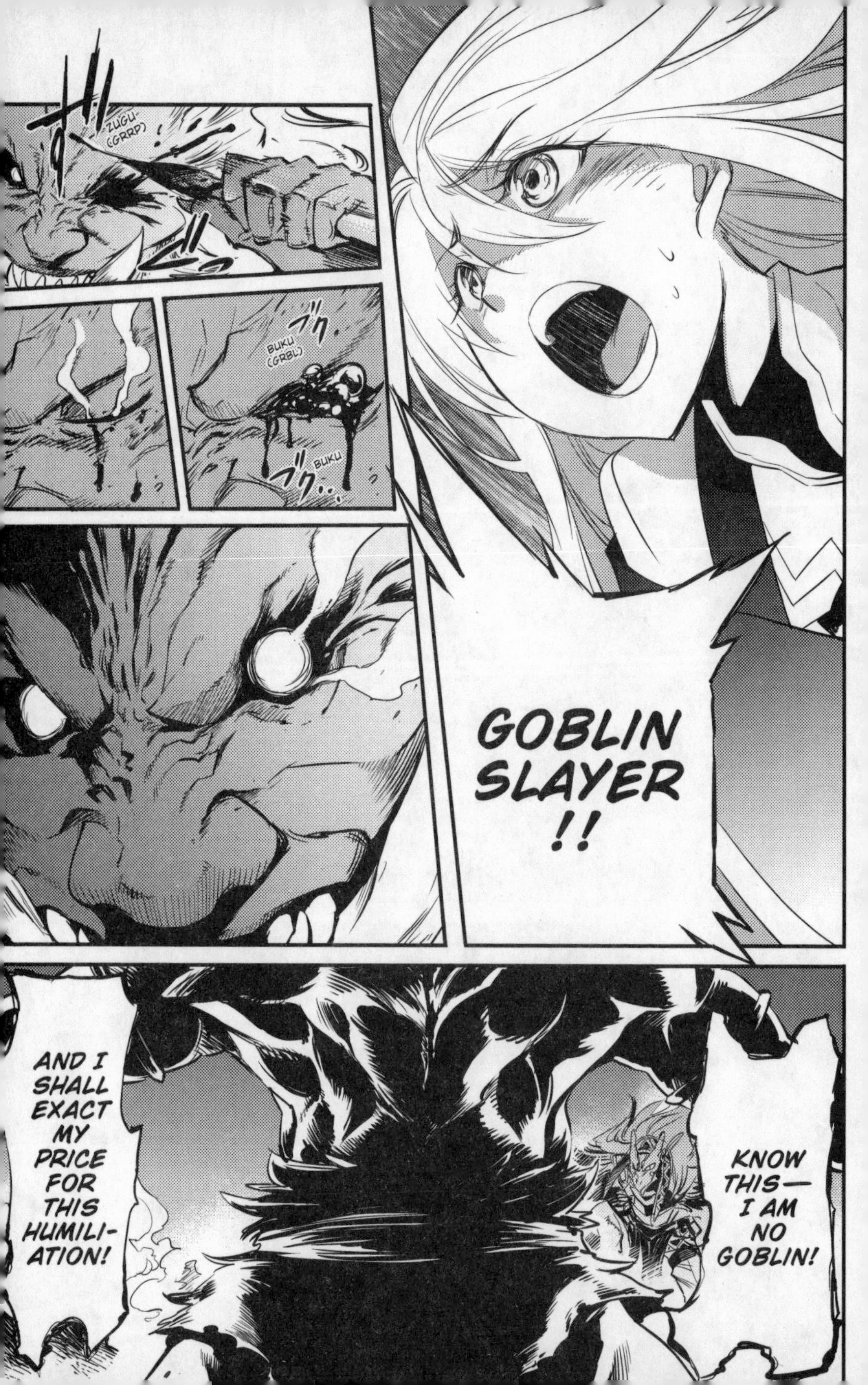
GOBLIN SLAYER !!
ZUGU (GRRP)
BUKU (GRBL)
BUKU
KNOW THIS— I AM NO GOBLIN!
AND I SHALL EXACT MY PRICE FOR THIS HUMILI-ATION!

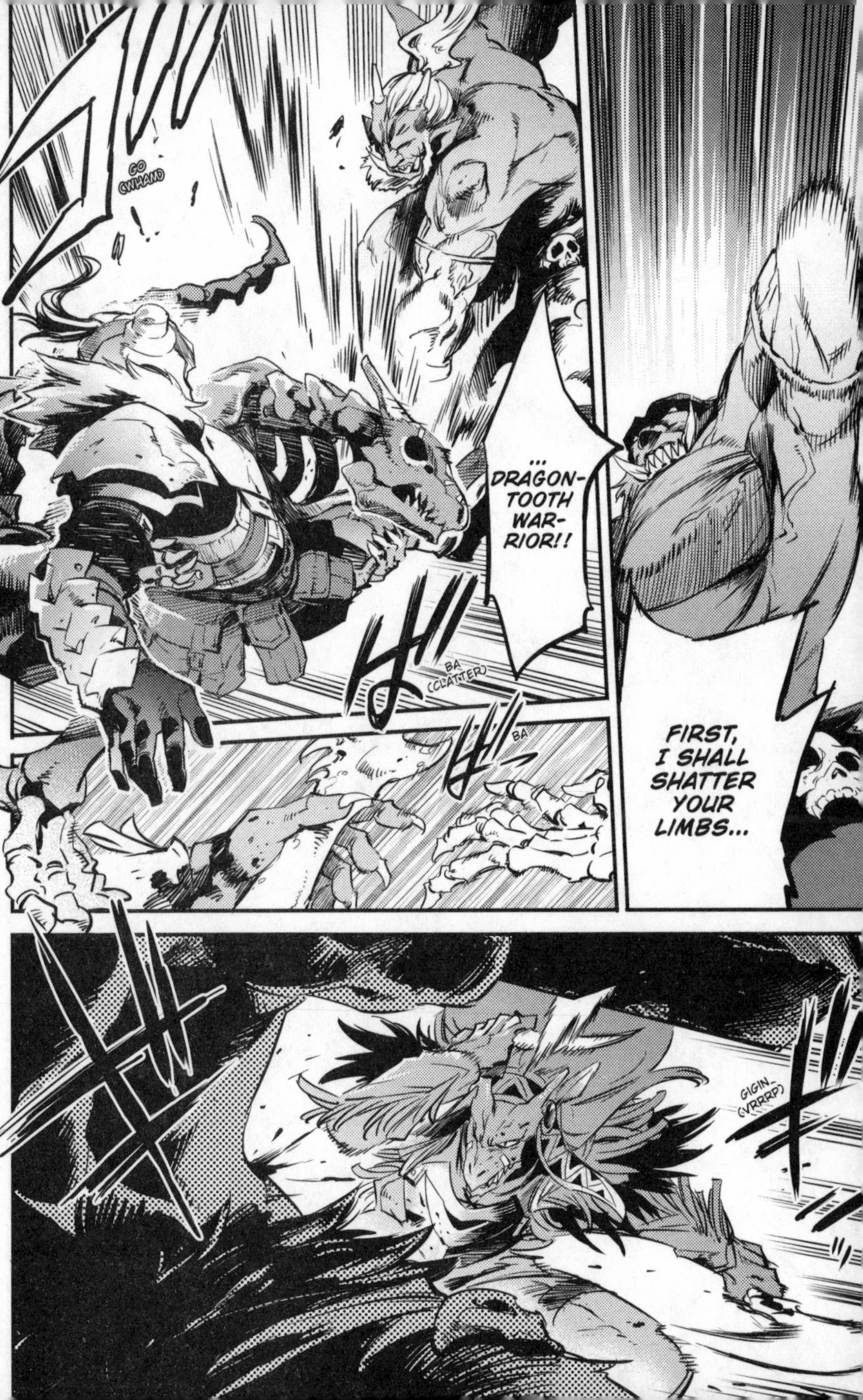
FIRST, I SHALL SHATTER YOUR LIMBS...
GO (WHAM)
... DRAGON-TOOTH WAR-RIOR!!
BA (CLATTER)
BA
GIGIN_ (VRRRP)

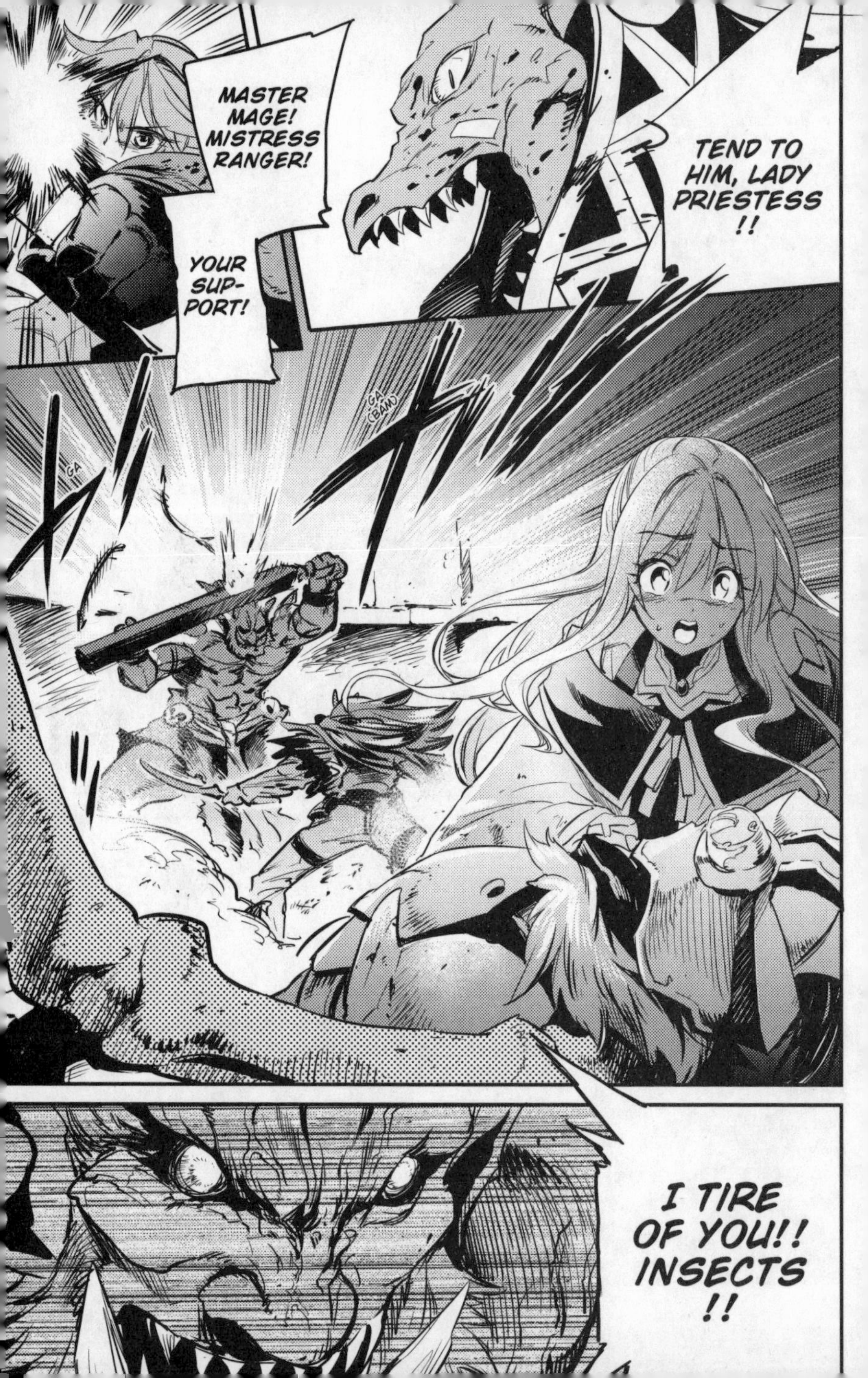
TEND TO HIM, LADY PRIESTESS !!
MASTER MAGE! MISTRESS RANGER!
YOUR SUP-PORT!
GA (BAM)
GA
I TIRE OF YOU!! INSECTS !!

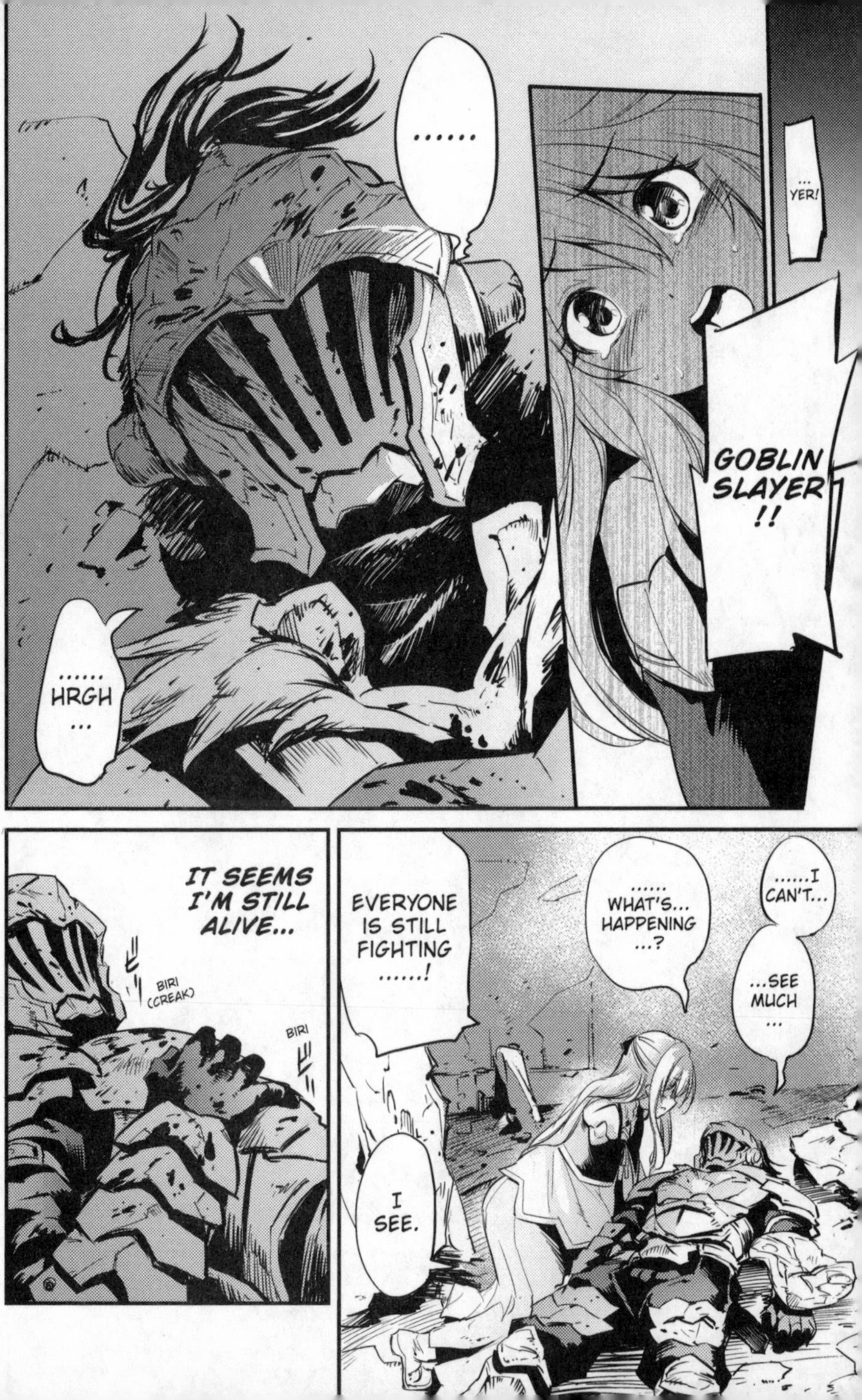
...YER!
GOBLIN SLAYER!!
......
......HRGH...
......I CAN'T...
...SEE MUCH...
......WHAT'S... HAPPENING...?
EVERYONE IS STILL FIGHTING......!
I SEE.
IT SEEMS I'M STILL ALIVE...
BIRI (CREAK)
BIRI

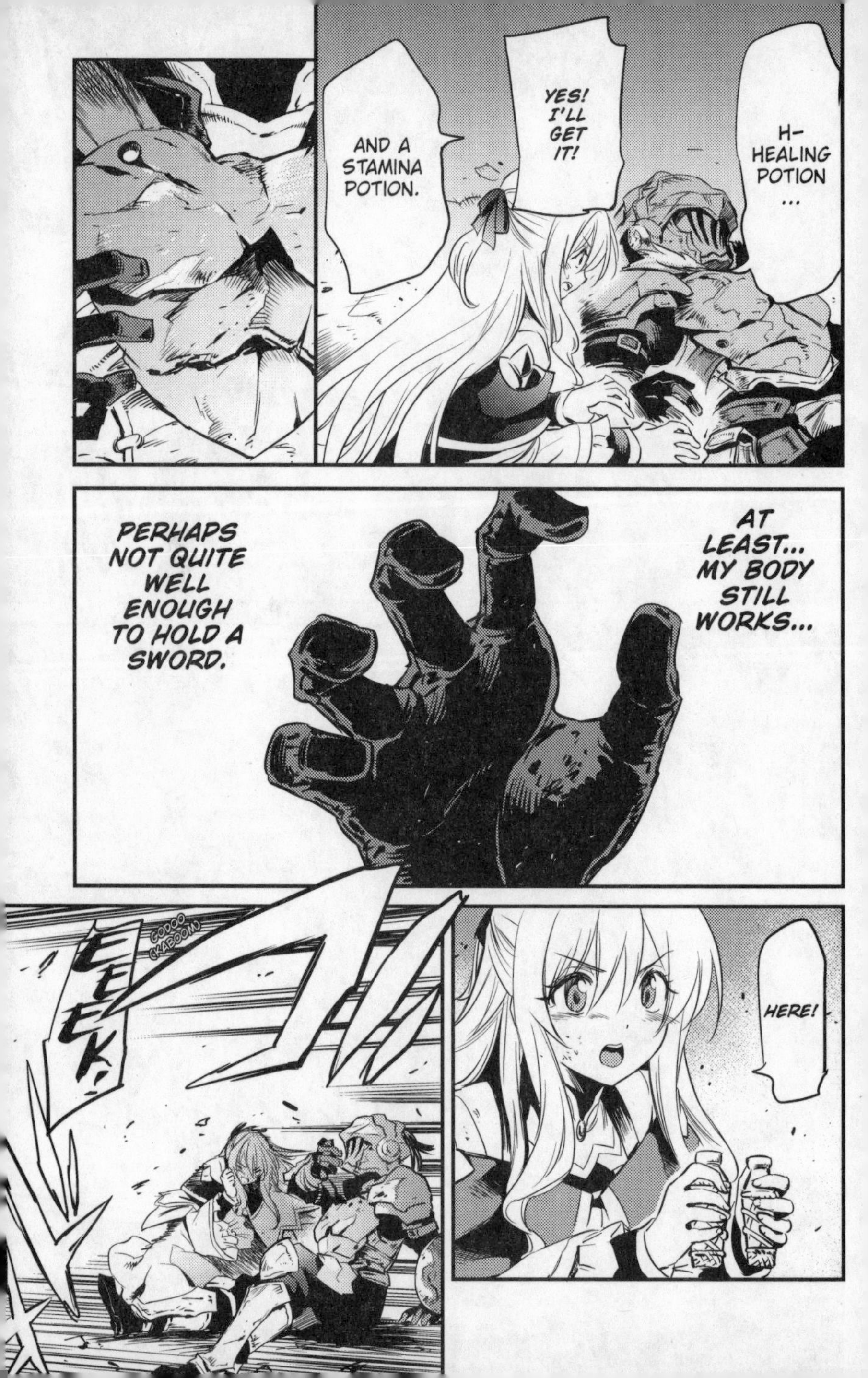
H-HEALING POTION...
YES! I'LL GET IT!
AND A STAMINA POTION.
AT LEAST... MY BODY STILL WORKS...
PERHAPS NOT QUITE WELL ENOUGH TO HOLD A SWORD.
HERE!
EEEK!
GODOO (KABOOM)

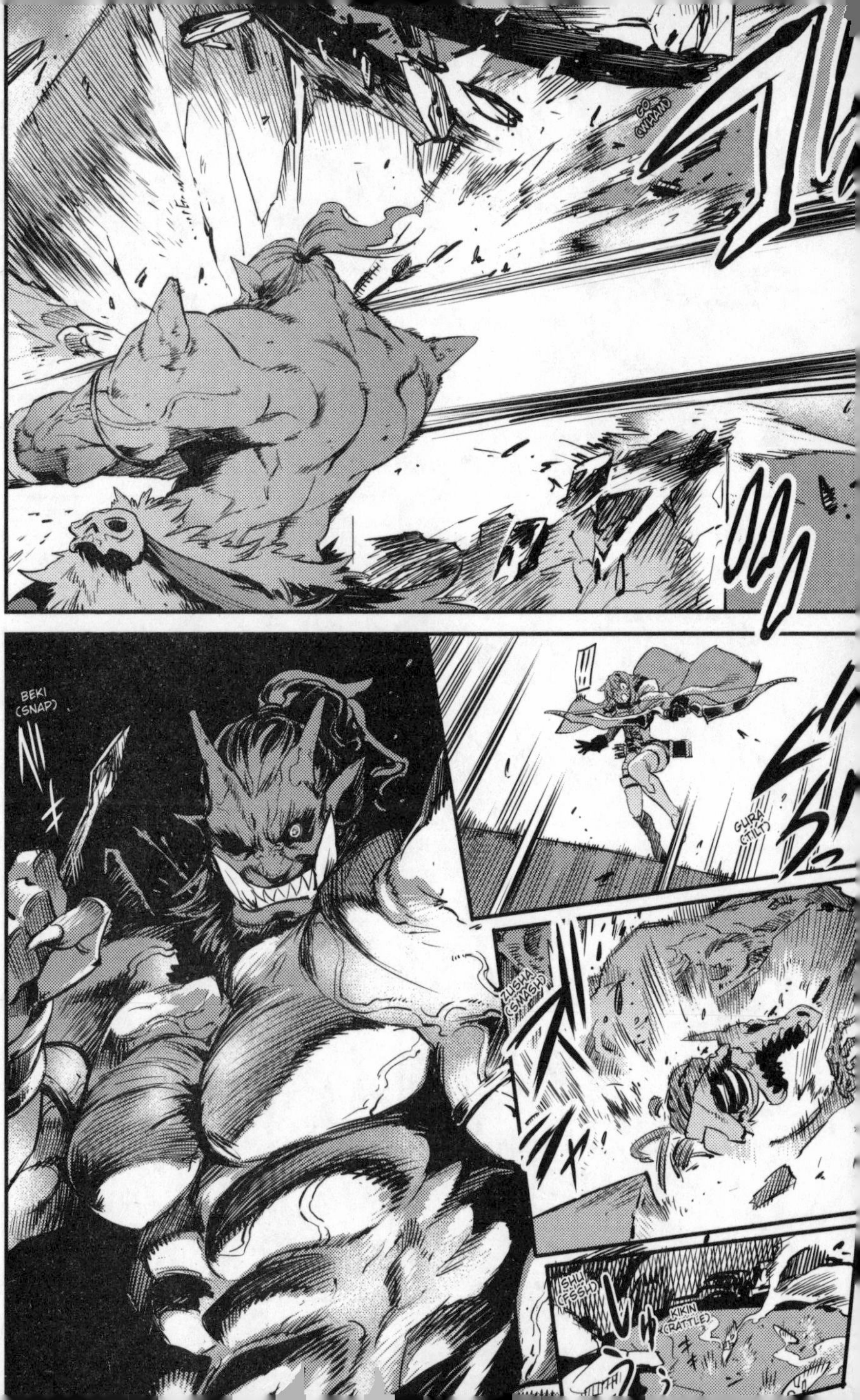
GO (WHAM)
GURA (TILT)
ZUSHA (SMASH)
ISHU (FSSH)
KIKIN (RATTLE)
BEKI (SNAP)

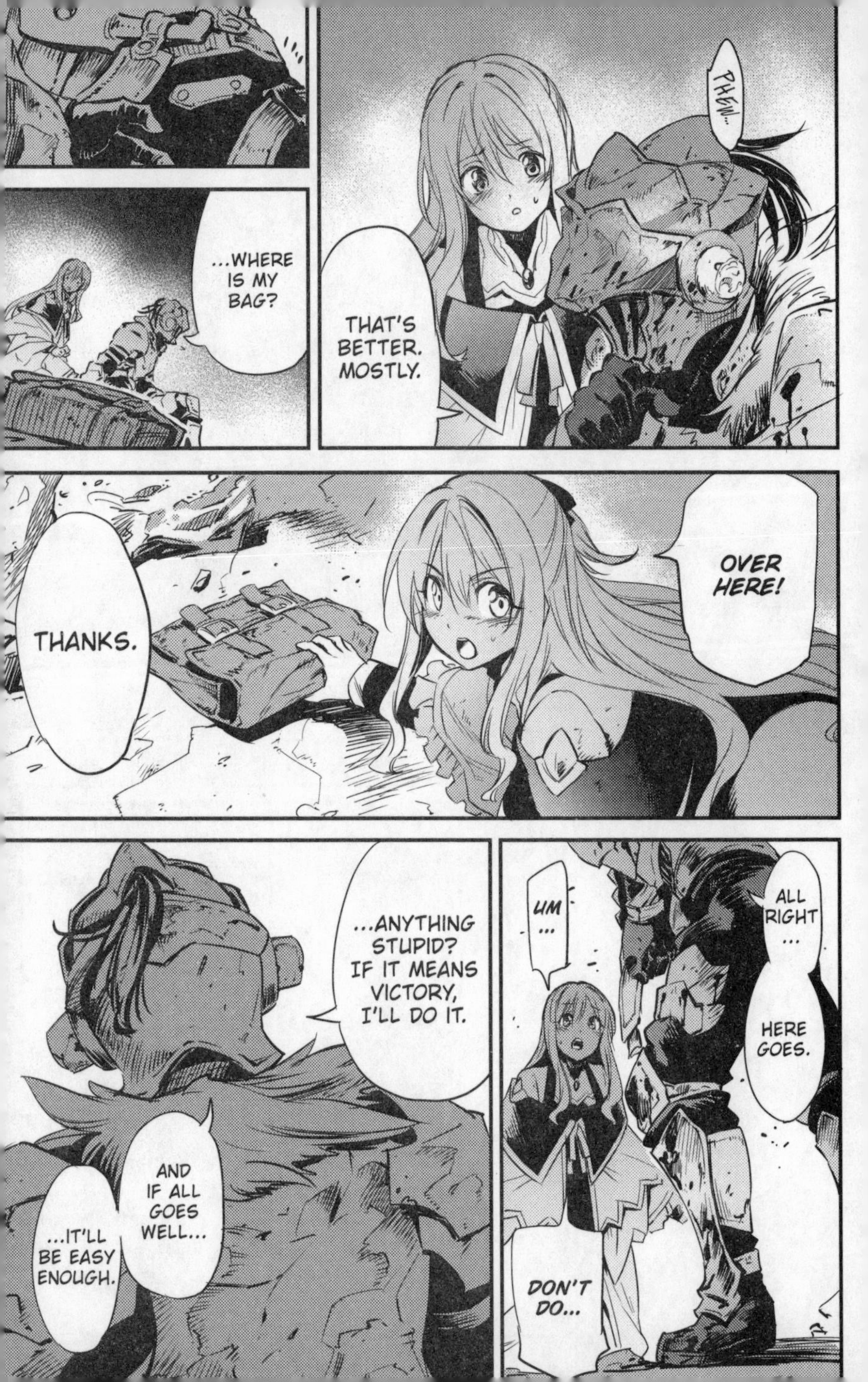
PHEW...
THAT'S BETTER. MOSTLY.
...WHERE IS MY BAG?
OVER HERE!
THANKS.
ALL RIGHT ...
HERE GOES.
UM ...
DON'T DO...
...ANYTHING STUPID? IF IT MEANS VICTORY, I'LL DO IT.
AND IF ALL GOES WELL...
...IT'LL BE EASY ENOUGH.

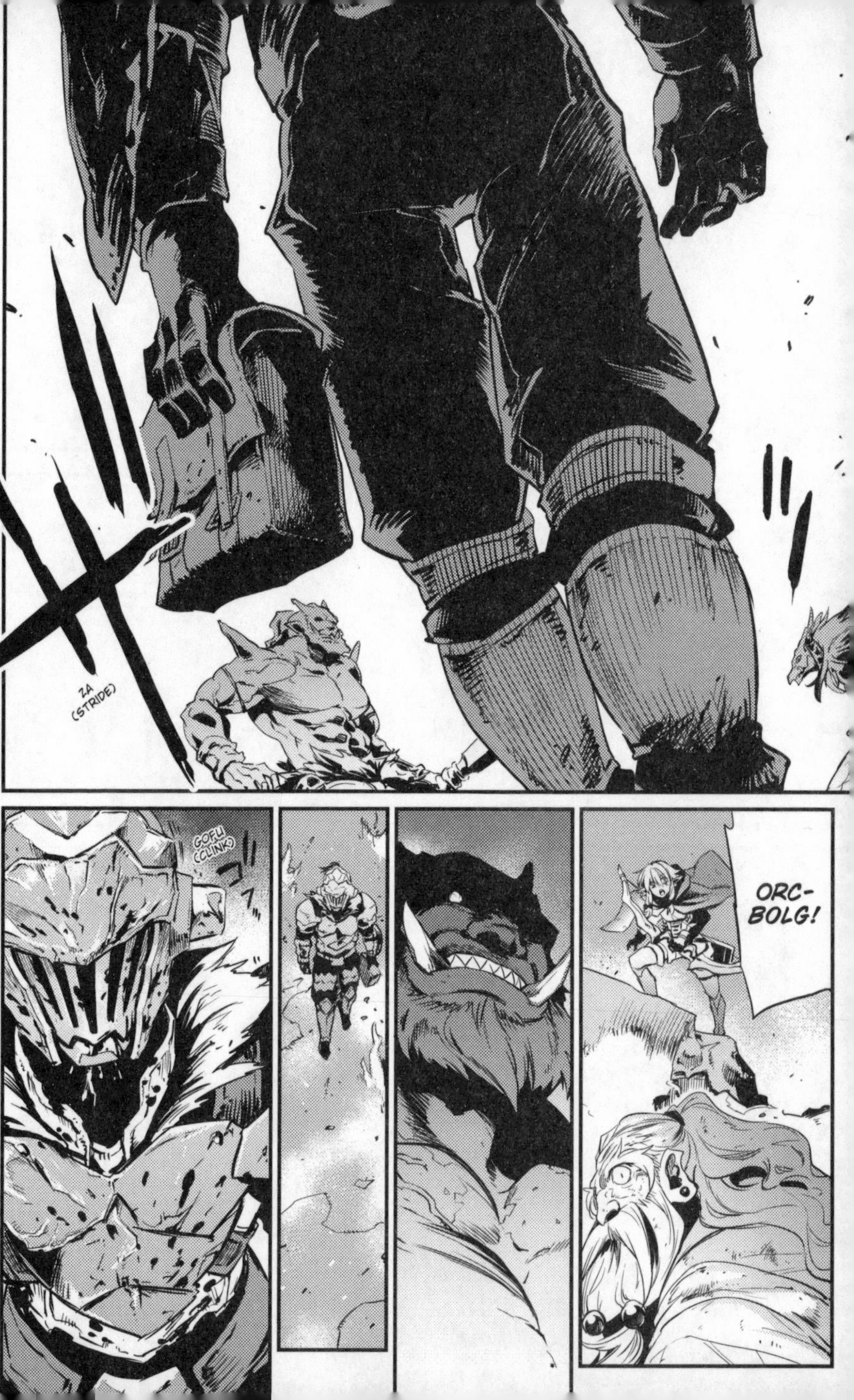
ZA
(STRIDE)
ORC-
BOLG!
GOFU
(CLINK)

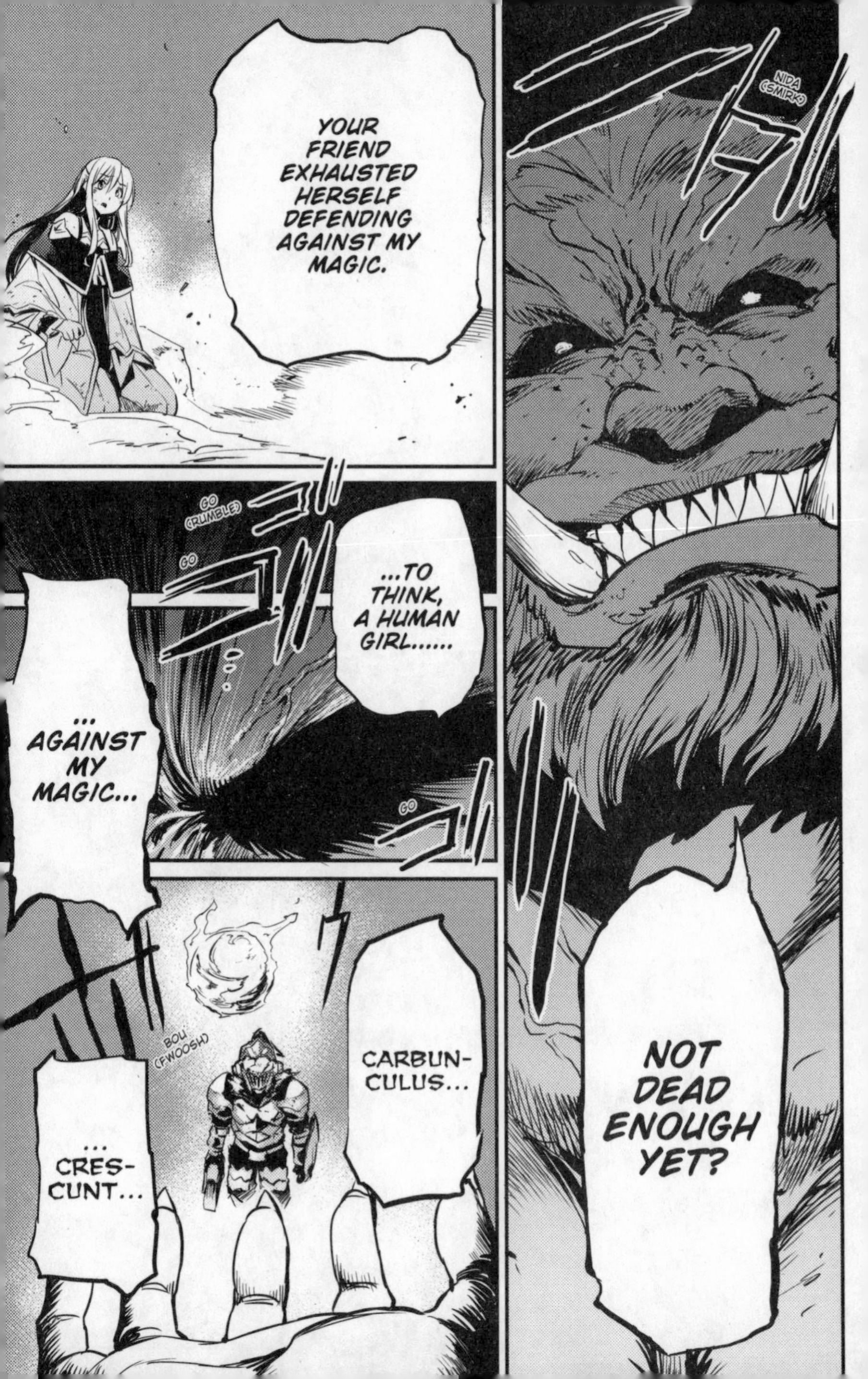
NIDA (SMIRK)
NOT DEAD ENOUGH YET?
YOUR FRIEND EXHAUSTED HERSELF DEFENDING AGAINST MY MAGIC.
GO (RUMBLE)
GO
...TO THINK, A HUMAN GIRL......
... AGAINST MY MAGIC...
GO
CARBUNCULUS...
BOU (F-WOOSH)
... CRESCUNT...

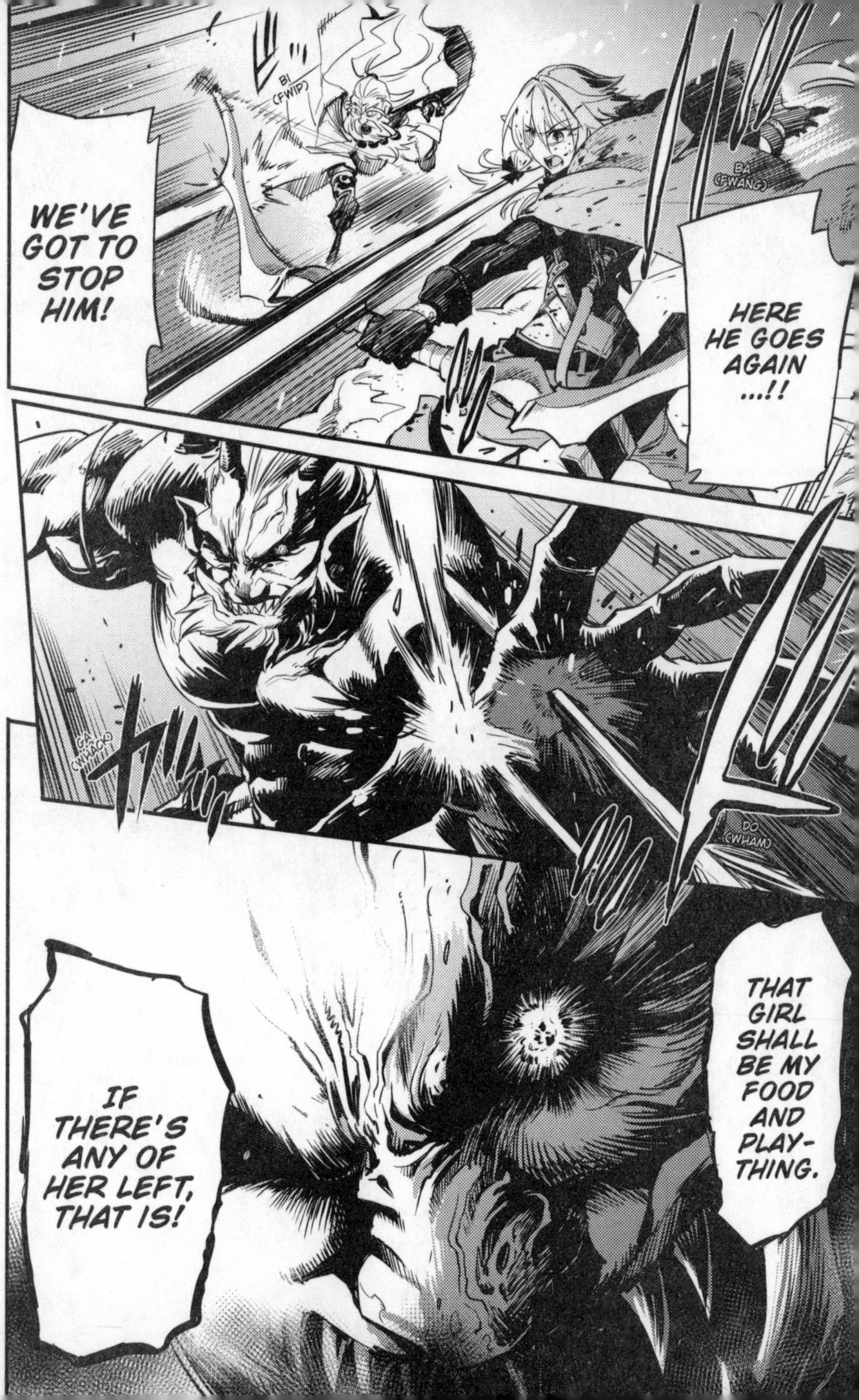
BA (FWANG)
HERE HE GOES AGAIN ...!!
BI (FWIP)
WE'VE GOT TO STOP HIM!
DO (WHAM)
GA (WHACK)
THAT GIRL SHALL BE MY FOOD AND PLAY-THING.
IF THERE'S ANY OF HER LEFT, THAT IS!

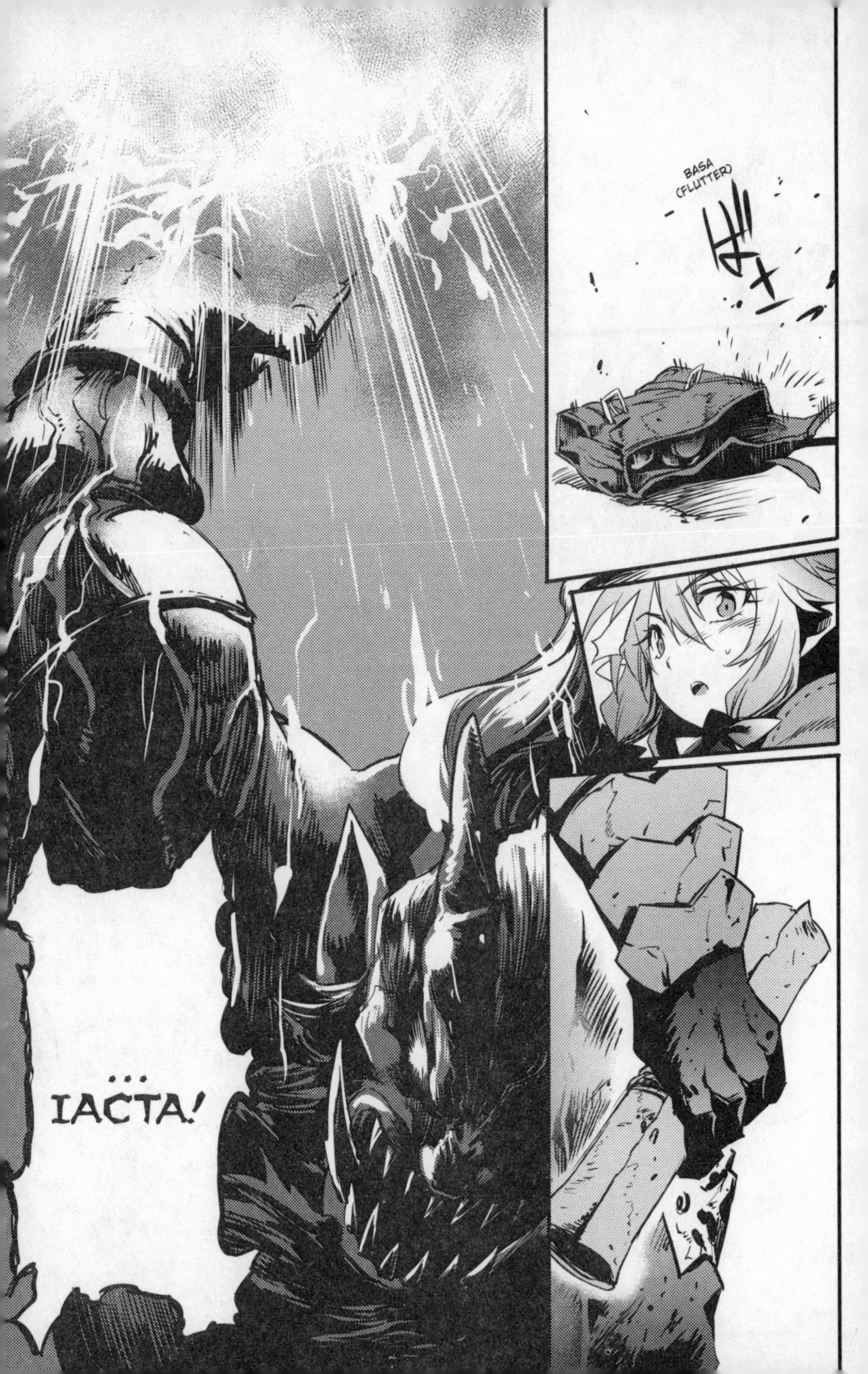
BASA (FLUTTER)
...IACTA!

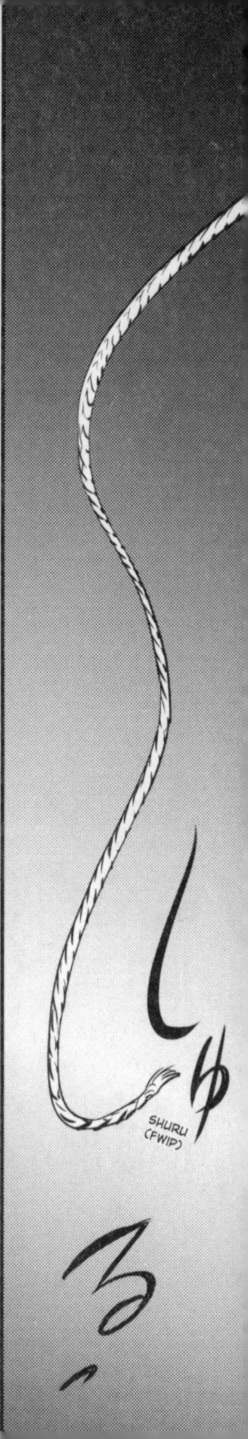
しゅる
SHURU
(FWIP)
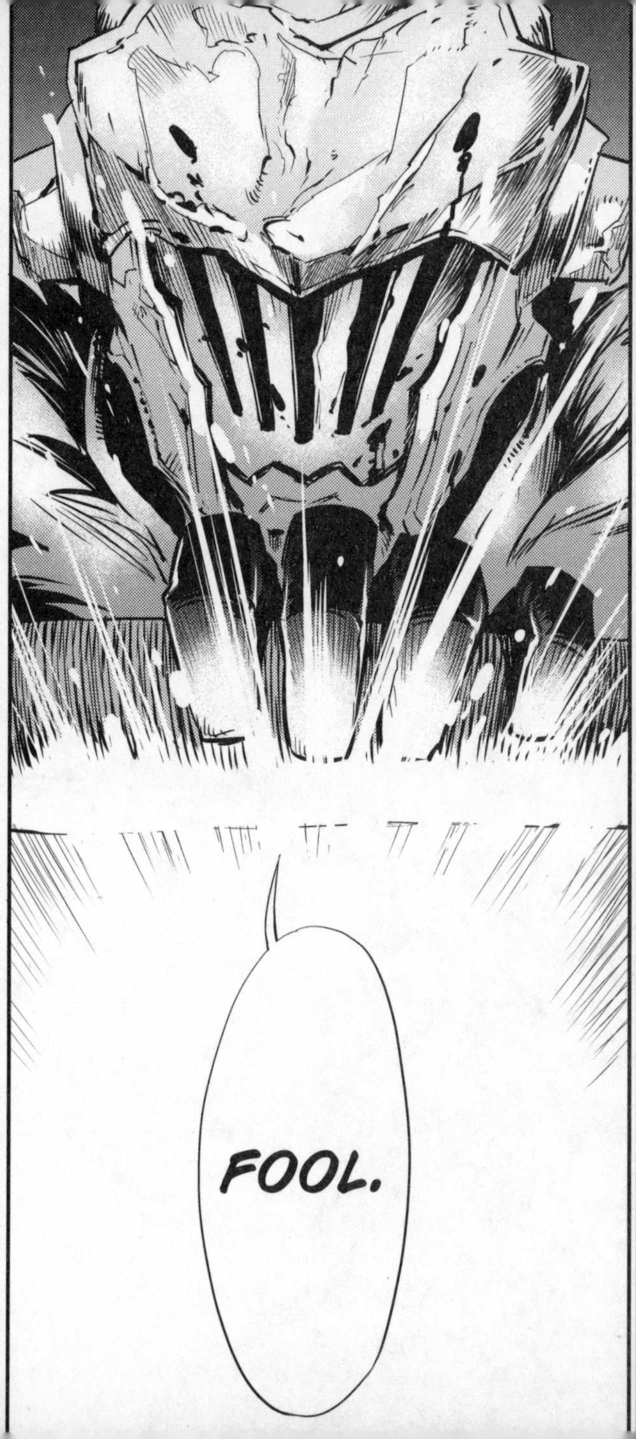
FOOL.

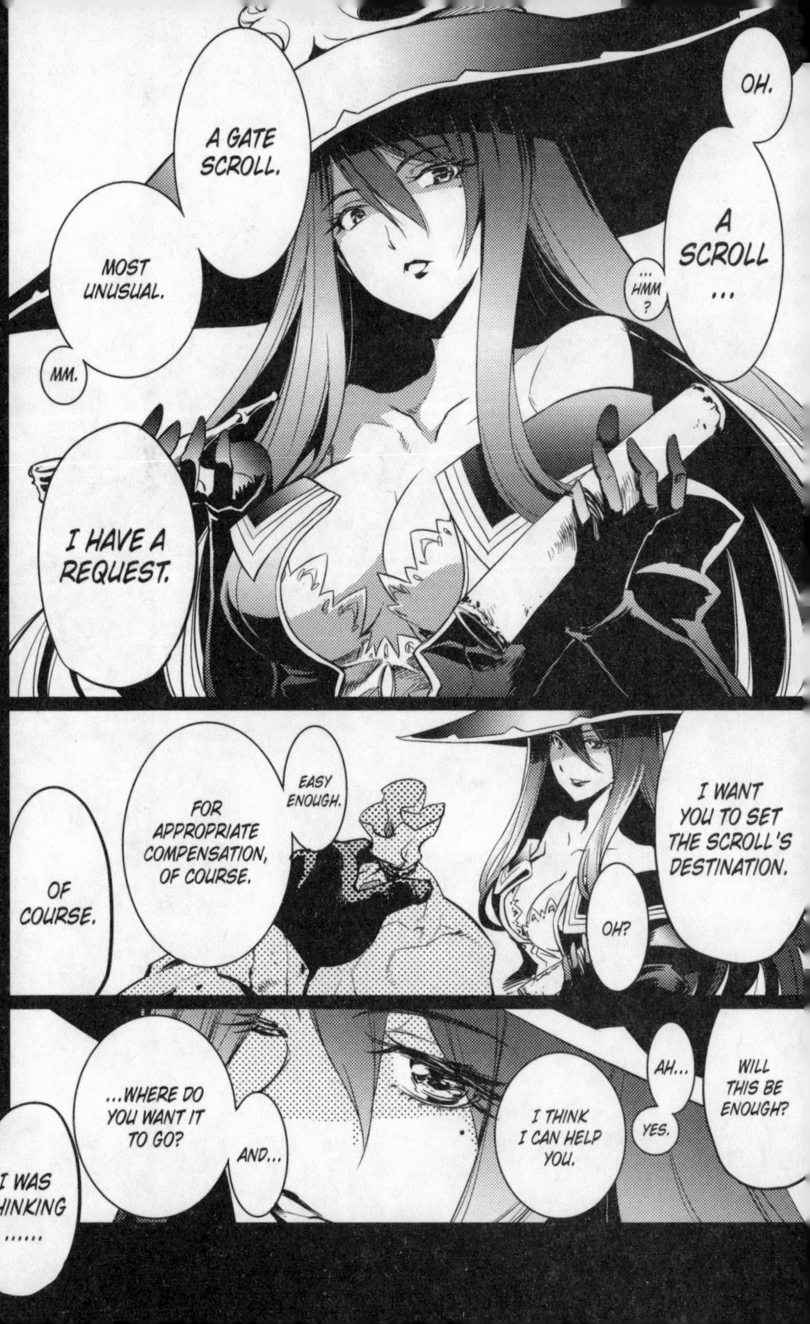
OH.
A SCROLL ...
...HMM?
A GATE SCROLL.
MOST UNUSUAL.
MM.
I HAVE A REQUEST.
I WANT YOU TO SET THE SCROLL'S DESTINATION.
OH?
EASY ENOUGH.
FOR APPROPRIATE COMPENSATION, OF COURSE.
OF COURSE.
WILL THIS BE ENOUGH?
AH...
YES.
I THINK I CAN HELP YOU.
AND...
...WHERE DO YOU WANT IT TO GO?
I WAS THINKING ......

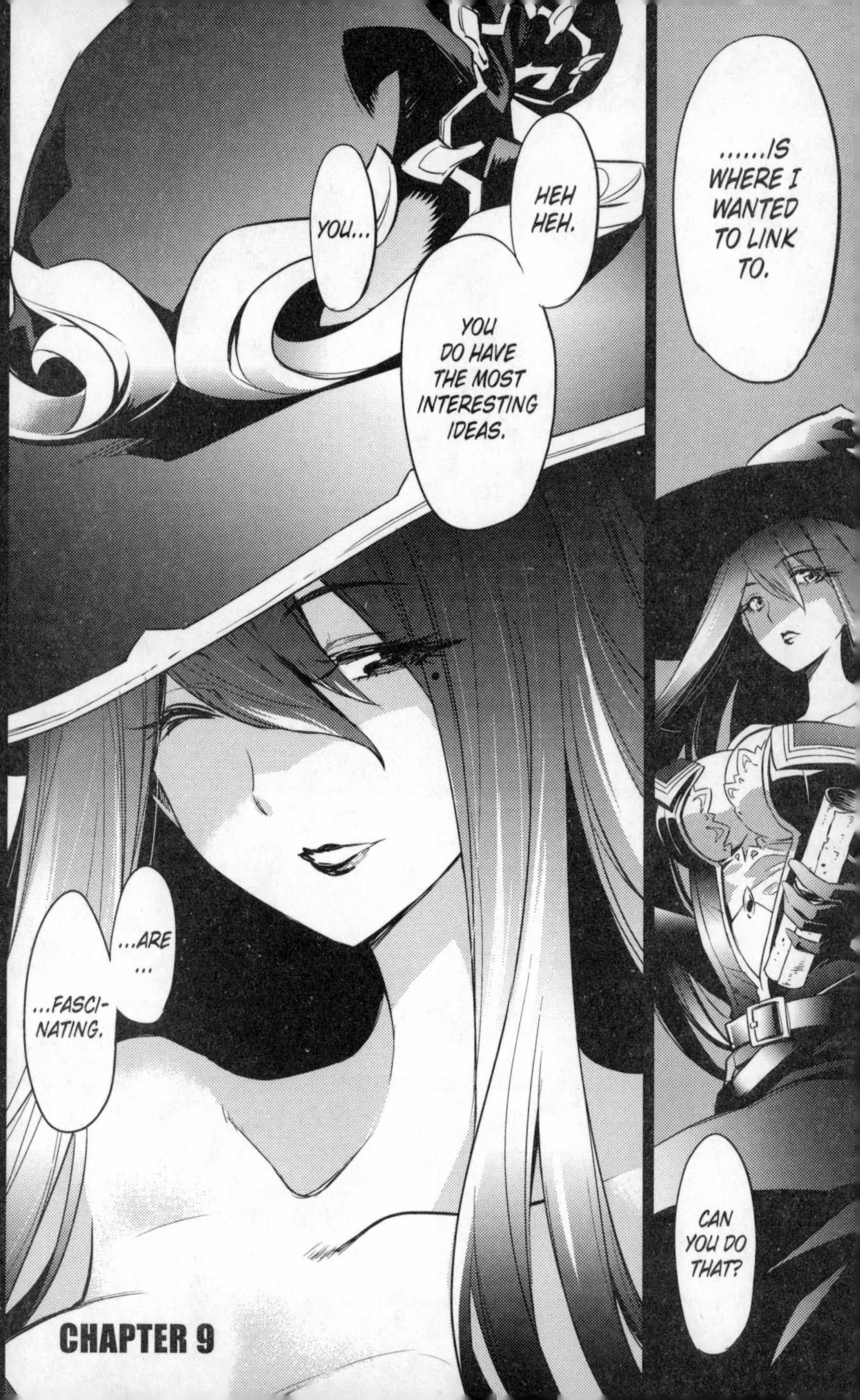
......IS WHERE I WANTED TO LINK TO.
CAN YOU DO THAT?
HEH HEH.
YOU...
YOU DO HAVE THE MOST INTERESTING IDEAS.
...ARE ...
...FASCINATING.
CHAPTER 9

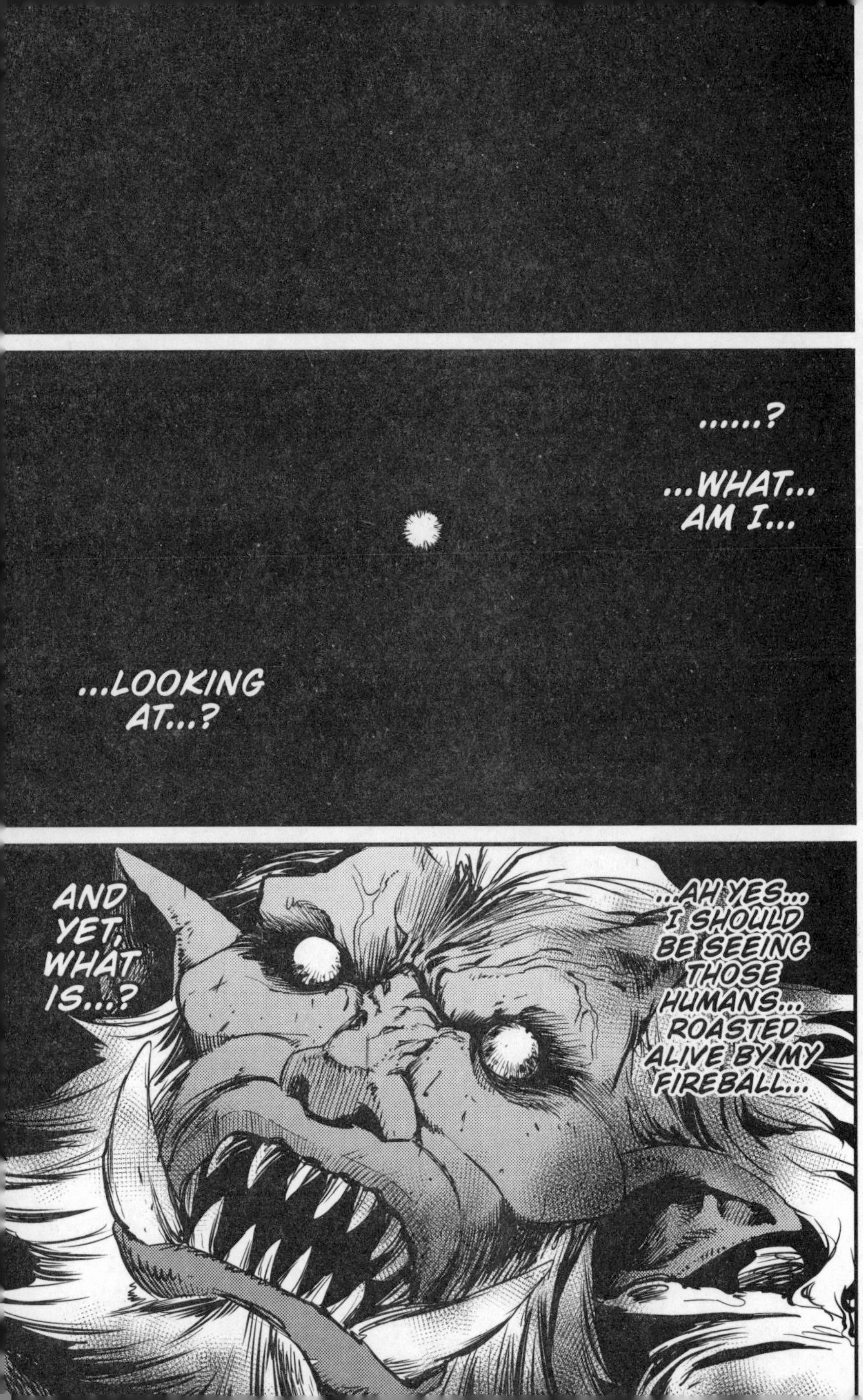
......?
...WHAT... AM I...
...LOOKING AT...?
...AH YES... I SHOULD BE SEEING THOSE HUMANS... ROASTED ALIVE BY MY FIREBALL...
AND YET, WHAT IS...?

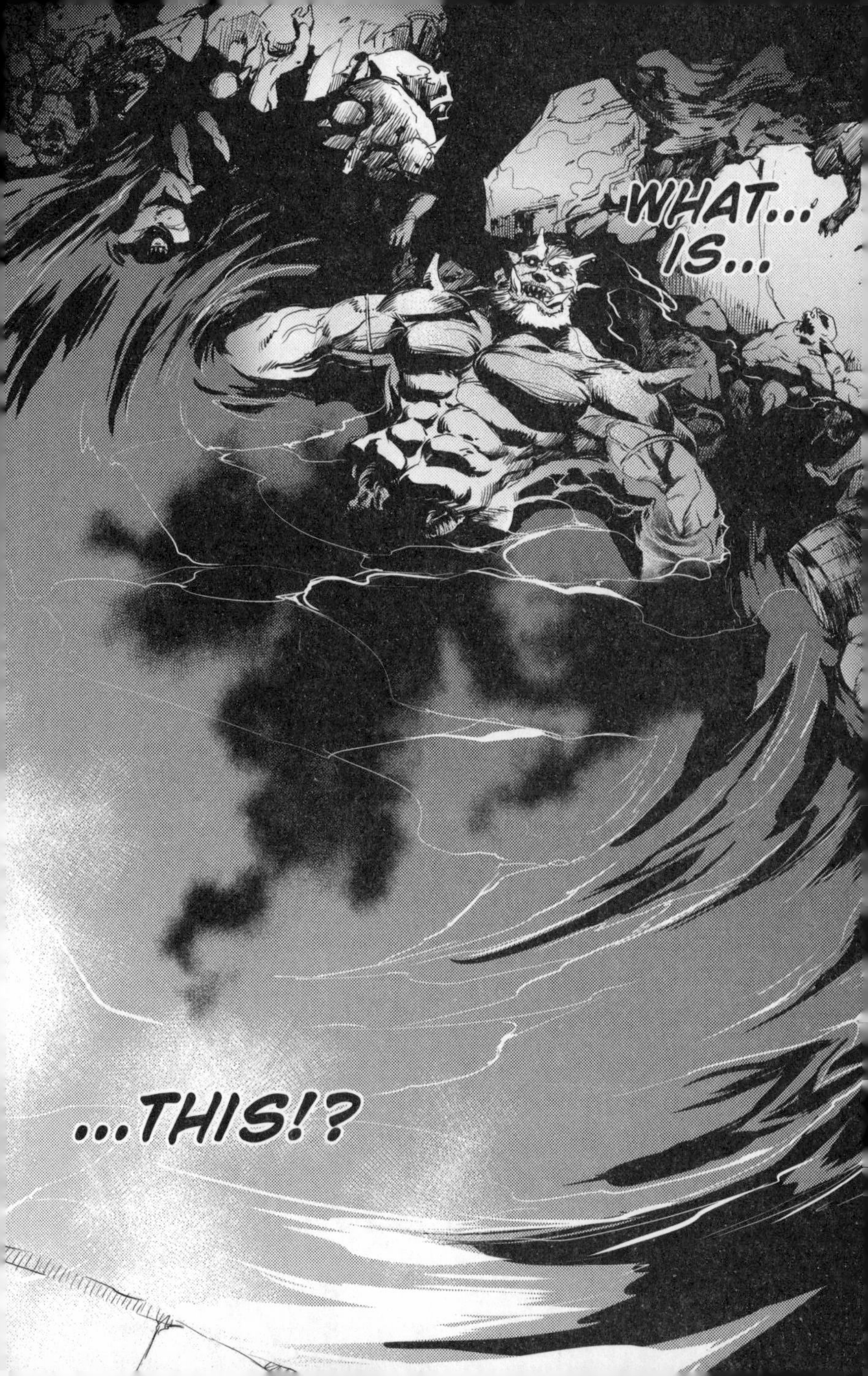
WHAT... IS...
...THIS!?

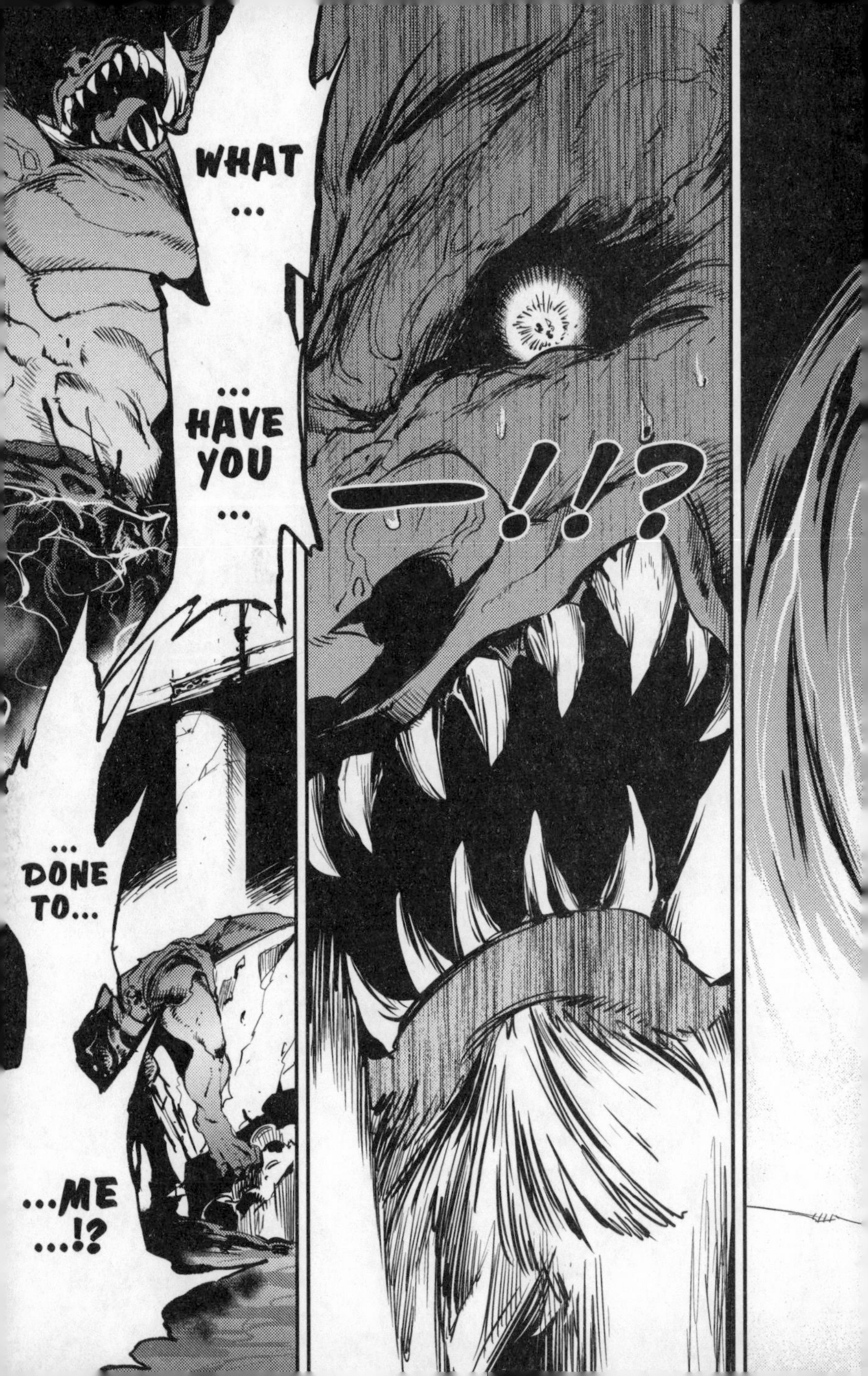
—!!?
WHAT
...
...HAVE YOU
...
...DONE TO...
...ME
...!?

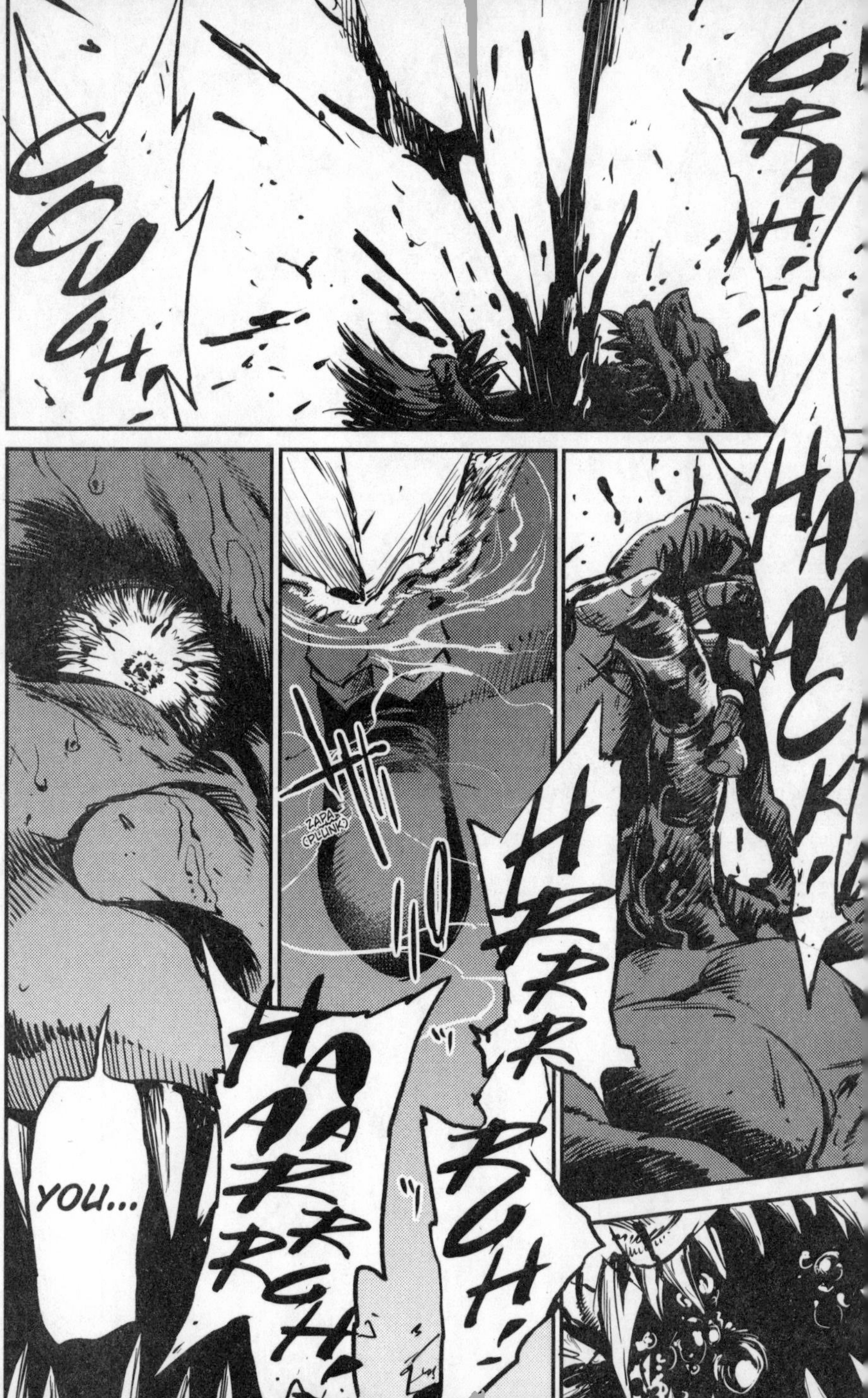
GRAHH!
OUUUH!
HAAACK!!
ZAPA (PLUNK)
HNRRRBUH!
HAAARRRGH
YOU...

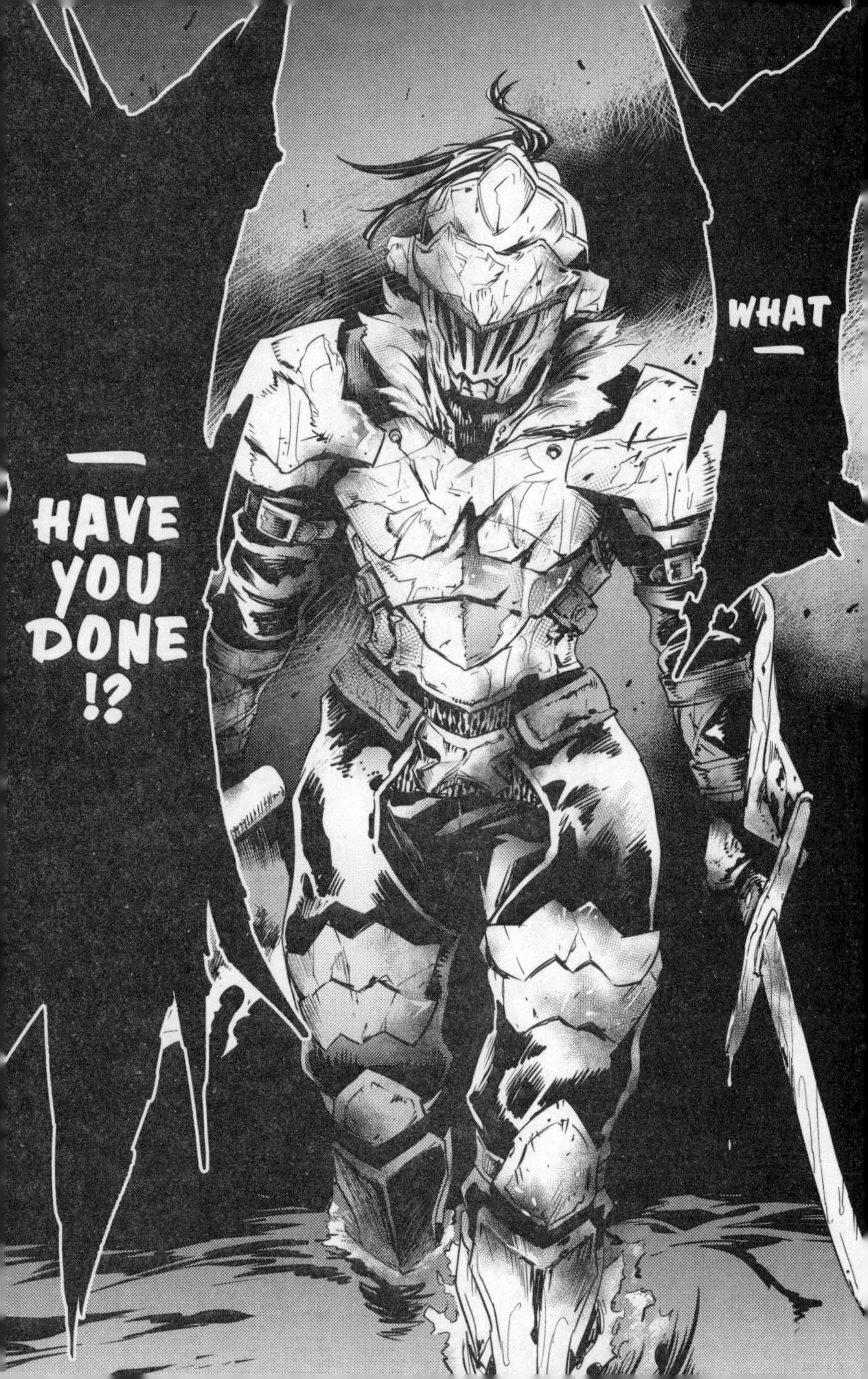
WHAT—
—HAVE YOU DONE !?

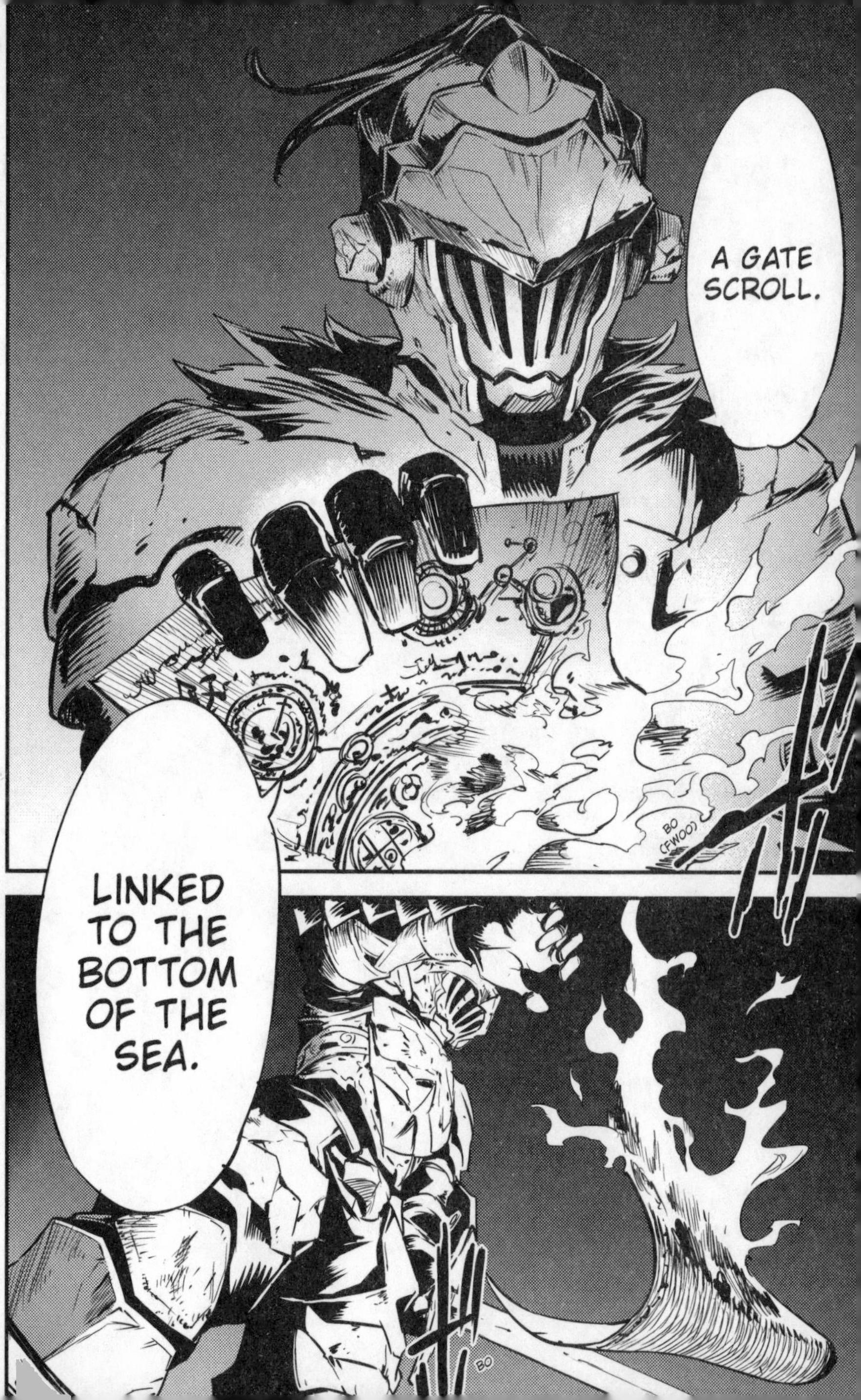
A GATE SCROLL.
BO (FWOO)
LINKED TO THE BOTTOM OF THE SEA.
BO

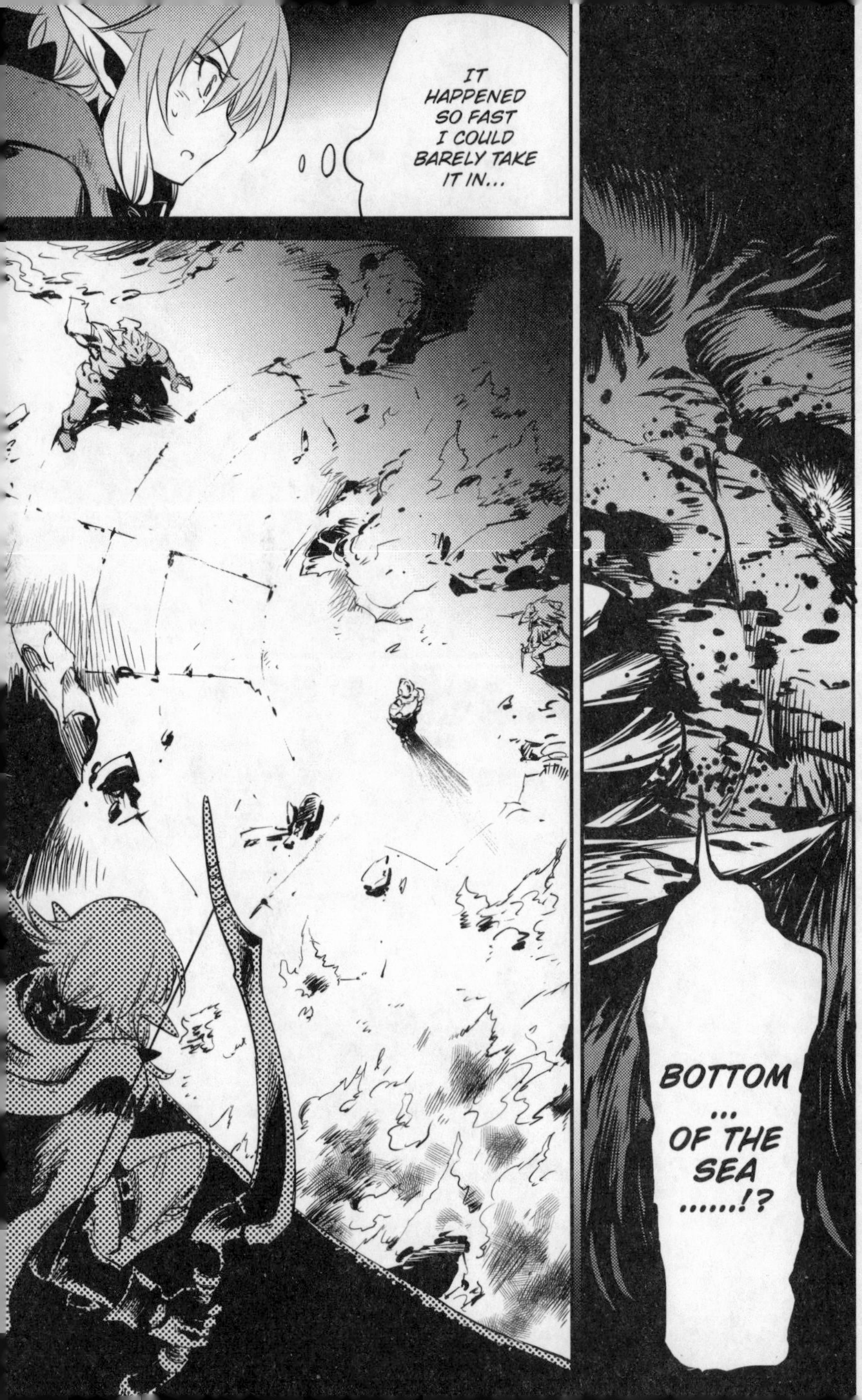
BOTTOM ... OF THE SEA ......!?
IT HAPPENED SO FAST I COULD BARELY TAKE IT IN...

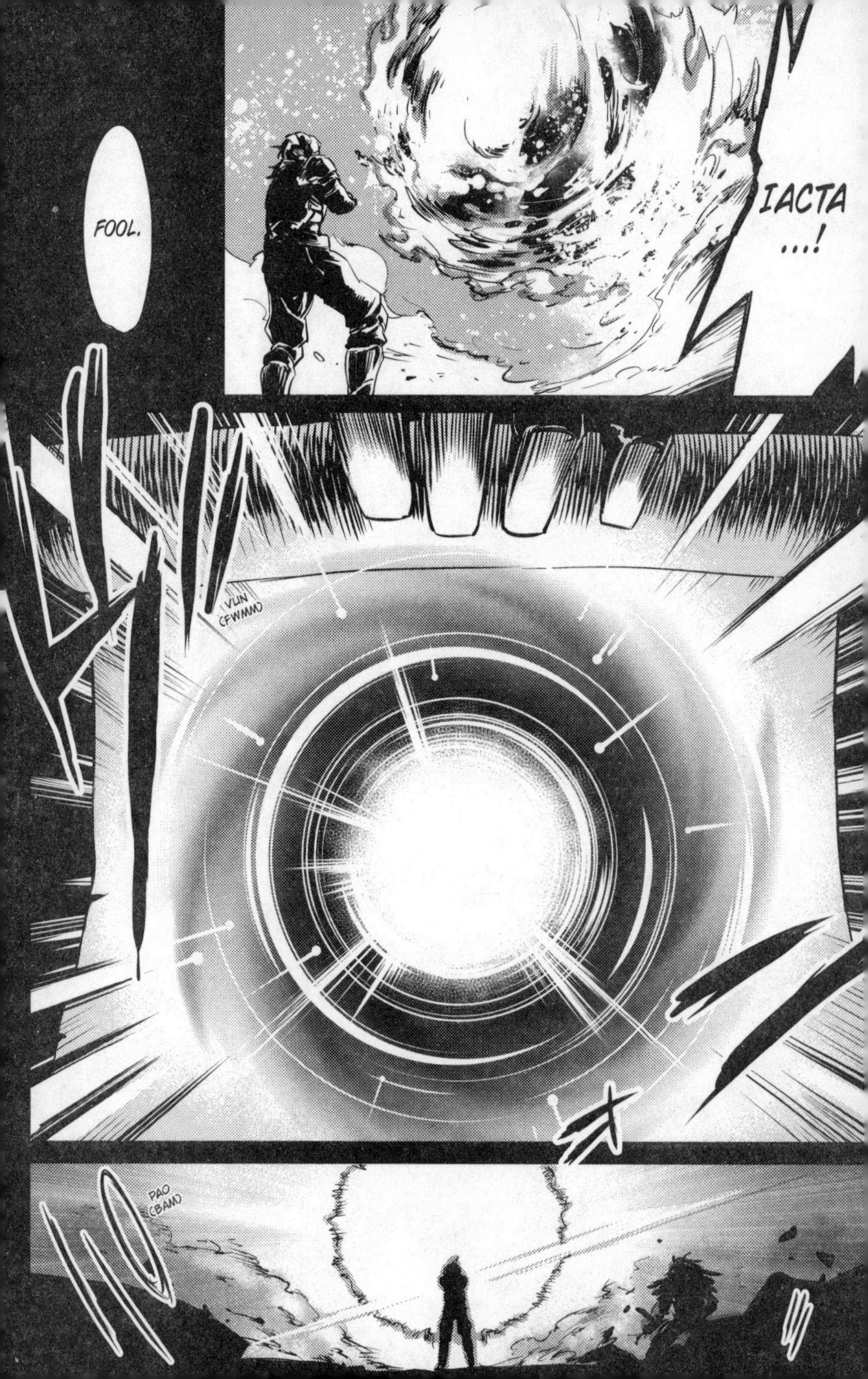
IACTA ...!
FOOL.
VUN (FWMM)
PAO (BAM)

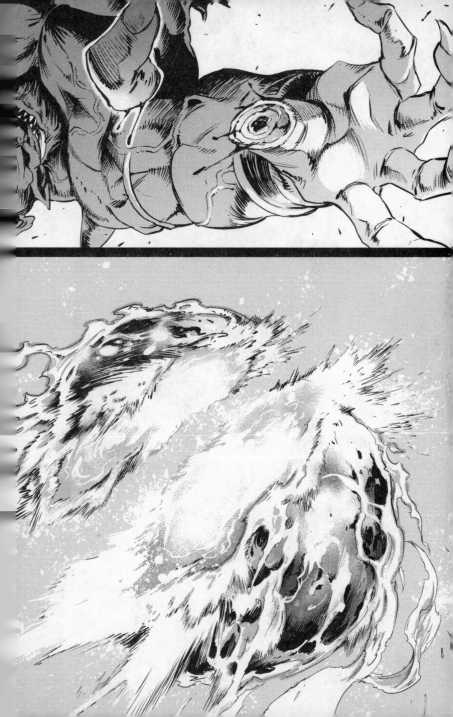

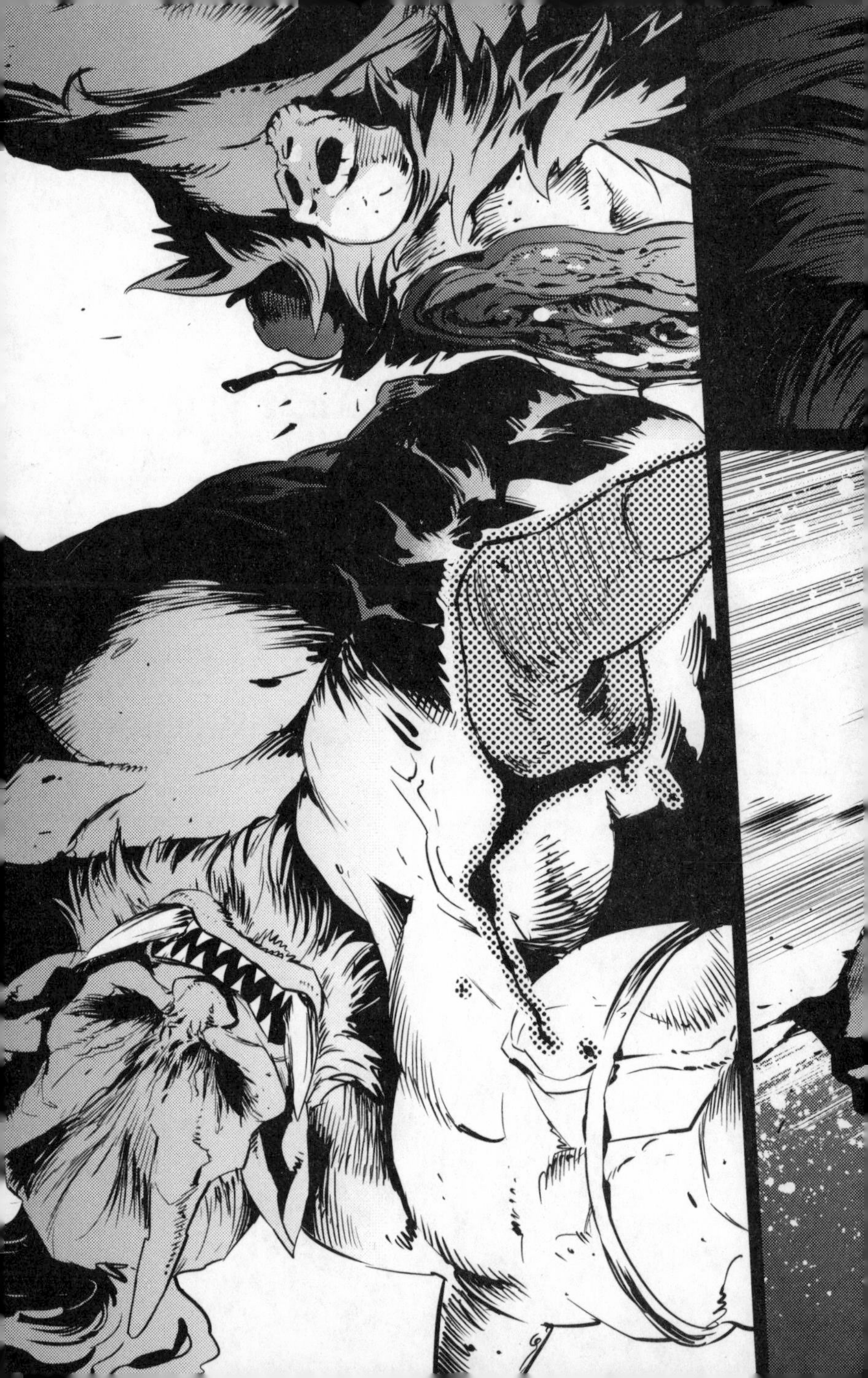

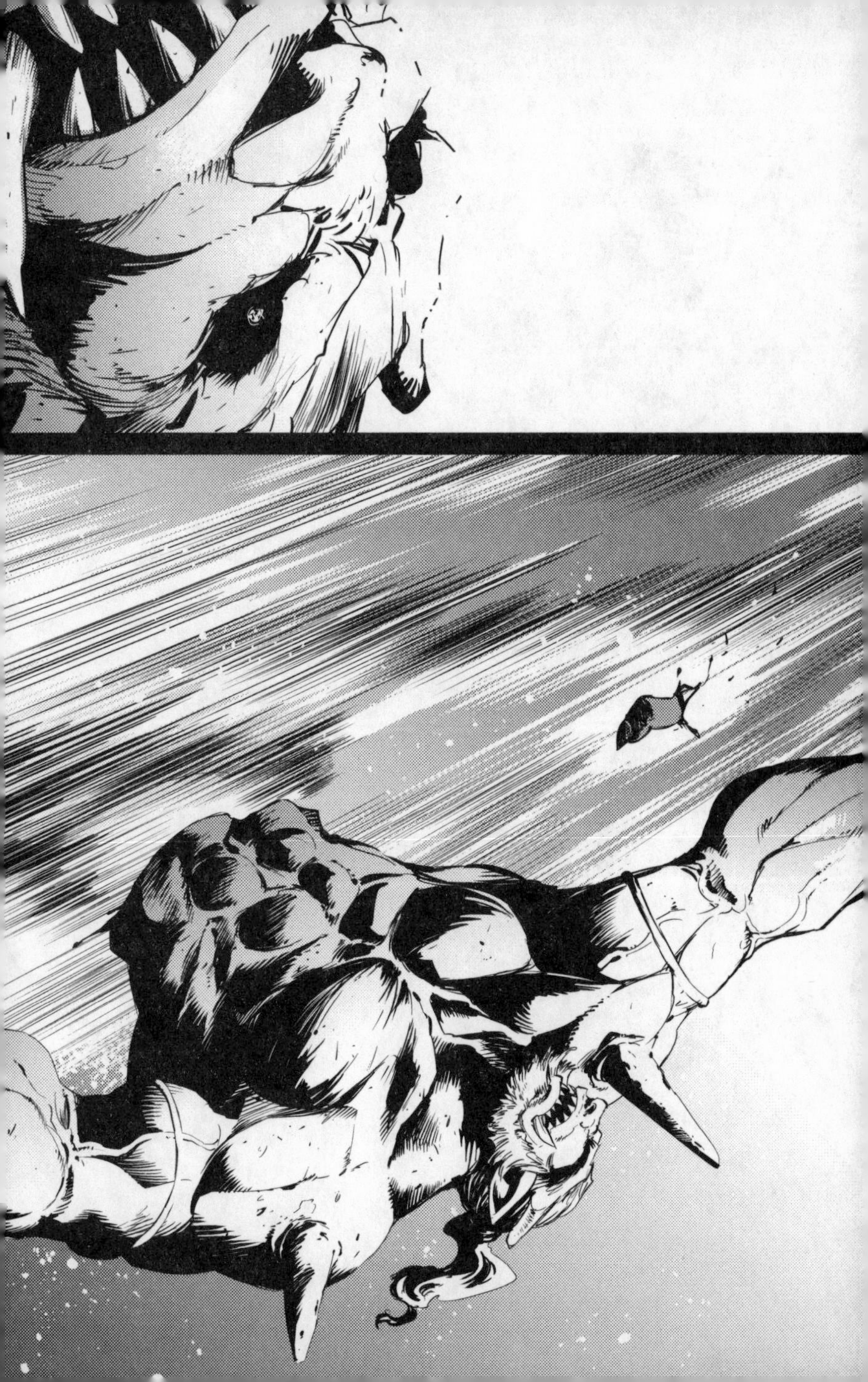

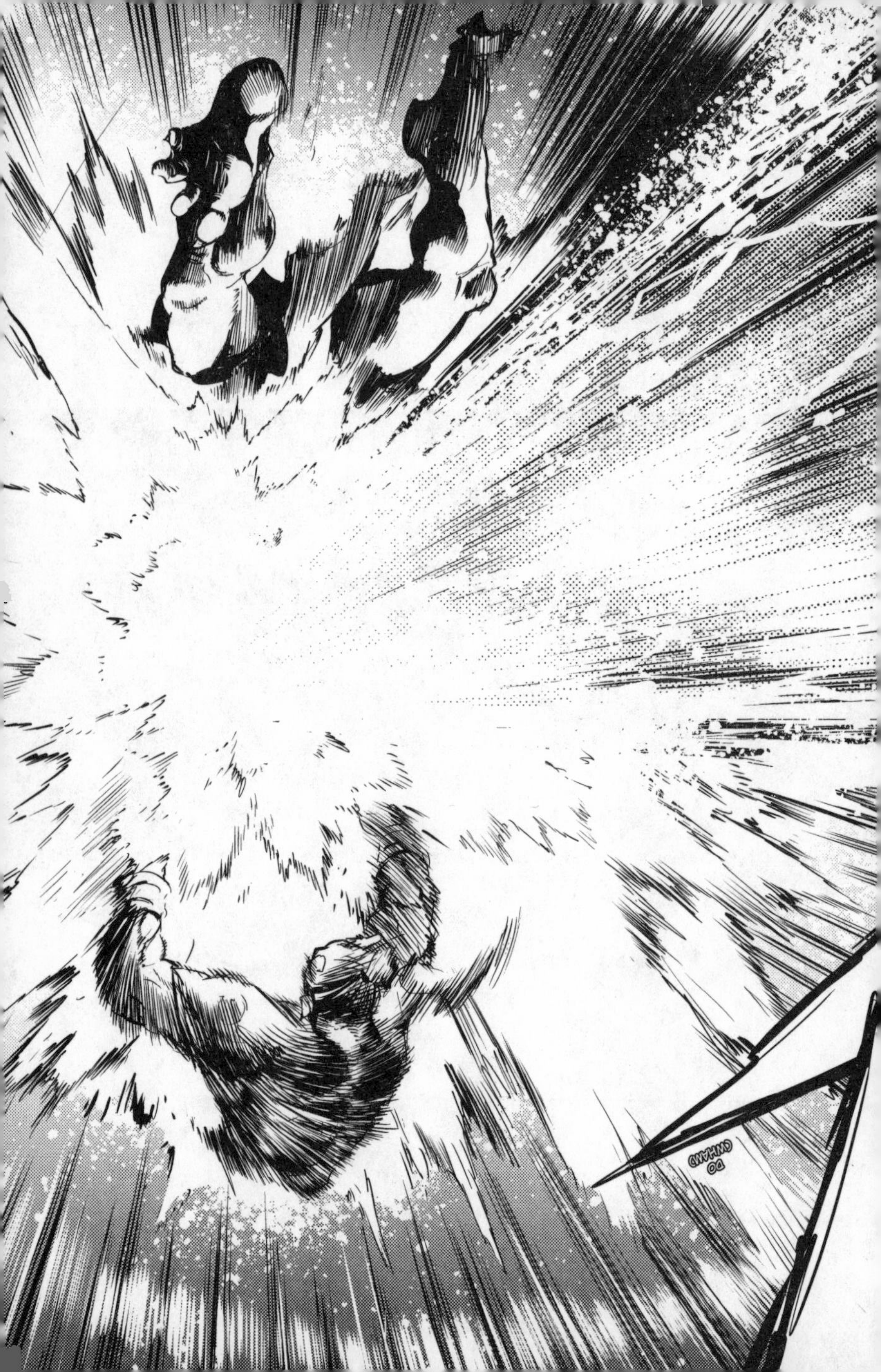
DO
(WHAM)

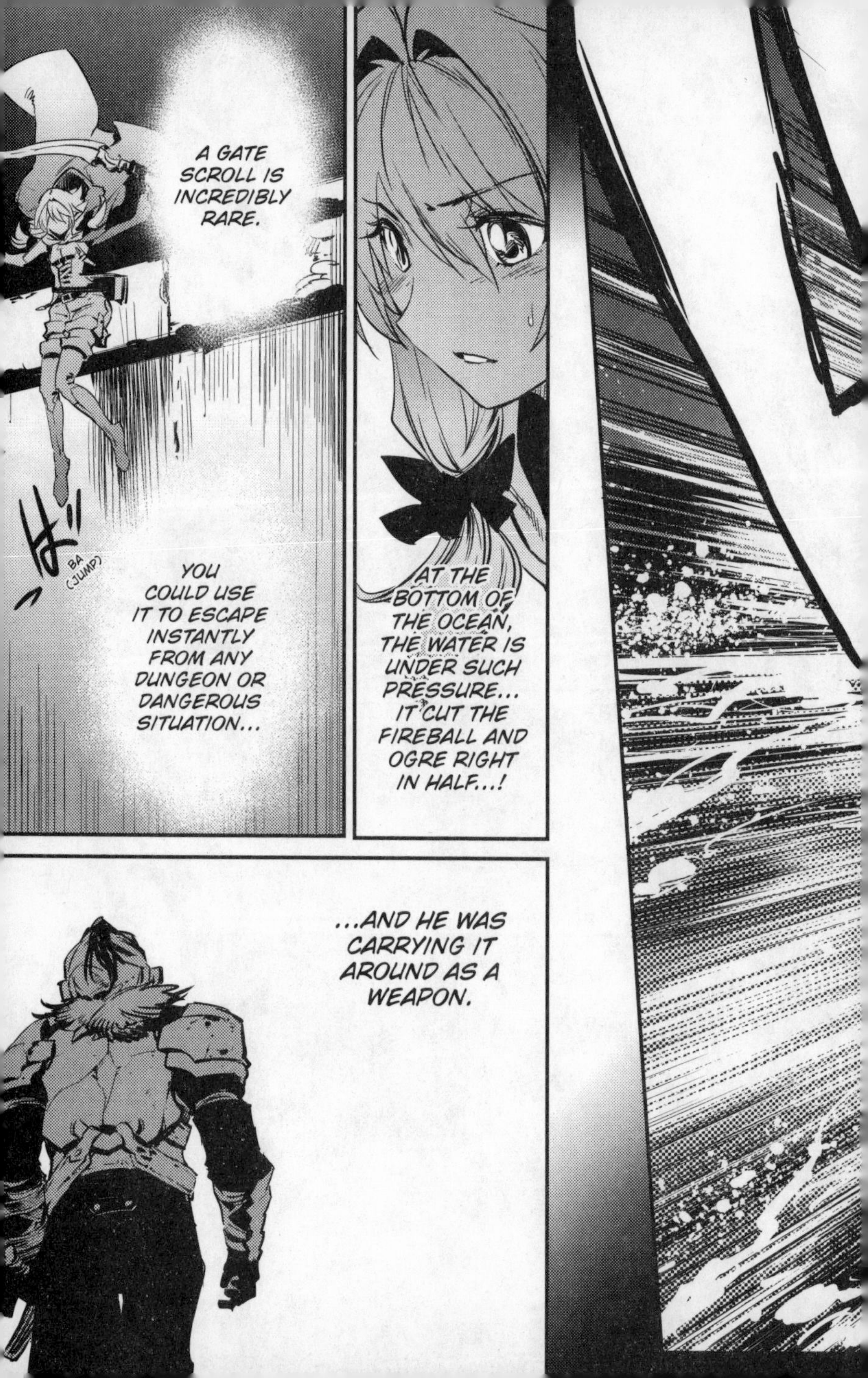
AT THE BOTTOM OF THE OCEAN, THE WATER IS UNDER SUCH PRESSURE... IT CUT THE FIREBALL AND OGRE RIGHT IN HALF...!
A GATE SCROLL IS INCREDIBLY RARE.
は
BA (JUMP)
YOU COULD USE IT TO ESCAPE INSTANTLY FROM ANY DUNGEON OR DANGEROUS SITUATION...
...AND HE WAS CARRYING IT AROUND AS A WEAPON.

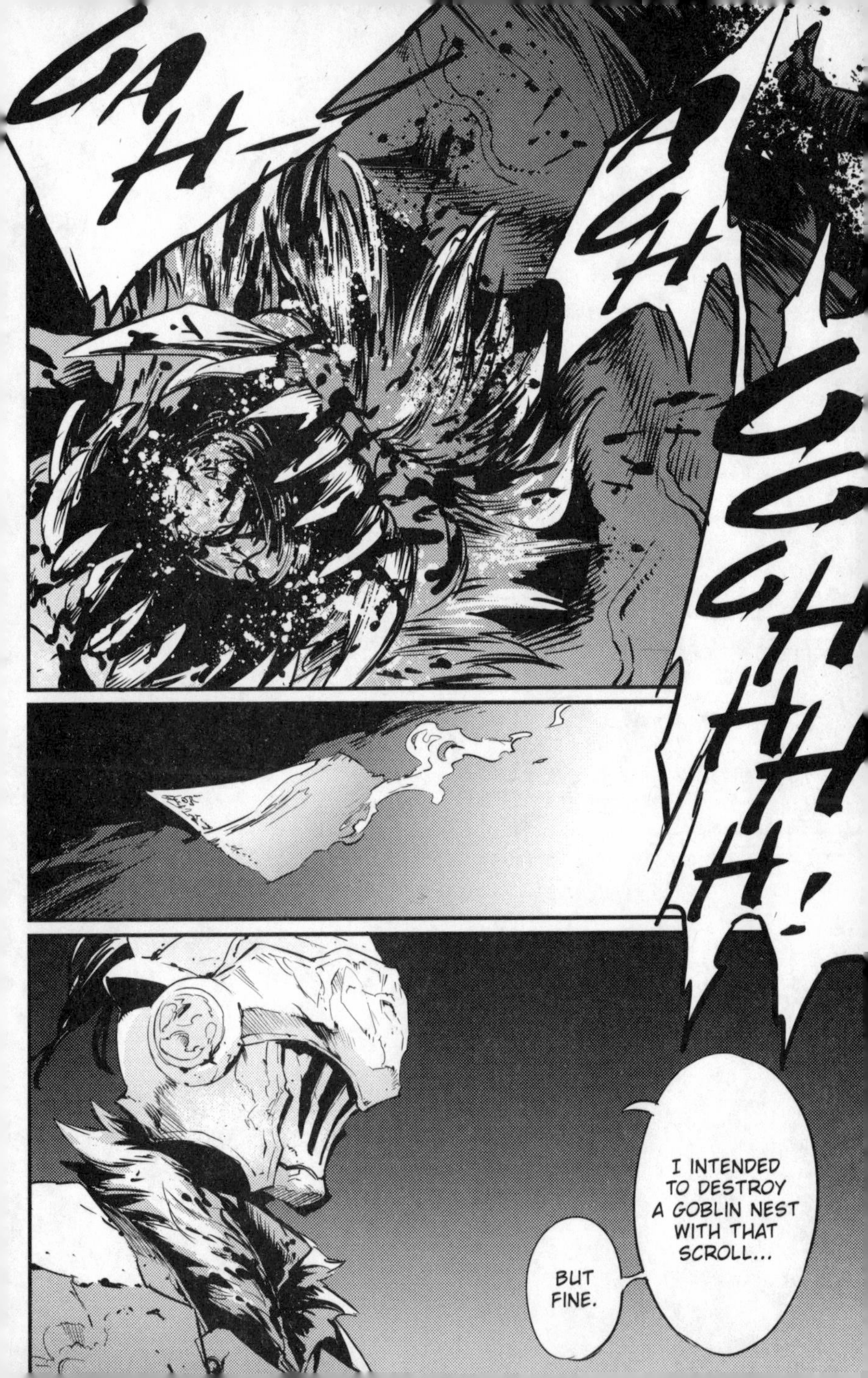
UGAH—
AUGHHHH!
I INTENDED TO DESTROY A GOBLIN NEST WITH THAT SCROLL...
BUT FINE.

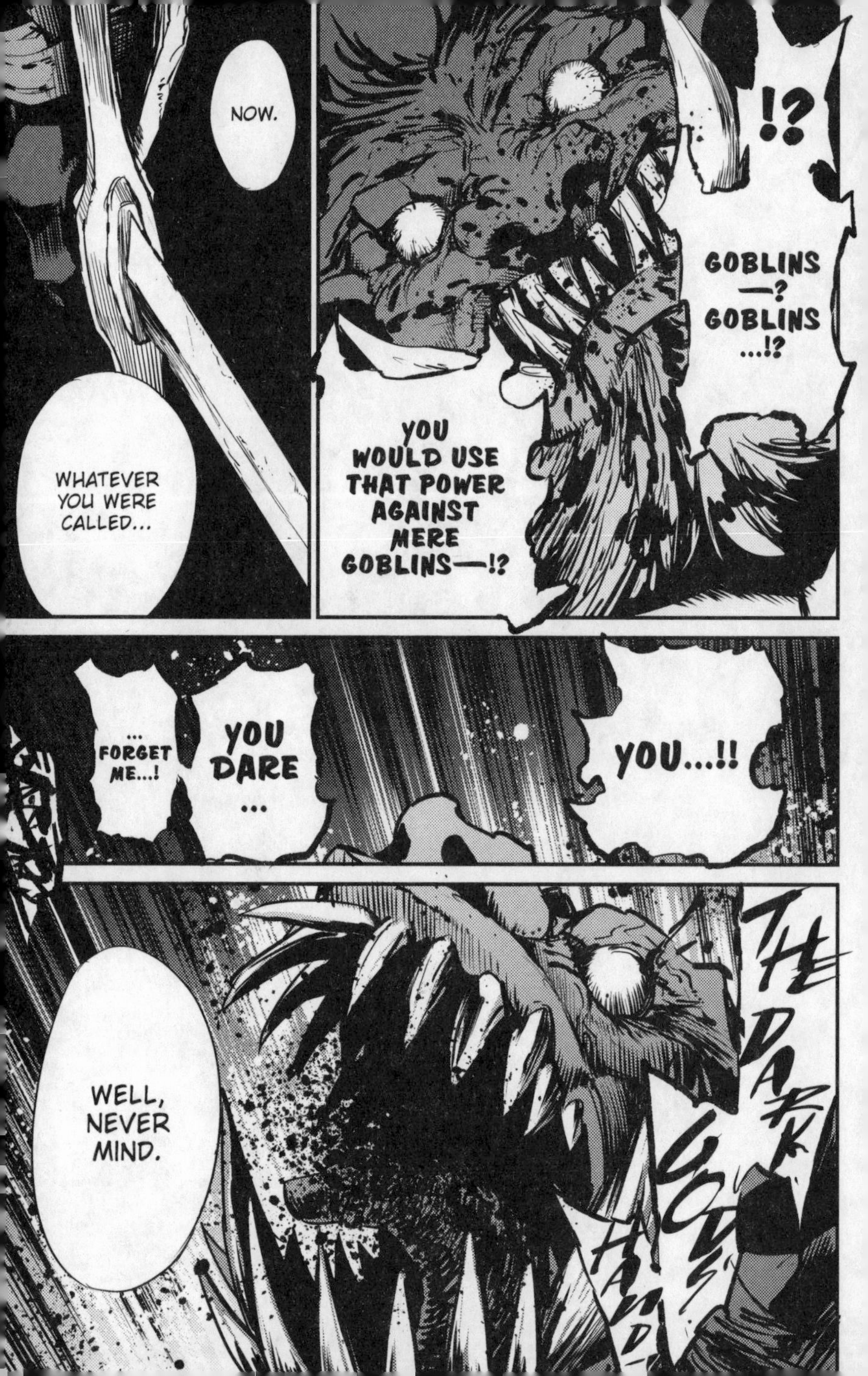
!?
GOBLINS—? GOBLINS...!?
YOU WOULD USE THAT POWER AGAINST MERE GOBLINS—!?
NOW.
WHATEVER YOU WERE CALLED...
YOU...!!
YOU DARE...
...FORGET ME...!
THE DARK ONE'S HAND—
WELL, NEVER MIND.

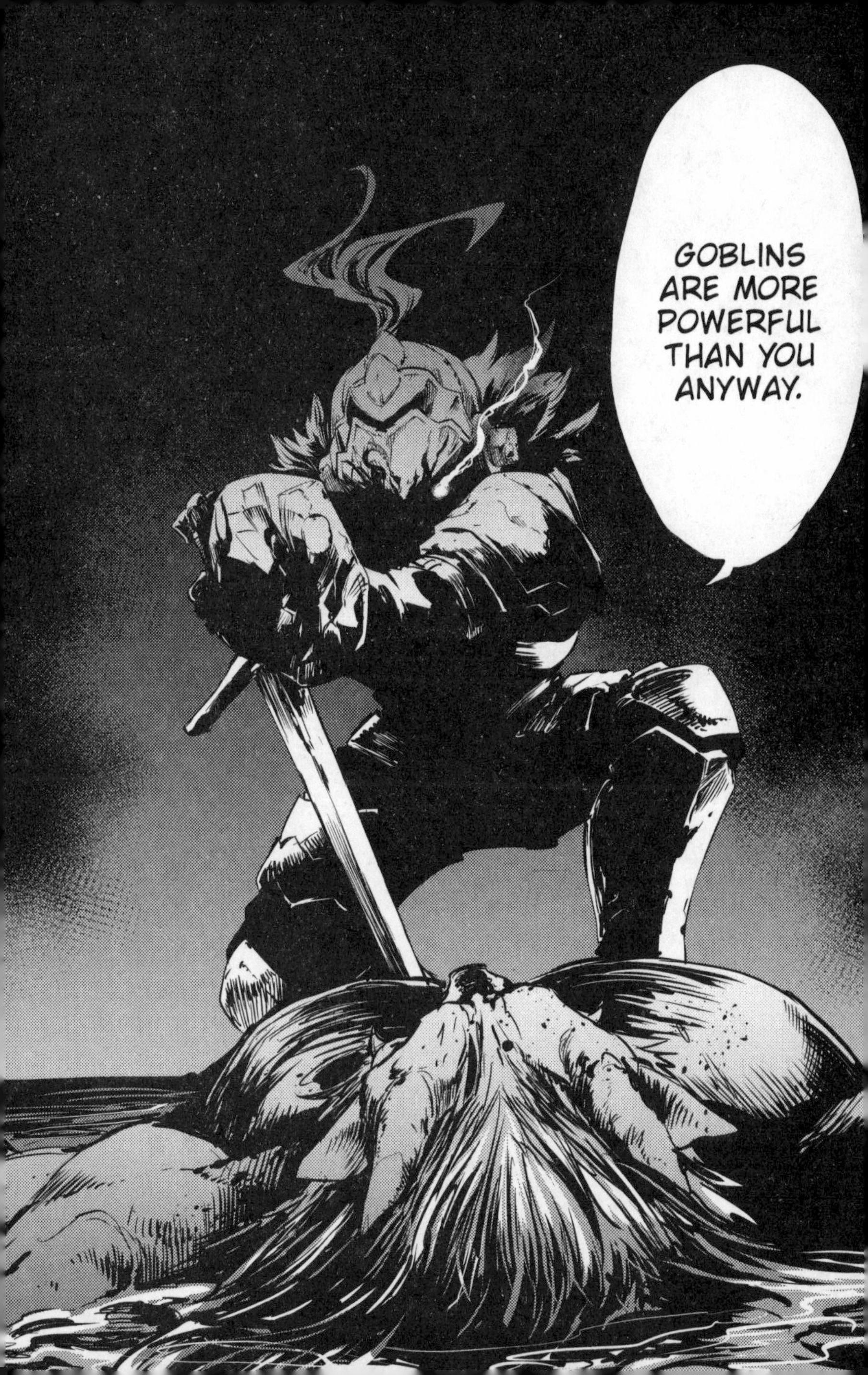
GOBLINS ARE MORE POWERFUL THAN YOU ANYWAY.

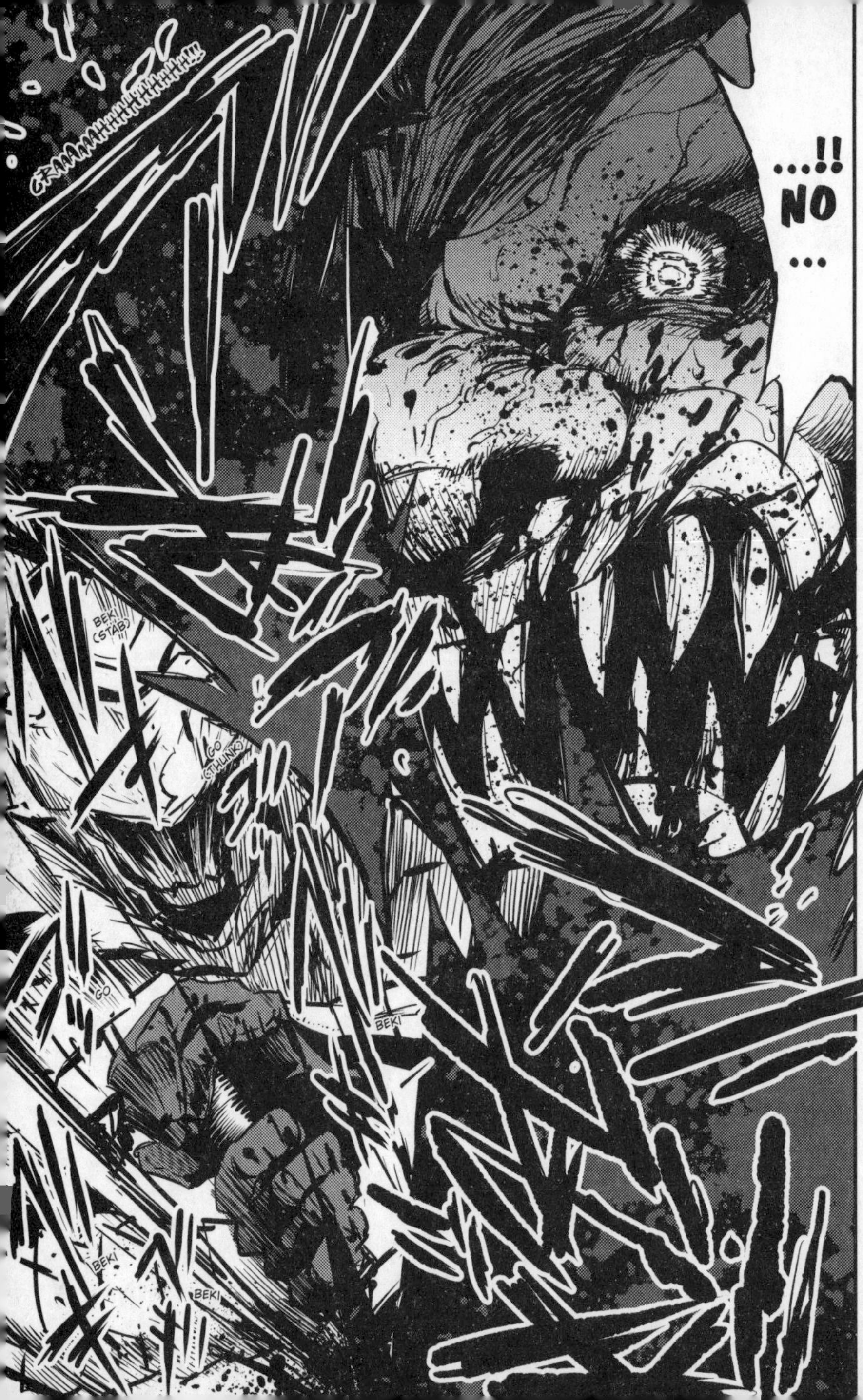
...!!
NO
...
GRAAAAHHHHHHHH!!!
BEKI (STAB)
GO (THUNK)
GO
BEKI
BEKI
BEKI

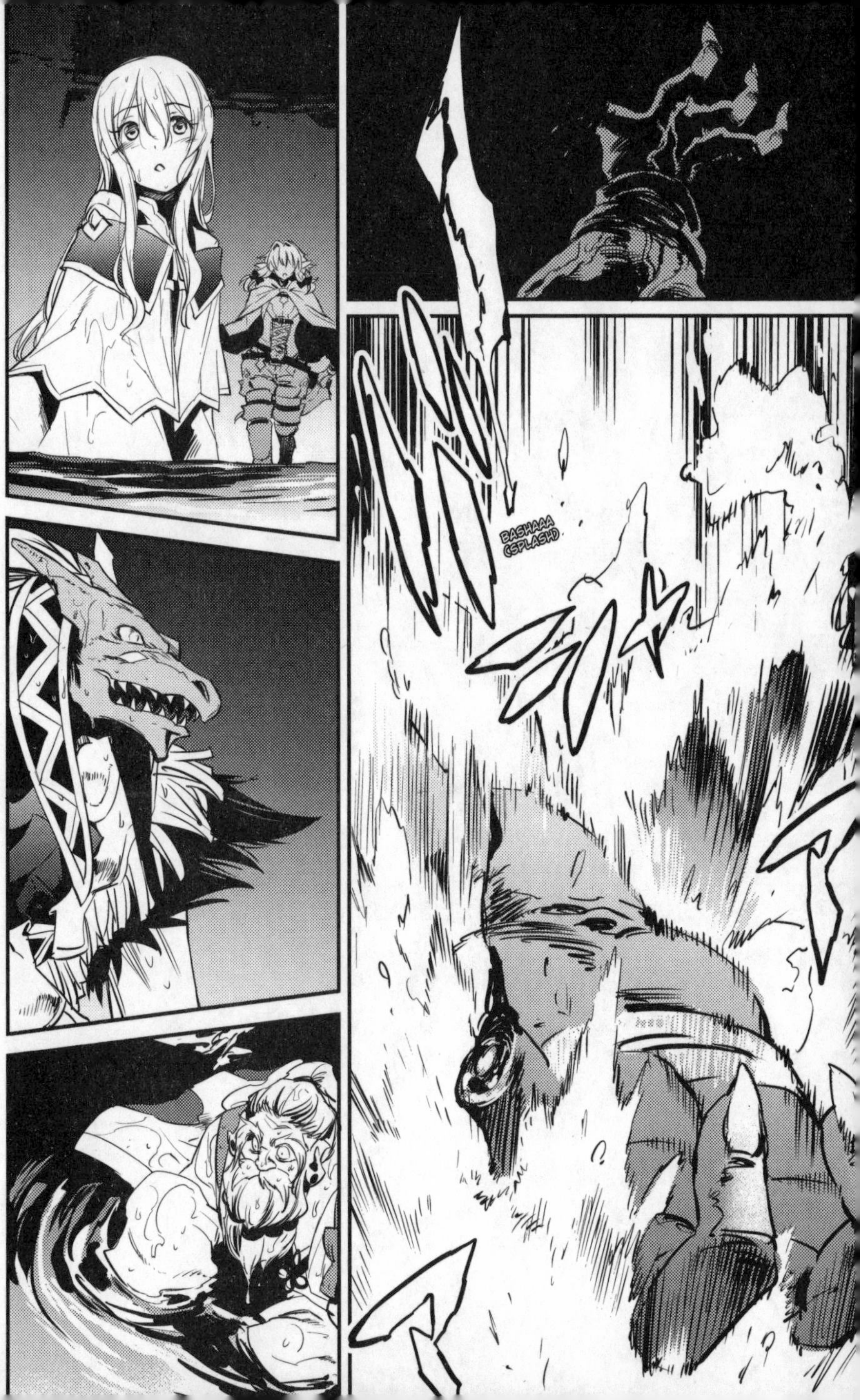
BASHAAA
(SPLASH)

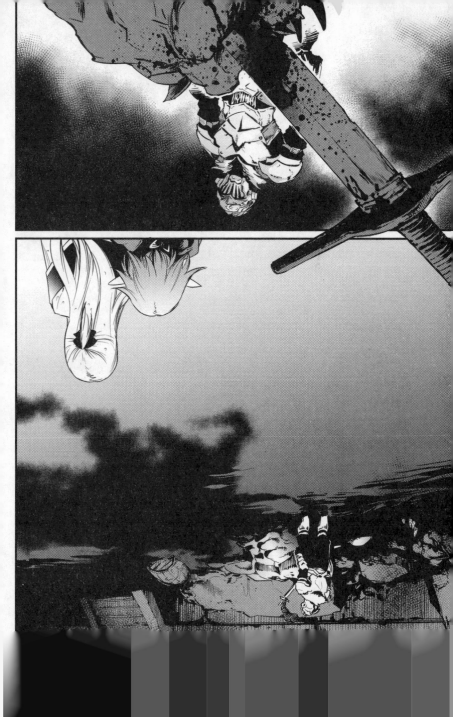

"...BEARD-CUTTER."

LET'S CALL IT A REST FOR TODAY...

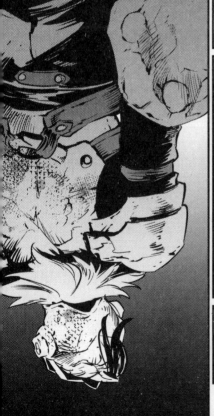

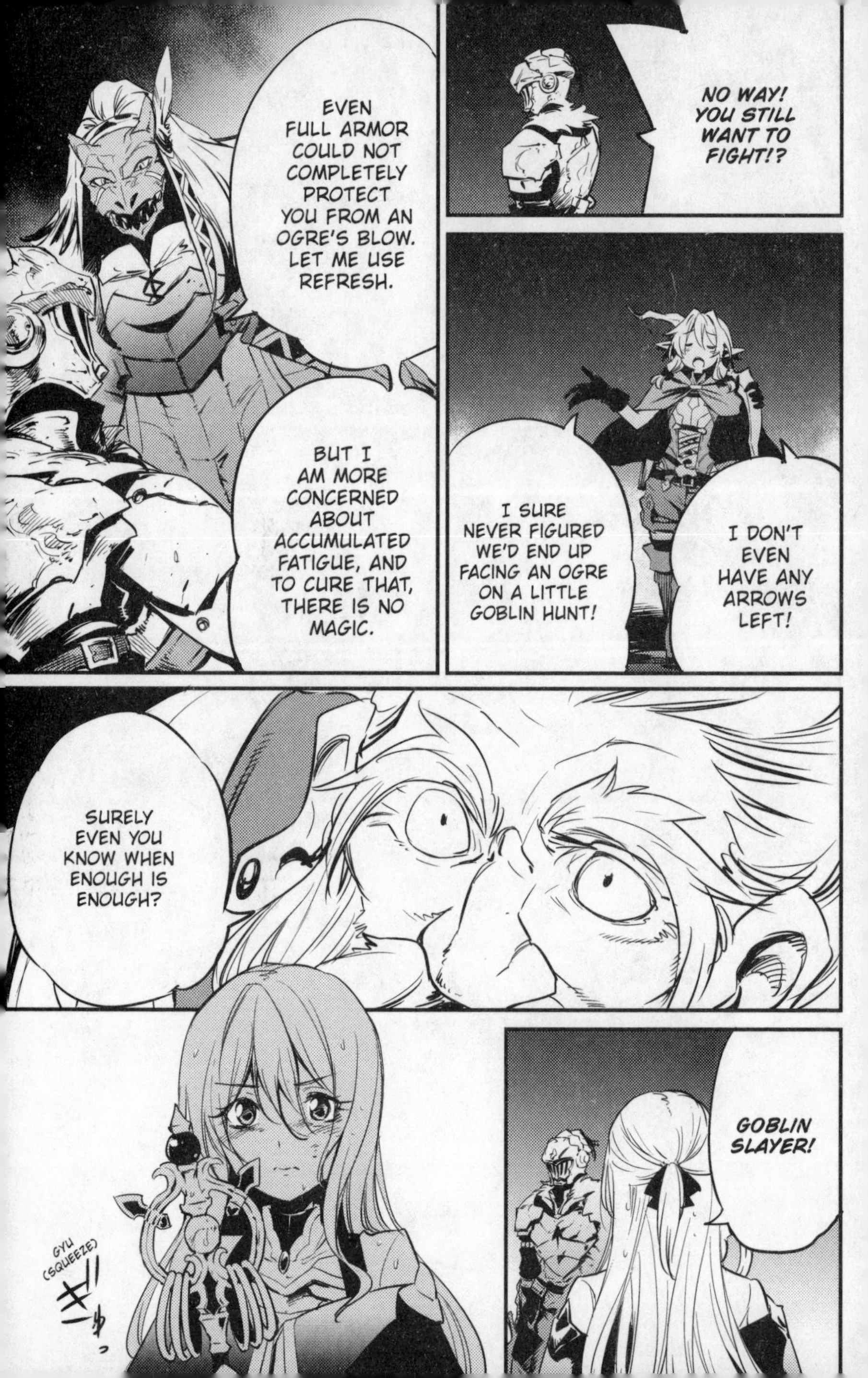
NO WAY! YOU STILL WANT TO FIGHT!?
EVEN FULL ARMOR COULD NOT COMPLETELY PROTECT YOU FROM AN OGRE'S BLOW. LET ME USE REFRESH.
BUT I AM MORE CONCERNED ABOUT ACCUMULATED FATIGUE, AND TO CURE THAT, THERE IS NO MAGIC.
I DON'T EVEN HAVE ANY ARROWS LEFT!
I SURE NEVER FIGURED WE'D END UP FACING AN OGRE ON A LITTLE GOBLIN HUNT!
SURELY EVEN YOU KNOW WHEN ENOUGH IS ENOUGH?
GOBLIN SLAYER!
GYU (SQUEEZE)

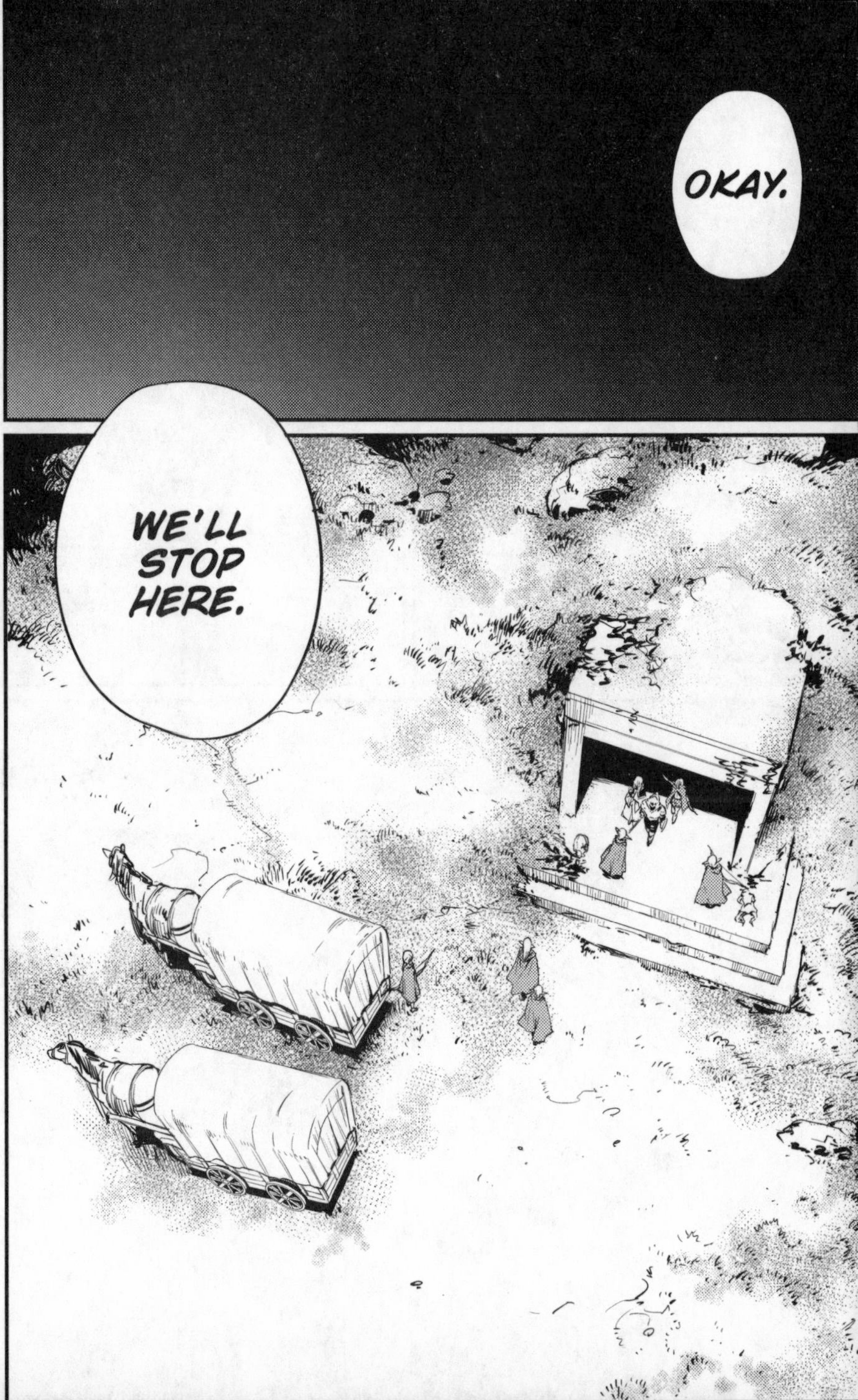
OKAY.
WE'LL STOP HERE.

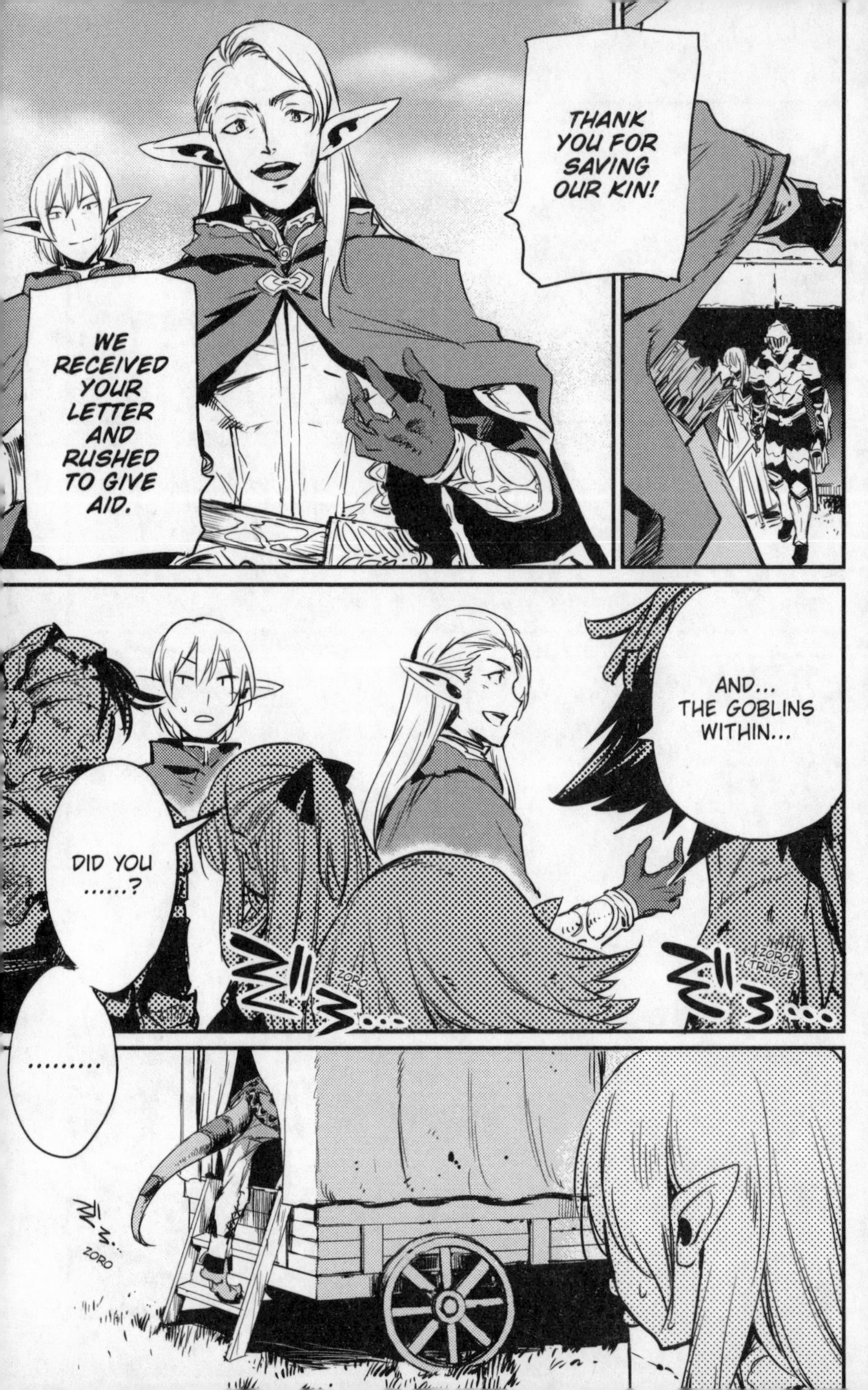
THANK YOU FOR SAVING OUR KIN!
WE RECEIVED YOUR LETTER AND RUSHED TO GIVE AID.
AND... THE GOBLINS WITHIN...
ZORO (TRUDGE)
ZORO
DID YOU ......?
....
ZORO

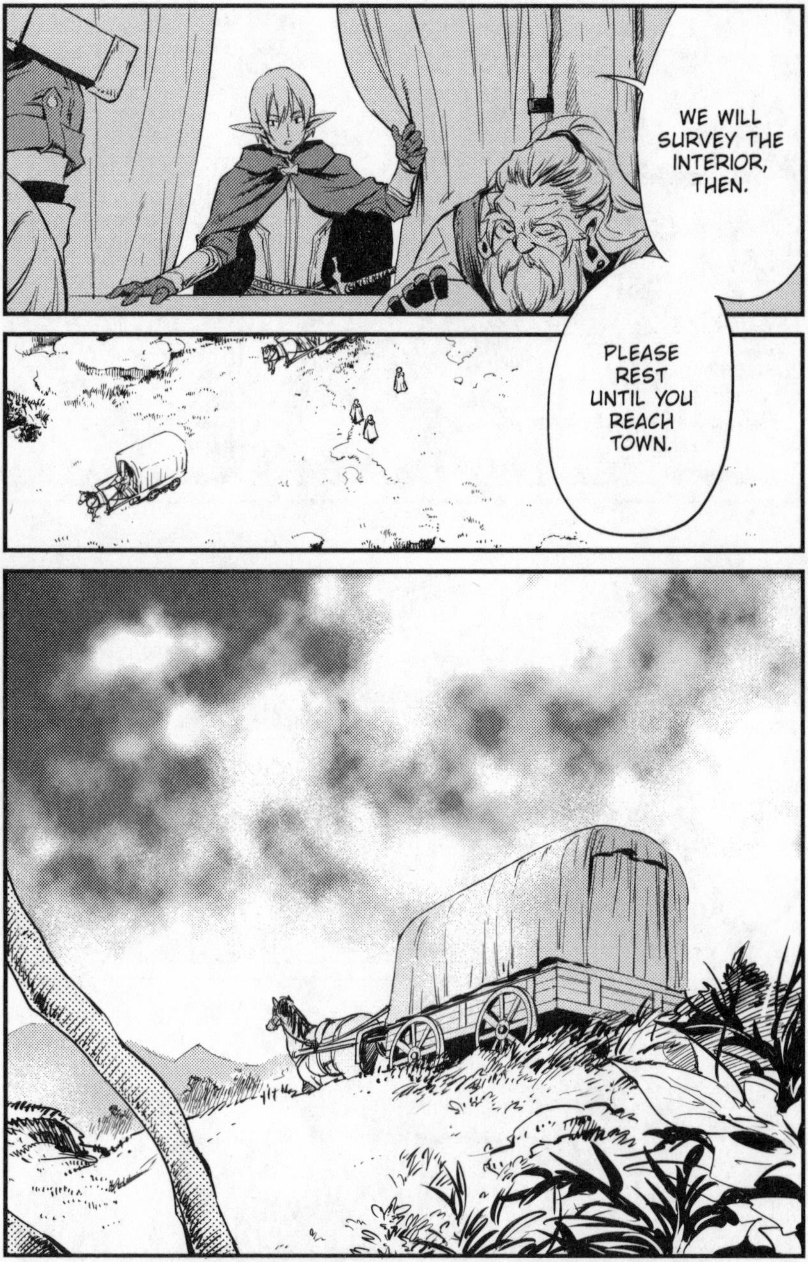
WE WILL SURVEY THE INTERIOR, THEN.
PLEASE REST UNTIL YOU REACH TOWN.

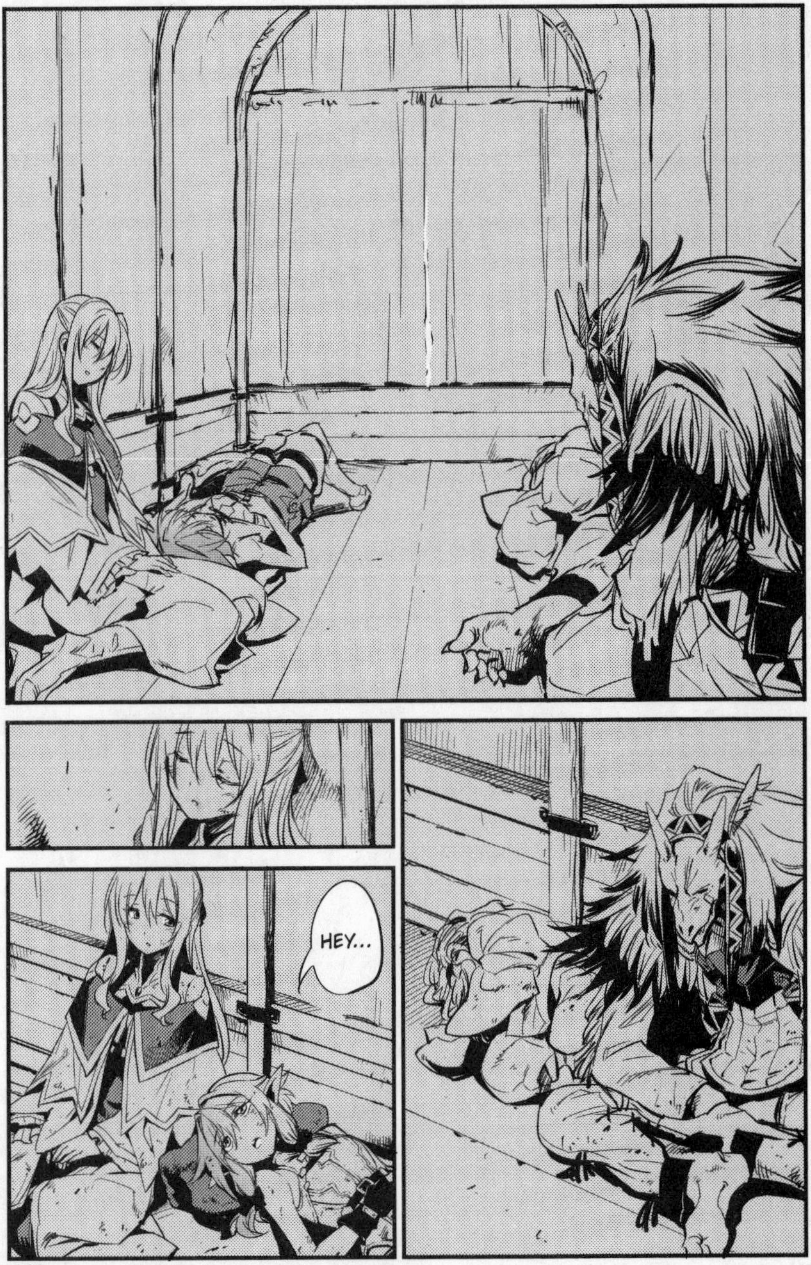
HEY...

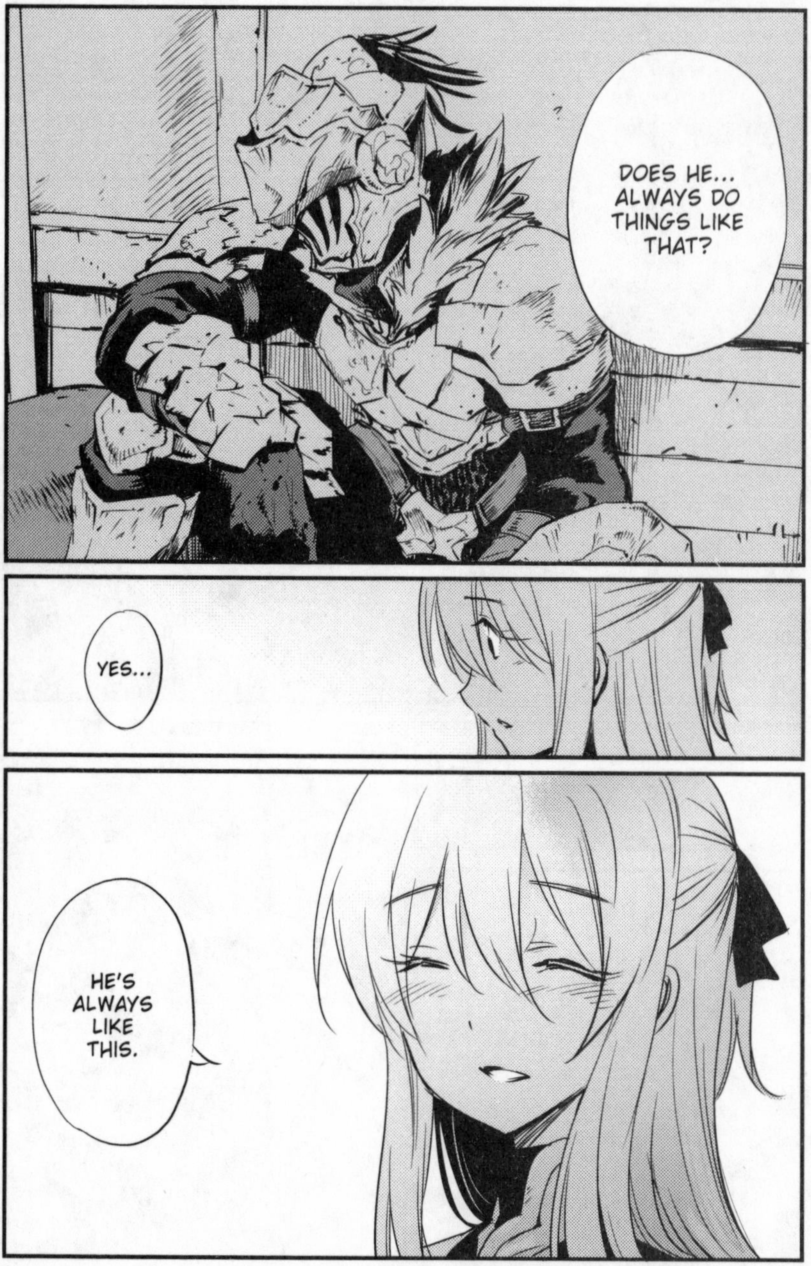
DOES HE... ALWAYS DO THINGS LIKE THAT?
YES...
HE'S ALWAYS LIKE THIS.

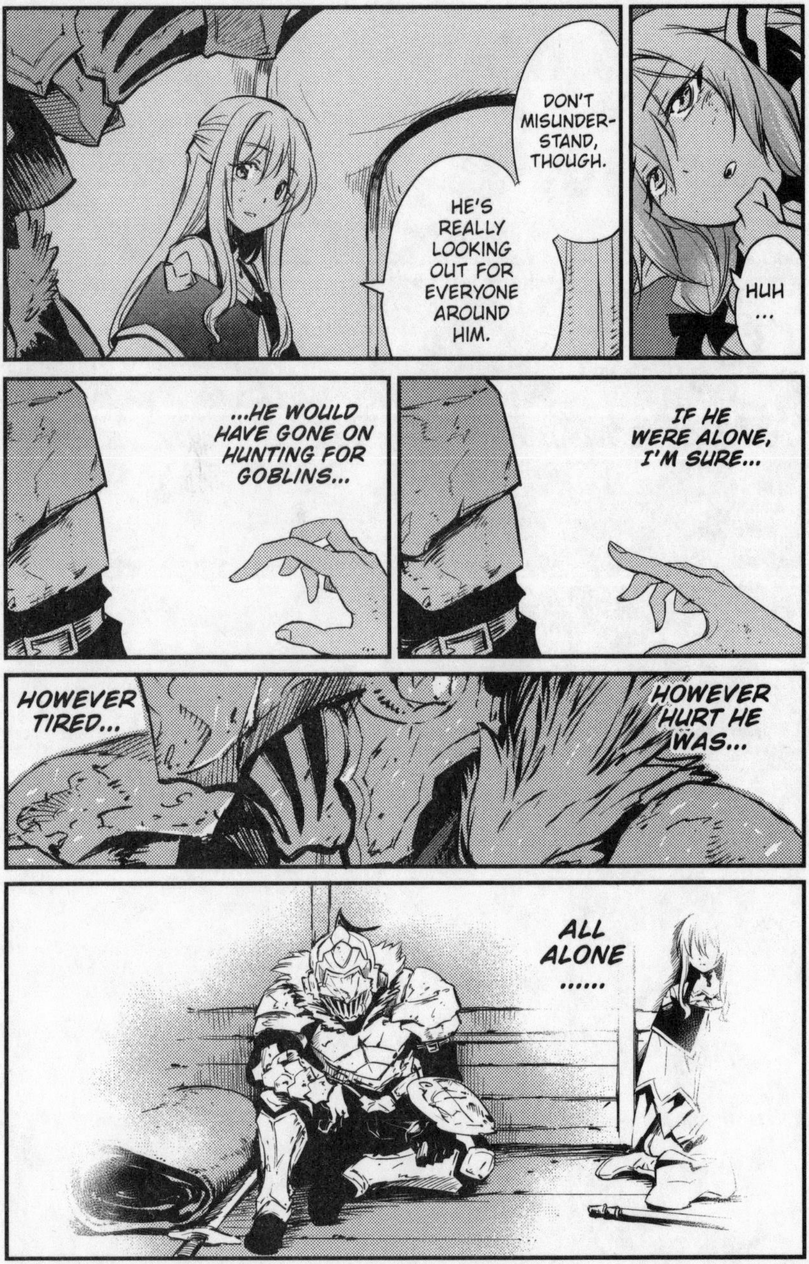
HUH ...
DON'T MISUNDER-STAND, THOUGH.
HE'S REALLY LOOKING OUT FOR EVERYONE AROUND HIM.
IF HE WERE ALONE, I'M SURE...
...HE WOULD HAVE GONE ON HUNTING FOR GOBLINS...
HOWEVER HURT HE WAS...
HOWEVER TIRED...
ALL ALONE ......

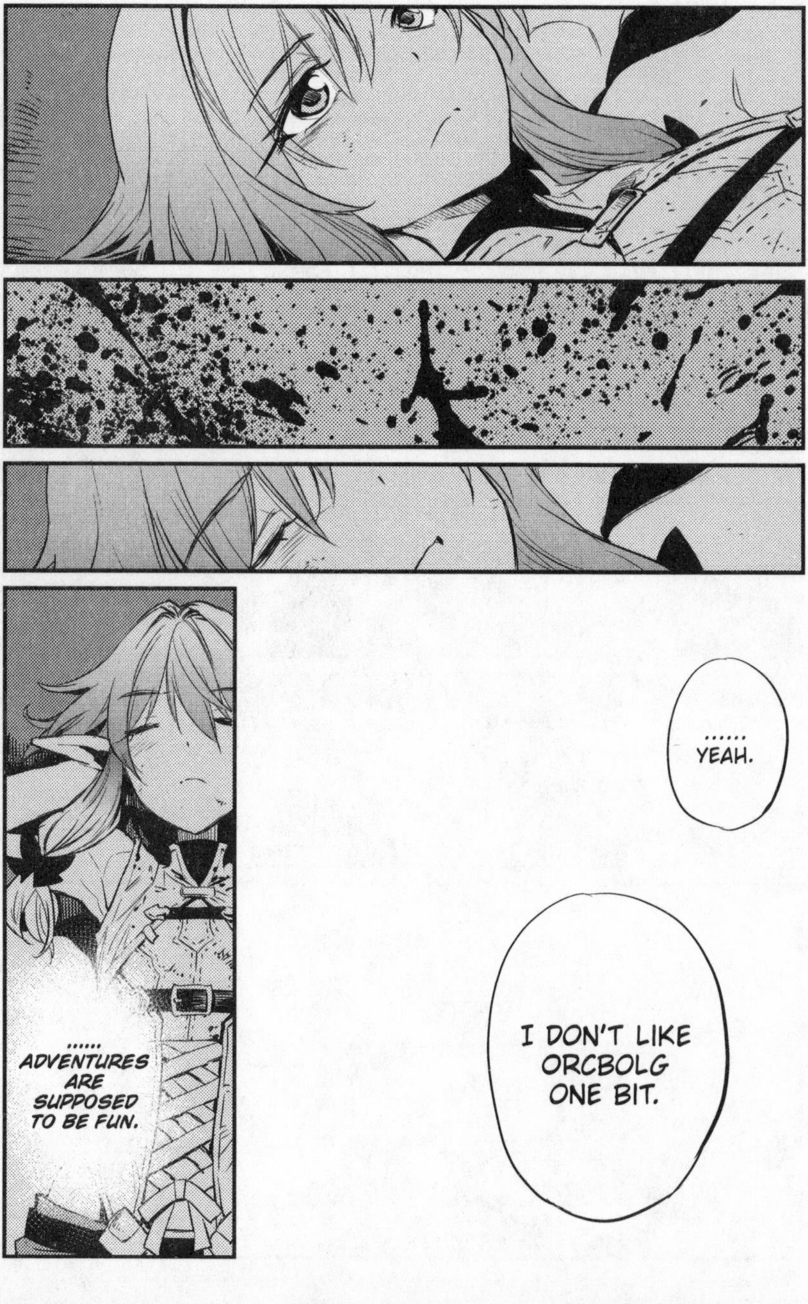
……YEAH.
I DON'T LIKE ORCBOLG ONE BIT.
……ADVENTURES ARE SUPPOSED TO BE FUN.

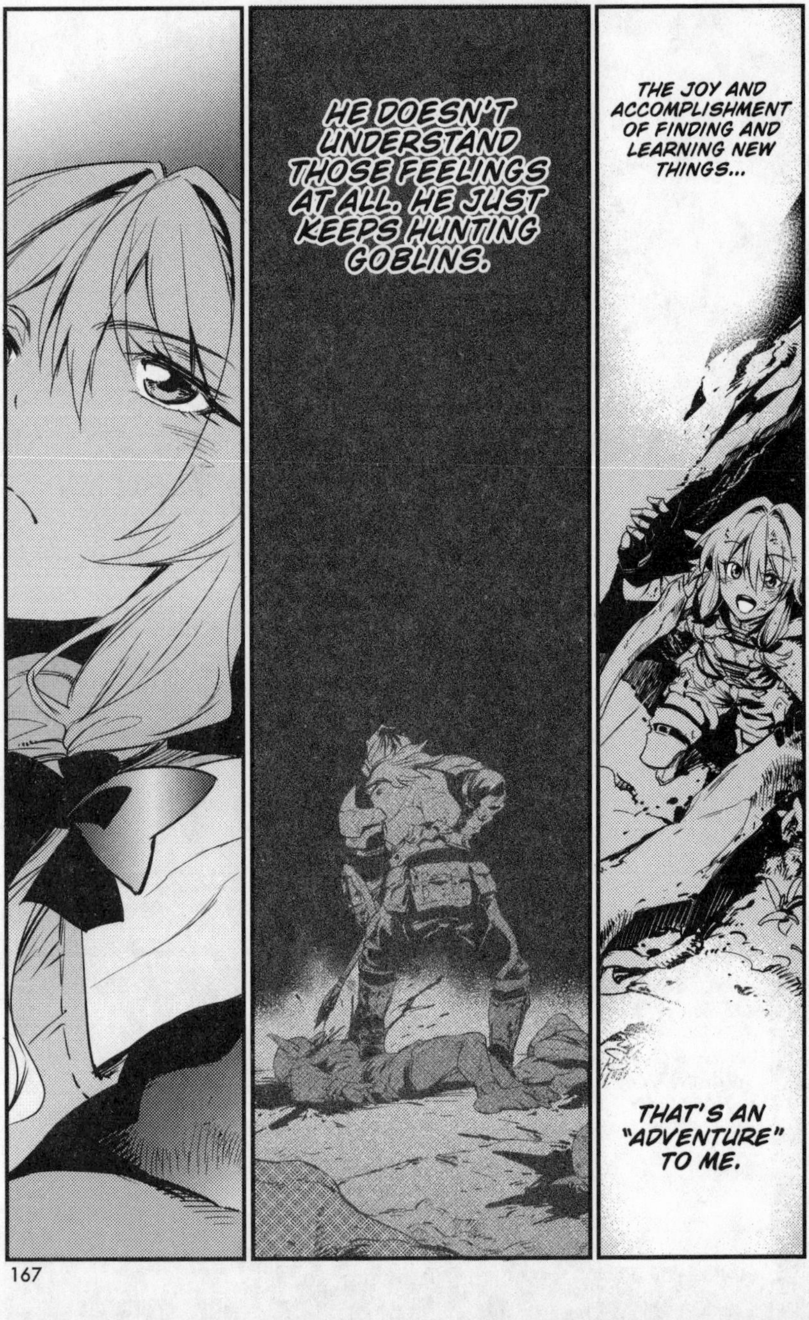
THE JOY AND ACCOMPLISHMENT OF FINDING AND LEARNING NEW THINGS...
THAT'S AN "ADVENTURE" TO ME.
HE DOESN'T UNDERSTAND THOSE FEELINGS AT ALL. HE JUST KEEPS HUNTING GOBLINS.

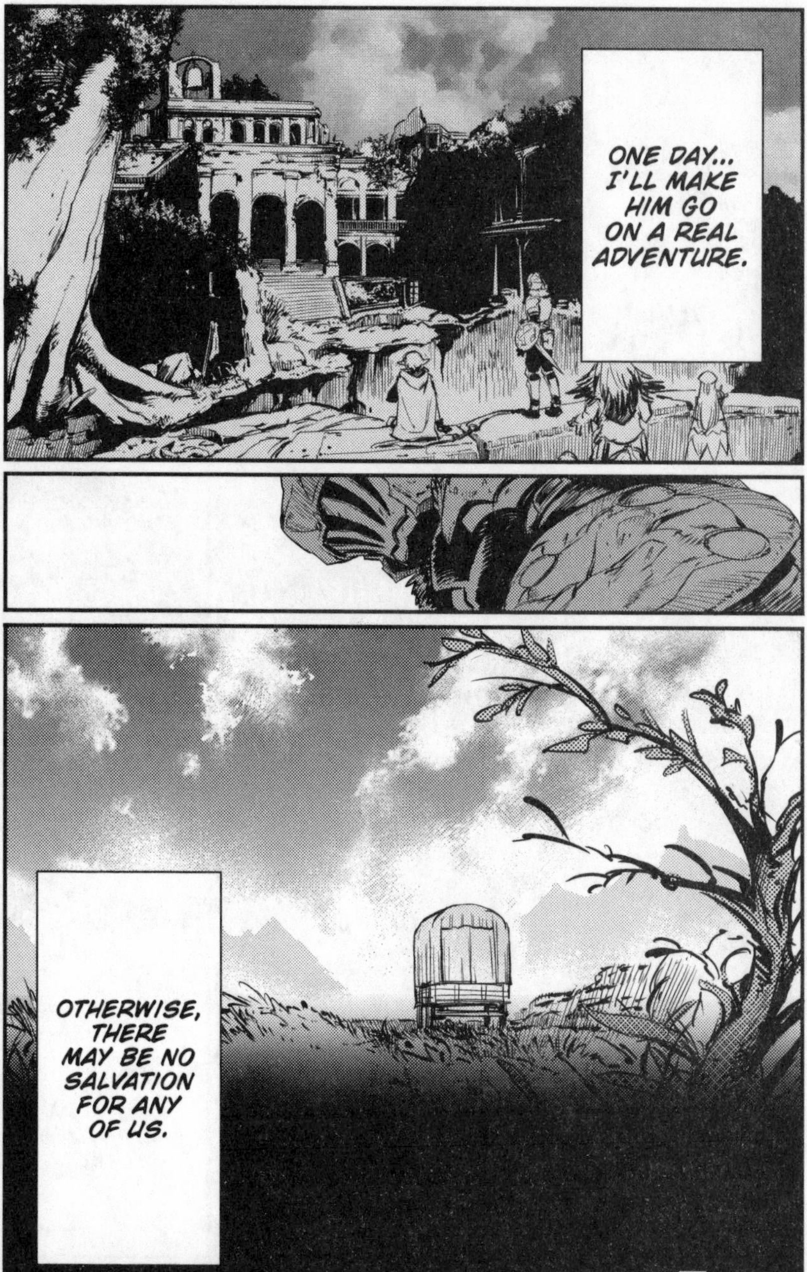
ONE DAY... I'LL MAKE HIM GO ON A REAL ADVENTURE.
OTHERWISE, THERE MAY BE NO SALVATION FOR ANY OF US.
GOBLIN SLAYER 2 THE END

HE DOES NOT LET ANYONE ROLL THE DICE.

A young Priestess joins her first adventuring party, but blind to the dangers, they almost immediately find themselves in trouble. It's Goblin Slayer who comes to their rescue—a man who has dedicated his life to the extermination of all goblins by any means necessary. A dangerous, dirty, and thankless job, but he does it better than anyone. And when rumors of his feats begin to circulate, there's no telling who might come calling next...

Light Novel
V. 1-2
Available
Now!

Check out the
simul-pub manga chapters
every month!

Yen
Press

YEN
ON

www.yenpress.com

Turn to the back of the
book for a short story by
Kumo Kagyu!

GOBLIN
SLAYER

"When the moons," he said, pointing to the sky with one gloved hand, "get to there. Considering the season."

"And then I can sleep through till morning, right?"

"You can do whatever you like," Goblin Slayer said with a long breath. "That's the idea, isn't it?"

"That's right," High Elf Archer said easily and laughed.

Then the adventurer called Goblin Slayer fell silent, the chin of his helmet drifting down.

Maybe he'd fallen asleep. The elf girl gave a small "hmph" and adjusted how she was sitting, taking out her bow. She loosened the string, restringing it with spider's silk as she looked up at the sky, where the moons and stars moved together.

It must be more difficult work than any other, causing the heavens and the earth to turn. Of course, it would take time.

"Well, I can wait," High Elf Archer said lightly. She relaxed and let the feeling of the night seep into her limbs.

The animals were singing, the wind was speaking, the moons were in harmony—and her traveling companions, too. She enjoyed even the sound of their breathing. This was the elvish way of life that she'd found for herself.

in the air. "Everything gets to live once and die once. Maybe its life is a little longer or a little shorter, but it's the same for everything that exists."

"...Is that so?"

"Yeah, it is," High Elf Archer said. For no real reason, a note of triumph entered her voice, and she puffed out her small chest. "So it's best to enjoy it, right?"

"Best?" There was a slight cock of the helmet.

"Uh-huh," the elf said with a nod. She continued melodically, "Flowers bloom, fruit ripens, seeds grow, birds fly, and fish swim." She narrowed her eyes with a chuckle and a placid smile. "If you can just enjoy that, I'd say your life is pretty happy."

"I never thought of it that way."

"Yeah, well, humans can only see what's right in front of them."

She glanced quickly at the grimy helmet. In the reflected light from the fire it looked a gruesome reddish black. The face within must have some expression, but she couldn't see it.

But when he spoke, it was in a clipped tone, almost like an obstinate boy. "And then we move on to the next thing. Until, eventually, we're finished."

"Gosh, I can barely keep my eyes open," High Elf Archer said with a yawn like a cat. Her ears twitched lazily. "Thinking about stuff like this makes me tired... When should I wake you up?"

Goblin Slayer looked up at the night sky. The light of the stars couldn't eclipse the two moons, red and green, that shone among them.

GOBLIN SLAYER

I just don't understand him.

High Elf Archer pulled her legs to her chest and rested her chin on her knees, gazing in his direction. The metal helmet, which hadn't moved, now turned and nodded ever so slightly in her direction. She smiled faintly.

"Take, for example," she said, pointing next to him, "that girl there."

"I don't have anything in particular to say about her."

High Elf Archer giggled with a sound like a bell at the brusque answer.

"You're so devoted to her. I was just sort of wondering why her dear teacher takes such good care of her."

He thought for a moment, then replied briefly, "I have been taken care of by others, in the past. So I thought I should do the same in my turn."

"Huh," High Elf Archer offered. "I wonder if that's just a human thing."

"What is?"

"That sort of...desire to leave some proof that you were alive."

"I don't know if that's what it is." The steel helmet moved slowly back and forth. High Elf Archer watched it with interest. "Do elves have no such desire?"

"It's only natural for the flower to bloom and then spread its seeds, right?" Just at that moment, a spark jumped into the air, illuminating her face. Her long ears, which marked her as an elf, twitched easily. "Wilted flowers, fallen leaves make the world turn. Nothing that exists is meaningless or without value." *Vwip.* Her pointer finger drew another circle every intention of showing him just how good an elf's eye for motion was, but...

"Then let me sleep."

Beside him, Priestess, wrapped in a blanket, was breathing in an easy rhythm. She had followed him around happily all day. She was like a little dog that thought it was an adventurer and would stick by its master. In sleep, everything about her relaxed, and her face appeared more innocent than her years.

There was no mistaking that she was still a child.

Human age just doesn't make sense to me.

With that thought in mind, High Elf Archer glanced at the ground. Lizard Priest and Dwarf Shaman were splayed out, sound asleep. High Elf Archer's long ears twitched in annoyance at the dwarf's gentle snoring.

Well, I guess the only person in this party whose age is easy to guess is the most grown-up——namely, me.

Having reached this conclusion, she spoke again. "Please?" she said in what sounded more than a little like a plea. "Being up all by myself is boring. Come on, just a little...!"

Goblin Slayer sat up wordlessly. He never took off his armor, even when he slept. High Elf Archer had grown tired of that habit——and there was something else that exasperated her, too.

"How can you possibly get any rest like that?" she had asked him, to which he'd replied, *"I loosen the fasteners."*

Sure, great. Loosen the fasteners. And how did that help with getting any rest?

But what really bothered her was that this man seemed to *think* he was getting rest.

GOBLIN SLAYER

Interlude:
Of a Night Camp – by Kumo Kagyu

"Hey, you awake? You are, aren't you?"

Pop, pop. Sparks crackled and danced weakly. In the sky were the stars and the two moons. In the spreading field was very little to distract from the view; the night was deep and vast.

They had spent an entire day walking across that field, the second day now not quite over.

High Elf Archer called out to the armored man near a tree, sword in hand.

"...Goblins?" Goblin Slayer said in a terribly quiet voice.

"No!"

"...Weren't we going to take the watch in shifts?" The words seemed to come from a hollow suit of armor. There wasn't the slightest motion, and High Elf Archer squeaked.

But fearlessness was, in her own estimation, one of her strong points. She swallowed with a gulp.

"L-let's talk."

To this Goblin Slayer responded coldly, "The spell casters must rest. Thus, the warrior and ranger will take turns on guard. I believe that's what we decided."

"I know that." High Elf Archer drew a circle in the air with her finger, unsure what to say.

The plan had been for her to take the earlier shift, him the later. She had been ready to play rock-paper-scissors for it if it came to that, but he'd agreed readily. She'd had

GOBLIN SLAYER 2

Original Story: Kumo Kagyu
Art: Kousuke Kurose
Character Design: Noboru Kannatuki

Translation: Kevin Steinbach ✛ Lettering: Bianca Pistillo

GOBLIN SLAYER Volume 2
©Kumo Kagyu / SB Creative Corp. Character Design: Noboru Kannatuki
©2017 Kousuke Kurose / SQUARE ENIX CO., LTD. First published in Japan in 2017 by SQUARE ENIX CO., LTD. English translation rights arranged with SQUARE ENIX CO., LTD. and YEN PRESS, LLC through Tuttle-Mori Agency, Inc., Tokyo.

English translation ©2018 by SQUARE ENIX CO., LTD.

Yen Press
1290 Avenue of the Americas
New York, NY 10104

Visit us at yenpress.com
facebook.com/yenpress
twitter.com/yenpress
yenpress.tumblr.com
instagram.com/yenpress

First Yen Press Edition: March 2018
The chapters in this volume were originally published as ebooks by Yen Press.

Yen Press is an imprint of Yen Press, LLC.
The Yen Press name and logo are trademarks of Yen Press, LLC.

Library of Congress Control Number: 2017954163

ISBNs: 978-0-316-44823-9 (paperback)
        978-0-316-44820-8 (ebook)

10 9 8

WOR

Printed in the United States of America